BOWMAN SCULPTURE

6 Duke Street St James's, London SW1Y 6BN
Tel. +44 (0) 207 930 0277

gallery@bowmansculpture.com
www.bowmansculpture.com

Edited by Robert Bowman

Text by Ben Hunter & Abby Hignell

Additional editing by Roberta Pisano

Photographic credits:

pp. 75–7, 121, 123 & 239 Unknown

All other photography & layout by Julian Jans

© 2014, Bowman Sculpture Ltd

All rights reserved

ISBN 978-0-9561204-1-0

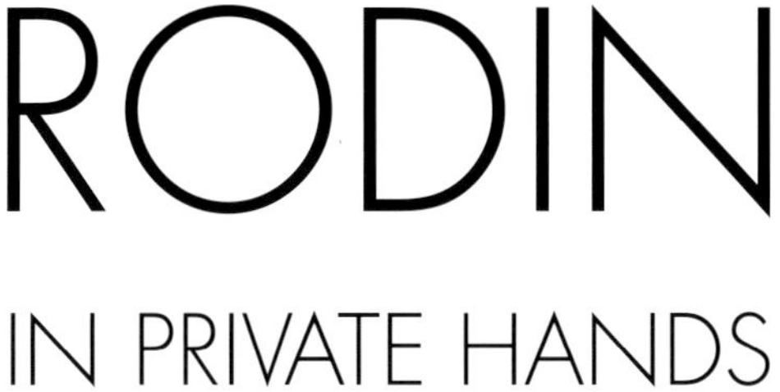

RODIN
IN PRIVATE HANDS

Contents

BOWMAN SCULPTURE

6 Duke Street St James's, London SW1Y 6BN

Tel. +44 (0) 207 930 0277

gallery@bowmansculpture.com

www.bowmansculpture.com

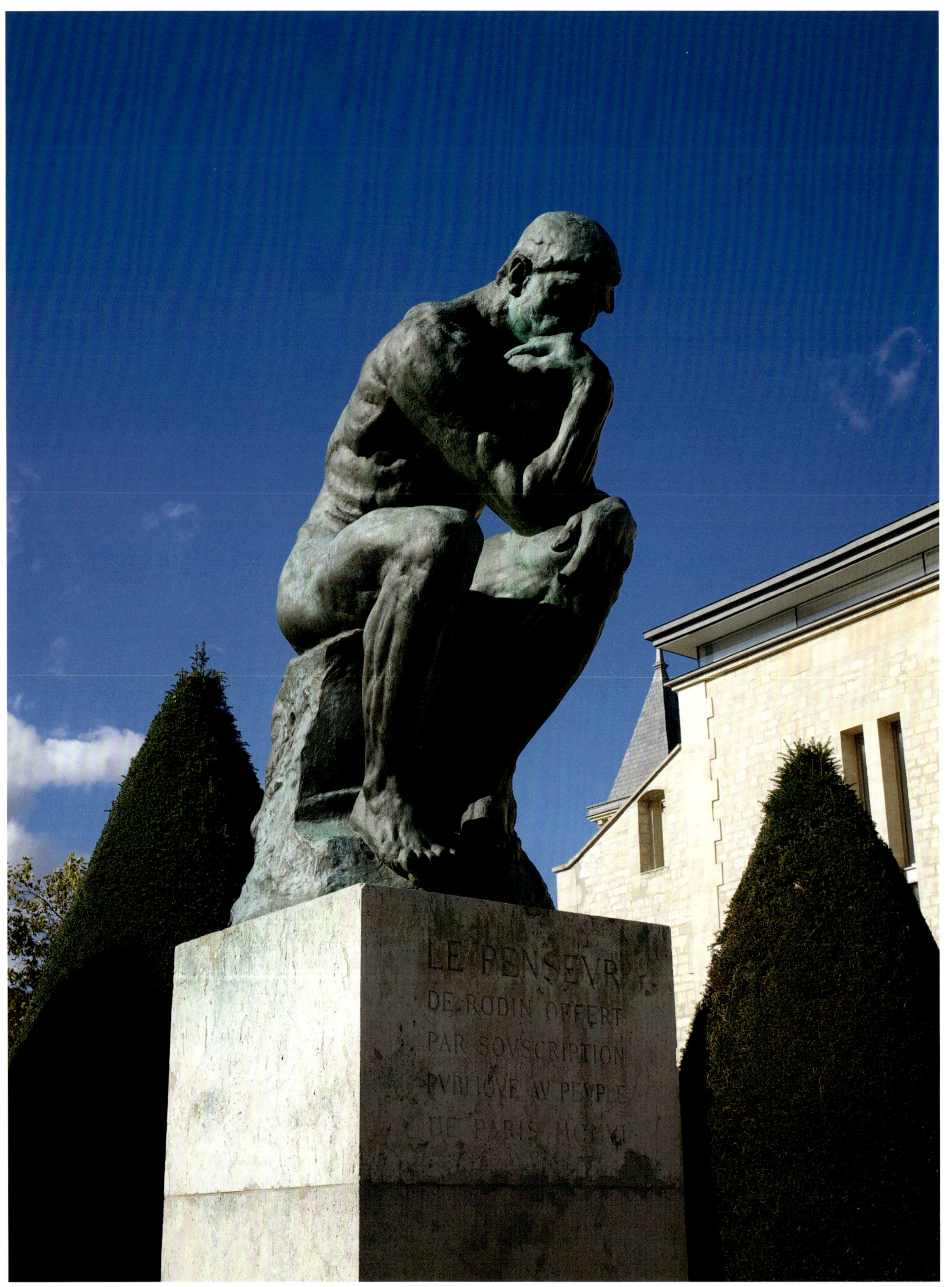

LE PENSEVR
DE RODIN OFFERT
PAR SOVSCRIPTION
PVBLIQVE AV PEVPLE
DE PARIS MCMVI

David Ekserdjian

Remarkably few sculptors are household names, but Rodin is unquestionably one of the happy few. He is also by far and away the most celebrated and best loved sculptor of the nineteenth century. Anyone who has been transfixed by the exuberance and energy of Jean-Baptiste Carpeaux's monumental group, *La Danse*, on the façade of the Opéra in Paris, or made the pilgrimage to the Père Lachaise Cemetery in the same city to gasp at Jules Dalou's extraordinary *cinéma verité* tomb of Victor Noir, will need no persuading that there are other great nineteenth-century sculptors. They are not all confined to France either, as admirers of Vincenzo Gemito and our own Alfred Gilbert—to name but two—will agree, but even so Rodin stands alone.

The sculptures of Auguste Rodin have become icons of modern art. *The Kiss* and *The Thinker* rank among the most famous images in the world, and are universally recognised even by those who have never set foot in a museum. Rodin came from a modest background and it was only after years of struggle that he rose to become one of the handful of great artists in any age who were both successful in their lifetime and revered ever after.

Seen from the perspective of today, it is hard to imagine the impact of Rodin's work upon an audience safe and comfortable with the cool, classical sculptural language of the period. What was so startling about Rodin's sculptures was their ability to convey raw emotion and individual character in a way that had never been seen before. Working in the same era as the Impressionists, whose canvases were often criticised for looking like unfinished sketches, Rodin's work pushed further still. Unafraid to unsettle the viewer, Rodin's figures, often partly encased in stone, looked alarmingly avant-garde. For all the same reasons, Rodin has rightly been considered to be the Father of Modern Sculpture ever since. Moreover, inspired by Michelangelo's unfinished works, specifically sculptural fragments of torsos and limbs, Rodin's figures single him out as a precursor of abstraction. His sculptures celebrated sensuality and sexuality and seemed to herald a new age. It was these qualities that threatened the French art establishment for so many years, yet which now assure his continued popularity. His sculptures feel as fresh and accessible today as they did a century ago.

Given where the present exhibition is taking place, it seems only right to recall the fact that Rodin enjoyed a special relationship with Britain. In 1882, he exhibited the *Bust of St John the Baptist* at the Royal Academy of Arts and other works at the Grosvenor and Dudley Galleries. The enthusiasm of early collectors such as Constantine Ionides and Lord Leighton, the President of the Royal Academy, helped to raise Rodin's profile, and he soon won over the cultural élite, who publicly hailed him as the greatest living sculptor and even more importantly collected his work. In November 1914, Rodin presented eighteen of his sculptures to the Victoria and Albert Museum in honour of the French and British soldiers killed in the First World War. This group of works is unique in public collections, having been personally selected and given by the artist himself, who described it as the collection he had been making all his life.

The Thinker
Musée Rodin, Paris

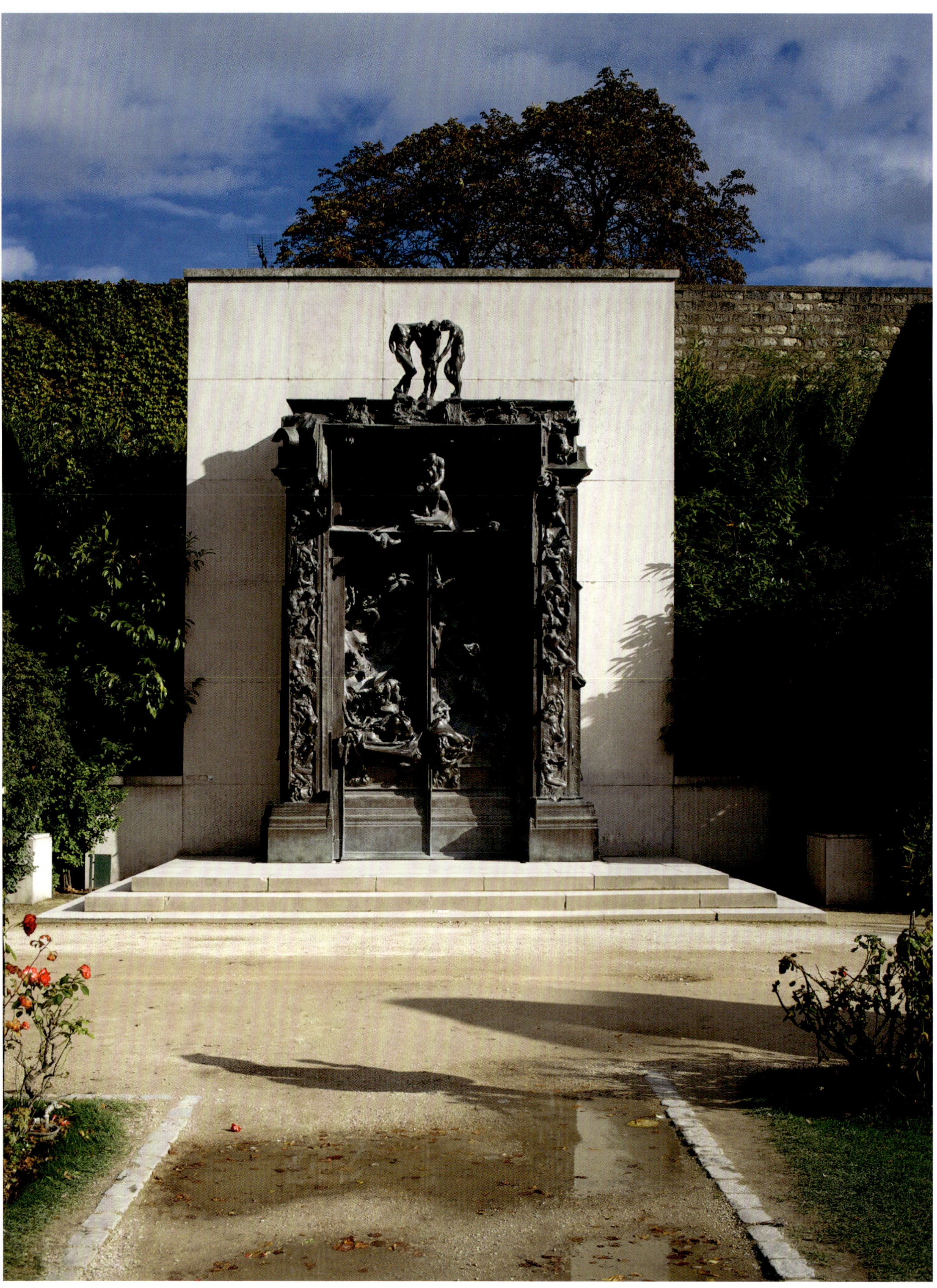

The benign shadow he has cast over the history of sculpture in Britain is long indeed. His influence on younger generations of sculptors—from Henry Moore to Anthony Caro, and on to Anthony Gormley, Richard Deacon and Tony Cragg—has been immense. They have all learnt their own highly personal lessons from Rodin, and without his inspiration there can be no doubt that their work would have been very different. This story is not at an end: *The Gates of Hell* were exhibited for the very first time in the UK in the Rodin Retrospective at the Royal Academy as recently as 2006, and it will be intriguing to see what kinds of impact they will have on the next generation of sculptors in this country.

Rodin employed a whole range of materials, but for many of us he is at his finest when working in bronze. His teacher was Albert Ernest Carrier-Belleuse, and the present exhibition includes an early collaboration between them in the form of the terracotta *Vase of the Titans*, a rare work which allows us to see the very thumb-print of the master. In another sense, however, Rodin's true master was Michelangelo, whom he revered, and referred to in 1875 or 1876 as 'the great magician'. Yet Michelangelo abhorred bronze, and only ever made two sculptures in the medium in his youth. One was a *David*, whose appearance we know from a preparatory drawing for it, but which has been untraced for centuries. In theory, therefore, it might still exist, but is unlikely to reappear at this late date. The other was a statue of Pope Julius II, the patron for whom the frescoes on the Sistine Chapel ceiling were painted, and the centrepiece of whose tomb in San Pietro in Vincoli in Rome is Michelangelo's *Moses*. Julius was a notoriously belligerent pontiff, and the statue was commissioned for Bologna, which he had recently conquered. It was colossal and was intended to tell Julius's new subjects who was boss. In his biography of Michelangelo, Vasari relates that when the fortunes of war turned and the Bolognese expelled the papal forces, the statue—regardless of the fact that it was the work of Michelangelo—was pulled down and sold to Duke Alfonso d'Este of Ferrara, who preserved the head, but melted down the rest and re-used it for a cannon that acquired the nickname 'the Giulia'.

In contrast, it is hard not to feel that Rodin's art was made for bronze. The often rough-hewn look of his bronzes is highly distinctive and involved a new spontaneity of surface. It also allowed for repetition and variation, and this selection features two versions of both the *Mask of the Man with the Broken Nose* and *The Eternal Idol*. Yet the categories into which these works may be grouped reveal Rodin as part of a long tradition stretching back to ancient times. Virtually all bronzes can be subsumed under a few admittedly at times porous categories, comprising figures, groups, heads, animals, and reliefs. The last two are not represented here, but are of course to be found in Rodin's oeuvre (the former admittedly only very occasionally), but there are two further categories that are in a way novelties—the extract and the fragment.

There is nothing surprising about this sense of belonging to a great tradition, because for Rodin the pressing need to break new ground was absolutely not in conflict with a profound engagement with the art of the past.

The Gates of Hell
Musée Rodin, Paris

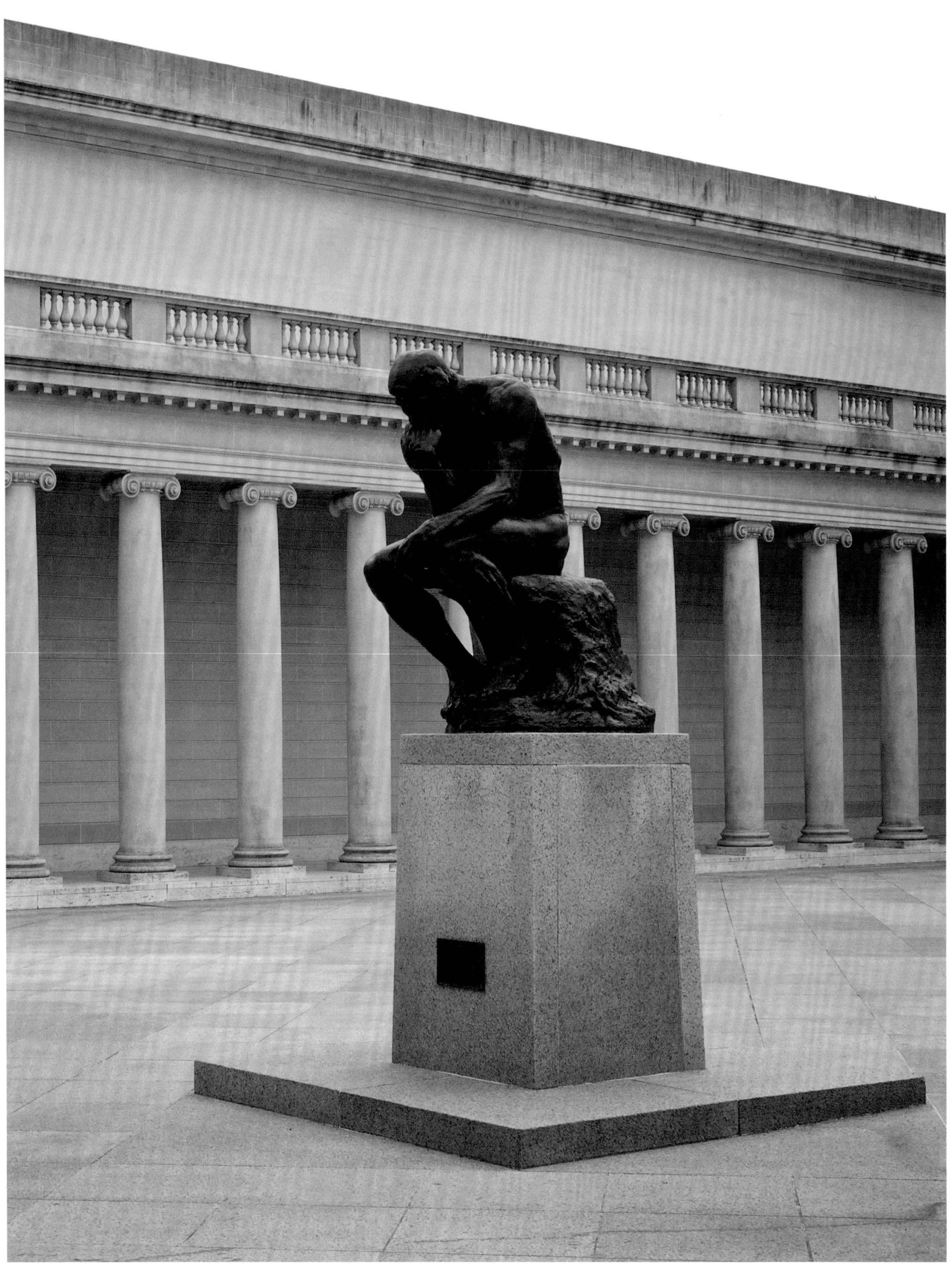

His study of it was often straightforward—how, for instance, could he have failed to revere the Elgin Marbles (for Rodin the so-called *Three Fates* from the pediment of the Parthenon were 'the most beautiful thing Greece ever produced')? At times, however, his homages were less predictable: an early drawing of *Two Figures* in the British Museum is directly based upon Adam and Eve in the woodcut of the *Temptation* from Dürer's *Small Passion*.

In the case of the single figure, the overwhelming impression is of variety. *Iris: Study with Head*, and *Nijinsky*—like *Balzac*, a figure which is at the same time a portrait—are both shown balanced on one leg. Thrilling evocations of movement, they take full advantage of the tightrope-walking daring which the medium of bronze encourages. Elsewhere, in such figures as *Balzac* himself, and *Jean d'Aire* from the group of the *Burghers of Calais*, the emphasis is on self-contained verticality. The former almost seems to sway as he leans backwards, whereas the latter is both solidly and defiantly planted on his base.

Two seated figures, the *Thinker* and *She who once was the Beautiful Helmet Maker's Wife*, are among the most unforgettable of all Rodin's works and underline his emotional range. Both are connected with *The Gates of Hell*, the project that runs like a thread through Rodin's career in the same way as the Tomb of Pope Julius II overshadows Michelangelo's. Rodin's *Gates*—which Dalou claimed would be 'one of the century's finest works of art, and perhaps the most original'—were inspired by Dante's *Inferno*, in which the poet describes entering Hell, and records the inscription on its gate, which concludes with the memorable line, 'Lasciate ogni speranza, voi ch'entrate' ('All hope abandon, ye who enter in' [Longfellow's translation]). In consequence, the *Thinker*, which was placed at the top of the great door, has sometimes been thought to represent the brooding figure of Dante himself, but this seems unlikely. In the *Inferno*, the sinners are naked, but Dante and his guide, Virgil, are not, and moreover neither the rippling muscularity of the body, nor the roughcast facial type fit with such an identification.

The visual source for the *Beautiful Helmet Maker's Wife* (*La Belle Heaulmière*) is a figure cast in relief towards the base of the *Gates*, while the title by which she is known—which may be a species of afterthought—is derived from a ballad by the great fifteenth-century French poet François Villon. In it, the *Belle Heaulmière* encourages young women to make the most of their beauty while it lasts, since—in her words—after their beauty is gone, they will be as much use as obsolete coinage. Whether Rodin had the poem in mind when he invented the figure or not, the idea of a connection between this shrivelled and defeated body and Villon's lament makes perfect sense.

Turning to the groups, Dante's *Inferno* was once again the inspiration for *The Kiss*, which was another component of *The Gates of Hell*. Although transformed into a universal archetype, these lovers are also Paolo and Francesca, whose reading about the equally adulterous liaison between Lancelot and Guinevere ended in a passionate kiss ('La bocca mi baciò tutto tremante'—'Kissed me on the mouth all palpitating'). So moved is Dante by Francesca's account of their tragic fate, which ends in their murder by her husband, that he loses consciousness ('E caddi come corpo morto cade'—'And fell, even as a dead body falls').

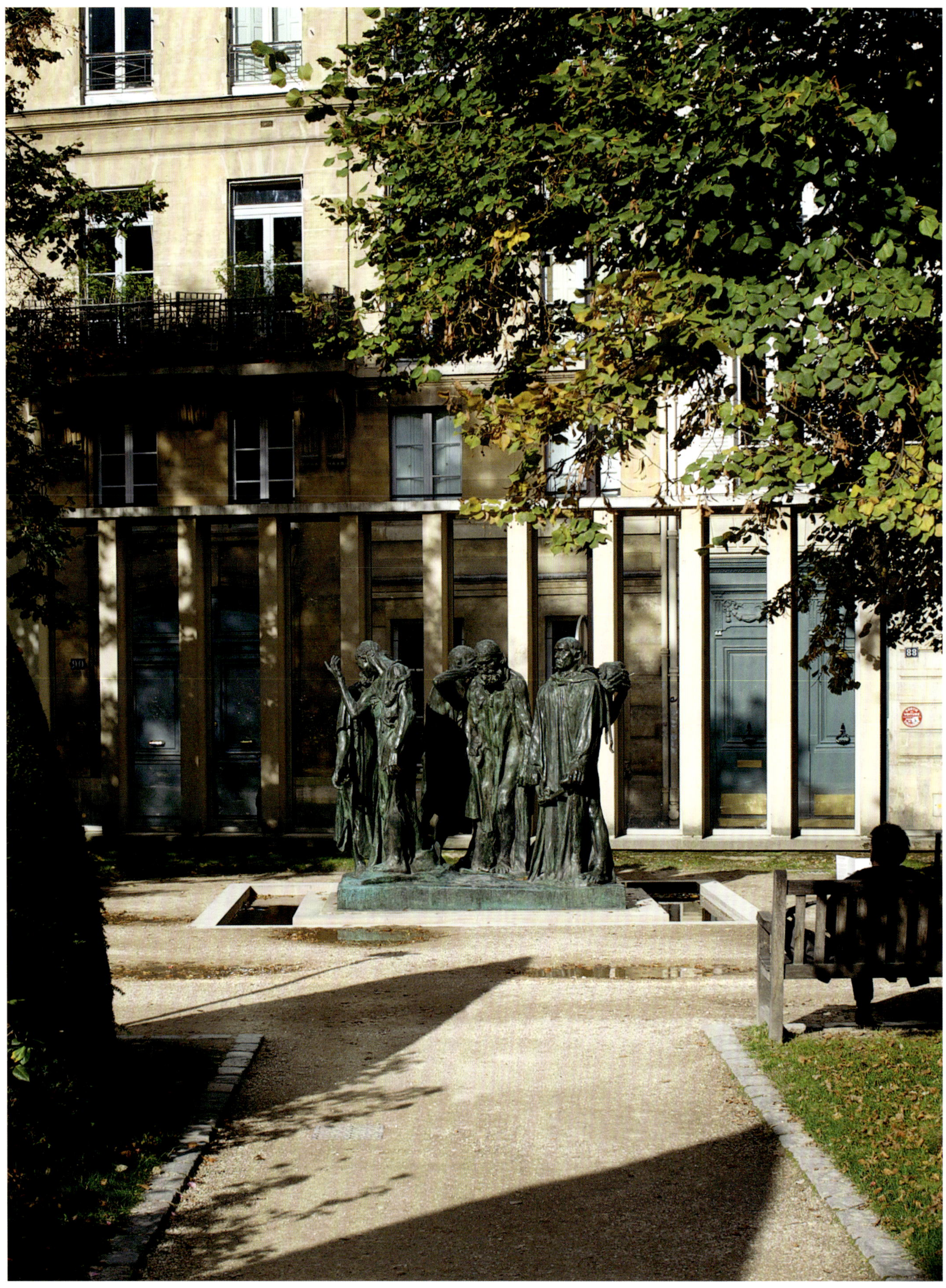

Conversely, for *The Burghers of Calais*—here shown in the form of a small maquette for the monumental group—the source is historical as opposed to fictional. Their heroic action during the Hundred Years' War had been chronicled by Froissart, and Rodin accoutred them with the halters and other attributes that were stipulated by the narrative. At the same time, however, he triumphantly ensured that their plight would acquire a timeless resonance.

Rodin was a remarkable portraitist, and by the end of his life he was also a considerable celebrity. As a result, he executed busts of other notables, including George Bernard Shaw (in 1906) and Gustav Mahler (in 1909)—in his own day best known not as a composer but as a conductor—but he also produced stunning likenesses of altogether less prominent or in effect anonymous individuals. One such is a masterpiece from the other end of his long career, the *Man with the Broken Nose* (1863–64), of which Rodin commented: 'It is the first good piece of modelling I ever did.' At the same time, like almost all artists he looked to the nearest available models—himself, and Rose Beuret, the woman who was his often betrayed mistress-cum-lackey for half a century, and only became Madame Rodin a fortnight before her death.

A number of extracts, by which I mean figures or groups designed for a particular context which Rodin isolated in independent sculptures, have already been discussed. The vast majority are taken from *The Gates of Hell*, although the single figure of *Jean d'Aire* has been isolated from *The Burghers of Calais*. In all such cases, the transformative effect of an exclusive focus upon them is palpable, and the connection with Rodin's fragments is highly suggestive.

In the nature of things, some sculptures—above all marbles from ancient Greece and Rome—now only exist in fragmentary form. Moreover, sculptors had always produced pieces that were in effect fragments in the preparatory process that led to the finished work of art. Such works, often in fragile materials like clay or wax, were in a sense the three-dimensional equivalents of the preliminary drawings for pictures routinely executed by painters. Even if not intended for public consumption, they did on occasion survive and some were even metamorphosed into 'finished' works of art, not least if they were subsequently cast in bronze.

What is so dramatically different about Rodin's practice is the idea of presenting such fragments as meriting exactly the same attention as all other sculptures. Most of them are of hands, but there are also torsos, which make the links with classical antiquity particularly compelling. Rodin likewise realised that there is no law that requires them to be small-scale: his *Monumental Torso* is over a metre high. In the case of the hands, the lyrically expressive side of his temperament comes to the fore, and never more so than in *La Cathédrale*. a work which—for all its slightly whimsical title and its extreme familiarity—is the very opposite of boring. Of course we know he brought it into being, and yet—like so many of Rodin's finest achievements—it is virtually impossible to imagine a world without it.

The Burghers of Calais
Musée Rodin, Paris

David Ekserdjian is Professor of History of Art & Film at the University of Leicester, and co-curated the acclaimed Royal Academy exhibition: 'Bronze'

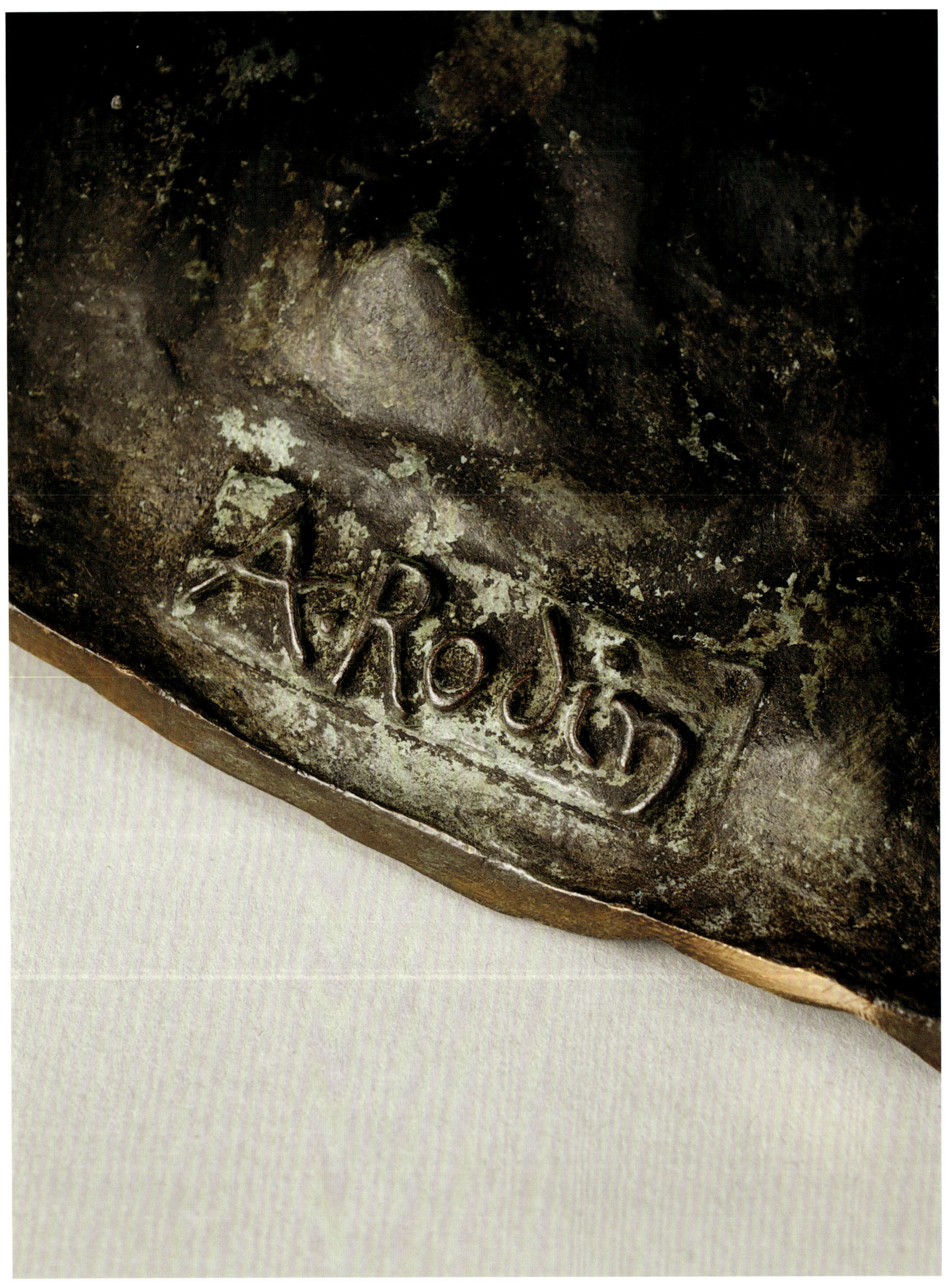

INTRODUCTION

Robert Bowman

My passion for Rodin started 35 years ago when I first saw *Iris Messenger of the Gods*. This started my journey into Rodin's sculpture beyond *The Kiss* and *The Thinker* and I discovered the pioneering works with which he really challenged the world of sculpture and rightly earned him the title of the father of modern sculpture.

What is most exciting for me is that every year the gallery finds another work I had not really fully appreciated before. As all collectors know its not until you have a sculpture in your possession and live with it every day, that you really get to understand it and appreciate it.

This catalogue is a selection of works we have available together with a selection of sculptures we have sold over the history of the gallery. It marks a point in time, as by the time it is published we will, no doubt, have found further works to offer our collectors and found homes for others.

When people discover we deal in sculpture by Rodin, the general response is incredulity, as a common misconception is that all Rodin's sculptures are now in Museum collections.

While Rodin's importance as a sculptor means that his work is a feature of almost all the major museums in the world, the nature of his output, working in bronze editions as well as making multiple works in marble and plaster, has ensured that there are still significant amounts of his sculpture available to the collector.

Almost all the works in this catalogue are owned by private individuals or are available to be privately owned. Some of our clients acquire a single work; others have formed collections based either on theme or style. We have clients who collect just sculptures of hands by Rodin, others who only buy the powerful dramatic works, others just torso's and of course, those who just collect what they find beautiful.

The availability of Rodin's sculpture is essentially down to the sculptor's desire for as many people as possible to enjoy his work. Rodin modelled all his works in plaster and then gave the plaster to a bronze foundry to make a mold of the work, to produce an edition in bronze. During Rodin's lifetime, if you wanted to own a particular work you would approach Rodin or one of his agents and request a cast of the work. Rodin would then authorise the foundry to make a bronze from the plaster version he had given them. These are what we term in the catalogue 'lifetime casts' and simply put, a lifetime cast is a work that was produced with Rodin's authority while he was still alive.

Certain very popular works, were given with the rights to cast, to a specific foundry. The best known of these is the Barbedienne Foundry who purchased the rights from Rodin for models including *The Kiss* and *Eternal Spring* and sent Rodin a commission for each cast they made.

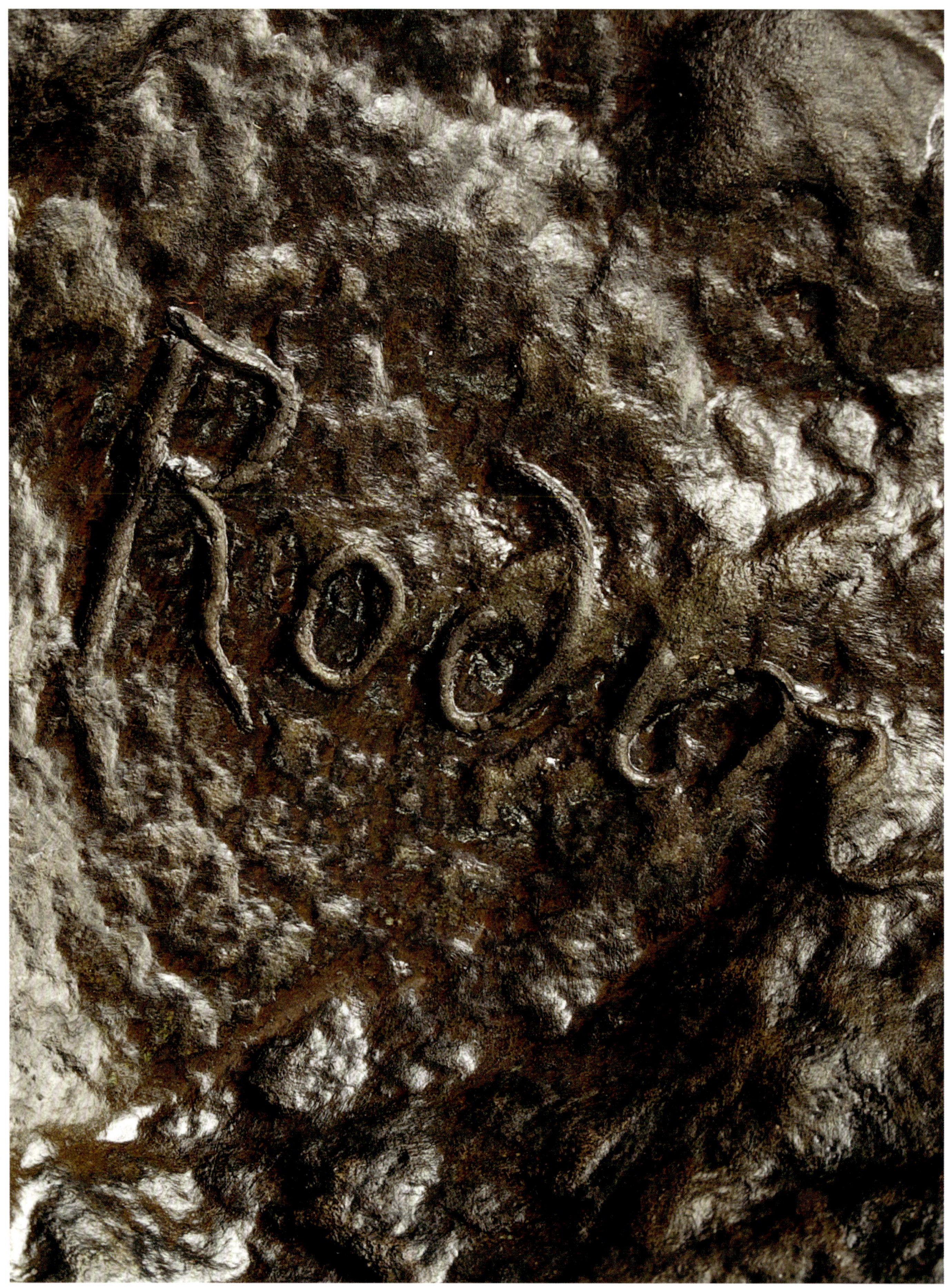
Rodin

By 1916 Rodin knew his health was starting to fade and he became very concerned that his work would stop being cast by his foundries, once he had died and his place in art history would therefore be diminished. He was also very concerned that unauthorised bronzes and copies would appear on the market without a control mechanism in place. To this end, he negotiated with the French government for his studio to become a museum and that on his death all the rights to his works would pass to that museum. The directors of the museum then took over the responsibility for bronze casts of Rodin's works to continue to be made. Therefore after 1917 bronze casts of Rodin's works were still made using the same molds made from the same plaster models that had been supplied by Rodin. In the case of works produced by the Alexis Rudier foundry, who had the right to cast certain models from 1902 to 1952, the only difference between a cast made in 1917 and one made in 1918 was that the former was authorised to be cast by Rodin and the latter was authorised to be cast by the Rodin Museum.

This situation continued until 1952 when the last contract with a foundry agreed by Rodin himself came to an end. After this date the Rodin Museum agreed that any further editions would be limited to 13, an edition of 12 and one cast for the Museum itself. It is at this point that the Museum looked to its huge inventory of sculptures left to them by Rodin, all with his express permission to be cast in edition if there was the public demand. These casts are known as Museum casts and in general, have the inscription copyright Musée Rodin.

There will of course always be a special value placed on bronzes cast during Rodin's lifetime. The differences between the castings of all periods are, however, tremendous, and there is no formula for acquiring a great cast. Some of the bronzes made in the 1920s and 30s for example are superior in quality to casts from the same mold made by the same foundry in Rodin's lifetime. One must remember that Rodin did not physically make any of the bronzes or indeed supervise their casting; he was simply too busy sculpting. So the quality of the bronze was down to the diligence and talent of the foundry workers who produced them. The key for the collector is to find a fine cast and this has many factors including the detail of the surface and the tones of the patina.

Some models are only available to be bought by collectors in an edition authorised by the Museum, as Rodin himself simply did not get some of his works cast in bronze. A good example of this is the magical sculpture of Nijinsky that Rodin left, in plaster form, to the Museum on his death, but was only cast in bronze for the first time in 1958.

Finally I must mention the fine work of Jerome Le Blay and the Comité Rodin. The Comité is a wonderful source of archive and expertise material, which has helped establish and stabilise the Rodin market. All works we offer for sale are sold with a letter from the Comité confirming the provenance and authenticity of the works.

Vase of the Titans (with A.E. Carrier-Belleuse)

Jardinière aux Titans (avec A.E. Carrier-Belleuse)

Signed A. Carrier-Belleuse
Terracotta
Height: 15½ inches (39.1 cm)

Provenance:
Private Collection, France
Robert Bowman Gallery, 2013
Private Collection, Turkey

Conceived circa 1877, the present example was cast under the authorisation of Albert-Ernest Carrier-Belleuse before 1887. According to the Comité Rodin, there are 6 distinct versions of the Vase of the Titans, with the current version being considered the finest. There are only three known examples of this version in terracotta.

The present model is an extremely fine terracotta cast of a work modelled by Rodin whilst he was in the employment of the eminent romantic sculptor, Albert-Ernest Carrier-Belleuse. At this time Carrier was director of the Sèvres porcelain works and employed a large studio to help him execute numerous public and private commissions.

It is clear from a drawing now in the collection of the Musée des Beaux Arts Calais, and also recorded by June Hargrove in 'Life and Work of Albert Carrier-Belleuse', that Carrier designed the vase himself before giving the project over to Rodin to execute.

The pencil drawing is typical of Carrier and shows languorous figures on top of an ornate pedestal supporting a large bulbous vase. The sculptural realisation of the design is however unanimously attributed to Rodin and the complicated contrapposto and strong introverted gestures are typical of his hand. Indeed the strong musculature, which was heavily influenced by Michelangelo, is typical of Rodin's output at this stage.

Between 1875 and 1876, the young sculptor had visited Italy and in a letter to his long-term partner Rose Beuret he states that during the visit he had managed to learn 'a few of the secrets of the great magician Michelangelo'. One can see a similar handling of the male form in Rodin's seminal *Thinker*, which he modelled three years after the present work in 1880.

The Vase of the Titans was exhibited in 1957 during the exhibition 'Rodin, ses collaborateurs et ses amis' at the Musée Rodin and was also produced in a glazed ceramic version that can be found in several museum collections, including the Victoria and Albert Museum and the Musée Rodin. However, the surface of the ceramic is devoid of the texture and detail of the terracotta works, which were cast in sections and then assembled and finished by hand.

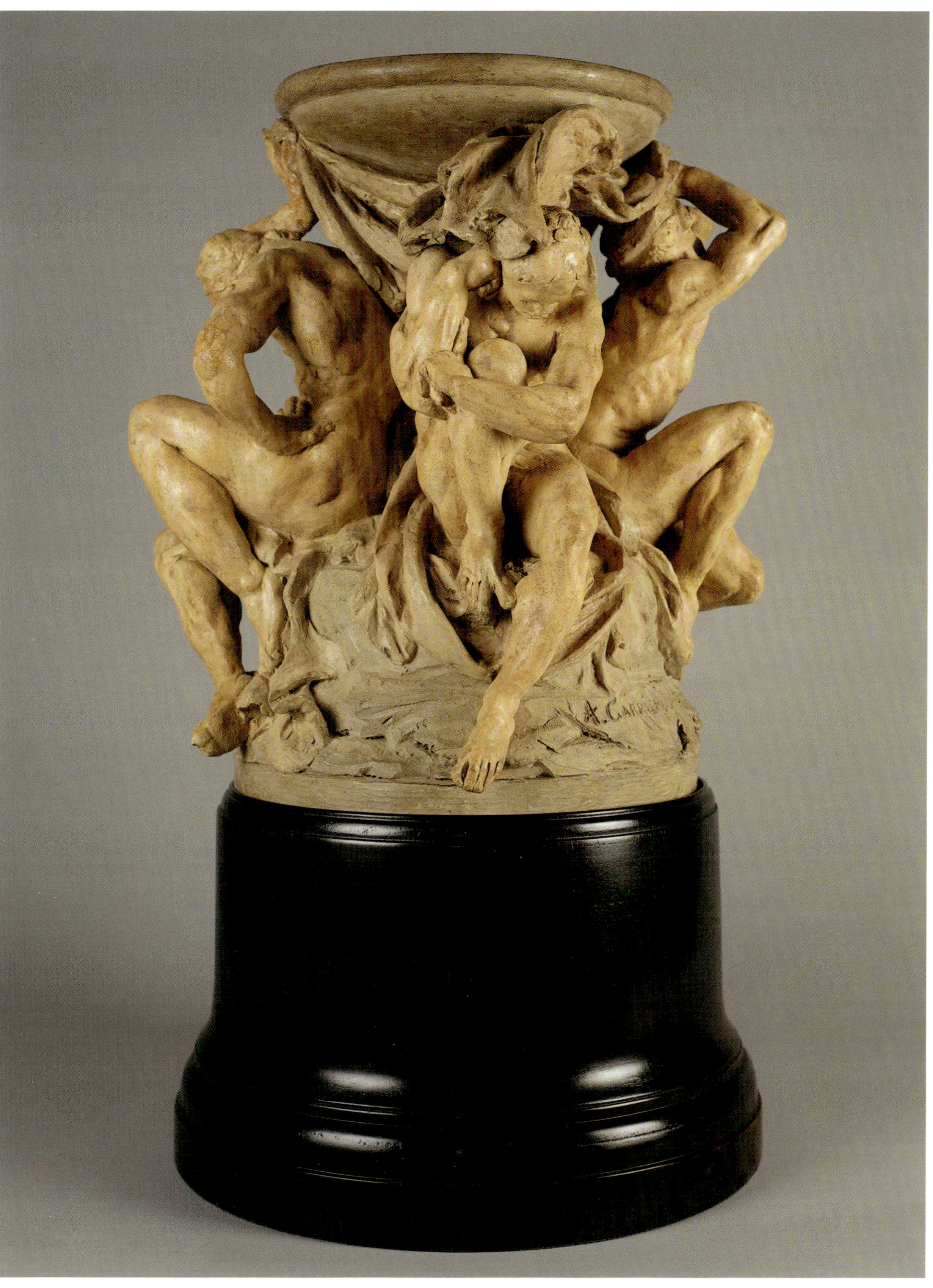

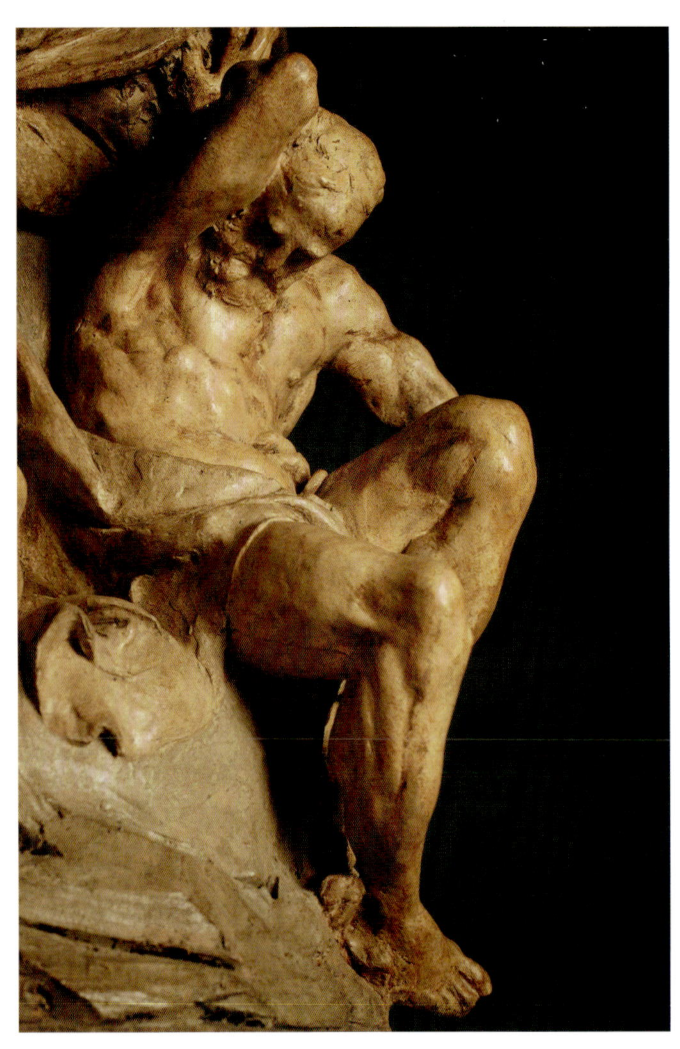
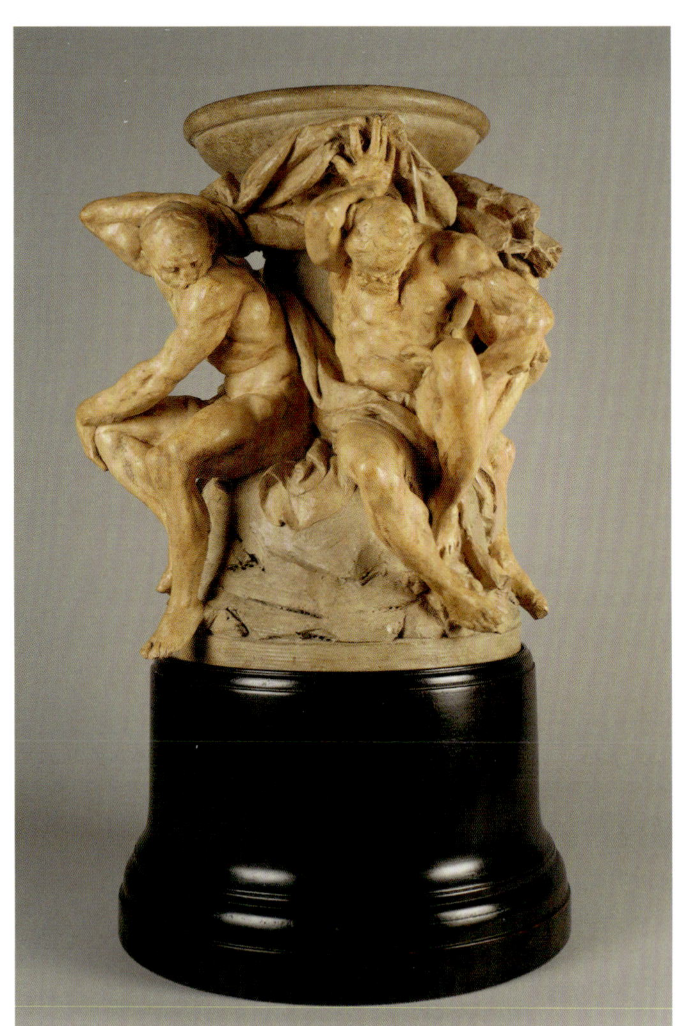

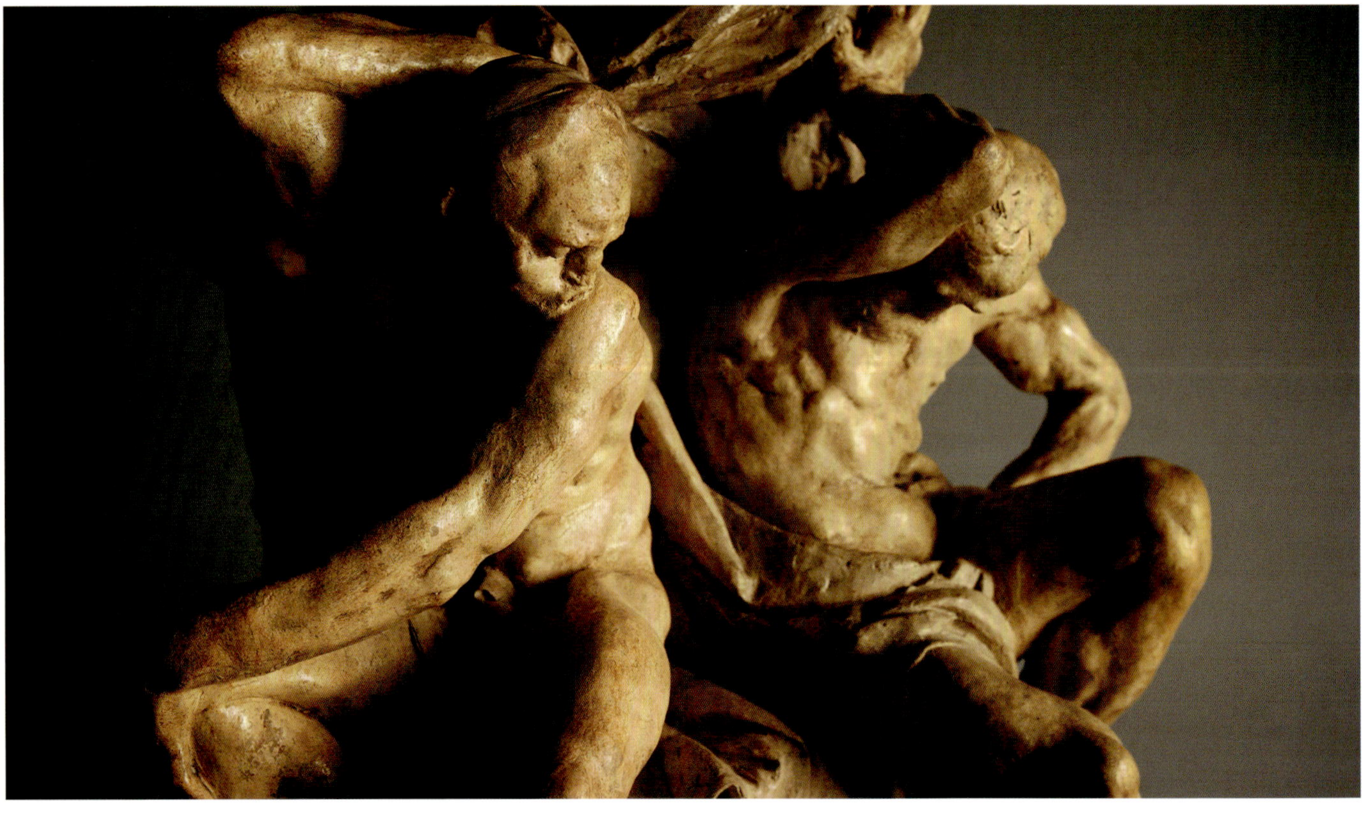

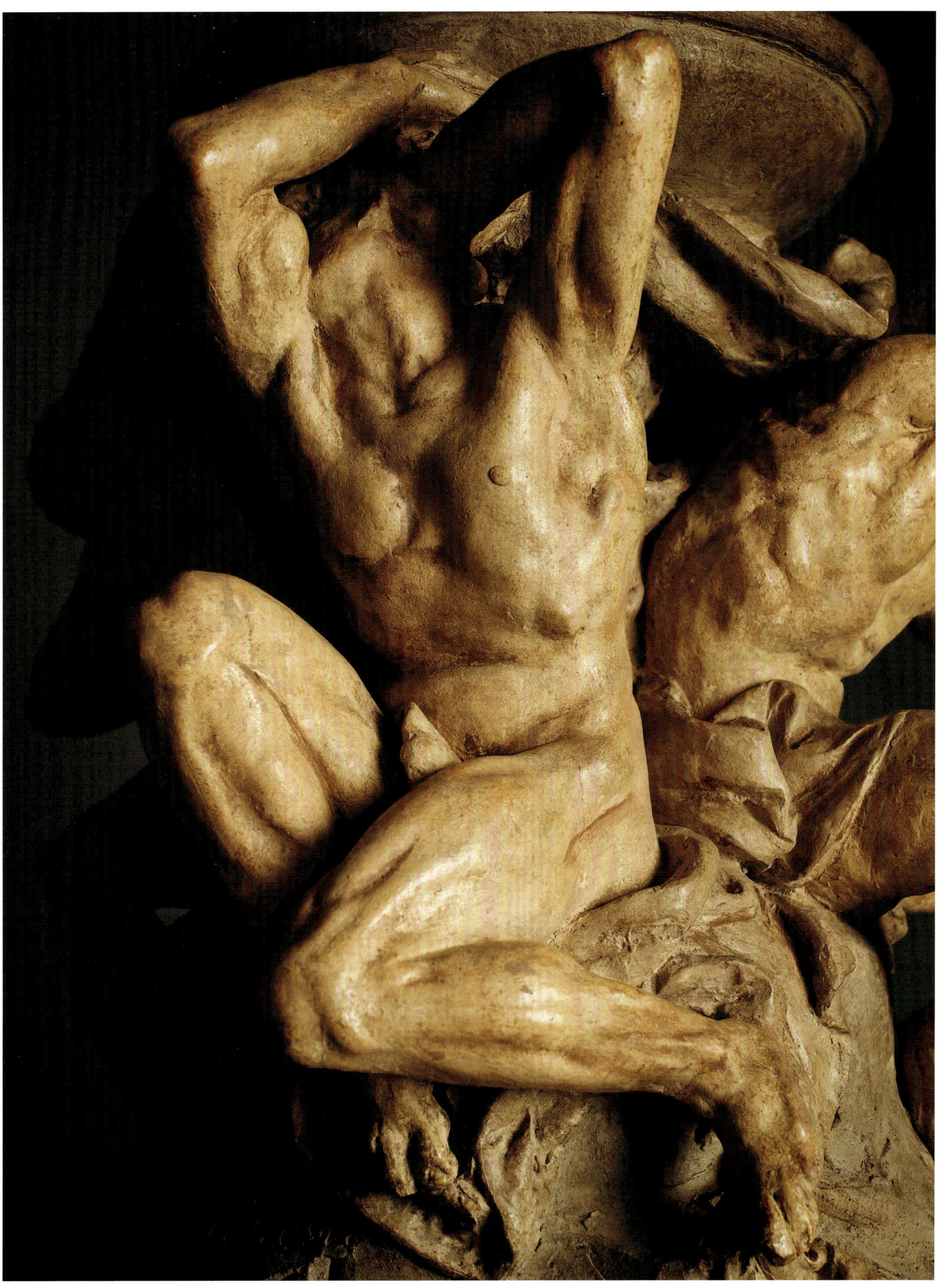

The Abduction of Hippodamie (with A.E. Carrier-Belleuse)

L'Enlèvement d'Hippodamie (avec A.E. Carrier-Belleuse)

Signed Carrier-Belleuse
With title plaque: L'Enlevement
Bronze with a rich green, mid and dark brown patination
Height: 25½ inches (65 cm)

Provenance:
Private collection, UK

Conceived circa 1871.

In 1864 Rodin joined the studio of the commercially successful Carrier-Belleuse. Rodin stayed in Carrier's employment until the outbreak of the Franco Prussian war in 1870. After a brief period in the National Guard, Rodin joined Carrier in Belgium, where he had set up a temporary studio away from the conflict. Rodin's relationship with Carrier deteriorated somewhat during the later 1870s, but he re-joined his old master in 1879 at the Sevres Porcelain factory where Carrier had become head of design.

Carrier himself had studied with David D'Anger before working with Carpeaux and Charles Garnier, designer of the Paris Opera House. In 1863 he sold his first work to Napoleon III, ensuring a number of private and public commissions, including the decoration of the Louvre and the Paris Opera House. Carrier's romantic style and expert eye for decoration made him incredibly commercially successful and by the 1870s he had a large group of artisans and sculptors working under his supervision.

The present work, first documented in 1871 when a terracotta version was included in a selection of models offered in Brussels, depicts Eurytus the centaur trying to abduct Hippodamie. The narrative is taken from the ancient Greek story in which the Lapiths, a peace-loving people of Thessaly, were celebrating the wedding of their King Pirithous, to Hippodamie. The Centaurs were invited but quickly began to misbehave. One of them, Eurytus, full of wine, tried to carry off the bride and soon a brawl ensued. Eventually the Centaurs were driven off, symbolising the victory of civilization over barbarism.

June Hargrove, author of the monograph Carrier-Belleuse, has demonstrated that the centaur's body, 'which ripples with a bold musculature', is characteristic of Rodin's models for the *Vase of the Titans*, another work from this period which was sculpted by Rodin but signed Carrier-Belleuse. The screaming face of the Centaur is also characteristic of Rodin's hand and can be seen repeated in his later model *Call to Arms* of 1878. It is therefore accepted that this work, while bearing the signature of Carrier-Belleuse, was created by his assistant Rodin.

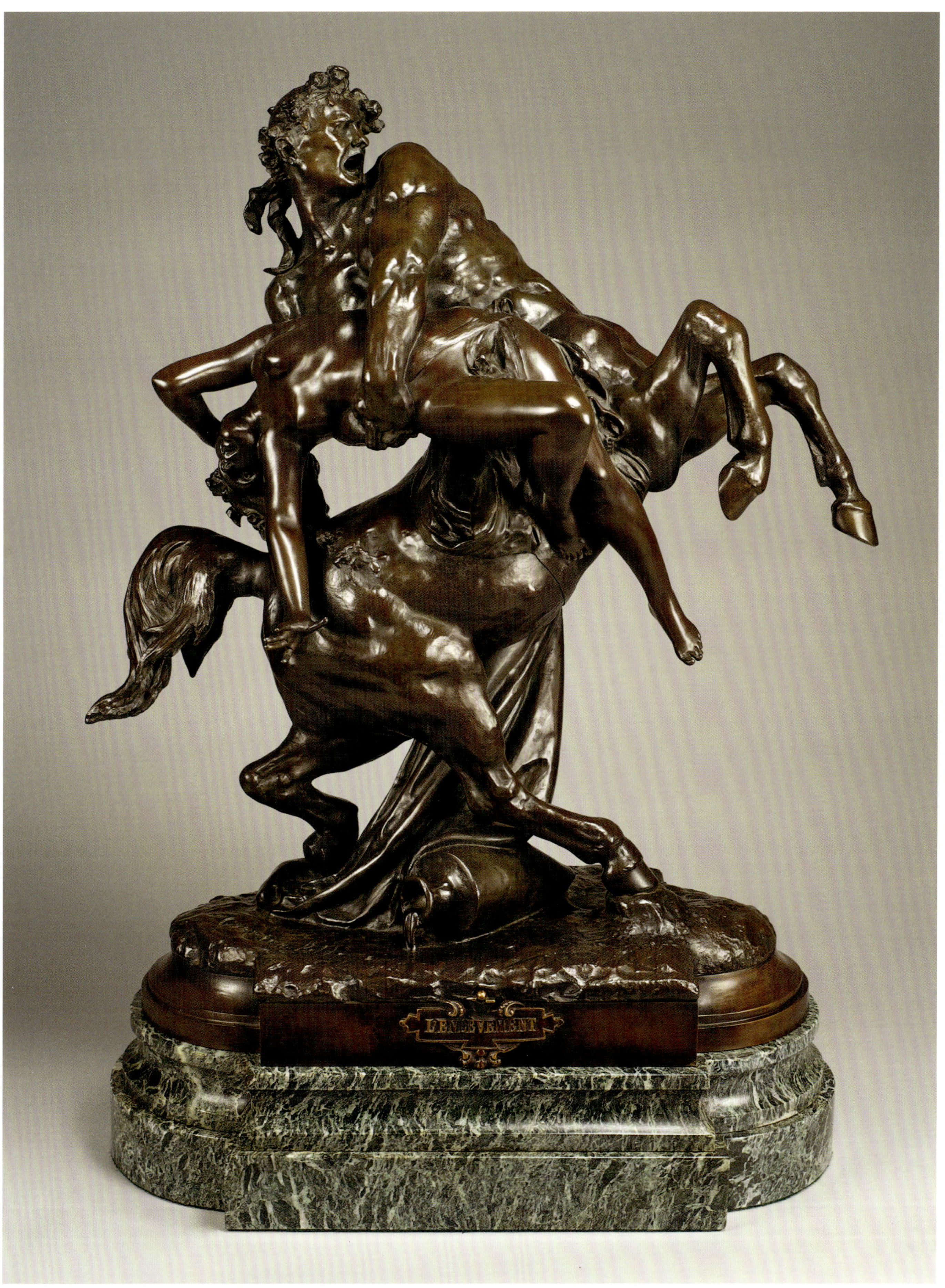
L'ENLÈVEMENT

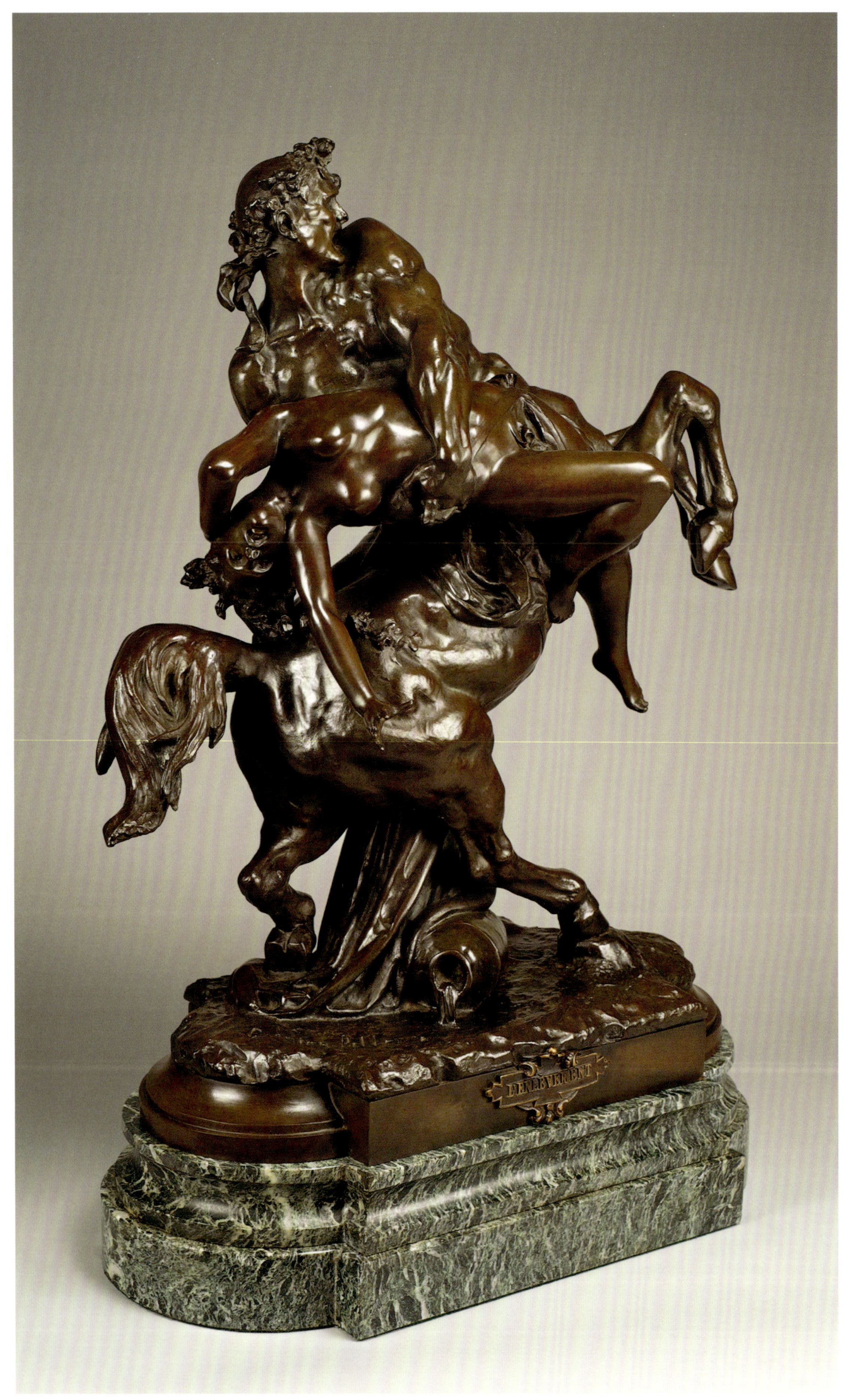
L'ENLÈVEMENT

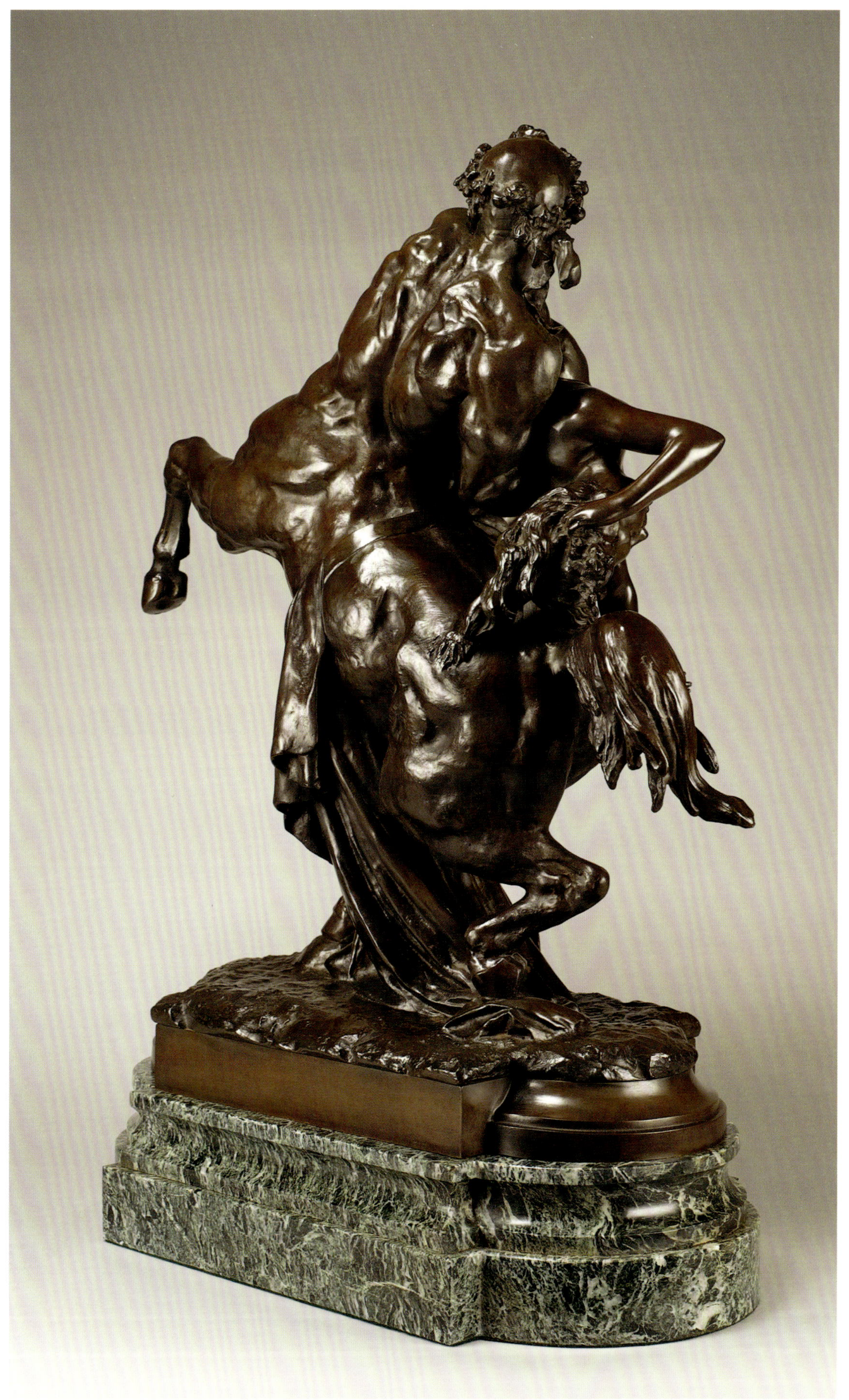

Eternal Idol, Large Model

Eternelle Idol, Grand Modéle

Signed A. Rodin with repeat raised interior signature
Inscribed Alexis Rudier Fondeur, Paris
Bronze with a rich dark brown patination
Height: 28¾ inches (72 cm)

Provenance:
Musée Rodin, Paris
Eugene Rudier, Le Vésinet, acquired Musée Rodin circa 1935
Private Collection, Florence
Private Collection, USA, acquired 1960 from a dealer in Florence
Robert Bowman Gallery, 2005
Private Collection, Turkey

Conceived in 1889, this example was cast in 1927. No lifetime casts of this model in this size were made. In total twelve casts in this size were made for the Musée Rodin between 1927 and 1978. The first four casts by the Alexis Rudier foundry, of which the present example was the first, and nine casts by the Georges Rudier foundry between 1967 and 1978.

Rodin originally conceived the sculpture whilst working on *The Gates of Hell*, incorporating both of the figures independently onto the right hand doorway. Sometime before 1890 the figures were combined into the group we now know. Rodin made a small 17cm high bronze (the only lifetime cast of this model), which was delivered to the collector Antoni Roux in 1891. Roux later encouraged Rodin to produce a larger version of the model, which was carved in marble by Jean Escoula. Rodin took a plaster cast of this marble in 1893 and it is from this plaster, now in the collection of the Musée Rodin, that the present bronze was cast.

The *Eternal Idol* is one of Rodin's most powerful groups and its emotive force has elicited a range of symbolic interpretations. The work is often seen as a depiction of tender adoration, the man's hands clasped behind his back in a symbol of respectful abstinence. Conversely, others have suggested the man's hands are not clasped in a respectful manner, but rather show that he is enslaved by the woman, unable to escape her power as she looks down pitifully upon him.

It is also impossible to ignore the similarities to Camille Claudel's *L'Abandon*, which was conceived in 1888, one year before the present work. Claudel's masterpiece uses a similar composition, but the two figures are shown in a loving embrace, rather than separated by the apparent gulf of emotional space in *Eternal Idol*. Perhaps the work echoed Rodin's own feelings towards his long-term lover and mistress who he was soon to reject forever.

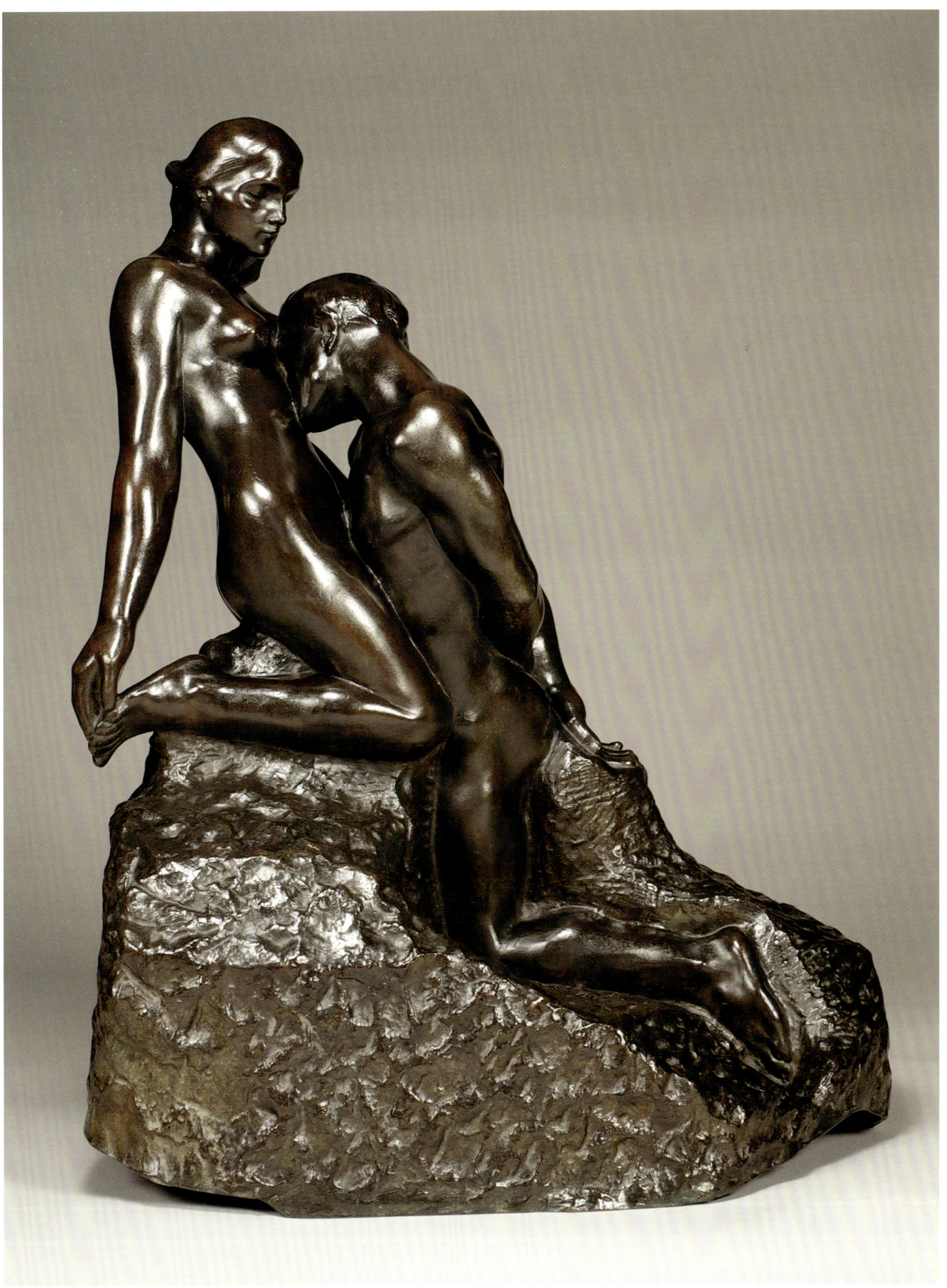

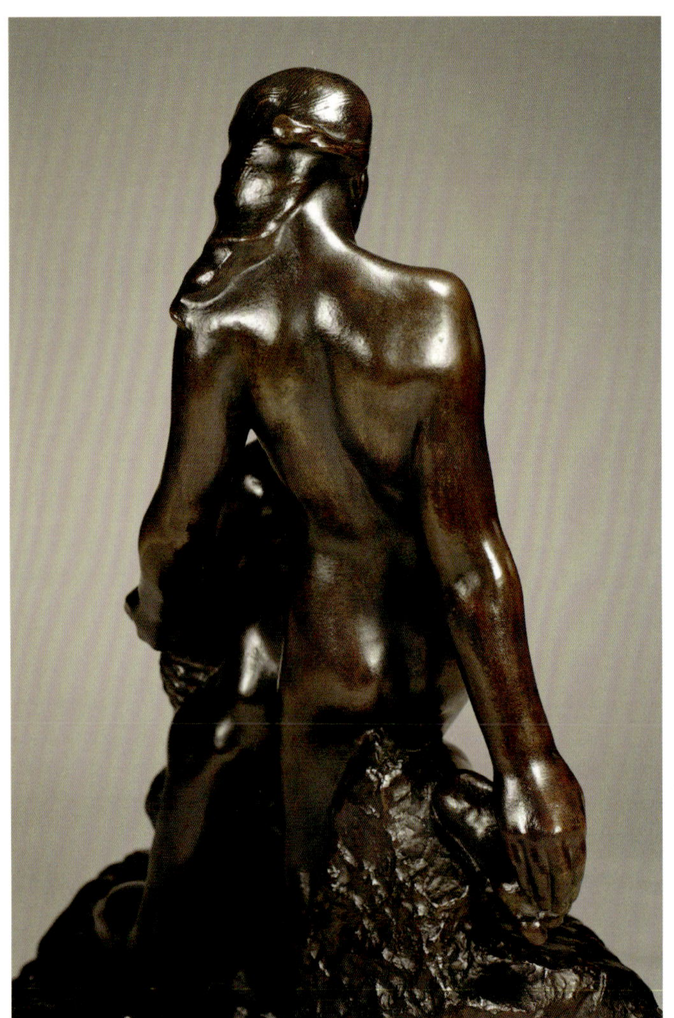 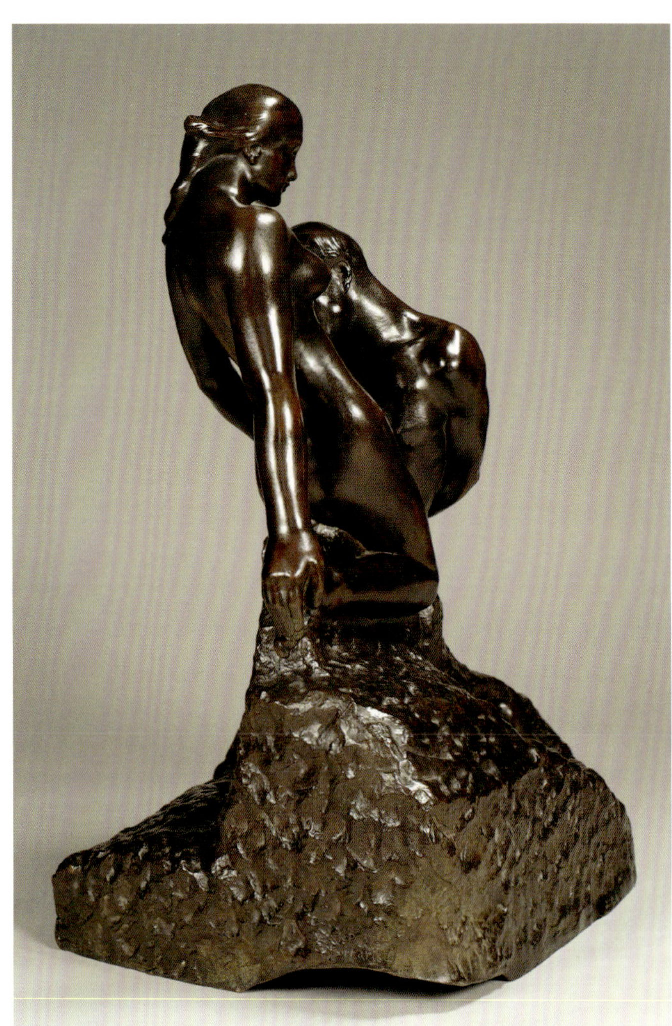

Jules Desbois, one of Rodin's many assistants offers the following account of the works inception. 'One day, from up on the scaffold where I was working on the Burghers of Calais, I noticed Rodin, who between some screens, was doing a nude sculpture, for which the model was a young woman, stretched out on a table. As the session was drawing to a close he bent over toward the woman and kissed her tenderly on the belly - a gesture of adoration of nature, which gave him much joy.'

Perhaps, like a number of Rodin's greatest masterpieces, the true power of the model lies in its ambiguity. The novelist and poet Rainer Maria Rilke, who wrote a monograph on Rodin in 1903, argued that 'a grandeur steeped in mystery emanates from this group. One dare not attribute a meaning to it. It has thousands… There is something like the atmosphere of Purgatory in this work. Heaven is near, but has not yet been reached; Hell is near, but has not yet been forgotten.'

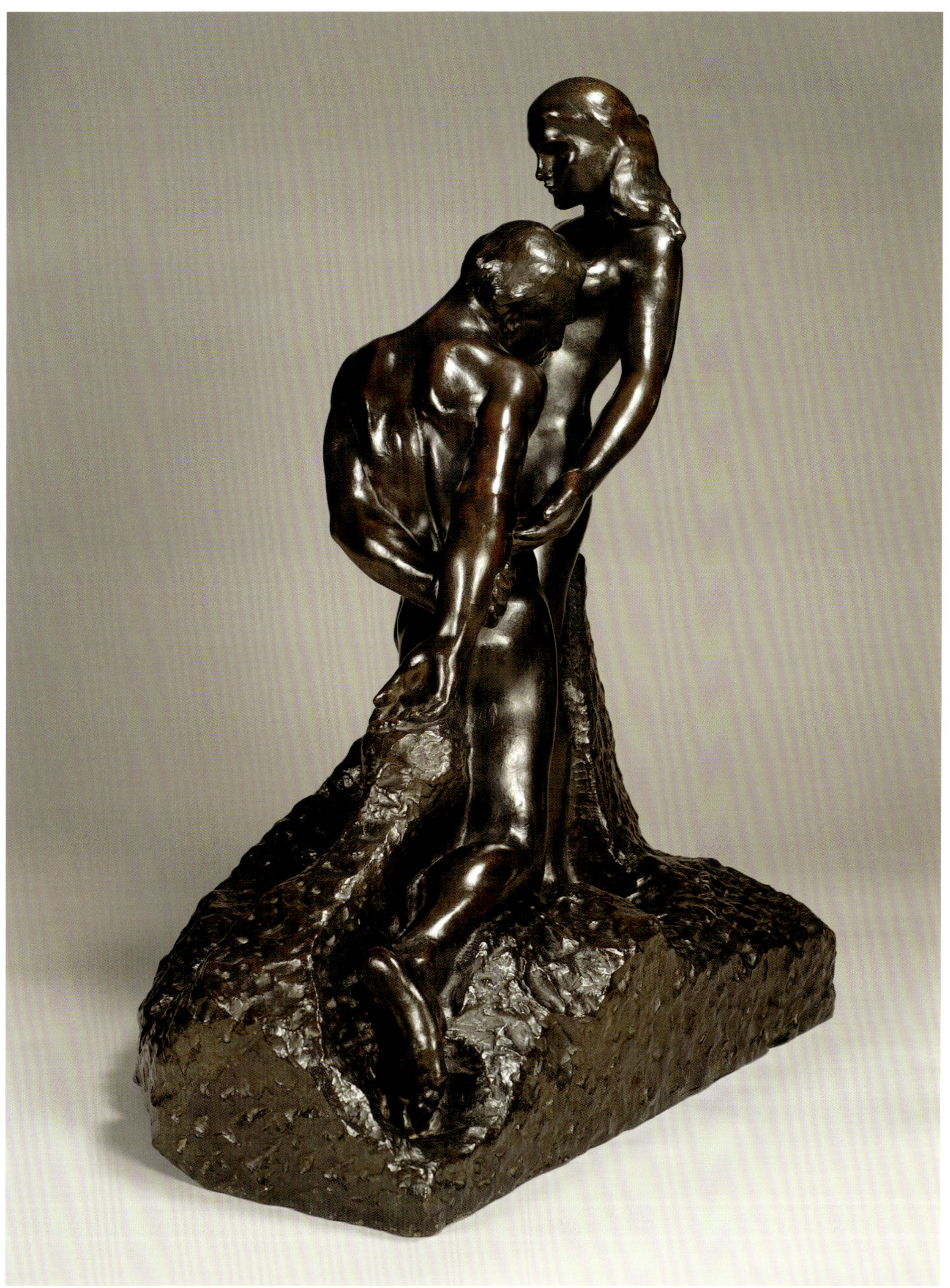

Eternal Idol, Small Model

Eternelle Idole, Petit Modéle

Signed A. Rodin
Inscribed Alexis Rudier Fondeur, Paris
Numbered 1
Bronze with a rich dark brown patination with light brown and green highlights
Height: 6¾ inches (17 cm)

Provenance:
Musée Rodin, Paris
Galerie Balzac, New York
Joan Whitney Payson
Charles Shipman Payson
Virginia Kraft Payson
Robert Bowman Gallery, 2005
Private Collection, Turkey

Conceived in 1889, this example was cast in 1927. Two casts of this model in this size were made during Rodin's lifetime. Sixteen further casts were made for the Musée Rodin. The first thirteen by the Alexis Rudier foundry between 1927 and 1945 (the present example is the earliest of these casts) and a final cast by the Georges Rudier foundry in 1958.

This is the original size of this model, conceived by Rodin in 1889. The first cast was delivered to the collector Antoni Roux in 1891.

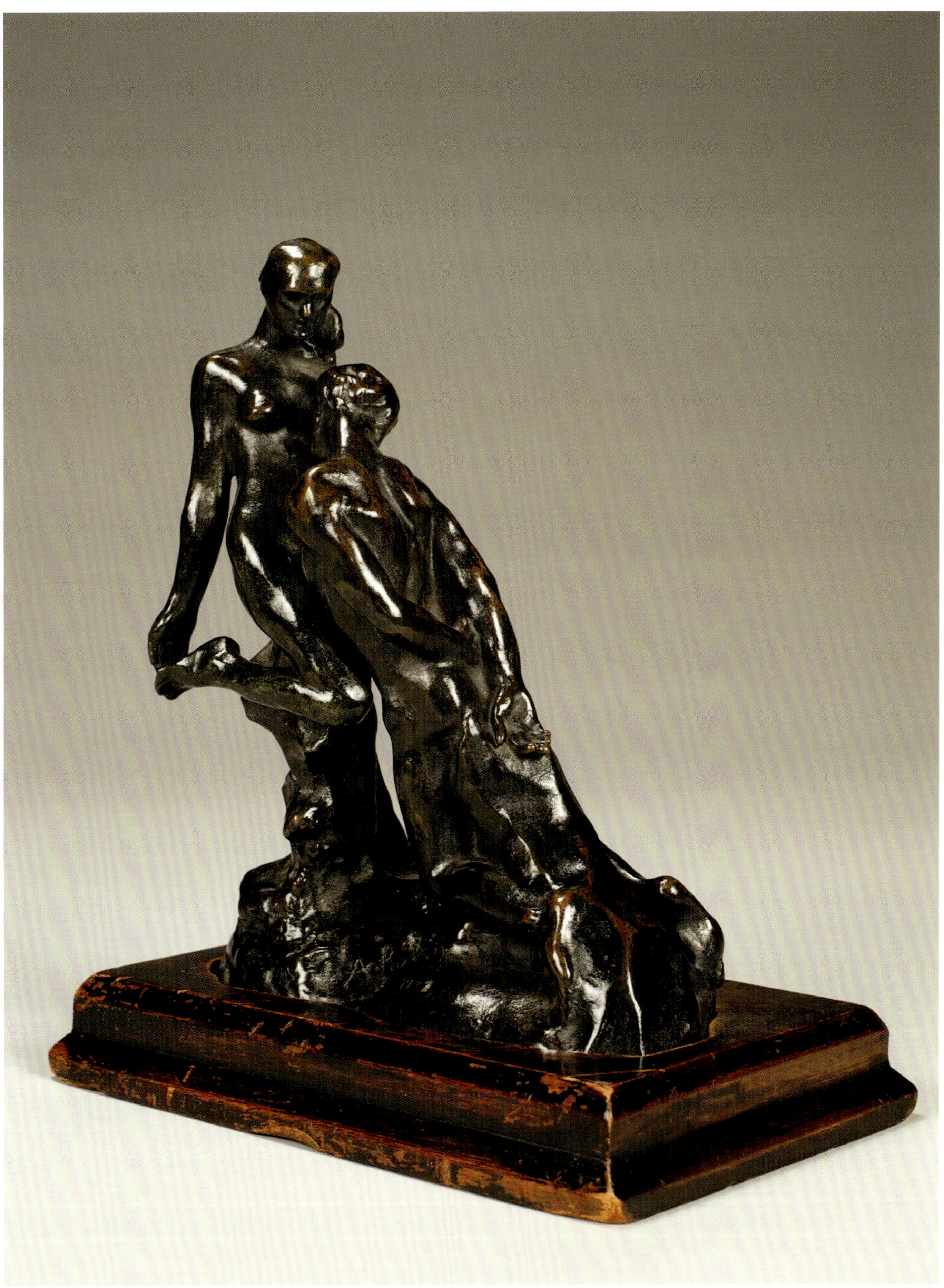

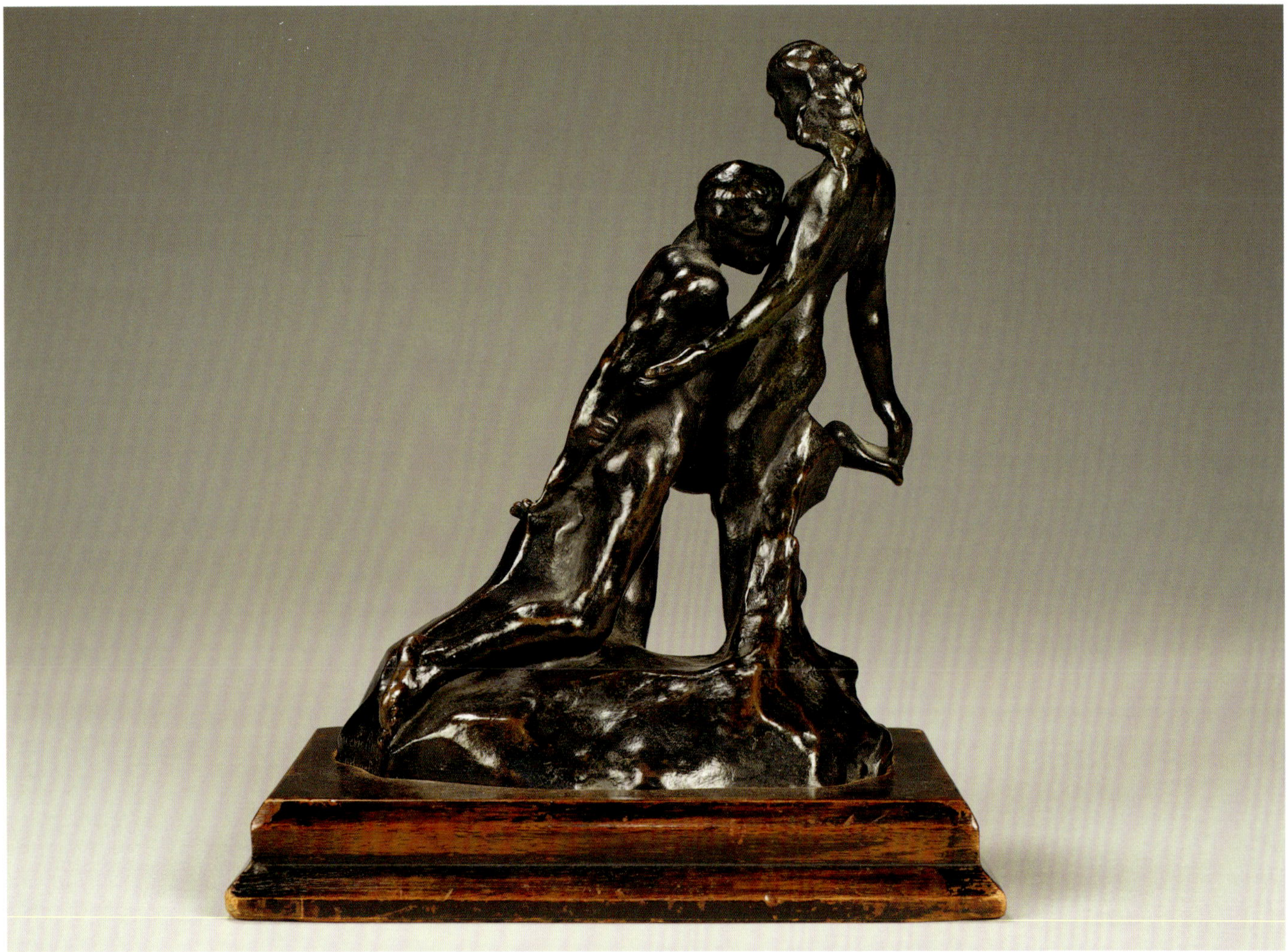

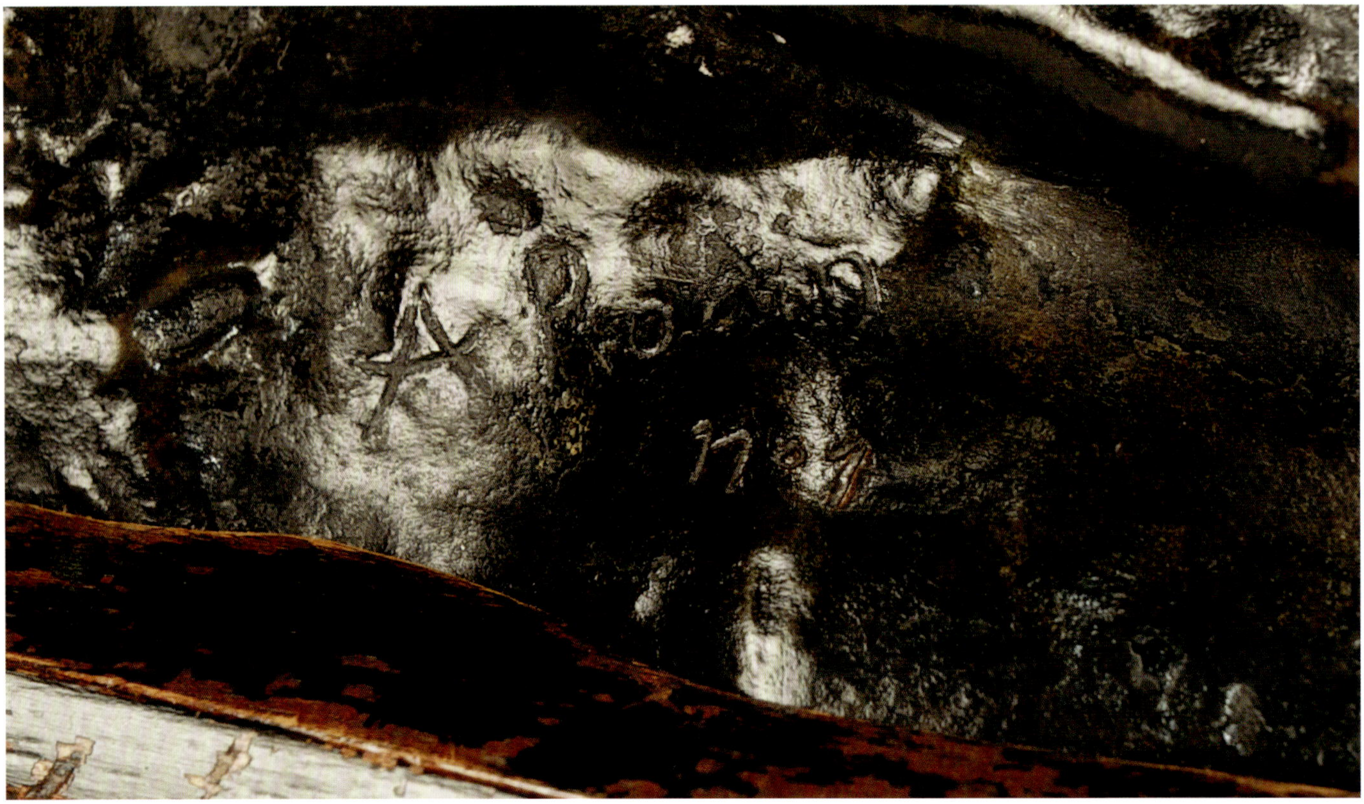

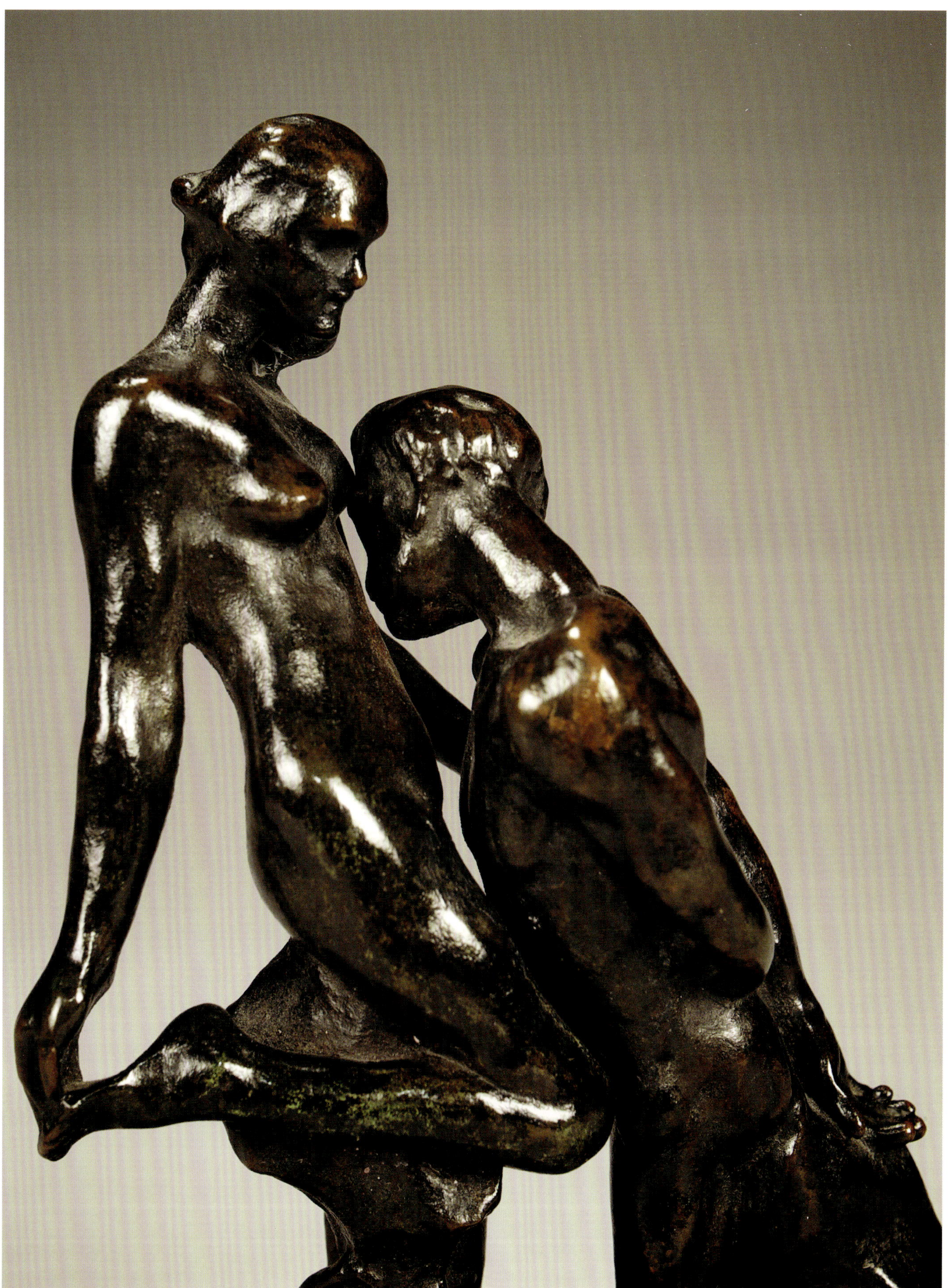

Eternal Idol, Mid-Size Model

Eternelle Idole, Moyen Modéle

Signed A. Rodin and with repeat raised interior signature
Inscribed Alexis Rudier Fondeur Paris.
Bronze with black and brown patination
Height: 11½ inches (29.2 cm)

Provenance:
Musée Rodin
Arthur Cowan, acquired from the above in 1957
Private Collection, USA
Robert Bowman Gallery, 2007
Private Collection, UK

Conceived in 1889, this example was cast in 1948. No lifetime casts of this model in this size were made. In total ten casts were produced for the Musée Rodin. The first two casts by the Alexis Rudier Foundry in 1927 and 1948, then a further eight casts were made between 1957 and 1970 by the Georges Rudier Foundry.

This version varies from the large version also featured in this catalogue as well as the small version. If one examines the underside of the cast the work is clearly cast in 2 sections and then joined together, the head of the man not quite touching the body of the woman. In the letter from Cecile Goldscheider, which accompanies this piece, she confirms that this was the model that was used to create the marble version that Rodin gave to his friend Eugene Corvient.

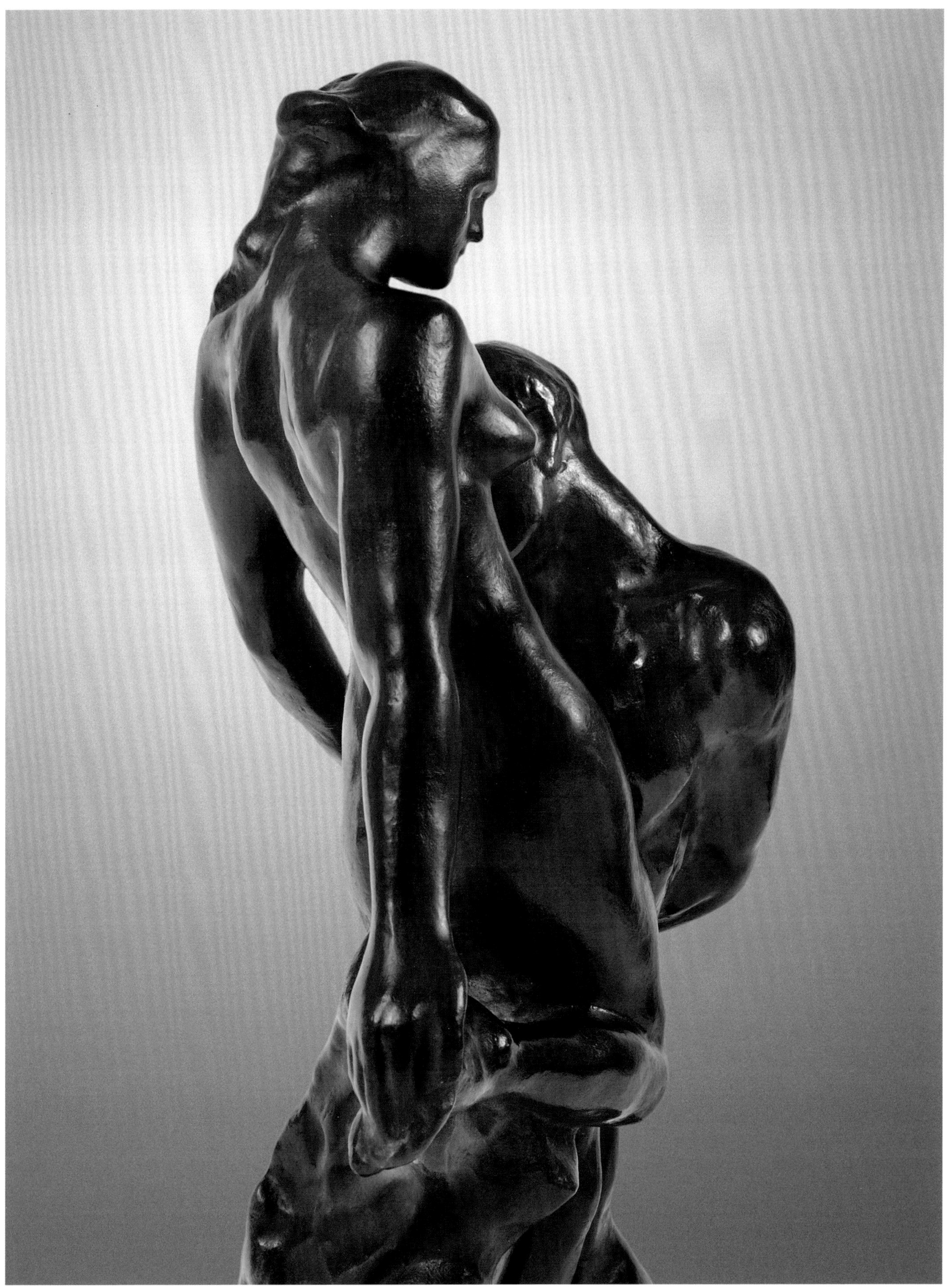

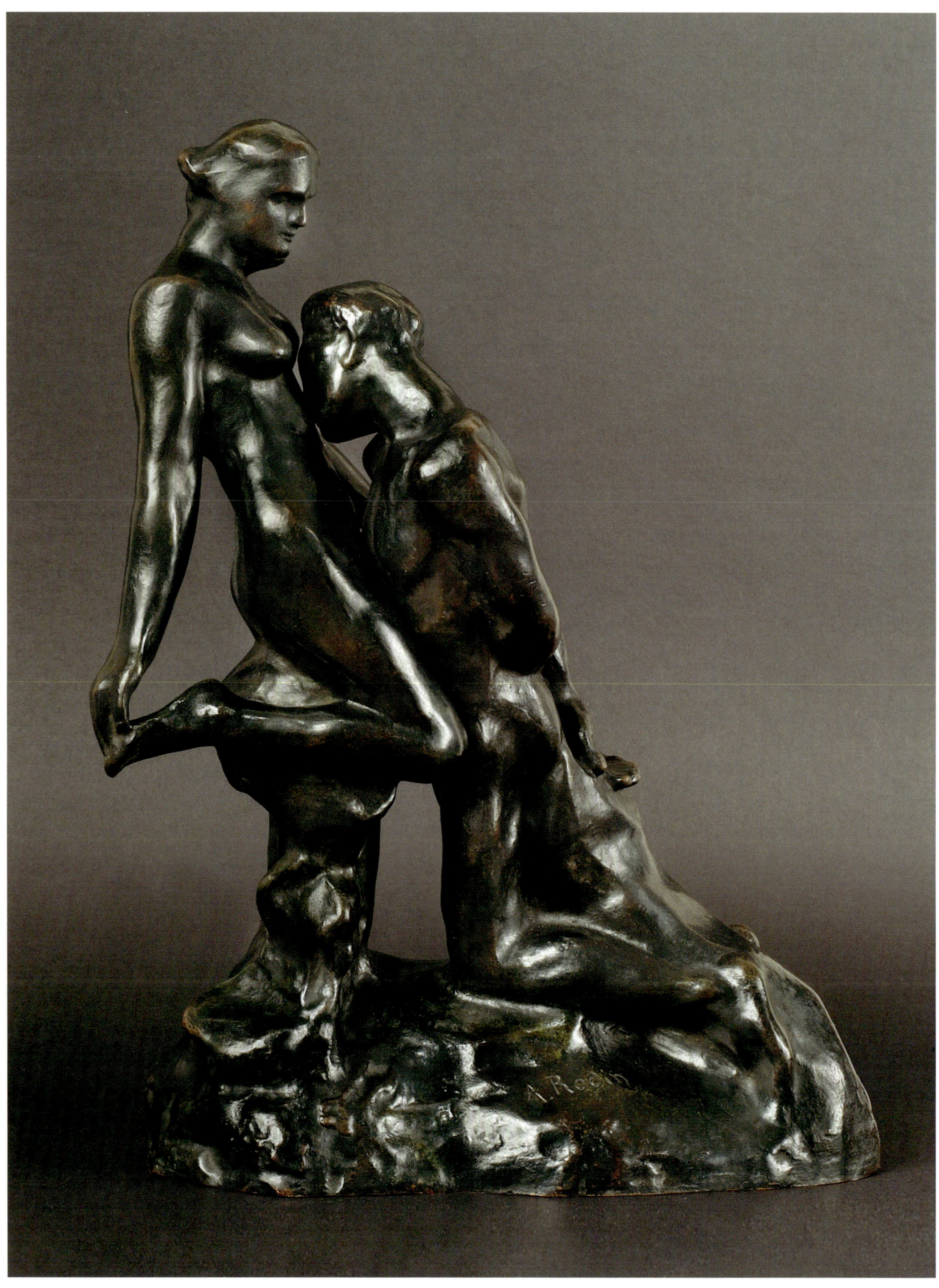

A. Rodin

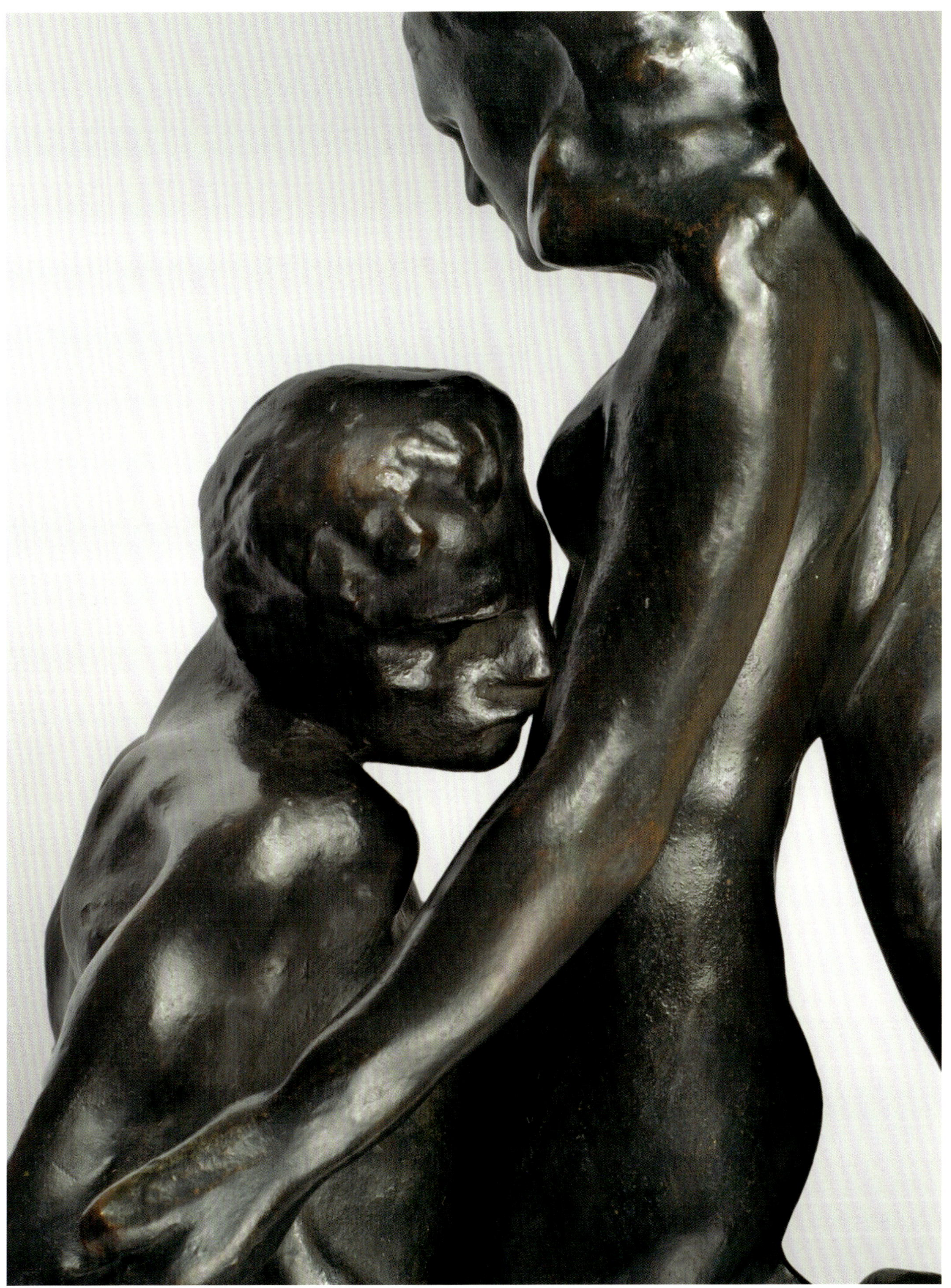

Death of Adonis

Mort d'Adonis

Signed A. Rodin with repeat raised interior signature
Inscribed © by Musée Rodin 1956 and Georges Rudier Fondeur Paris
Bronze with a brown and dark green patination
Height: 10⅝ inches (27 cm)

Provenance:
Musée Rodin 1956
Private Collection, UK
Robert Bowman Gallery, 2011
Private Collection, Turkey

Conceived between 1885 and 1887, this example was cast in 1956. At least one cast of this model was made during Rodin's lifetime. An edition of twelve casts was produced for the Musée Rodin between 1918 and 1966.

Between 1887 and 1888 Rodin was commissioned to illustrate a leather bound copy of Baudelaire's *The Flowers of Evil*, which was owned by the publisher and book lover Paul Gallimard. The book contained the poem *Poison*, and it is in the margin of this poem that an illustration and early design for the present model can be found.

Some years later, when the sculptural work was first exhibited in Brussels, it was entitled *Venus and Adonis*, alluding to the moment when Venus tried to seduce Adonis before the young warrior went out hunting. In 1898, the work was exhibited in London with the title *Hero and Leander*. The title suggested the moment, again from Greek mythology, when Leander leapt from her tower to join the dead body of Leander, who had perished whilst trying to swim across the Dardanelles to see her.

The final title describes the death of Adonis, the Greek God of beauty and desire, who was killed by a wild boar whilst hunting and died in the arms of Aphrodite. As was typical of his work, Rodin's depiction of the story is full of ambiguity and sexual charge, not least because the figure of Adonis can be identified as the female figure from *Man and his Thought*, which appears on the upper lintel of *The Gates of Hell*.

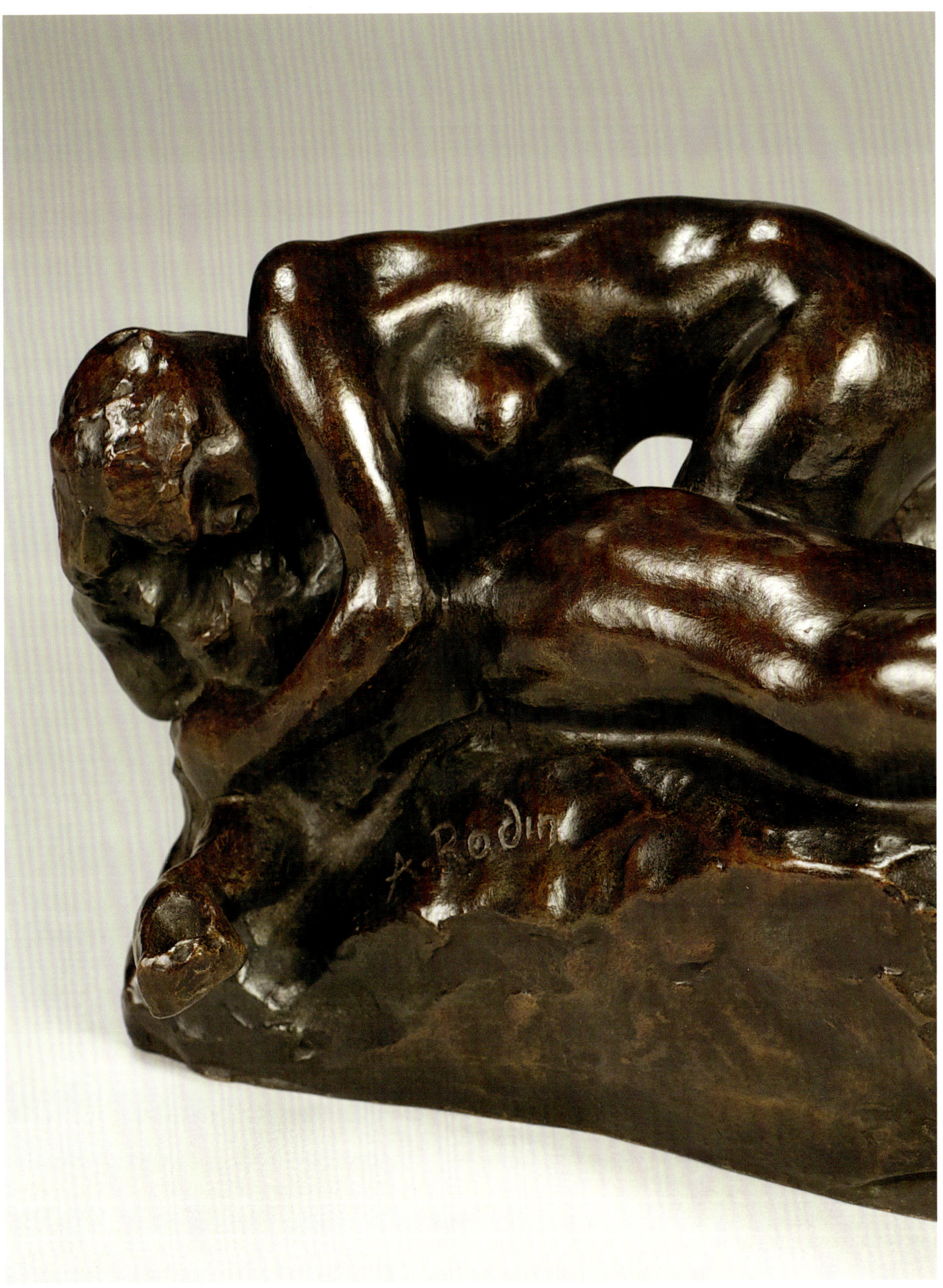

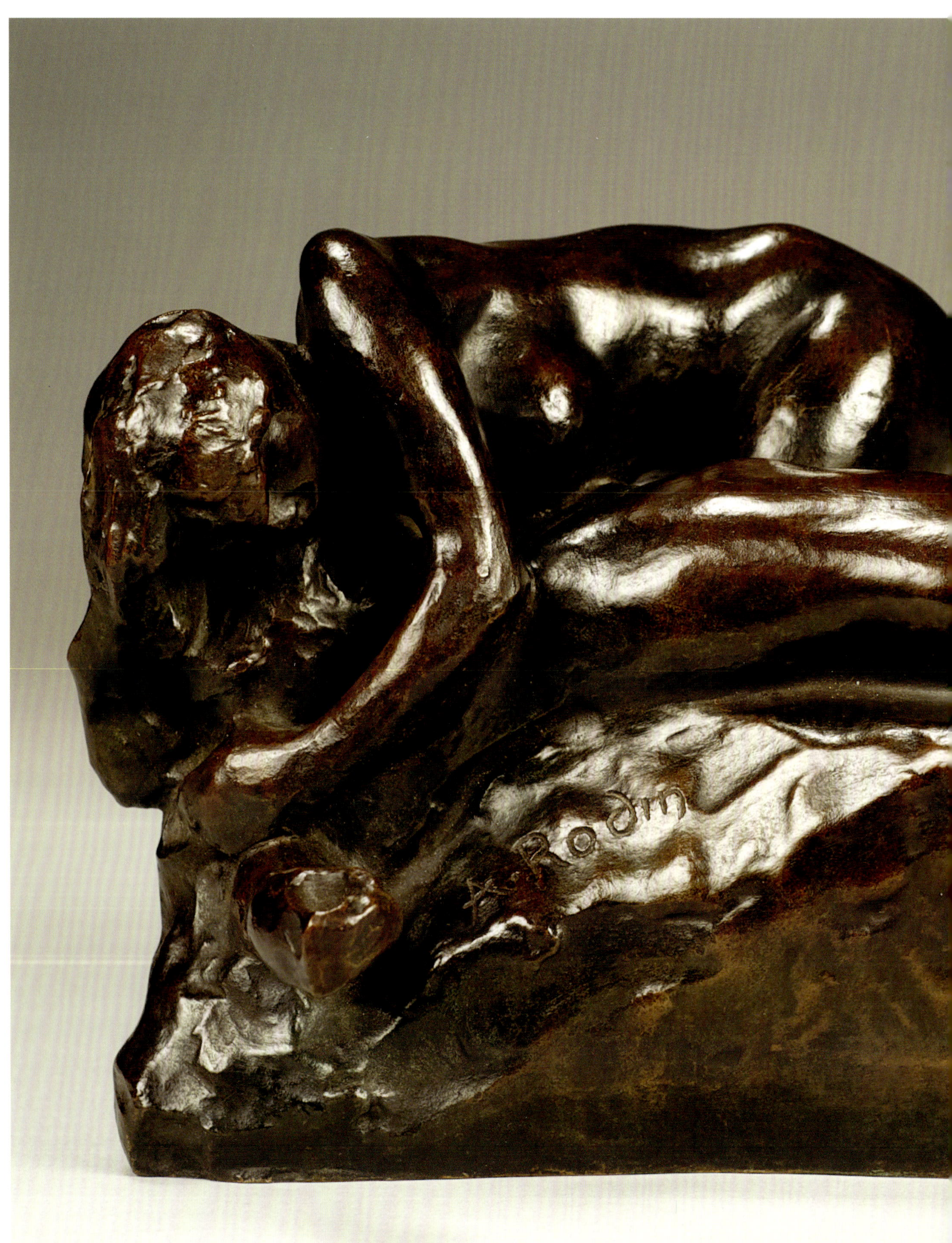

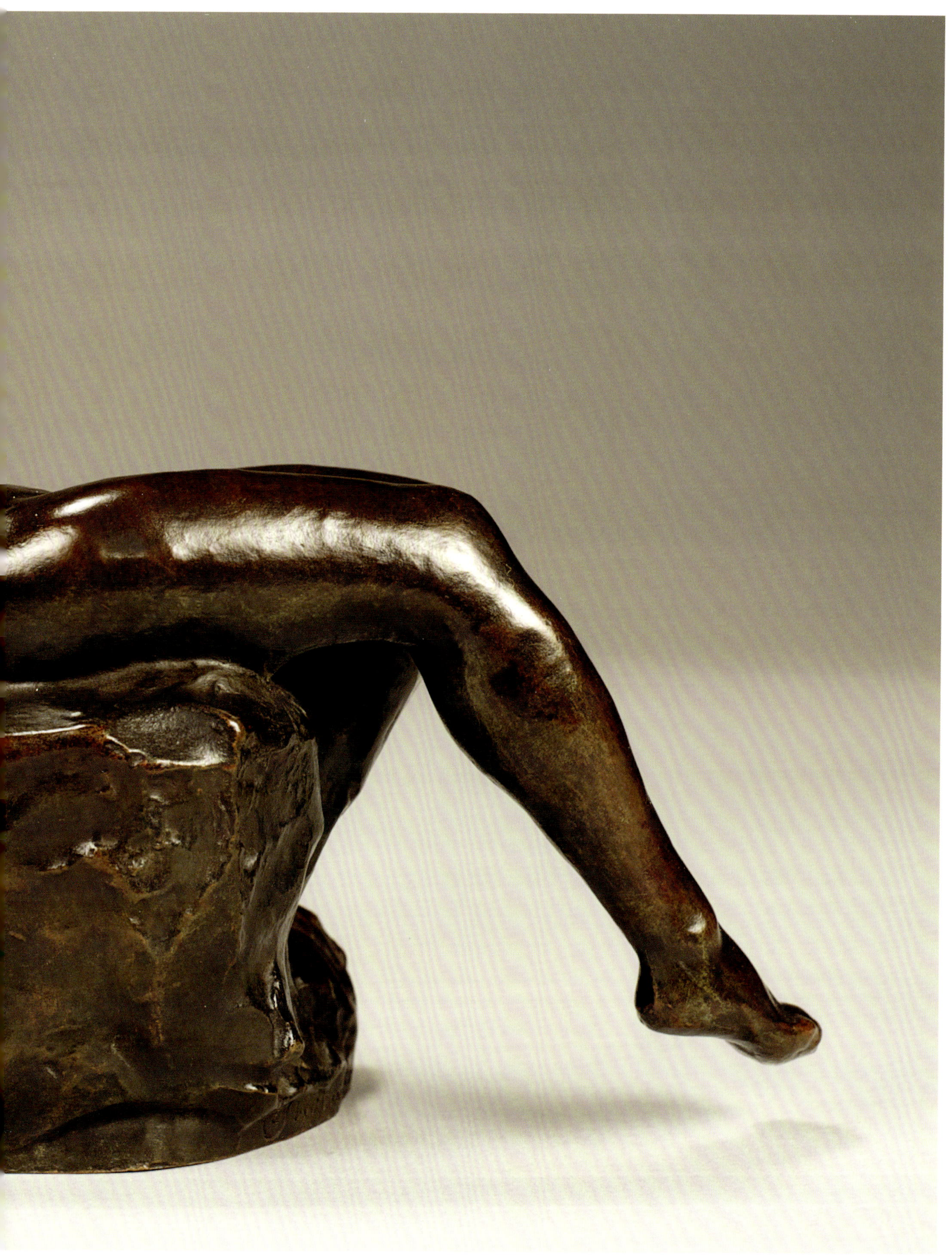

Triumphant Youth

La Jeunesse Triomphante

Signed A. Rodin
Inscribed Thiebaut Fres Paris Fumière et Cie. Suc
Bronze with a rich golden brown and dark brown patination
Height: 20½ inches (52 cm)

Provenance:
Fritz Roeber (Director of the Royal Academy of Arts in Dusseldorf 1908–1921), acquired between 1906 and 1918.
Sold Christie's London 29 June 1976 lot 240
Private European Collection
Robert Bowman Gallery, 2005
Private Collection, Turkey

Conceived in 1894, this example was cast between 1906 and 1918. In 1898 Thiebaut Freres, Fumiere & Gavigniot successeurs began a ten year contract to produce an unlimited edition of this model. In 1908 the contract was renewed for a further ten years. It is known that at least fifty bronzes were cast between 1898 and 1918.

Rodin first modelled the old woman seen in this group as a single figure in 1885 known as *She Who Was The Helmet Maker's Beautiful Wife* after a poem by François Villon. Albert Elsen comments:

'When one looks closely at Rodin's *Old Woman*, the longer the figure is studied, the more conscious the viewer becomes not of biography but of sculpture. Far from illustrating a medieval French poem about an ageing beauty lamenting her lost youth, Rodin found a timeless experience in the living model's own rich story and the capacity of her aged body to inspire a stunningly powerful form.'

This sculpture is an assemblage of the old woman combined with that of a reclining young woman, which Rodin also produced as an individual sculpture, known as *Fatigue*. Throughout his career Rodin pioneered the technique of creating entirely new works by reusing sculptures he had already made and assembling them into groups, sometimes repeating the same figure as with his *Shades*. Rodin's ingenuity resides in the fact that he took casting in multiples, the intrinsic method of making bronzes, and made it a systematic part of his creative process.

The work was first exhibited publically in 1896 in marble at the Paris salon, a bronze version being shown in Berlin in 1903. This work has several different titles, *Triumphant Youth, Eternal Youth, Fate* and *The Convalescent*, the *Grandmother's Kiss, Old Age* and *Adolescence, Young Girl* and *Fate*. The symbolic interpretations are always a source of discussion but contrary to the most accepted title, youth is in fact embracing old age, as all mortals have to in the end.

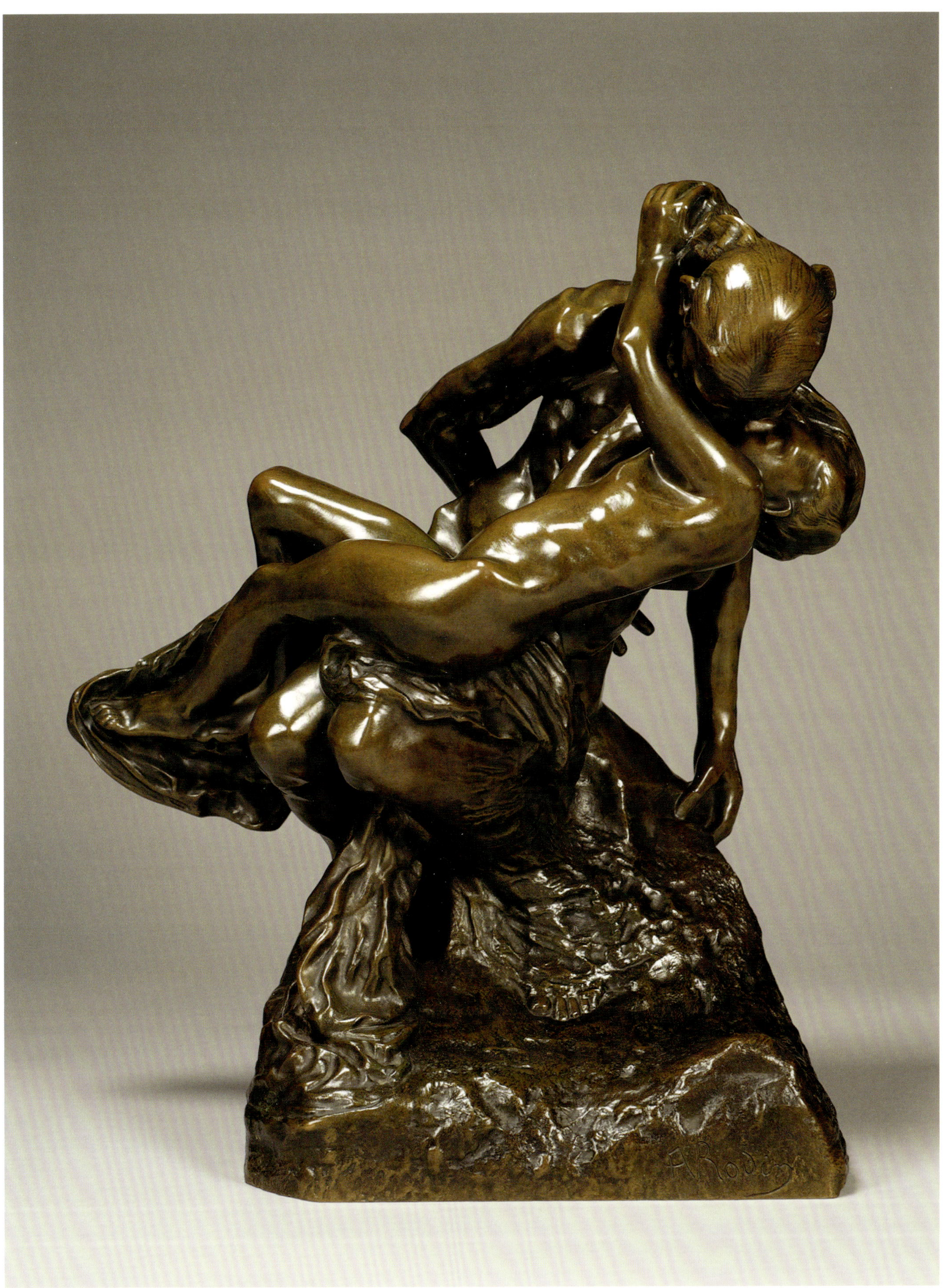

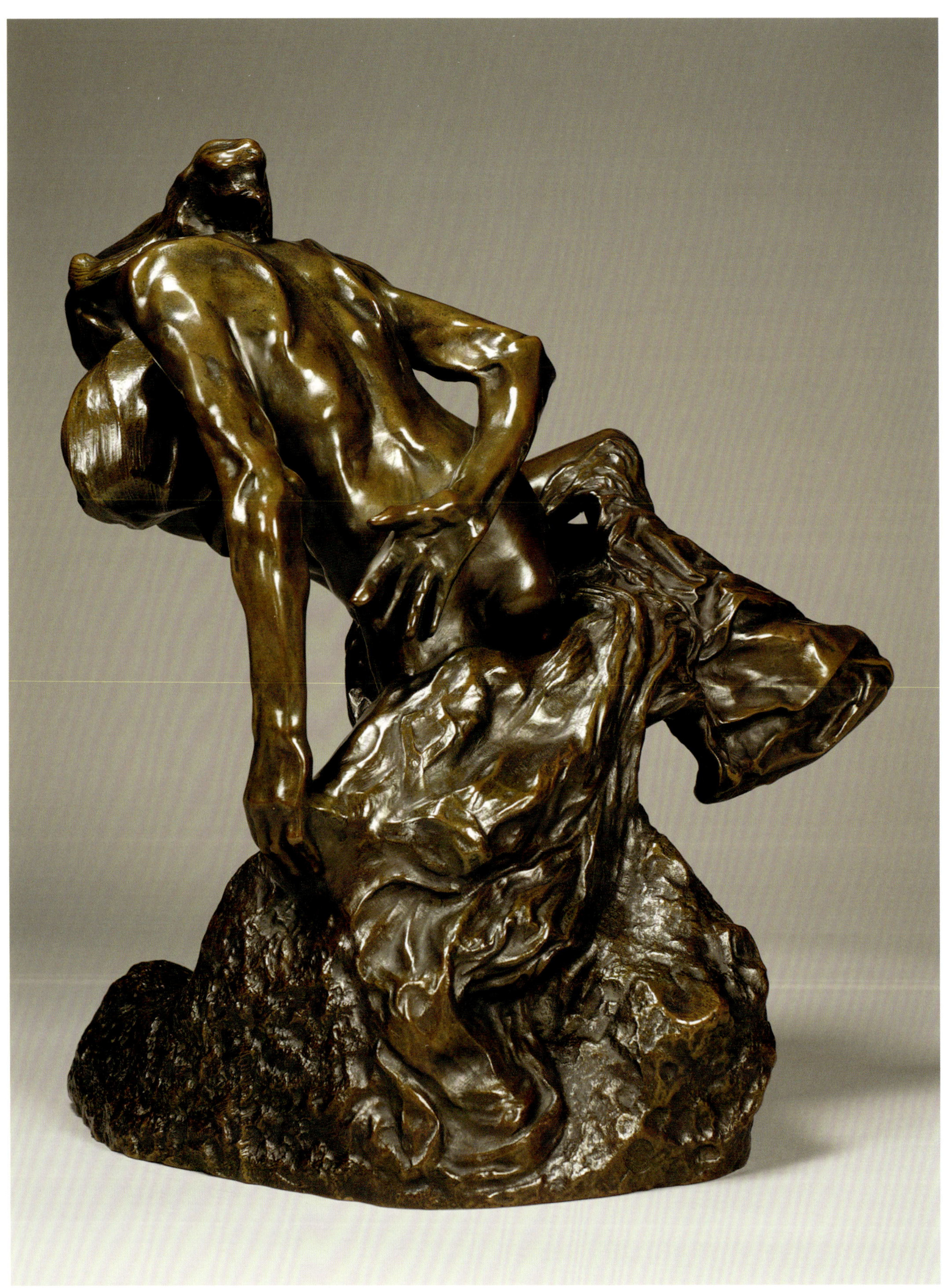

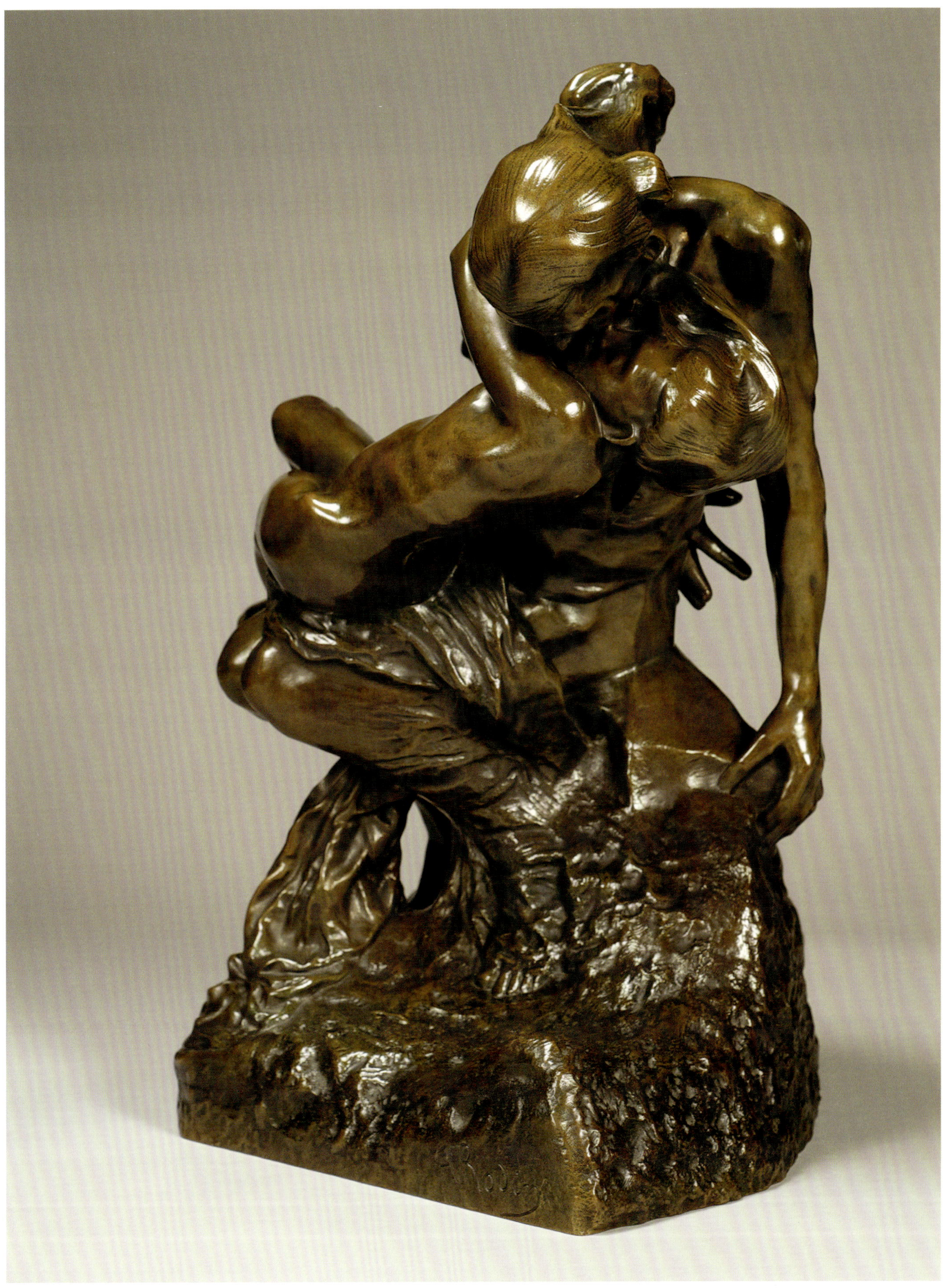

Brother and Sister

Frère et Sœur

Signed A. Rodin with repeat interior signature
Inscribed Alexis Rudier Fondeur, Paris
Bronze with a dark brown and green patination
Height: 15 inches (38 cm)

Provenance:
Jean Alvarez de Toledo (Paris)
Jourdan Barry Collection
Private Collection, UK

Conceived between 1890 and 1891, this cast was executed in 1905. According to the Comité Rodin, around thirty casts were made during Rodin's lifetime. A further twenty casts were produced for the Musée Rodin, firstly by the Alexis Rudier foundry between 1926 and 1950, then by the Georges Rudier foundry between 1962 and 1965.

The present model is particularly unusual in Rodin's oeuvre in that it incorporates a variation of a model by Camille Claudel. The sister figure seen here is taken from Claudel's *Young Girl with a Sheaf* (1887) from which Rodin later also developed his model *Galatea* (1888). The figure of the young boy relates to a number of works produced by Rodin during the 1870s and 1880s.

In 1897, the François Rudier foundry produced a bronze cast of the work, although it was a plaster that was first exhibited in Vienna the following year and then in Brussels and the Netherlands in 1899.

The group proved highly successful with a number of bronzes being cast and Rodin having the model transferred into marble. It provided a charming counterpoint to the vigor and chaos of Rodin's *The Gates of Hell*, which he was working on at the time.

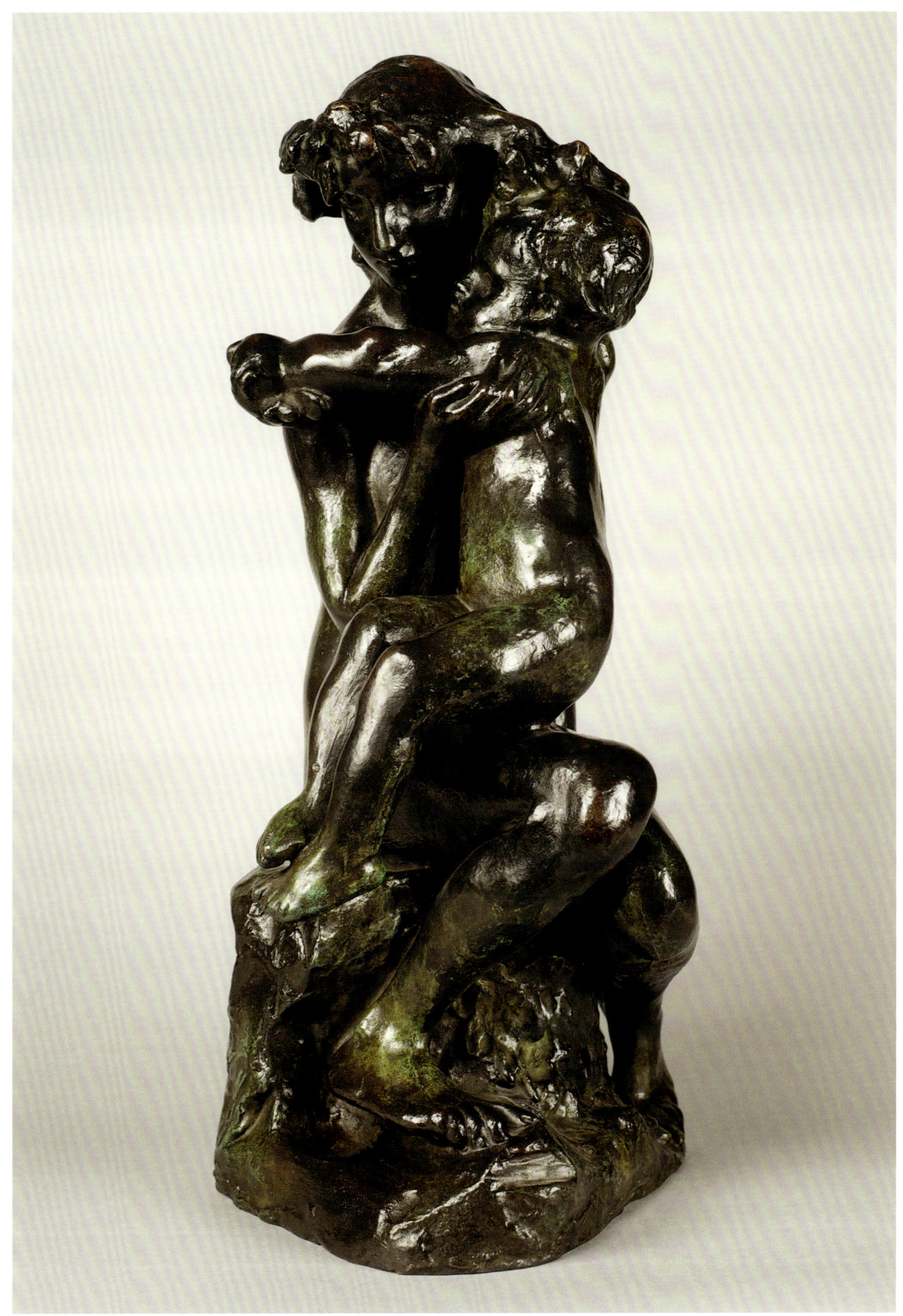

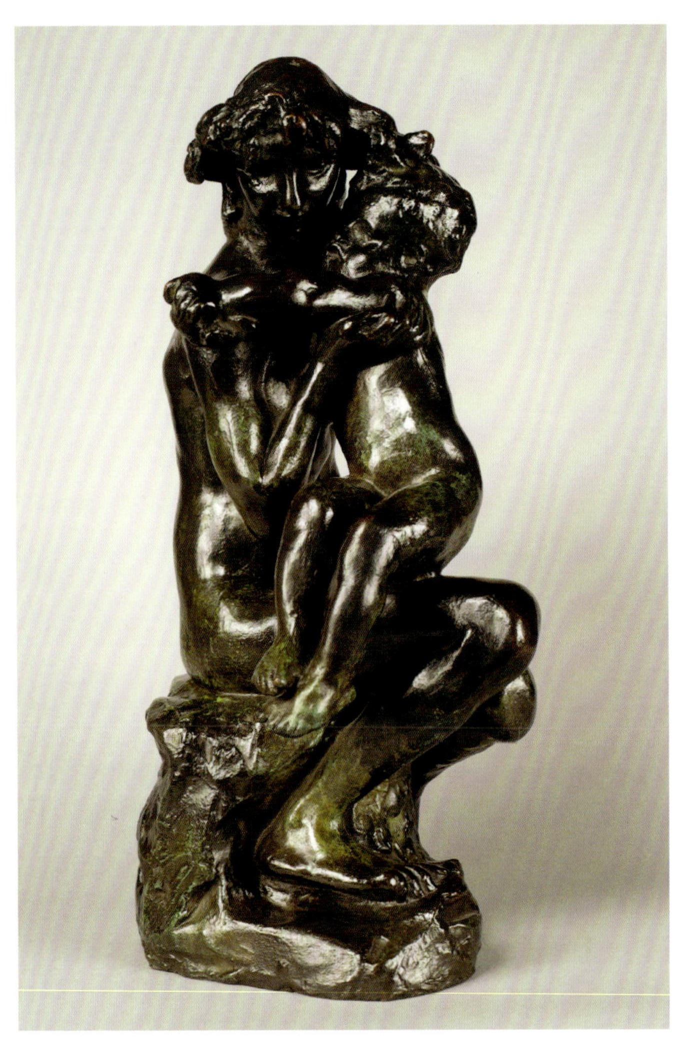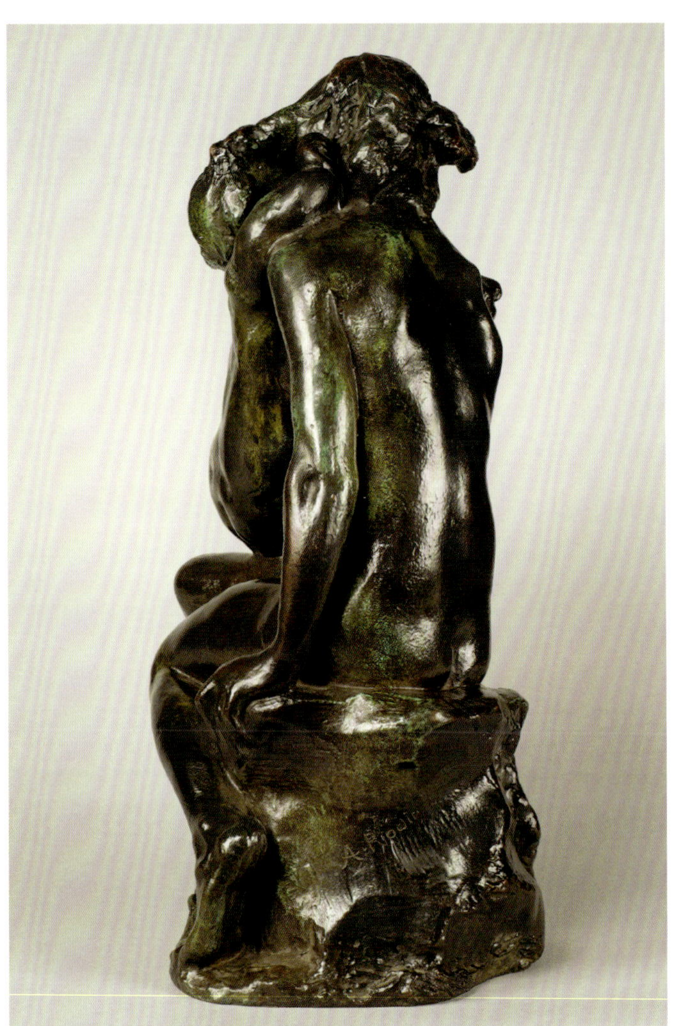

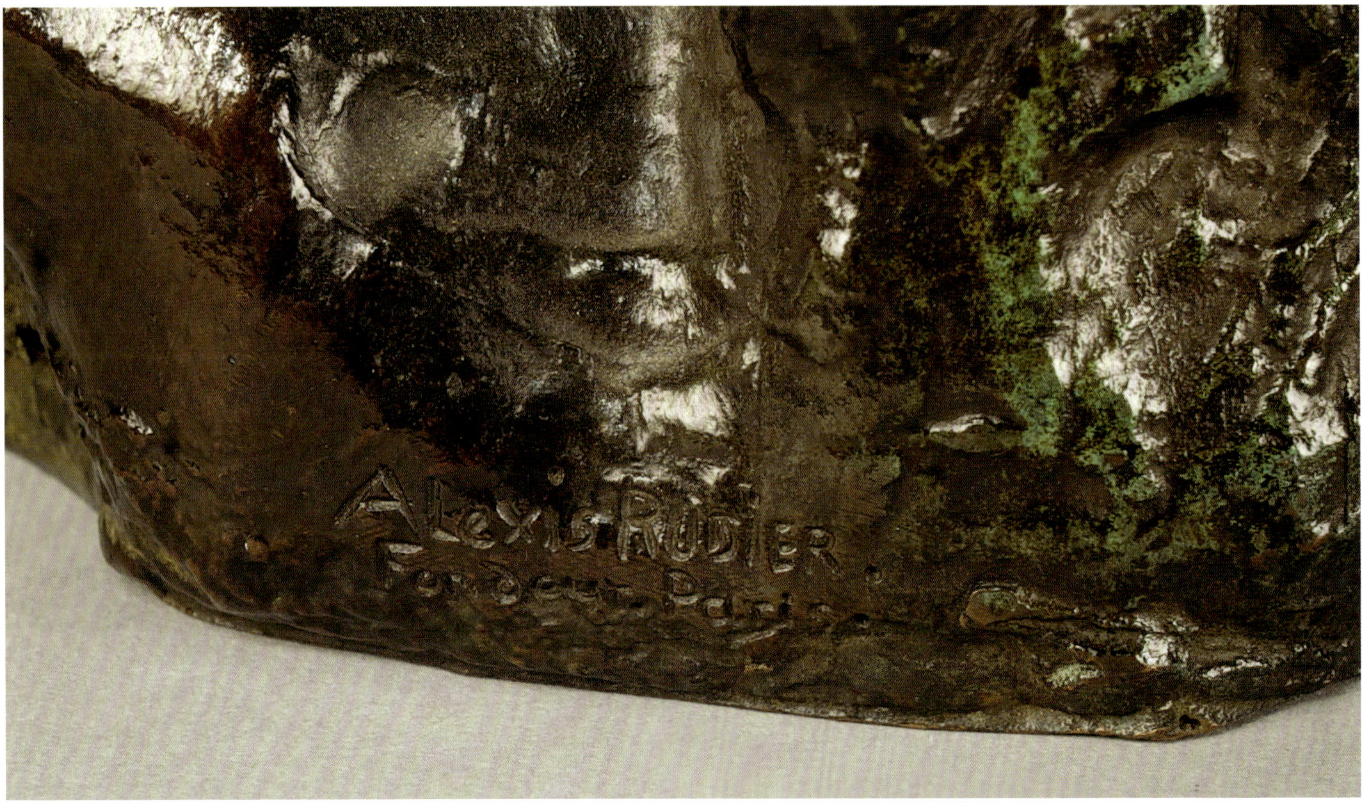

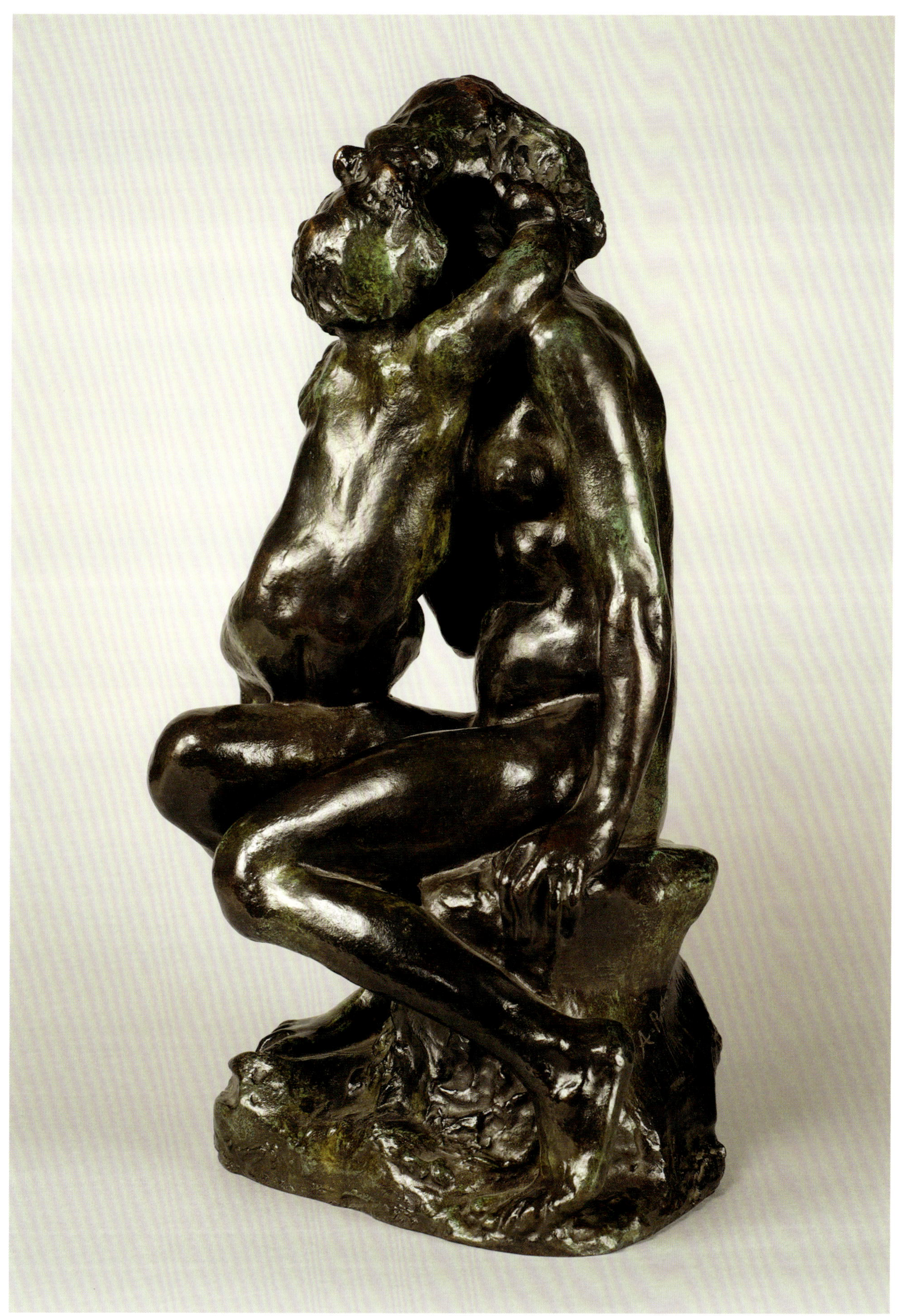

Young Mother

Jeune Mère

Signed A. Rodin 2^{éme} epreuve
Inscribed Fcois Rudier Fondeur Paris
Bronze with a dark brown and green patination
Height: 15⅜ inches (39 cm)

Provenance:
Eugéne Rudier, Le Vésinet
M. Knoedler & co., Inc., New York (stocks no 15573, acquired from the above, 1923)
Mr. Emil Winter, Pittsburgh
Mme Geraldine Rockefeller Dodge, Madison, New Jersey
Rose Faggen
Private European Collection

Conceived in 1885, the present example was cast between 1887 and 1901. Eighteen lifetime casts of this model were made by the foundries Perzinka, Gruet Fils, Griffoul et Lorge, François Rudier and Alexis Rudier. Fourteen further casts were made for the Musée Rodin. The first eight casts by the Alexis Rudier foundry between 1927 and 1945, then six casts by the Georges Rudier foundry between 1955 and 1963.

Rodin was greatly taken by the subject of maternal love, developing the theme in three small sculptural groups. The first of these, modelled in high relief and known as *Young mother in the Grotto*, was originally conceived to adorn the left hand pilaster of *The Gates of Hell* where it probably represented *Venus and Amor*.

In 1888 Rodin reconfigured the pilaster, replacing *Young mother in the Grotto* with *The Fallen Caryatid with a Stone*. The sculptor no longer considered the tranquil image of a loving mother and her child to be appropriate for an assemblage of works based around Dante's *Inferno*.

The present model, which is certainly one of Rodin's most charming, is a free standing version of *Young mother in the Grotto*. The tender intimacy between the mother and child is expertly rendered and the child reaches out to touch his mother's hair whilst staring intently at her.

The work was probably first carved in marble in 1889, and Rodin revisited the composition in 1890 when he modelled *Frere et Soeur*. As Antoinette Le Normand-Romain comments, these works 'reflect a side of Rodin's work in the 1880s that served as an indispensible counterpoint to the tragic universe of *The Gates of Hell*.'

By tackling the subject of maternal love, Rodin also invites comparison with both Albert Ernest Carrier-Belleuse and Jean Baptiste Capreaux, both of whom had also modelled groups depicting a mother and child. This point would not have escaped art connoisseurs of the time, and reminds us of Rodin's own debt to these masters of the 19th century Romantic tradition.

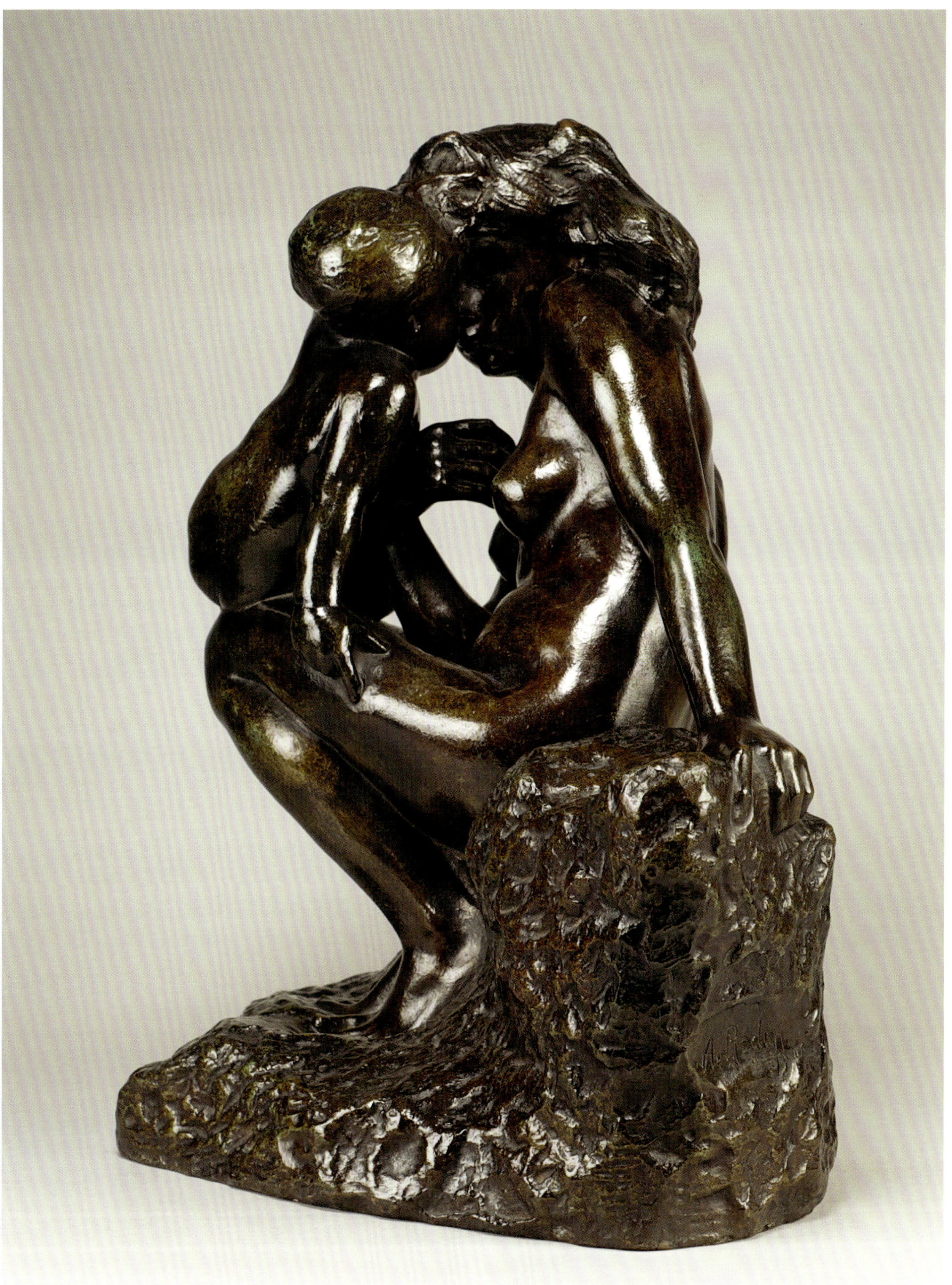

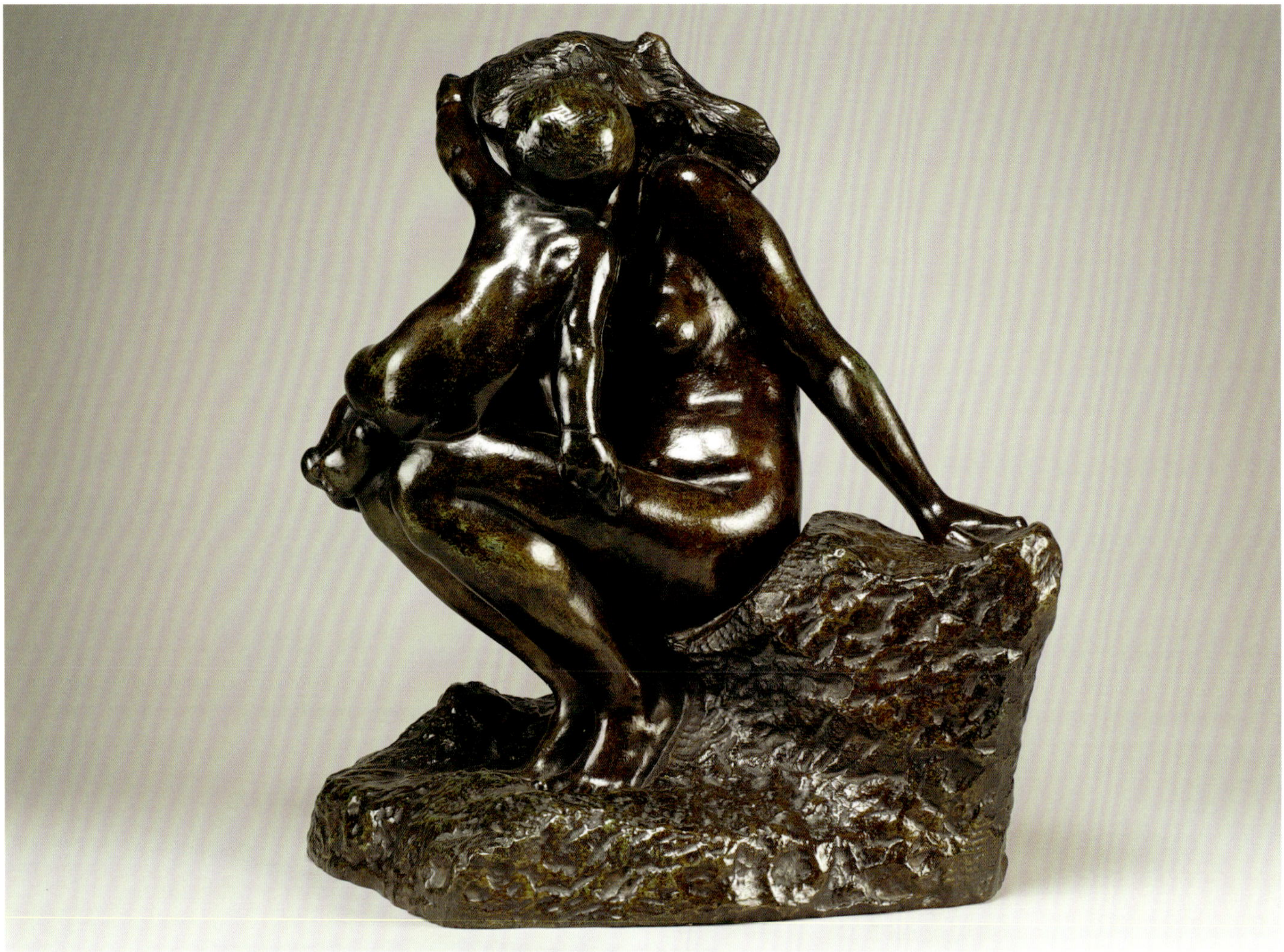

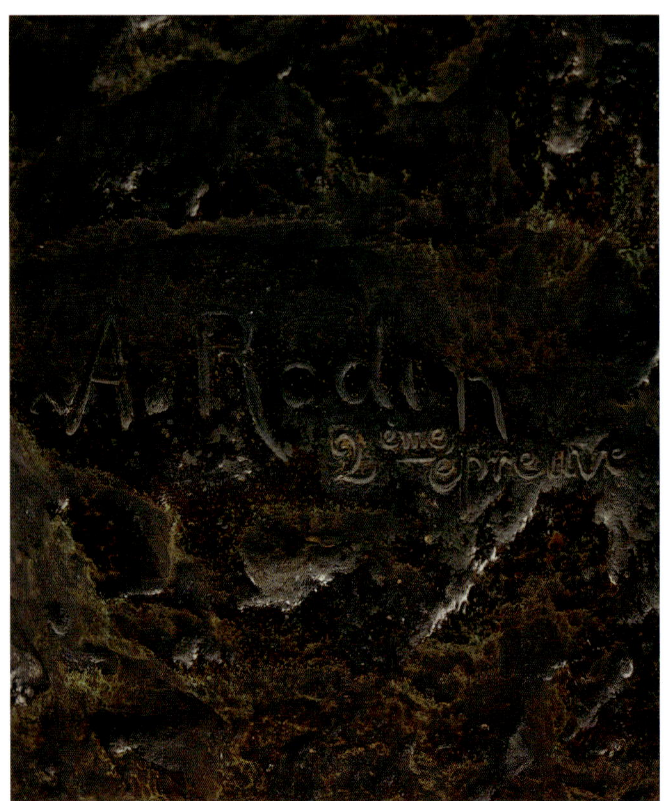
A. Rodin
2ème épreuve

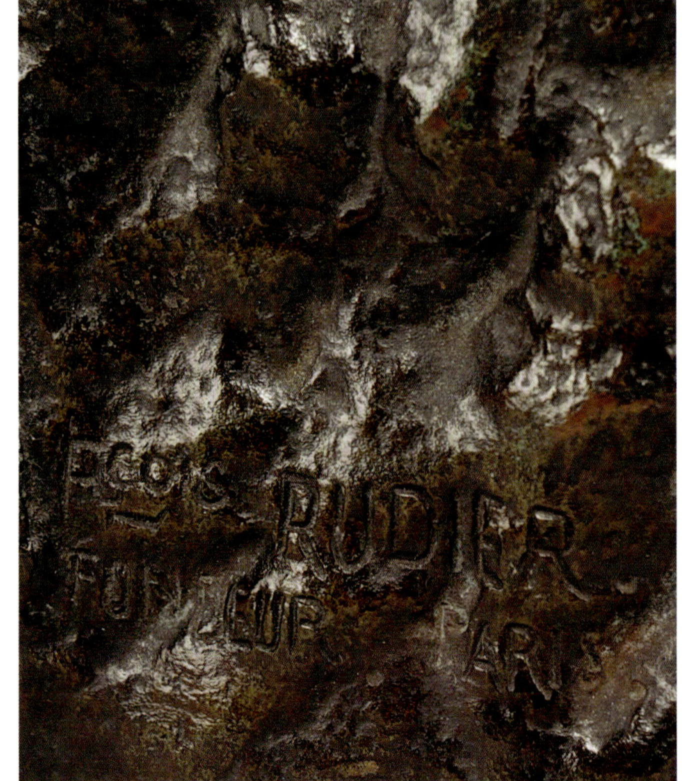
ECOIS
FONDEUR
RUDIER
PARIS

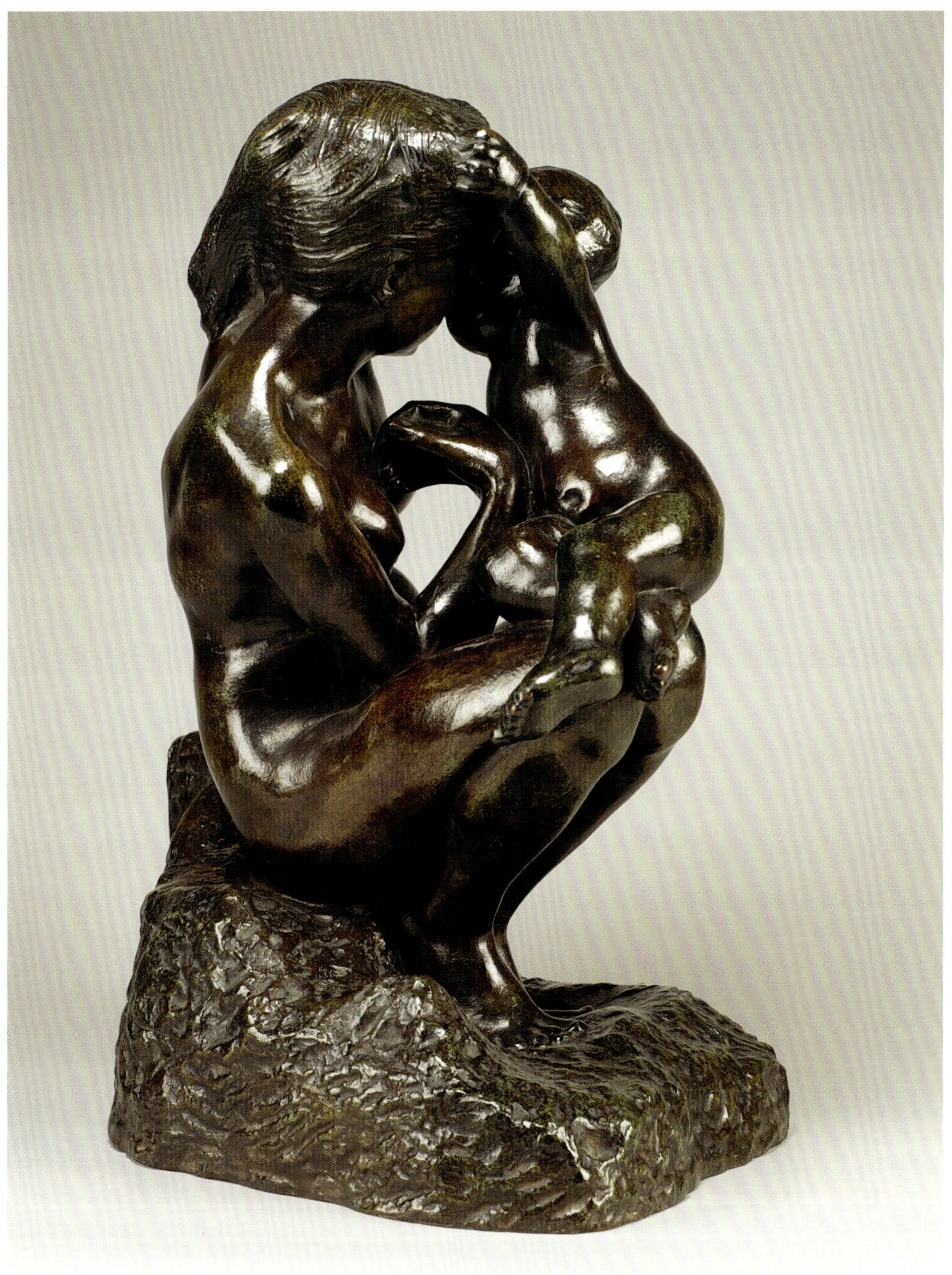

Pas-de-deux, Study Type B

Pas-de-deux, Étude Type B

Signed A. Rodin
Inscribed © by Musée Rodin 1964 and G. Rudier Fondeur, Paris
Bronze with a brown patination with red highlights
Numbered 11
Height: 12¼ inches (31.5 cm)

Provenance:
Musée Rodin, Paris
Dominion Gallery, Montréal
Galerie Walter Klinkhoff, Canada
Christies New York, 3 November 1993, Lot 129
Christies New York, 1 May 1996, Lot 104
Private Collection, USA

Conceived circa 1911, this example cast in 1964. No lifetime casts of this model were made. Thirteen casts were made for the Musée Rodin by the Georges Rudier foundry between 1964 and 1966.

Rodin's dancers were influenced by his nights at Paris' famous Folie-Bergère nightclub and here he portrays two dancers performing chahuts, high kicks that feature prominently in the cancan.

Throughout his career, Rodin experimented with assemblages, incorporating previous sculptures (or parts of sculptures) into new works with slight modifications. The *Dance Movements* series comprised nine different movements labeled A through I and incorporate this technique.

In *Pas de deux, étude type B*, Rodin repeats the forms used in *Pas de deux, étude type G*, also conceived circa 1911. While the figures in *Pas de deux, étude type G* face away from one another, the dancers in *Pas de deux, étude type B* face the same direction and are unified in their intimate performance, seemingly moving as one.

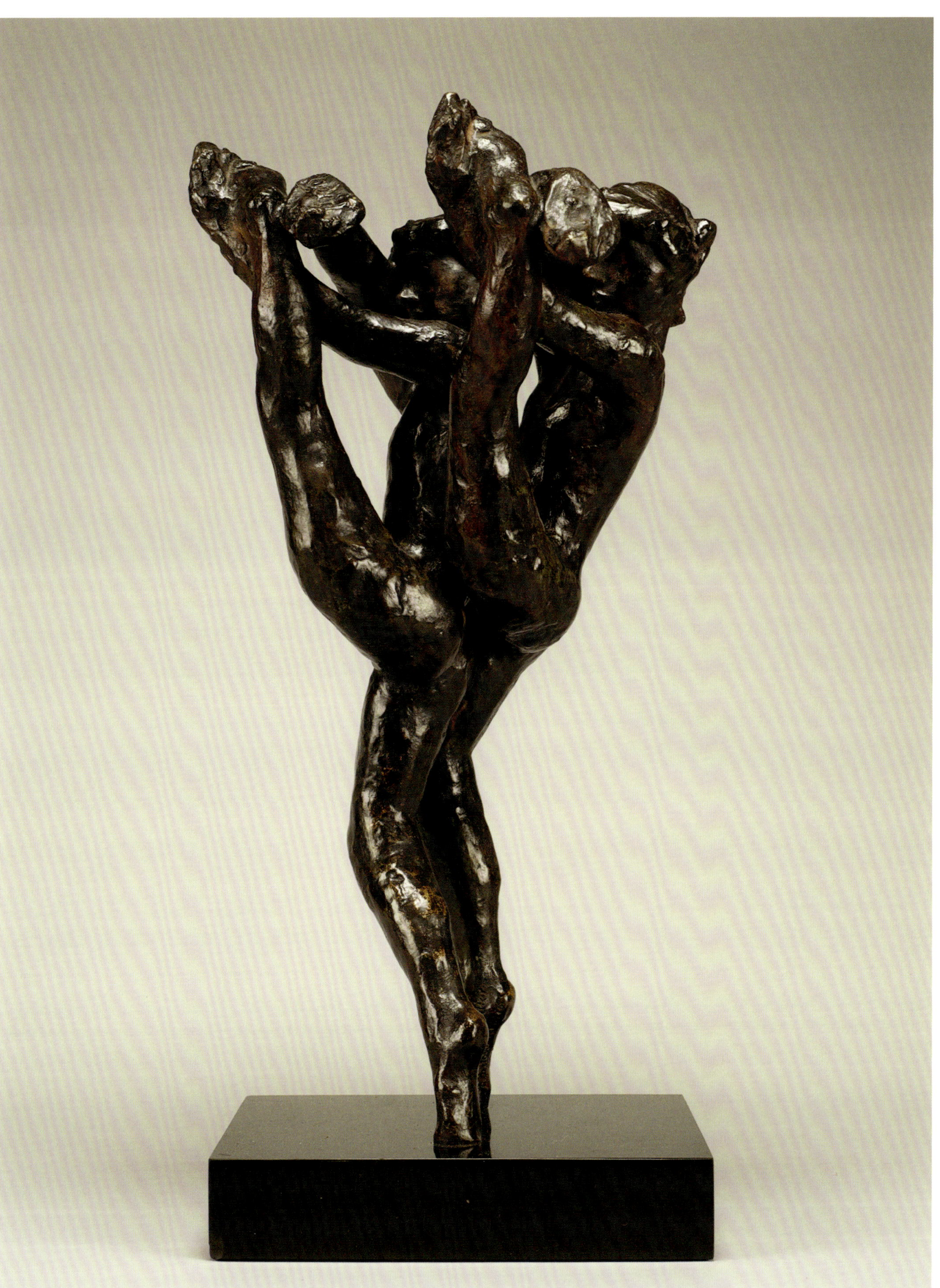

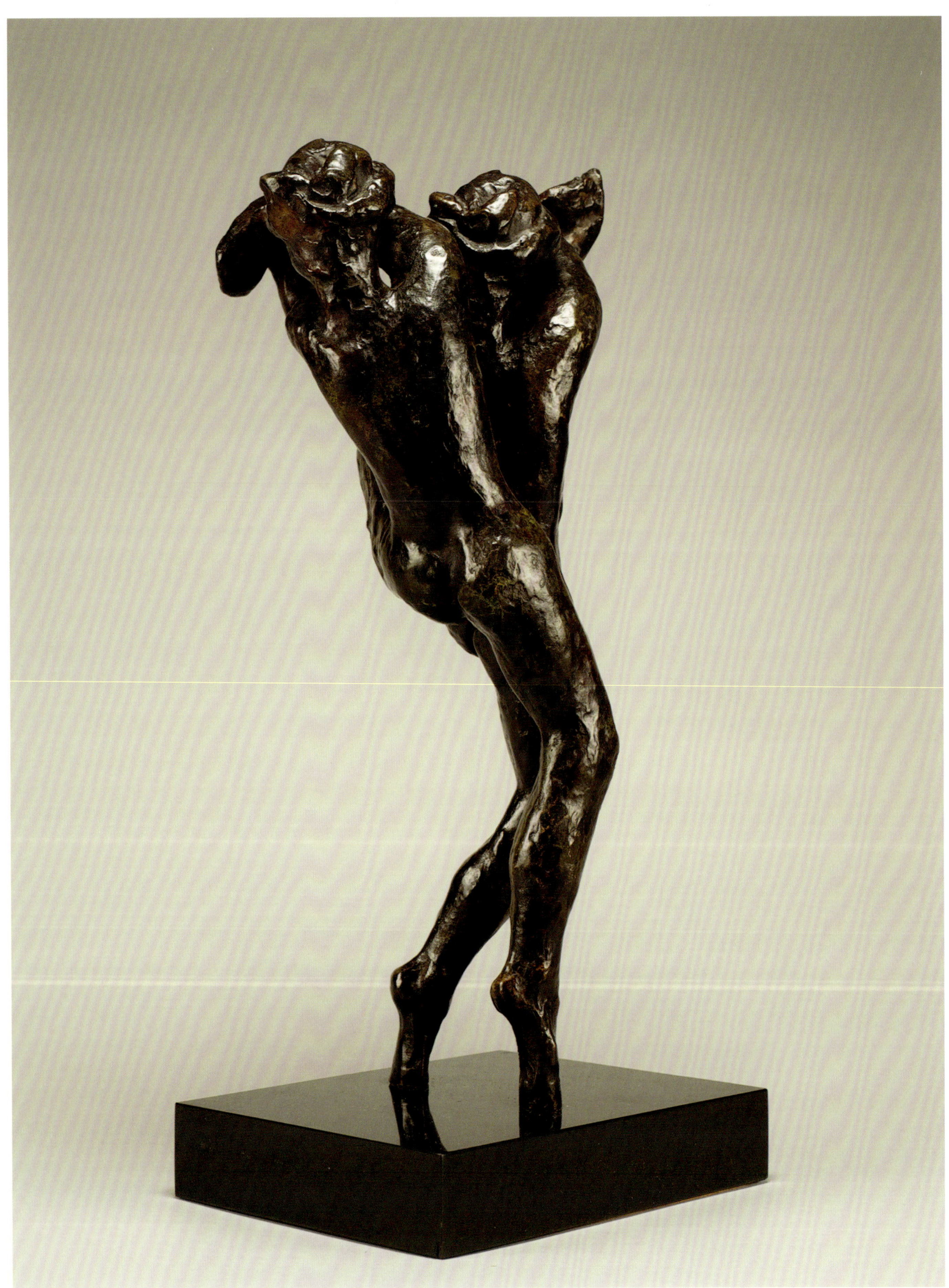

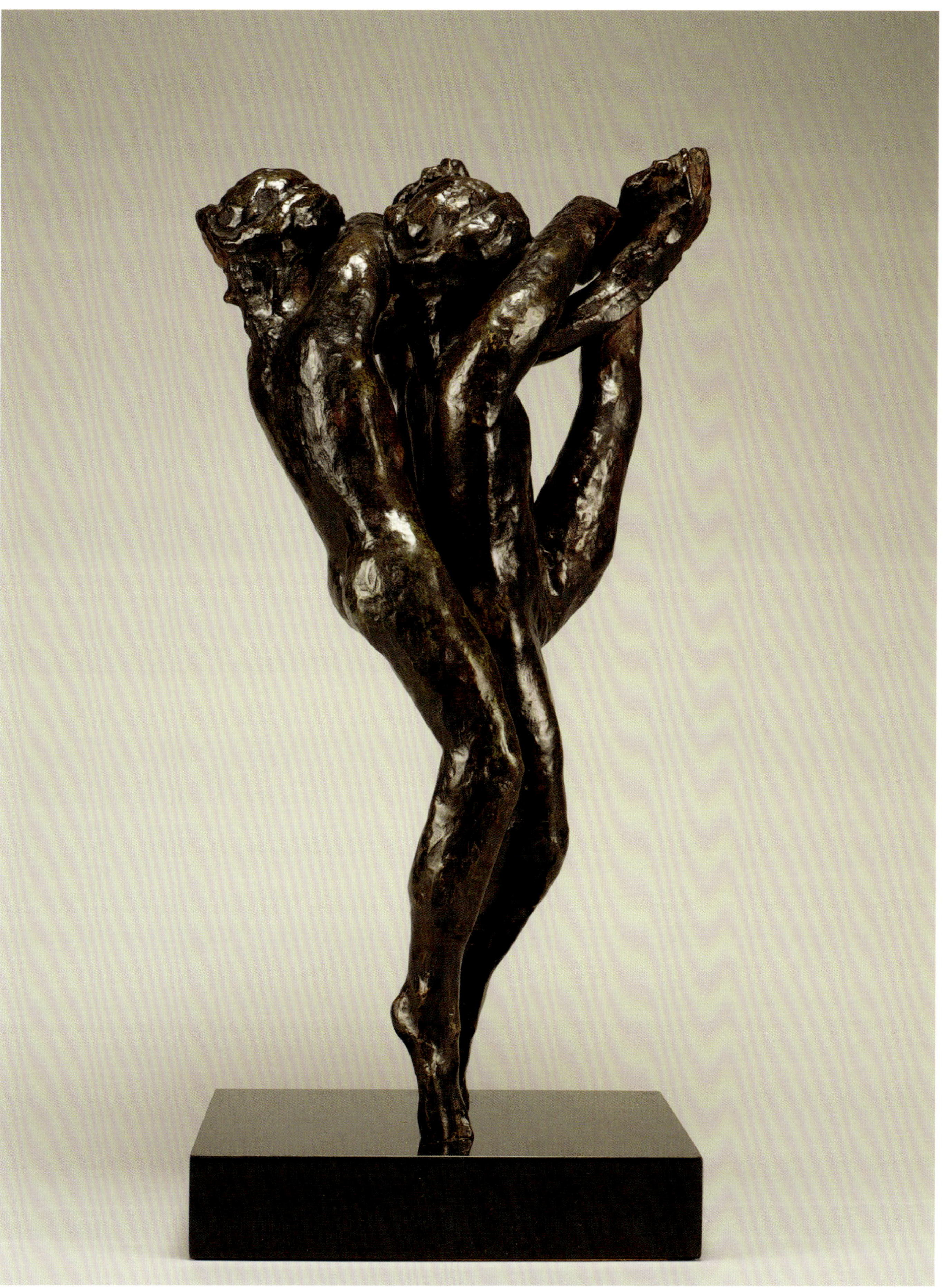

Iris Awakening a Nymph

Iris Éveillant une Nymphe

Signed A. Rodin with repeat raised interior signature
Inscribed Alexis Rudier Fondeur Paris
Bronze with a rich brown patination
Height: 13¼ inches (33.9 cm)

Provenance:
Musée Rodin, Paris
M. Hachard, Paris (acquired November 1943)
Collection of Mme Herbin, France (acquired between 1950 to 1965)
By Descent, 1970
Robert Bowman Gallery, 2010
Private European Collection

Conceived in 1885, the present example was cast in 1943. The model was cast five times during Rodin's lifetime. Twelve casts were made for the Musée Rodin, firstly five casts by the Alexis Rudier foundry between 1931 and 1945, then five casts by the Georges Rudier foundry between 1965 and 1976. Two final casts were made by the Godard foundry in 1979.

Rodin was an avid collector of objects from classical antiquity and often utilised themes from Greek mythology in his own sculptures. In this work he depicts *Iris*, the messenger of the gods, leaning over to awake a beautiful young maiden as she sleeps. The elevated emotional state between the two female forms is evident and combined with the smooth finishing of the figures; the work is somewhat reminiscent of *The Kiss*.

Here, Iris is depicted as a delicate and feminine figure, rather than the muscular and provocative messenger, which Rodin created some six years later. Given the sculptor's working methods at this period and the fact that the present work suggests an assemblage of two pre-existing models, it is likely the figures were originally created for *The Gates of Hell*.

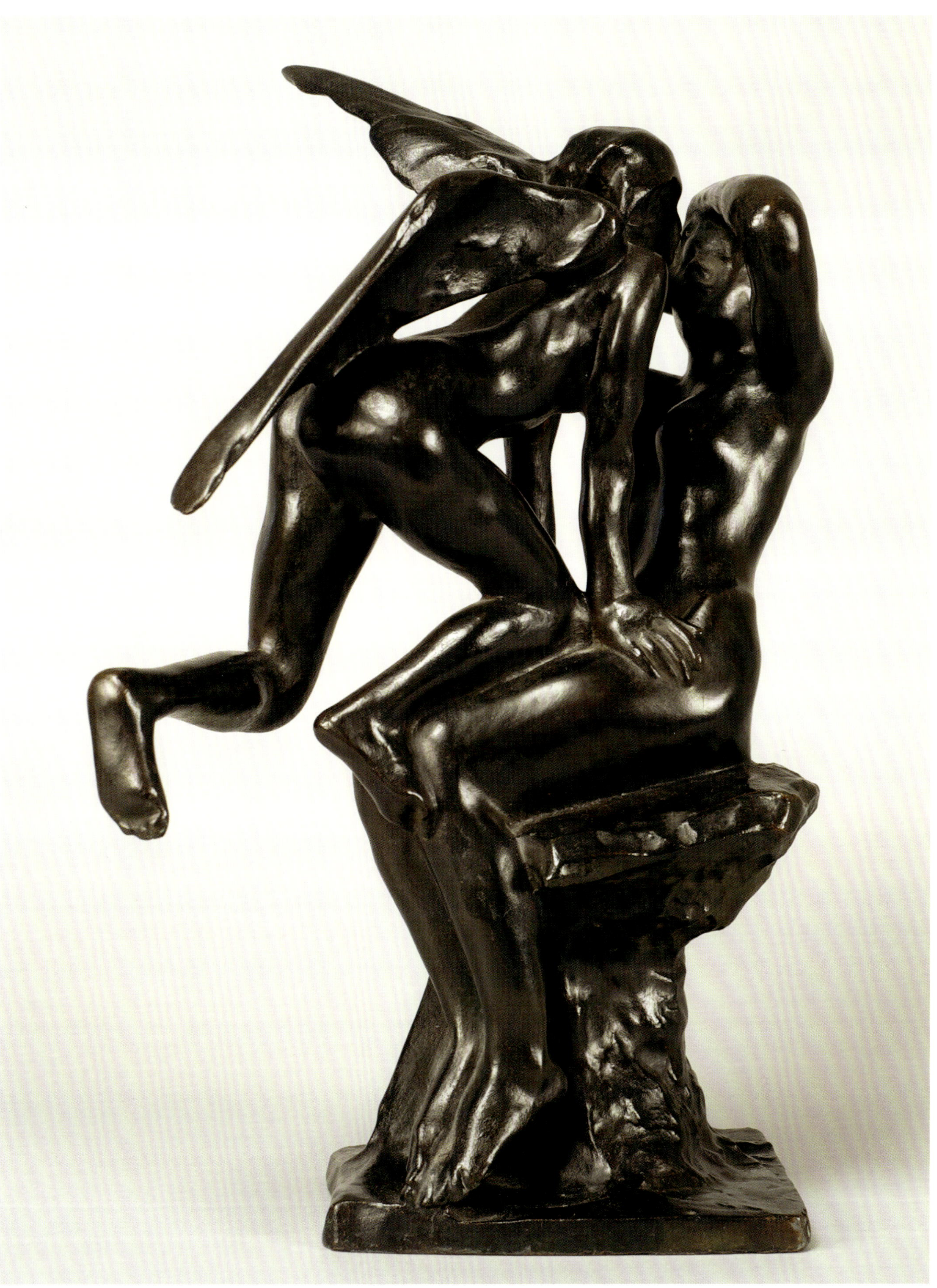

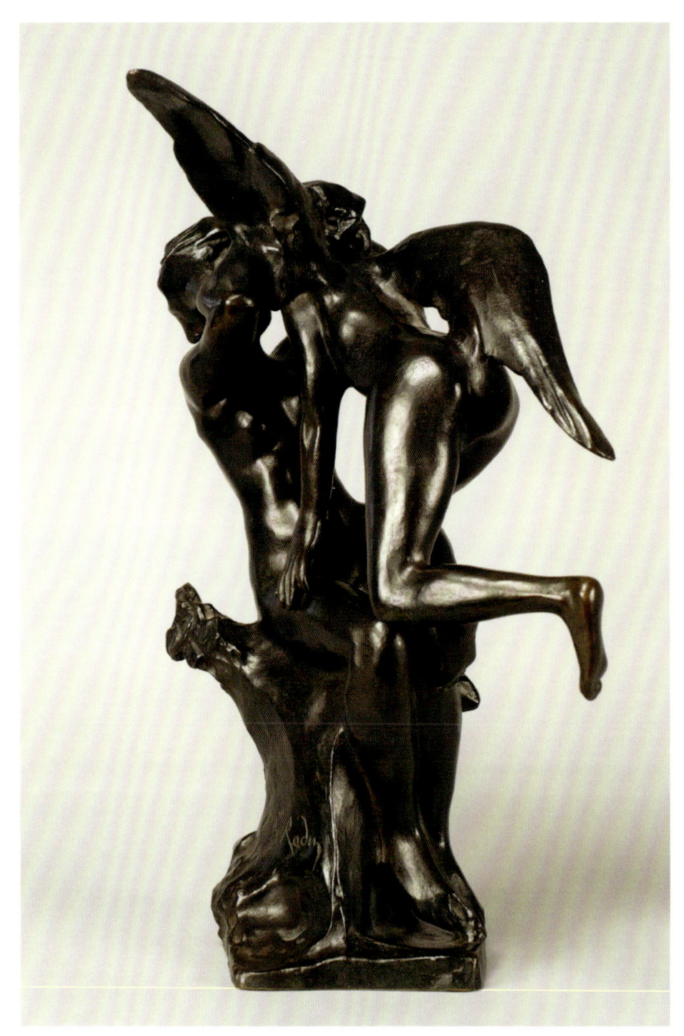 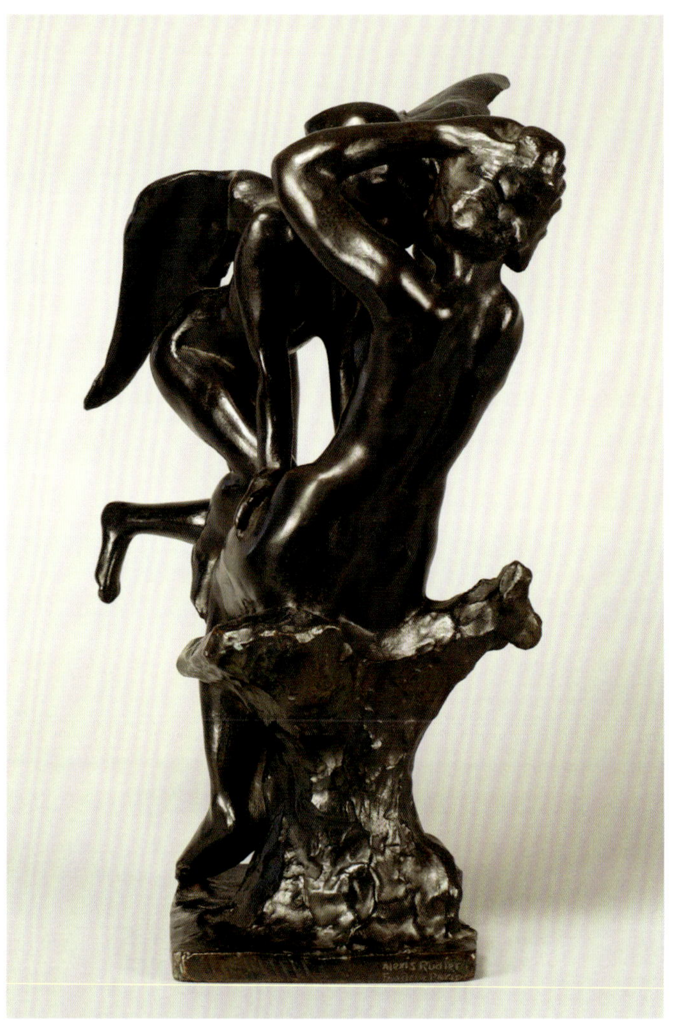

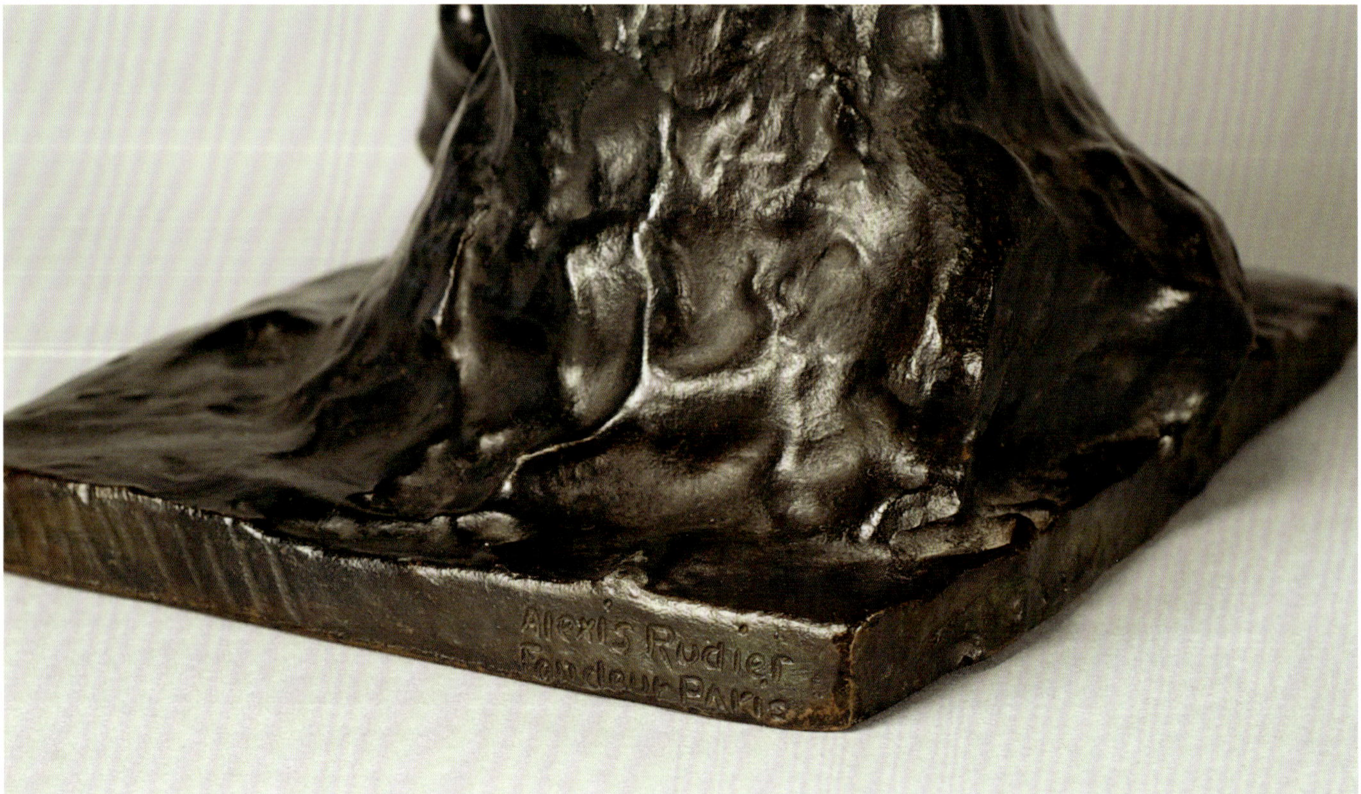

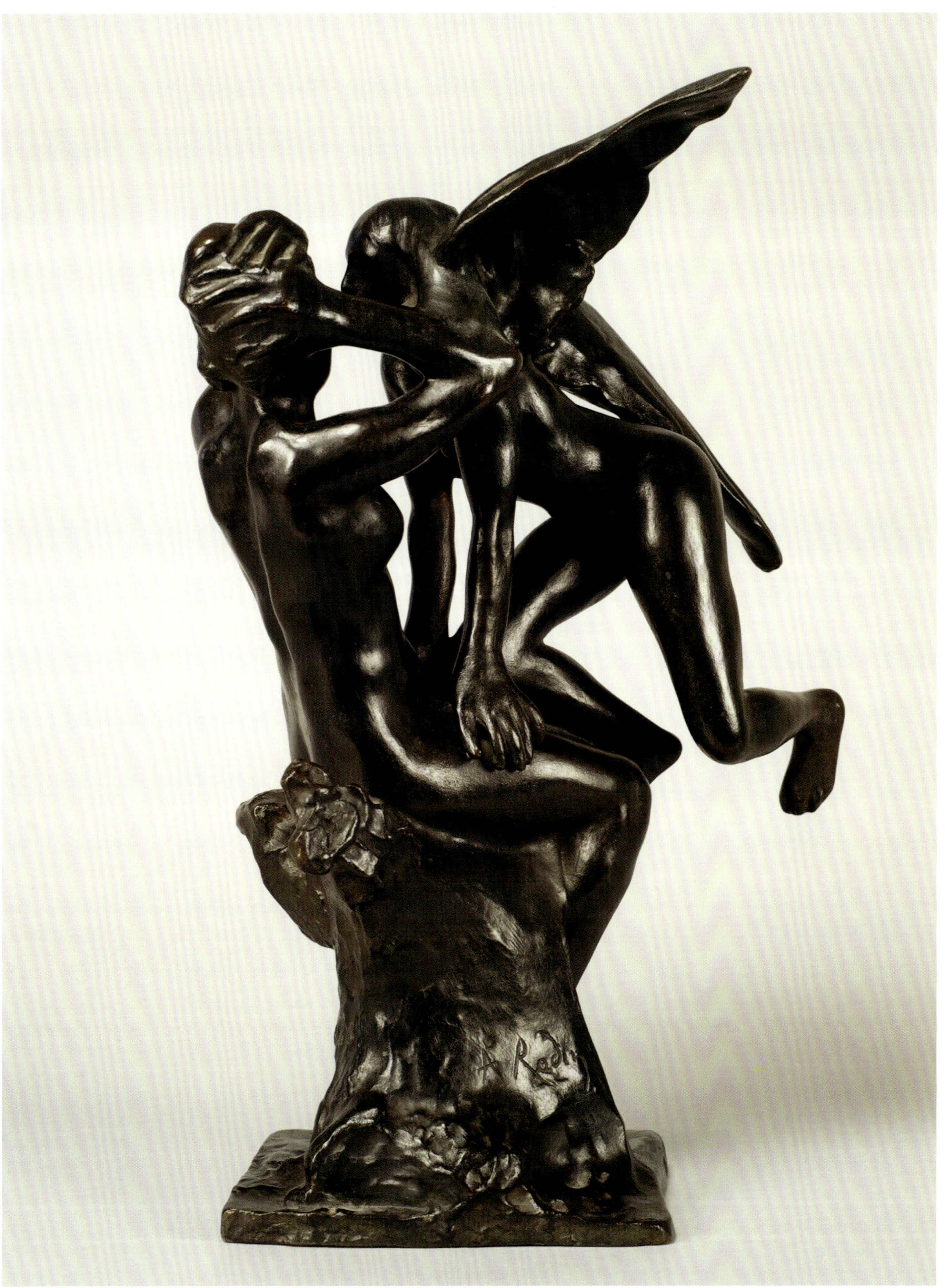

The Kiss, 1ˢᵗ Reduction

Le Baiser, 1ᵉʳᵉ Réduction

Signed Rodin
Inscribed with the foundry mark F. Barbedienne Fondeur
Bronze with a rich dark brown patination
Height: 29 inches (72 cm)

Provenance:
Private Collection, Germany
Sale: Kunsthaus am Museum-Van Ham, Cologne, 23rd October 1983, lot 2463
Private Collection, Germany
Robert Bowman Gallery, 2006
Private Collection, Norway

Conceived in 1886, this example cast circa 1910. The Barbedienne foundry executed forty-nine casts of this model in this size between 1904 and 1918. Rodin agreed a ten year renewable contract for the Barbedienne foundry to produce an unlimited edition of the model in 1898. The foundry produced four sizes of this model, 72cm, 60cm, 40cm and 25cm.

The Kiss is one of Auguste Rodin's most famous sculptures. It was originally conceived as part of *The Gates of Hell* and first exhibited as an independent group in 1887 in both Paris and Brussels. In 1898 Rodin exhibited a lifesize marble at the Salon de la Société National des Beaux-Arts.

The Kiss was initially intended to represent the tragic love story of Paolo and Francesca. Dante's *Inferno* tells the passionate tale of the young lovers Paolo and Francesca da Rimini who were tragically condemned to hell for their illicit love. Francesca, daughter of an important citizen of Polenta, had been forced to marry Gianciotto, the deformed son of the Lord of Rimini. It was a loveless marriage and before long the young bride fell desperately in love with Gianciotto's younger brother, Paolo. They became lovers, but tragedy struck when Francesca's husband discovered them and immediately stabbed the pair to death. The pair descended to hell, eternally damned.

Rodin's depiction of the embracing lovers met with a mixed reception during his lifetime. Five years before it was rapturously received at the Salon de la Société National des Beaux-Arts, the sculpture was selected to be part of the 1893 Chicago World's Fair. On arrival, the work was relegated to an inner chamber at the fair as it was considered unsuitable for general display and only a select few were admitted to view it. Eleven years later, the life-size marble, now in the collection of the Tate Gallery, was loaned for public display to a town hall in Sussex. Local residents quickly covered it in drapes concerned that it would encourage the ardour of soldiers billeted in the town.

Today, with its blend of eroticism and idealism, *The Kiss* is considered an iconic image of love and passion and is one of the world's most recognisable sculptures.

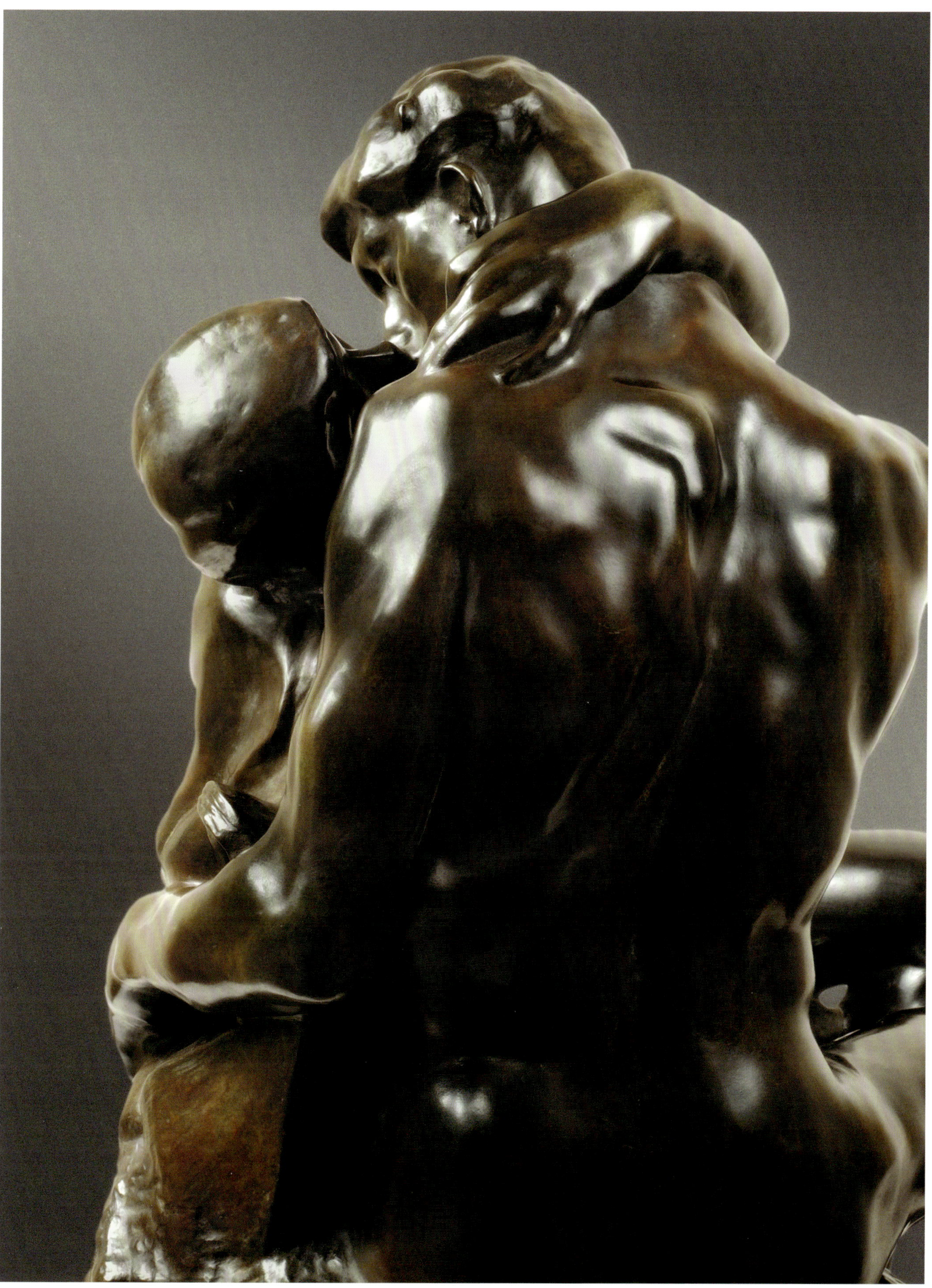

The Kiss, 2nd Reduction

Le Baiser, 2ème Réduction

Signed Rodin
Inscribed F. Barbedienne Fondeur and the letter J stamp and 13 on the underside
Bronze with a rich mid and dark brown patination
Height: 23½ inches (59.8 cm)

Provenance:
Gift of the French Government to the M. J.B. Abel (1863–1921) Governor of Algeria
Captain de Vaisseau Abel, by descent
J.F. Dufour, Paris by descent
Robert Bowman Gallery, 2001
Private Collection, UK
Robert Bowman Gallery, 2009
Private European Collection

Conceived in 1886, this reduction conceived in 1904. This example cast between 1904 and 1918. The Barbedienne foundry cast between sixty-five and sixty-nine casts of this model in the size between 1904 and 1918. Rodin agreed a ten year renewable contract for the Barbedienne foundry to produce an unlimited edition of the model in 1898. The foundry produced four sizes of this model, 72cm, 60cm, 40cm and 25cm.

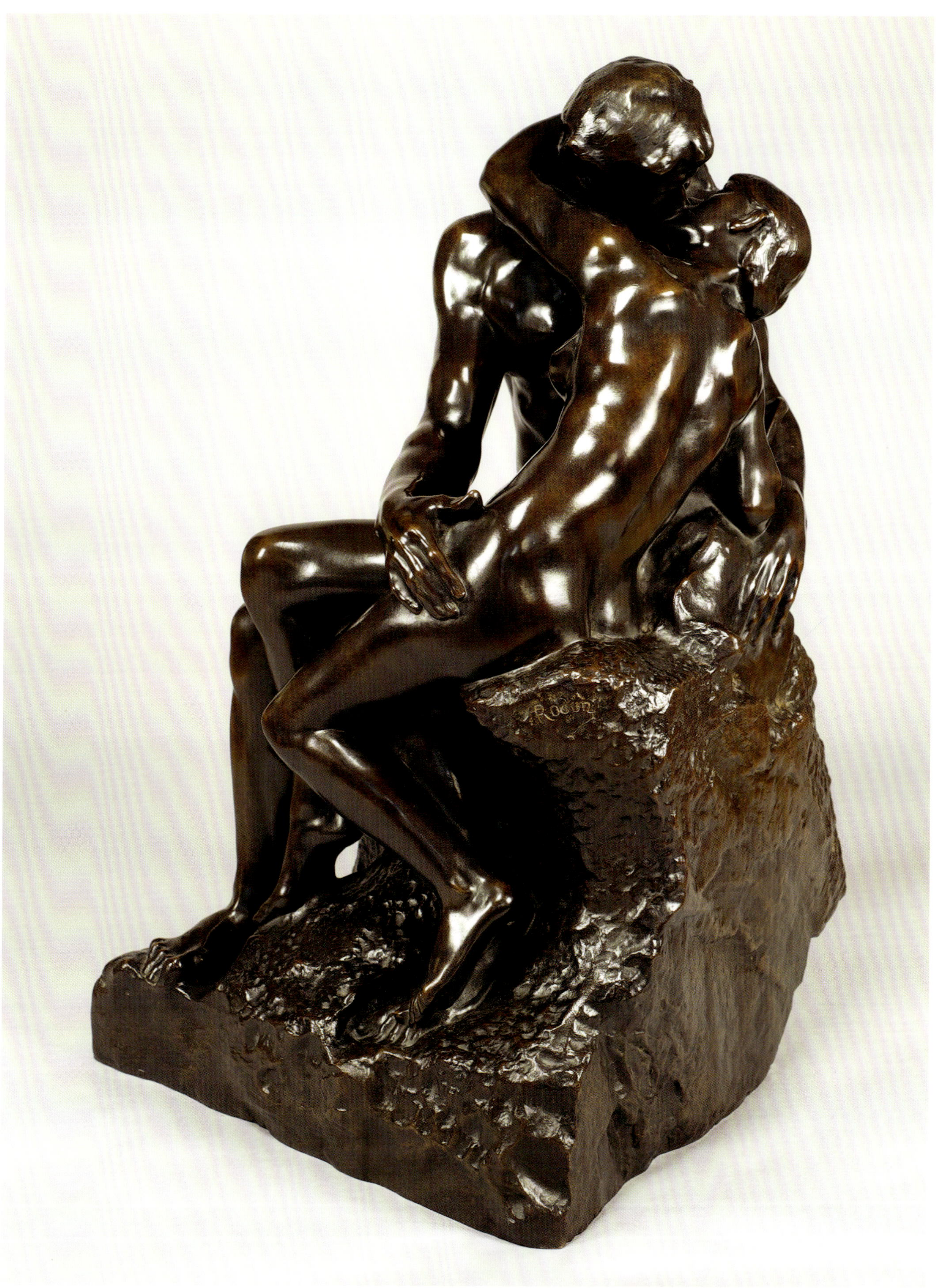

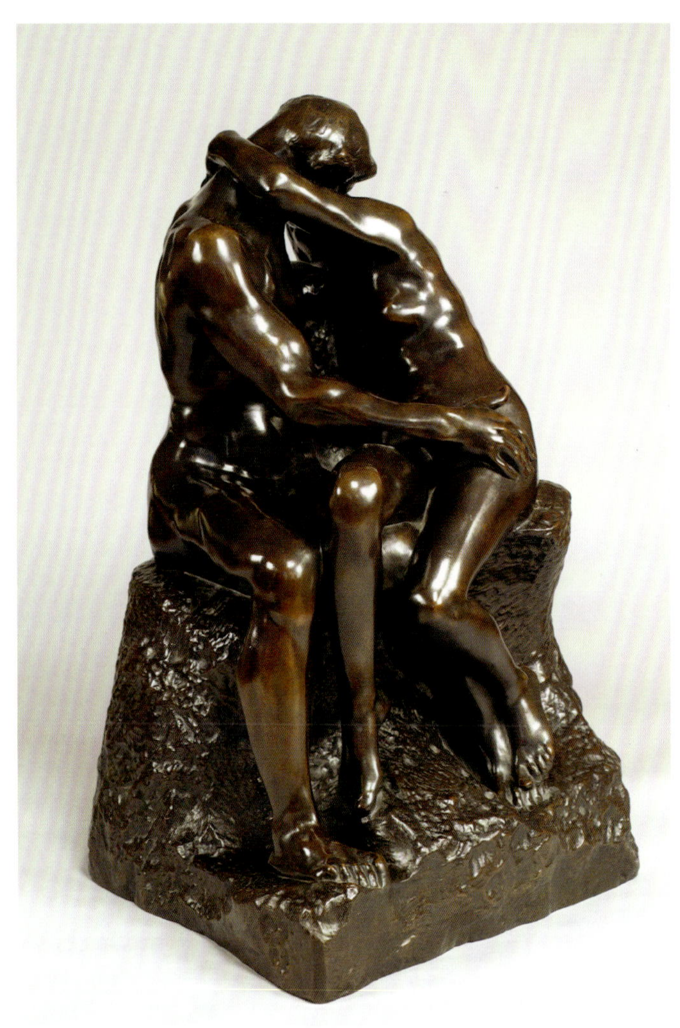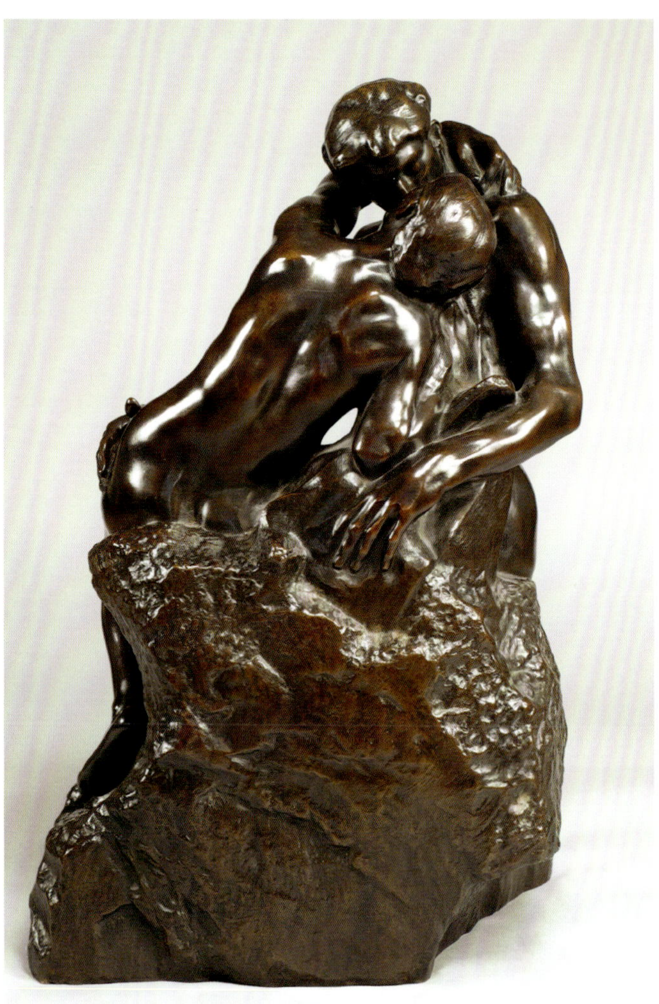

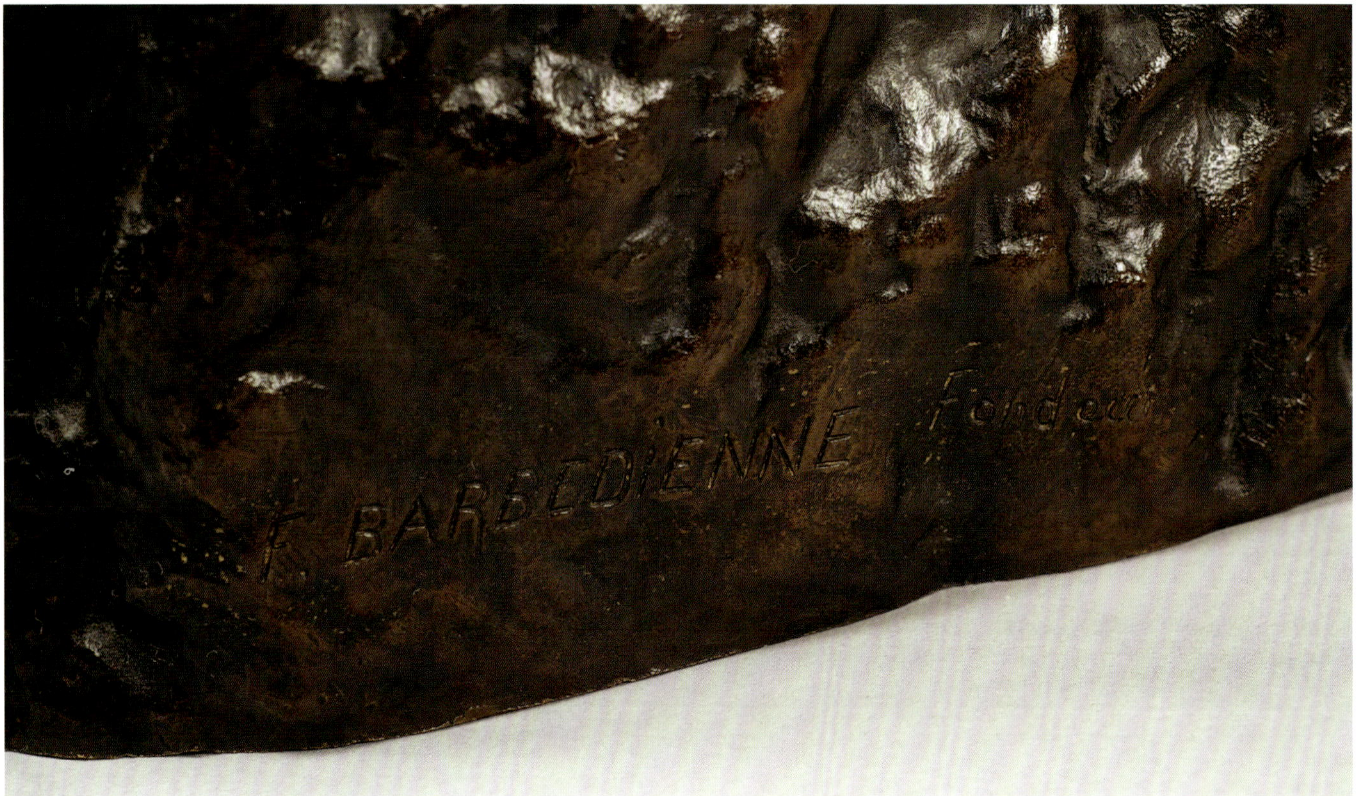

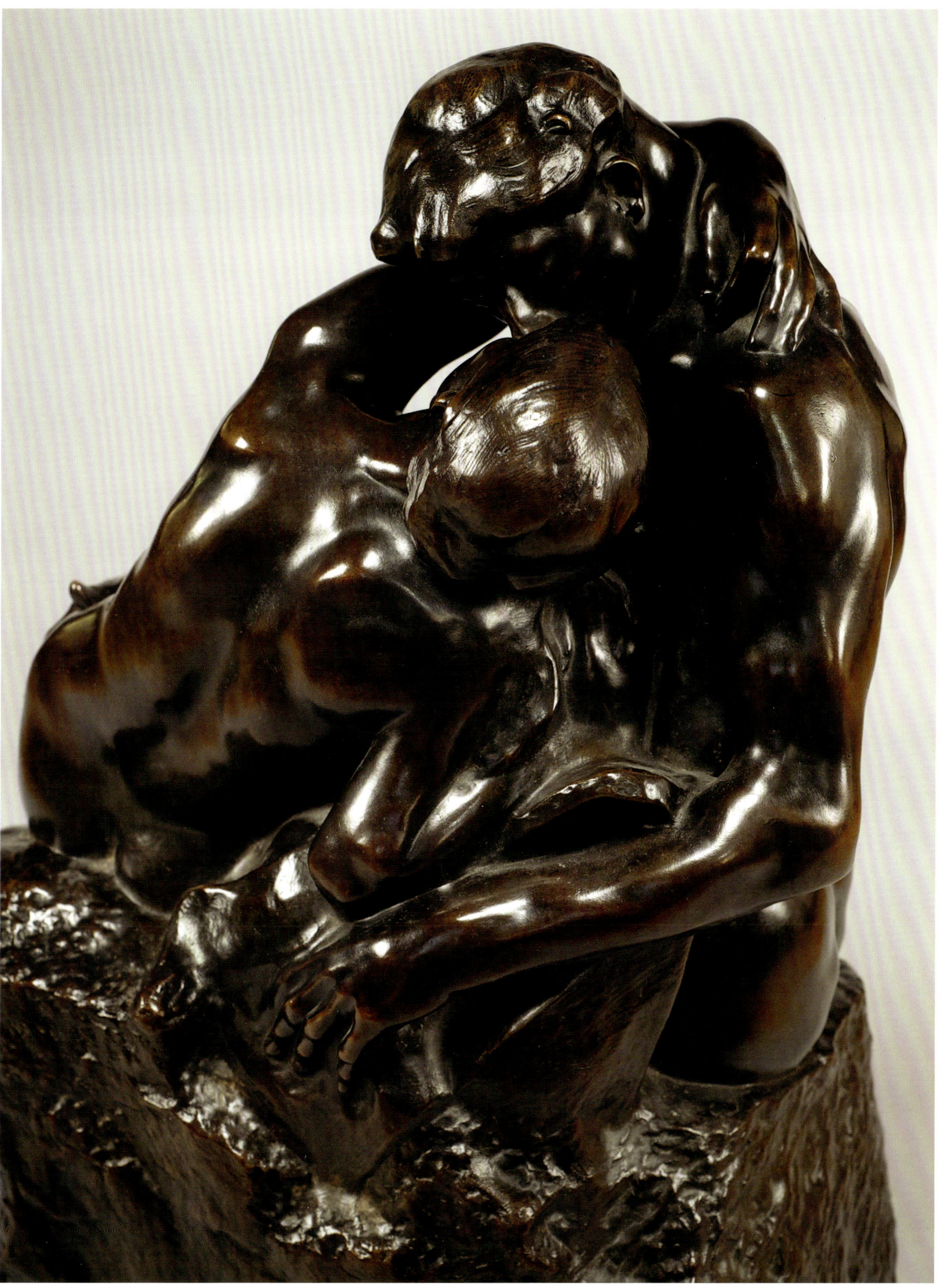

The Kiss, 3rd Reduction

Le Baiser, 3ème Réduction

Signed Rodin
Inscribed with the foundry mark F. Barbedienne Fondeur
Numbered 798, with the letter 'S' and '66921 osl' on the interior.
Bronze with a rich dark brown patination
Height: 15½ inches (39.5 cm)

Provenance:
Collection Nougayrol, Toulouse
By Descent

Conceived in 1886, this reduction was conceived in 1901. This example cast on the 15th December 1906. The Barbedienne foundry cast between one hundred and five and one hundred and nine casts of this model in this size between 1904 and 1918. Rodin agreed a ten year renewable contract for the Barbedienne foundry to produce an unlimited edition of the model in 1898. The foundry produced four sizes of this model, 72cm, 60cm, 40cm and 25cm.

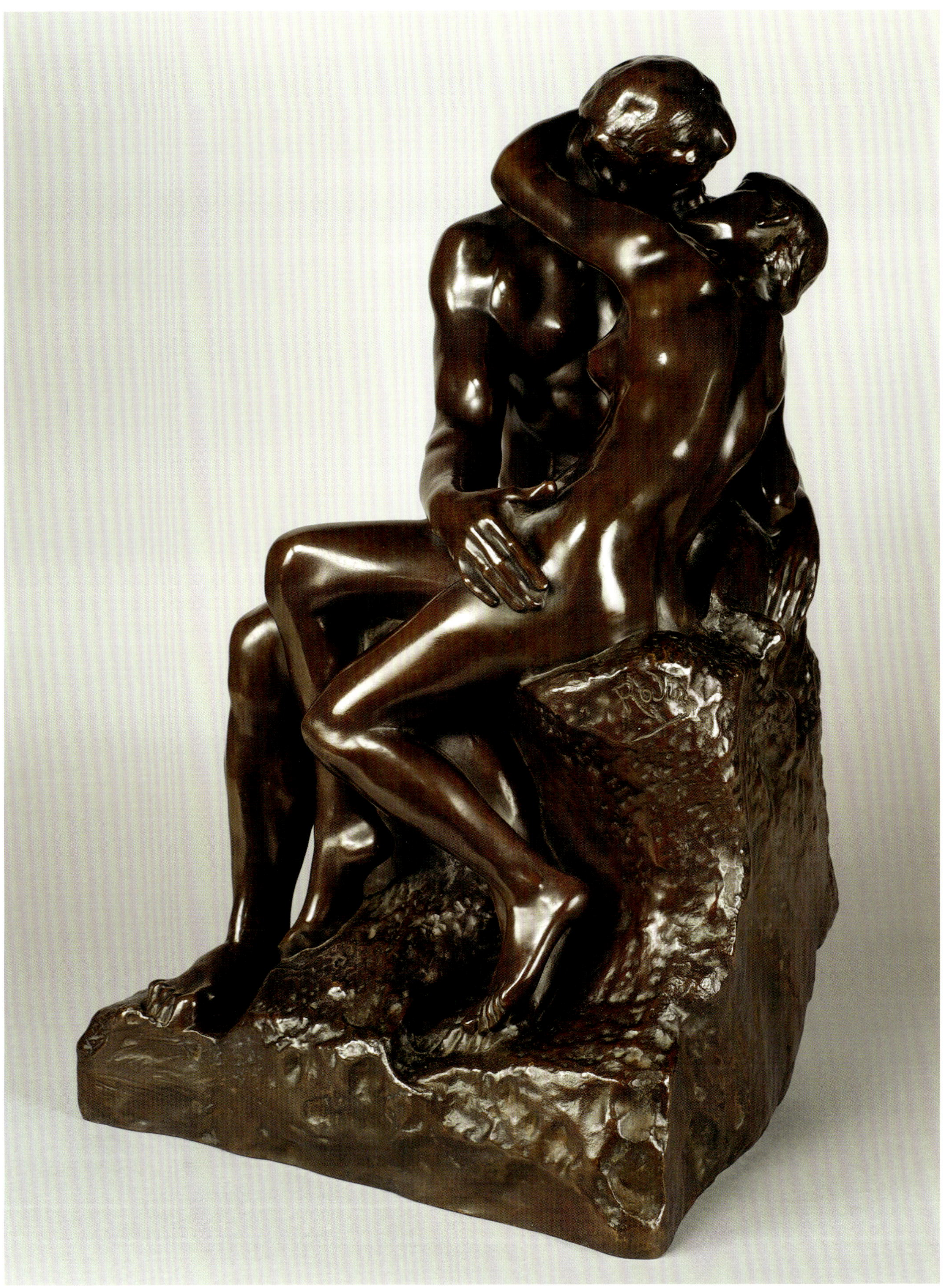

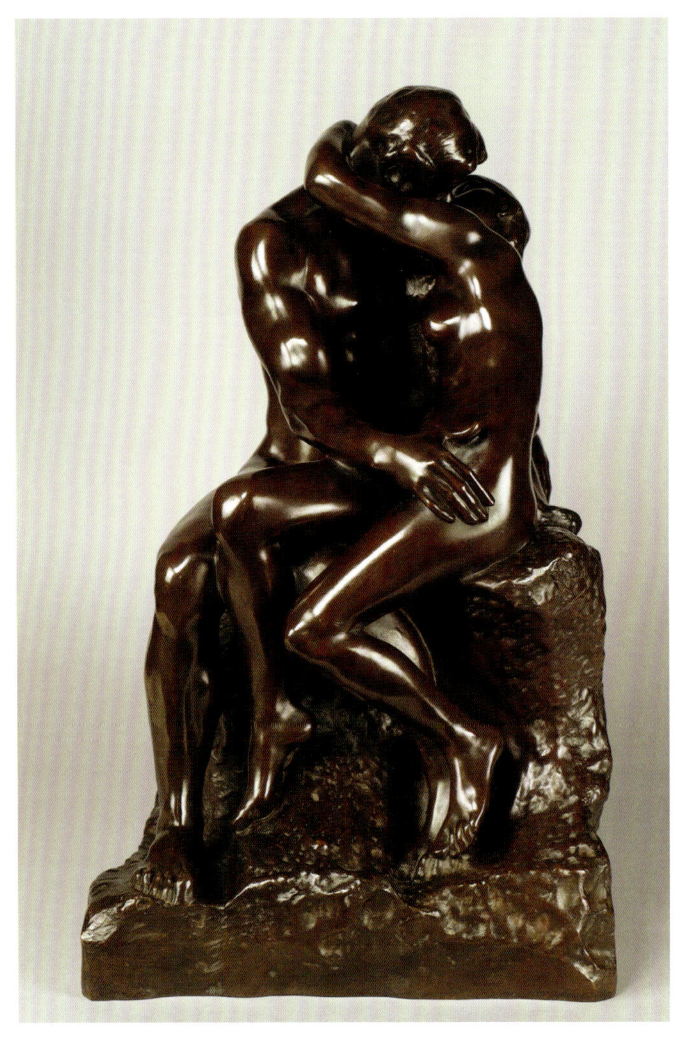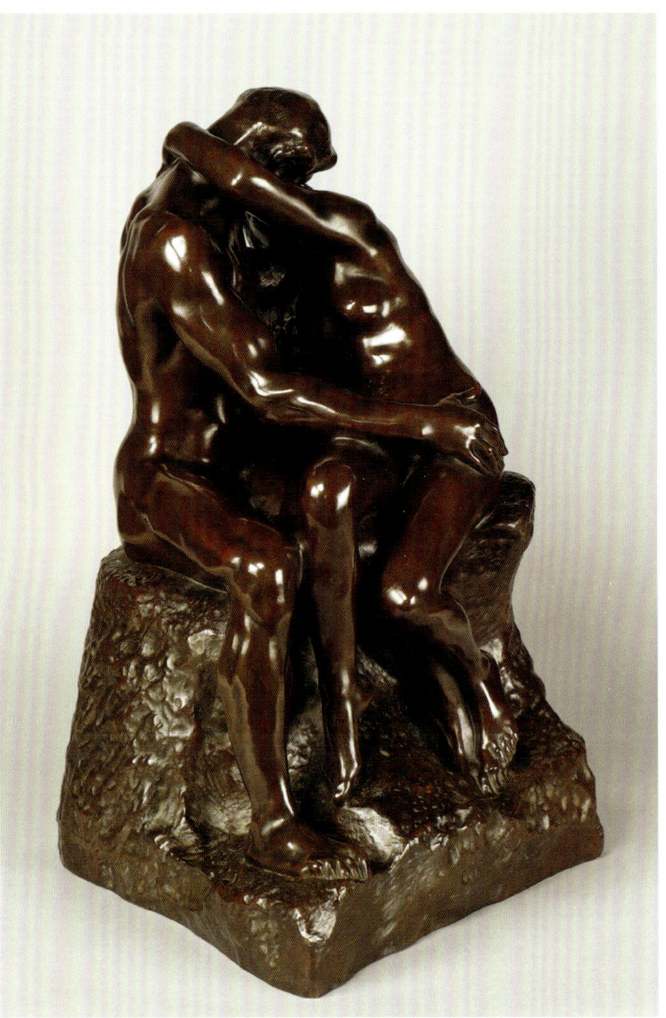

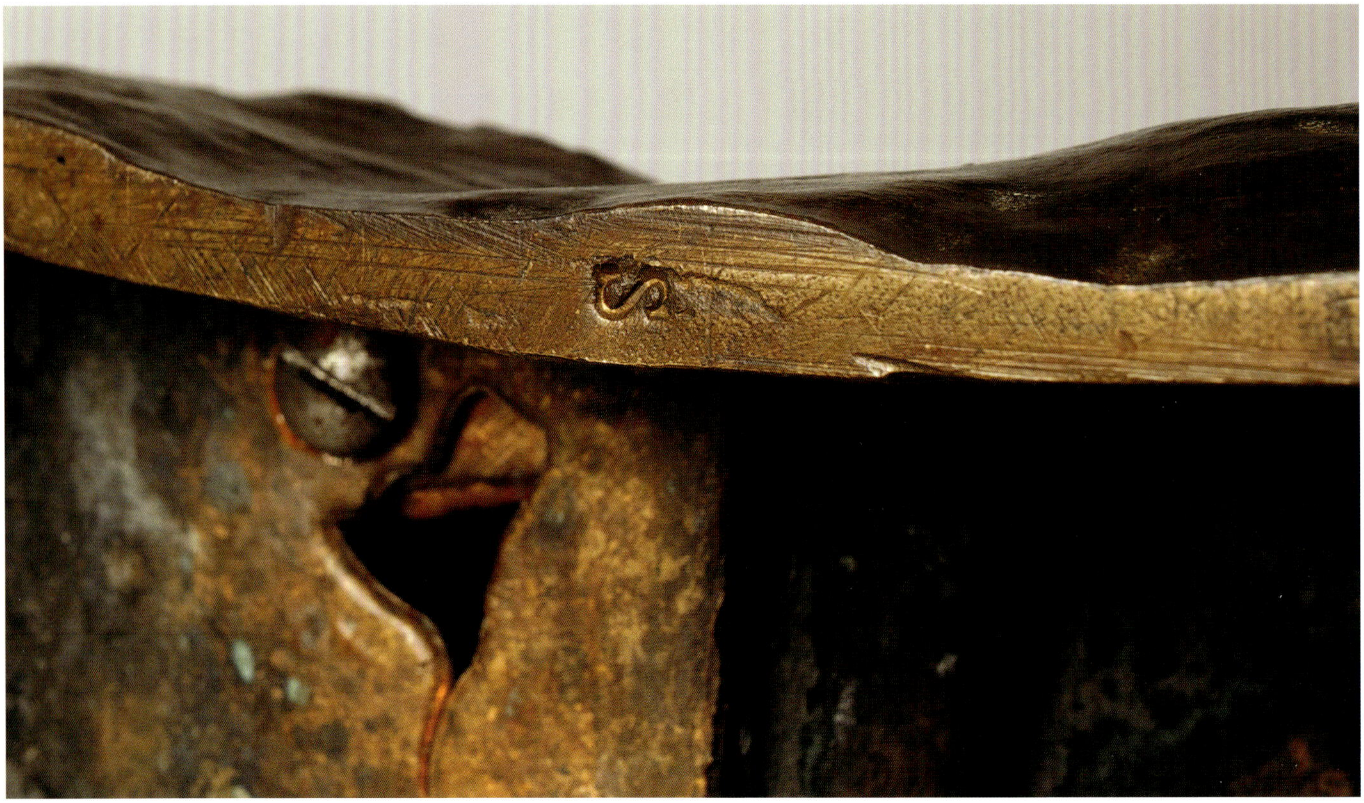

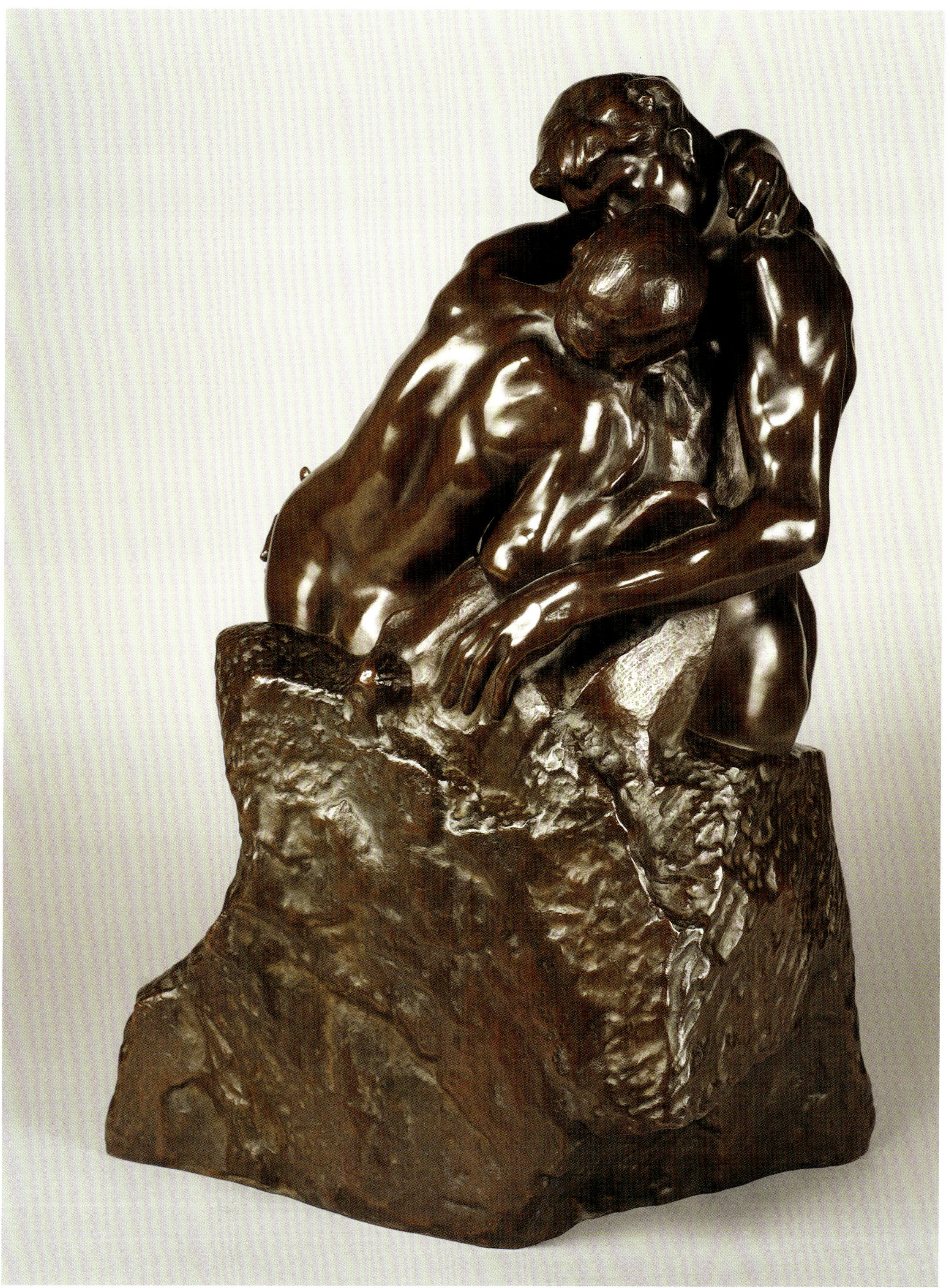

The Kiss, 4th Reduction

Le Baiser, 4ème Réduction

Signed Rodin
Inscribed F. Barbedienne Fondeur
Bronze with a rich brown and dark brown patination
Height: 10 inches (26 cm)

Provenance:
Private Collection, France
Sotheby's New York, 7 May 2003, Lot 116
Robert Bowman Gallery
David Smith, USA

Conceived in 1886, this reduction conceived 1898. This example cast between 1898 and 1918. The Barbedienne foundry cast between ninety three and one hundred and three casts of this model in this size between 1898 and 1918. Rodin agreed a ten year renewable contract for the Barbedienne foundry to produce an unlimited edition of the model in 1898. The foundry produced four sizes of this model, 72cm, 60cm, 40cm and 25cm.

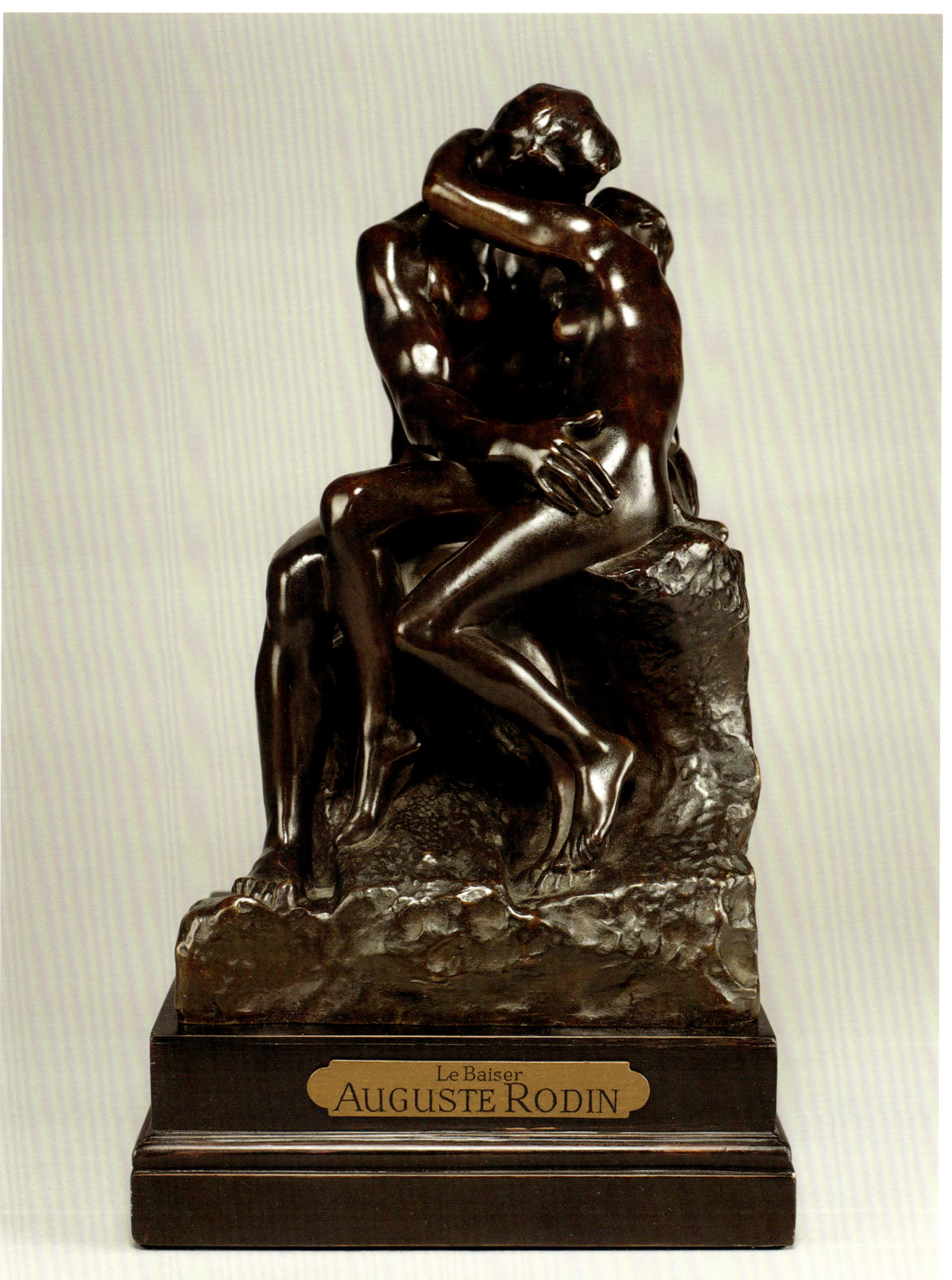
Le Baiser
AUGUSTE RODIN

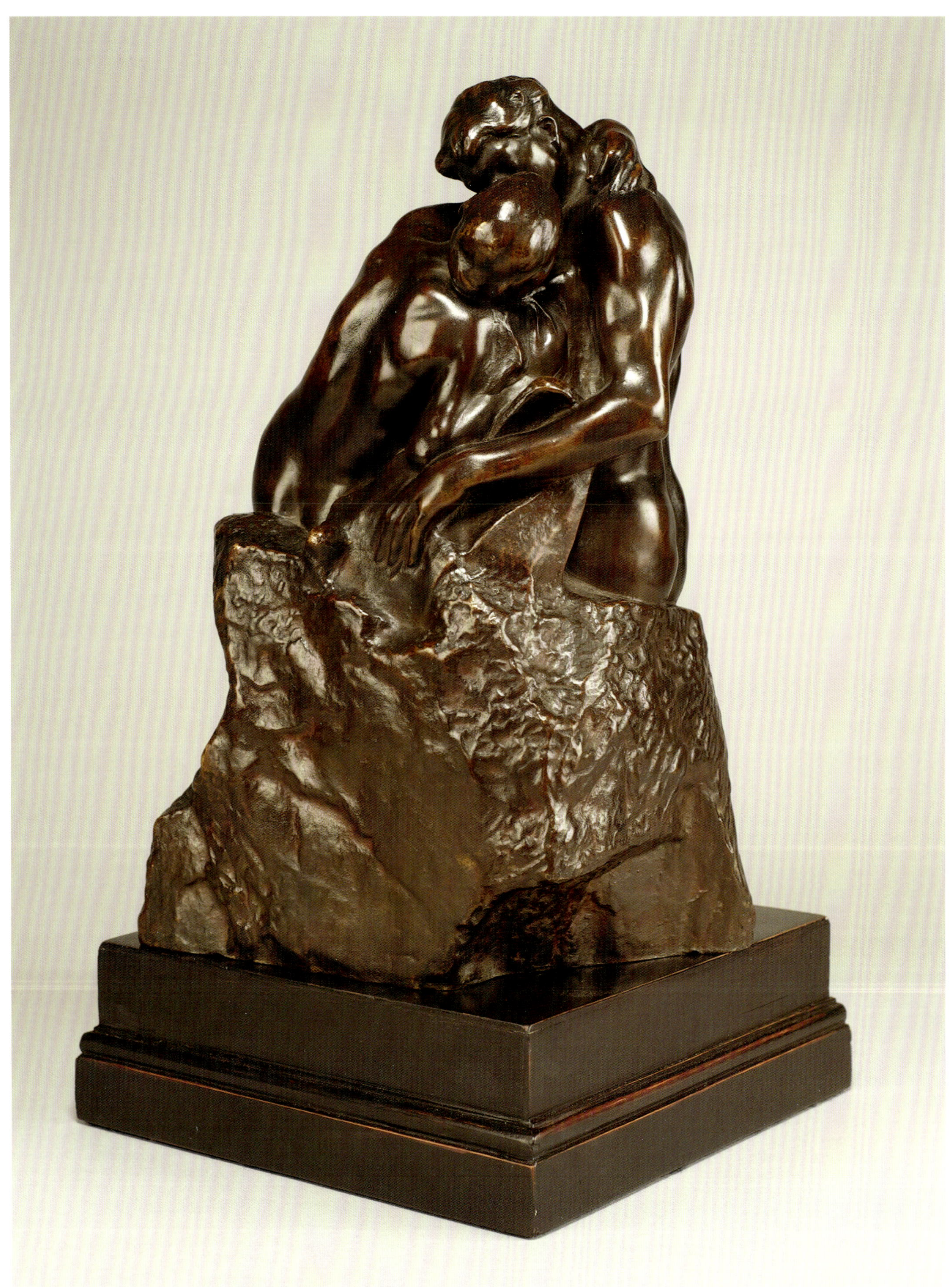

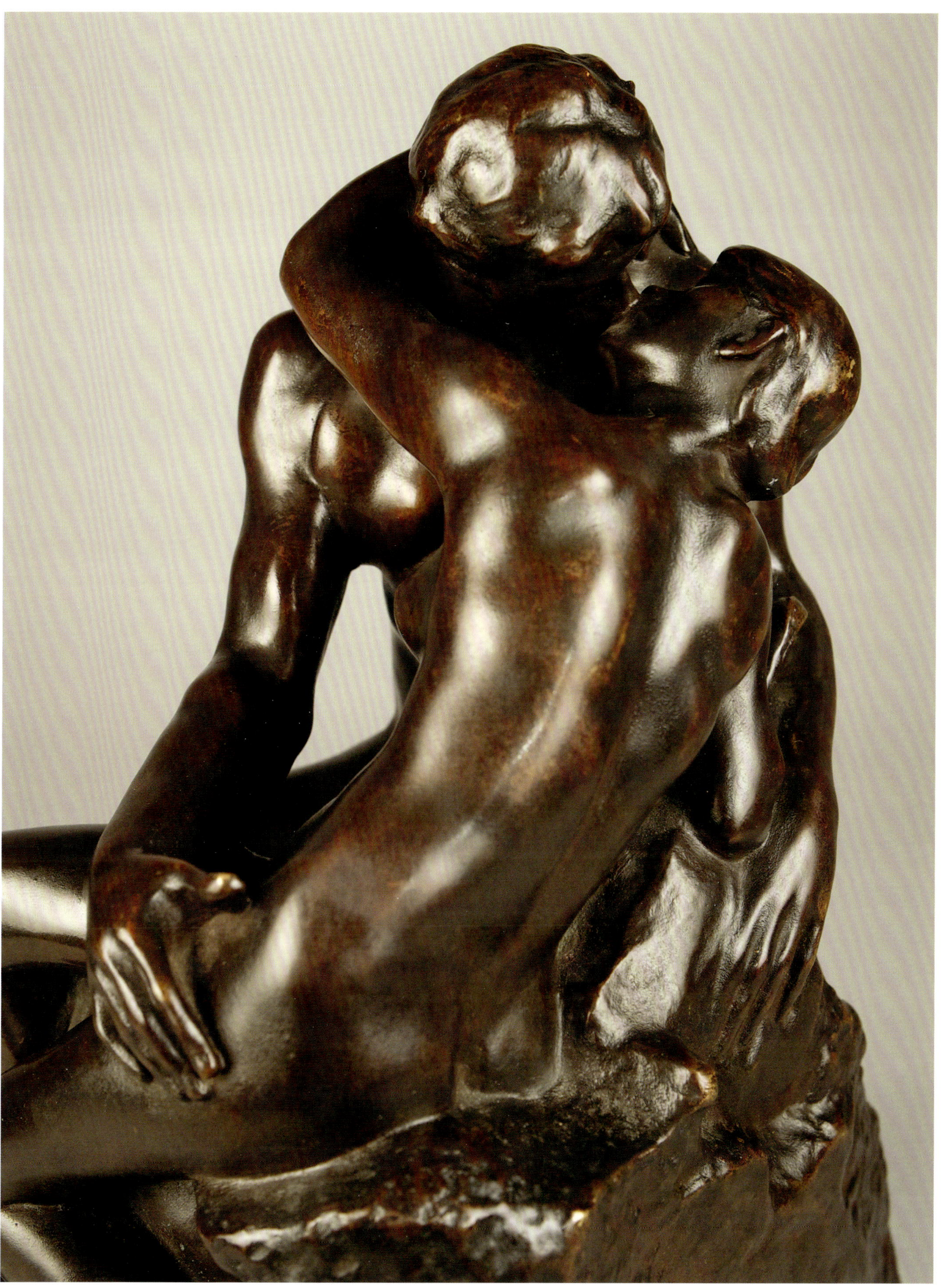

Fugit Amor, Large Model, Second Version

Fugit Amor, Grand Modèle, Deuxième Version

Signed A. Rodin with repeat raised interior signature
Inscribed Alexis Rudier Fondeur Paris
Numbered 1
Bronze with a rich mid and dark brown patination
Height: 21 inches (53.2 cm)

Provenance:
Musée Rodin, Paris
Eugène Rudier, Paris
Mrs Eugène Rudier, Paris (by descent in 1952)
Private Collection, Paris
Drouot, Paris, 29 April 1994, Lot 32
Private Collection, Switzerland

Conceived in 1887, this version conceived in marble between 1894 and 1895. This cast executed between 1944 and 1945. Four casts of this model, with varying bases corresponding to different marbles, were cast during Rodin's lifetime. Two bronzes were then cast for the Musée Rodin by the Alexis Rudier foundry in 1944 (numbered 1) and 1945 (numbered 2).

Originally conceived as part of *The Gates of Hell*, the two figures known as *Fugit Amor* can be seen twice on the right hand door of the great portal. A vertical configuration leaping from the surface of the gates is coupled with a second horizontal composition that appears alongside *The Awakening*. It was common in Rodin's practice to reuse his figures, the male figure in the present model was original conceived for one of the children in his group *Ugolino*. The same figure would later be used in *Prodigal Son*.

Inspired by the story of Paolo and Francesca from Dante's *Inferno*, the sculpture was known by several different names, including, *The Sphinx*, *The Dream*, *The Memory* and *The Evening*, before finally being titled *Fugit Amor*.

The work was first conceived in 1887. Between 1894 and 1895 Rodin had an enlargement carved in marble, which he considered to be one of his most important works. Rodin later exhibited this marble in his 1900 solo exhibition at Place de l'Alma before selling it to the collector Albert Kahn.

After this original marble enlargement, Rodin ordered three further marbles, each of which differed slightly around the base. Two of these marbles are now in the collection of the Musée Rodin, Paris and the third is in the collection of the Museum of Art, Shizuoka, Japan. Rodin had four bronzes cast after these marbles using the foundry Gruet Fils.

Two further bronzes, including the present example, were cast for the Musée Rodin by the Alexis Rudier foundry from a plaster taken from the original Albert Kahn marble. The present example is the only bronze still in private hands.

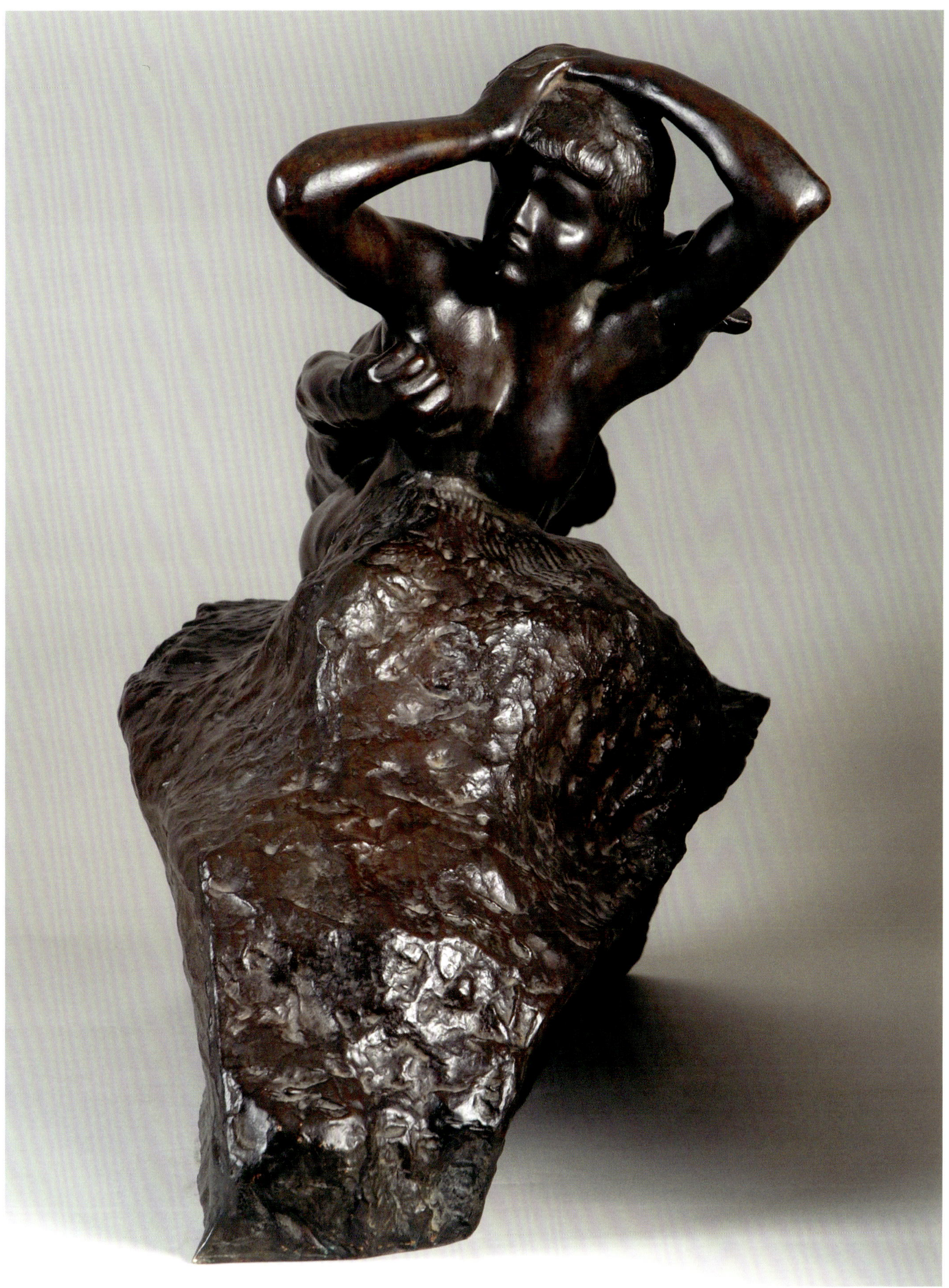

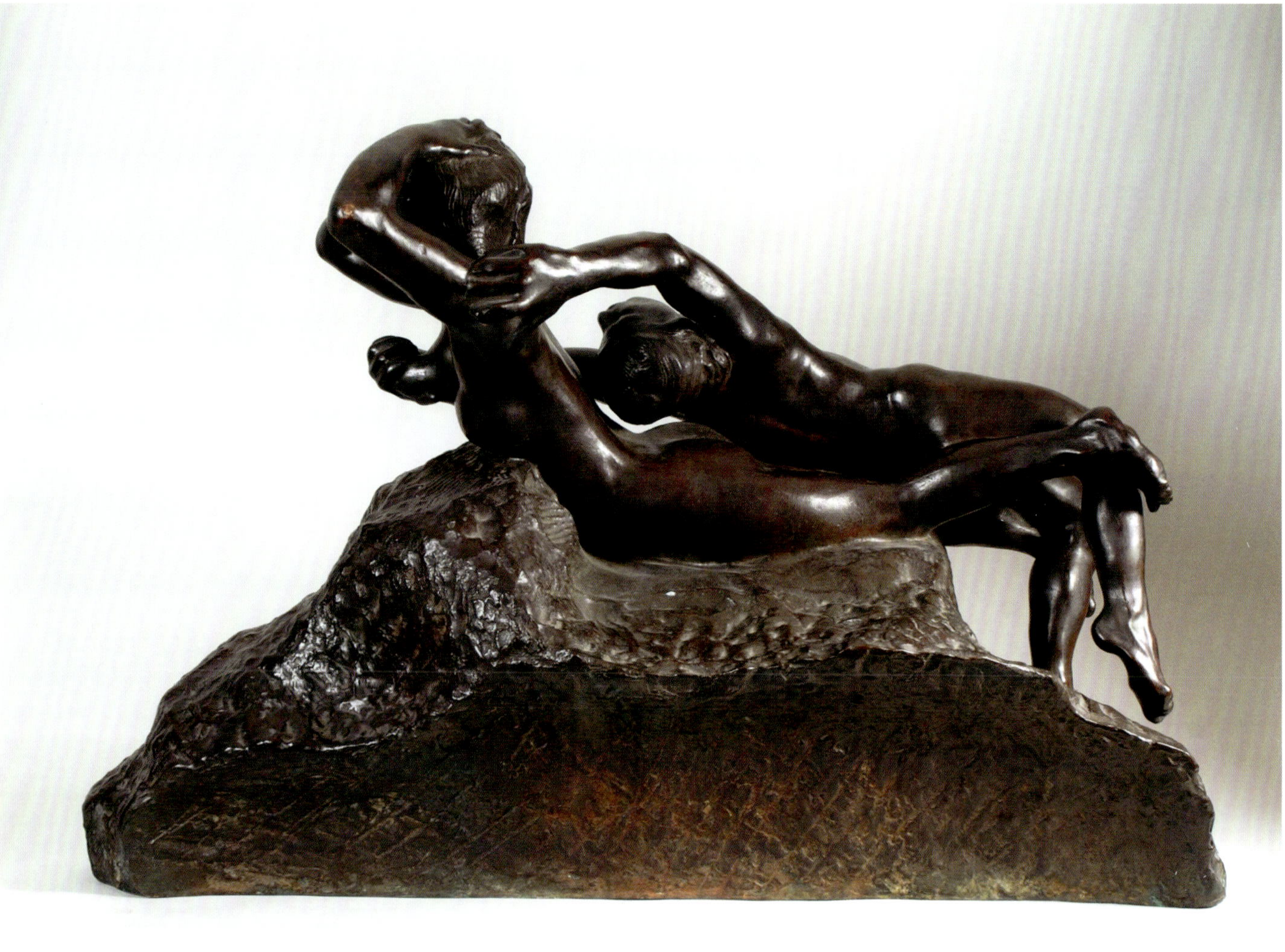

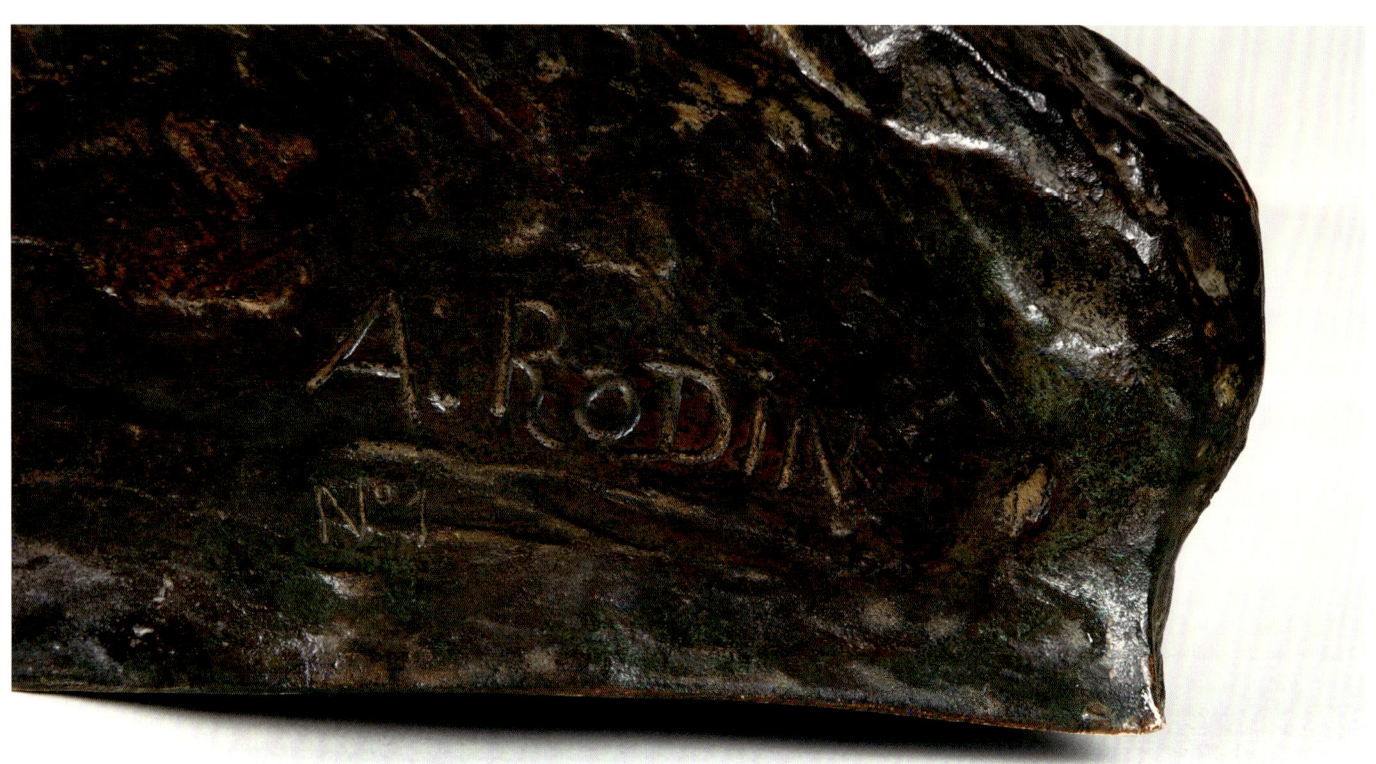

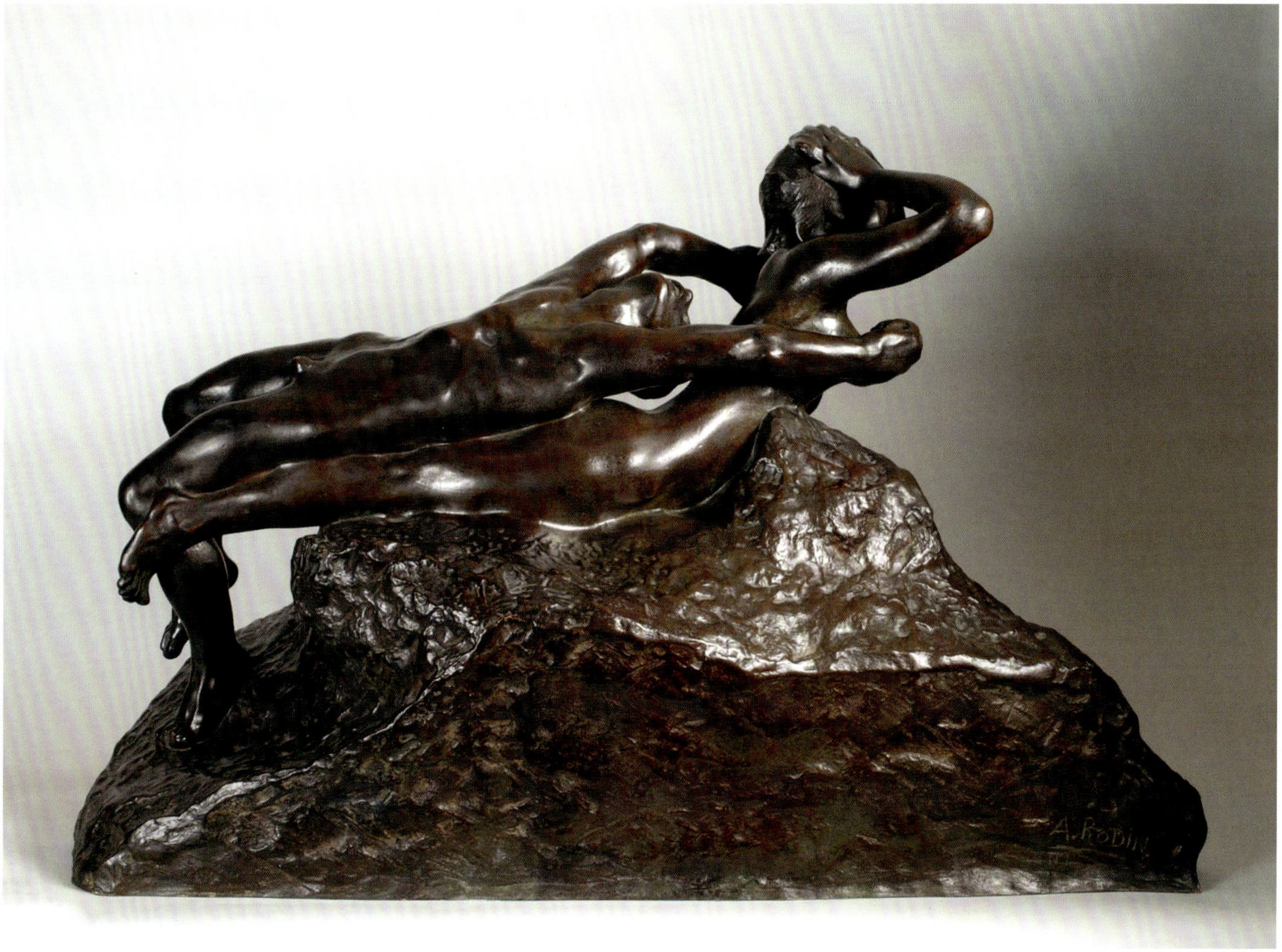

A. RODIN

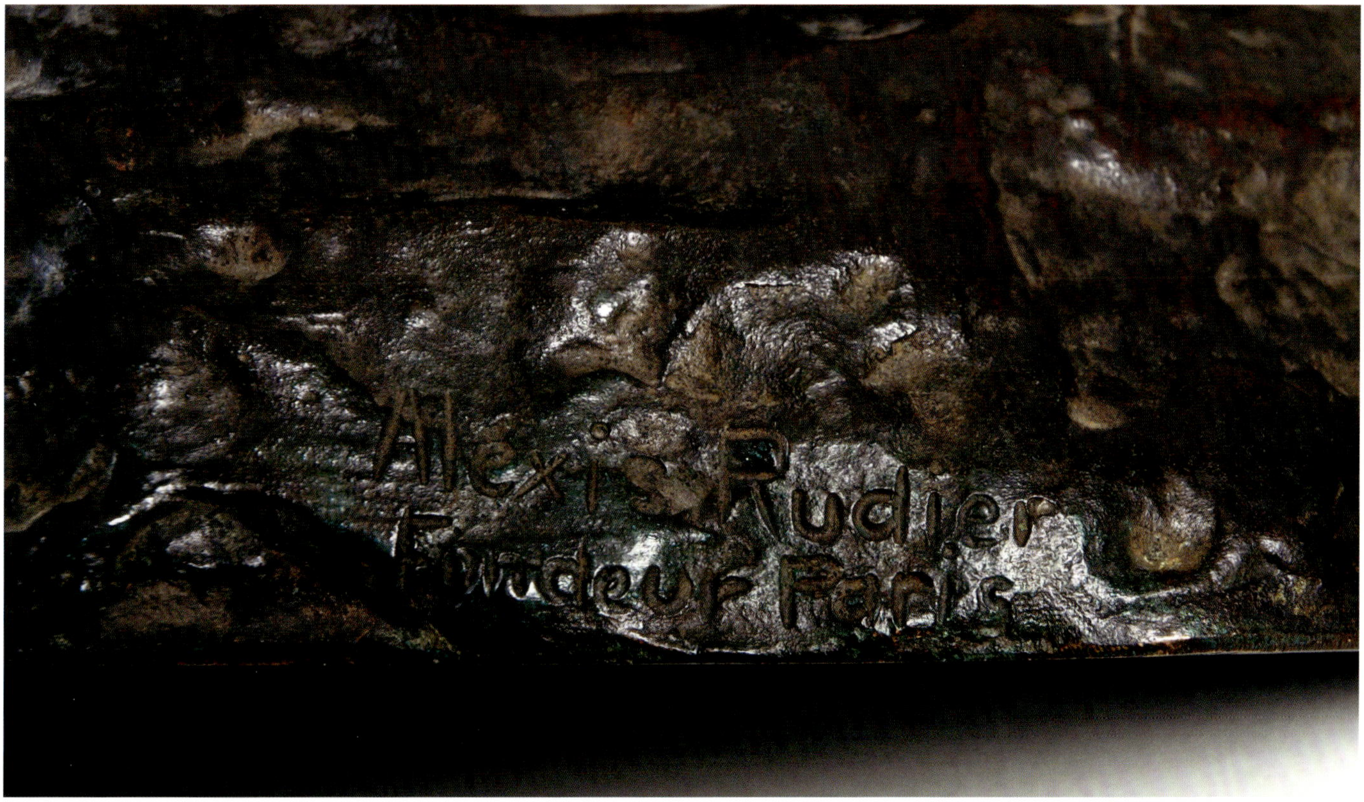

Alexis Rudier
Fondeur Paris

The Sirens, Large Model

Nereides, Grand Modèle

Signed A. Rodin and dated 1902
Bronze with a green patination
Height: 17 inches (42.3 cm)

Provenance:
Purchased from Rodin by Oscar Schmitz in 1902
Mme Mary Munchmeyer-Schmitz by descent 1933
Taken by the Soviet forces 1945
Dresden Museum from 1950
Returned to the descendents of Oscar Schmitz
Robert Bowman Gallery, 2012
Private European Collection

Conceived before 1887, this example cast in 1902. Two casts in 1899 by Leon Perzinka, two casts in 1900 by Francois Rudier (one for Count Tolstoy and one for the Musée des Beaux-Arts de Budapest), two casts in 1900 by Sevin and two casts in 1902 by Alexis Rudier of which this cast is one. The Musée Rodin continued the edition with Alexis Rudier with less than four casts made between 1918 and 1927, then seven casts by Georges Rudier between 1967 and 198, making a total of 19 casts.

The Sirens appear both halfway up the left door of *The Gates of Hell* and were then reworked for *The Monument to Victor Hugo.*

The sculpture can be seen as the three Furies from the *Inferno*. Dante is warned not to stare at the Furies, as they would summon Medusa, who would turn him to stone. Rodin melds this story with that of three water-nymphs The Rhinemaidens from Wagner's *The Ring* and the Greek Myth of The Sirens, who, like the nymphs, were often depicted as mermaids and who used their beauty and charms to lure sailors to their death.

Mermaids became a popular subject matter for the Art Nouveau artists of the time. Their sensuous femininity and intertwined bodies perfectly expressed the curvilinear style. In this sculpture we see Rodin at his closest to this artistic style, however, his sculpture shows three women and so explores sensuality and the dangers of seduction in modern terms. This cast features a beautiful green patina conveying its association with the sea.

Rodin described them as: 'three entwined women, three powerful forms moving like a wave, which has thrown them at the hero's feet, sisters, through the momentum and the rhythm, to the Rhine Daughters, murmuring the songs of the world which he will transcribe in verse. An admirable allusion drawn from the very heart of nature!'

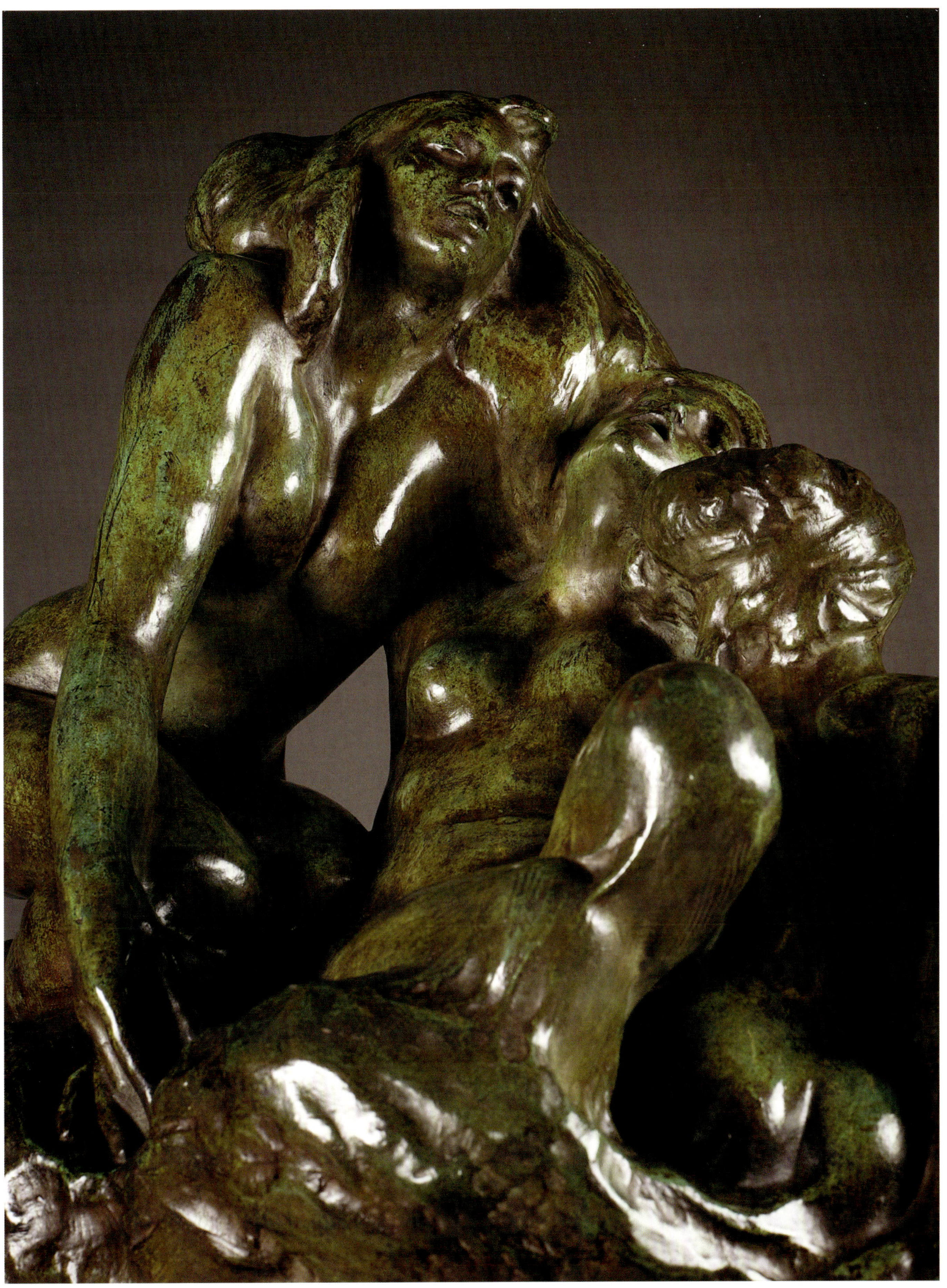

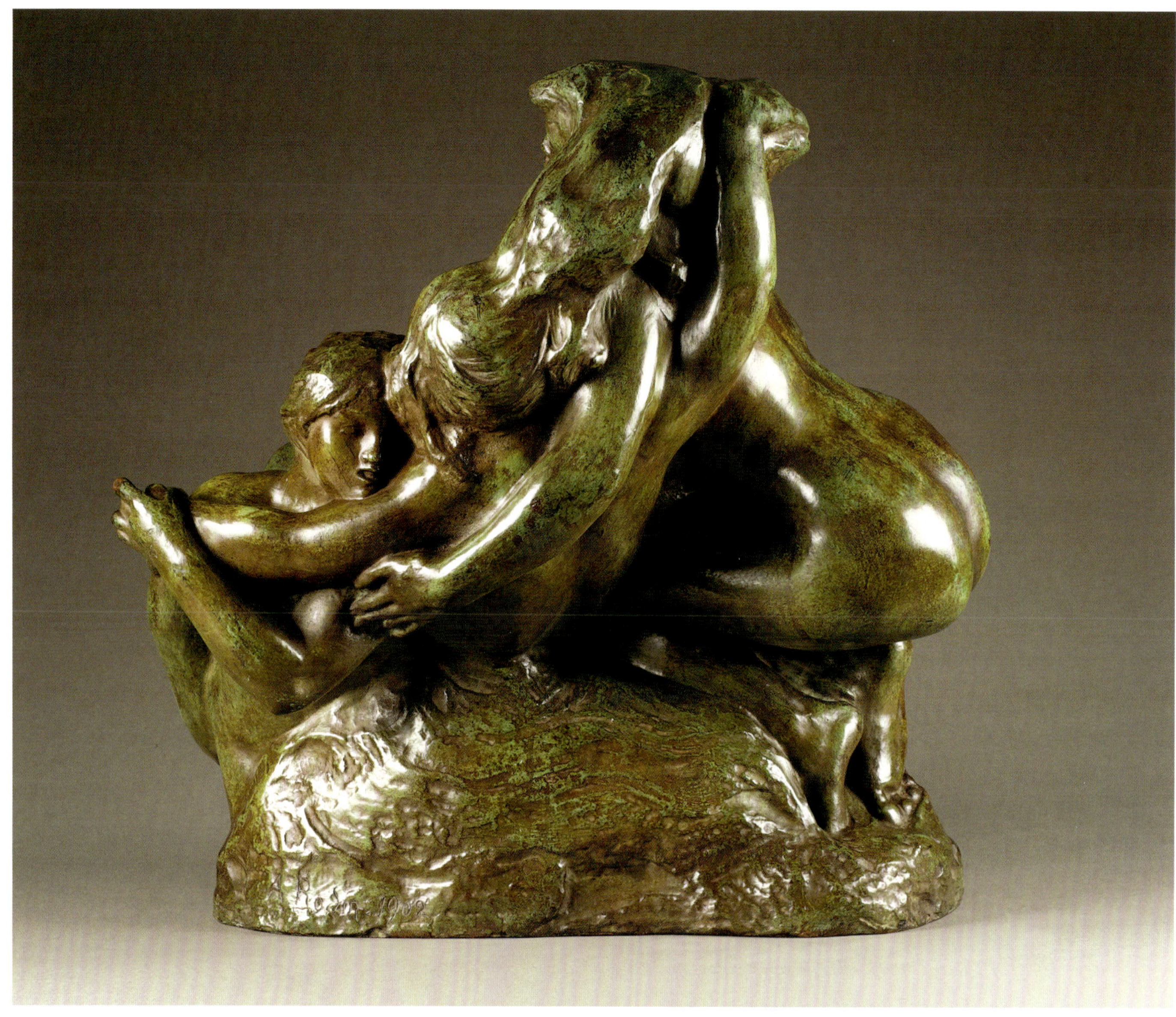

This cast of *The Sirens* or *La Vague*, as it was sometimes known, was commissioned by Oscar Schmitz, one of the great art collectors of the twentieth century. At this time the Schmitz collection already included works by Cezanne, Renoir, Monet and Van Gogh.

In 1902 Schmitz had moved from Le Havre, France where he had been working for his father, to Dresden, Germany. In February of that year, Schmitz wrote to Rodin requesting a bronze version of *The Sirens*. On the 1st March Schmitz visited Rodin's studio and agreed to commission this bronze, he then wrote to Rodin in March 'to add the date to the signature.' This cast is the earliest known Rodin sculpture to be cast by the Alexis Rudier foundry who were to become his preferred casting company.

In 1945 Soviet forces seized this cast when they moved into Dresden and subsequently deposited it in the State Museum of Art in Dresden. The sculpture was later returned to the descendants of Oscar Schmitz.

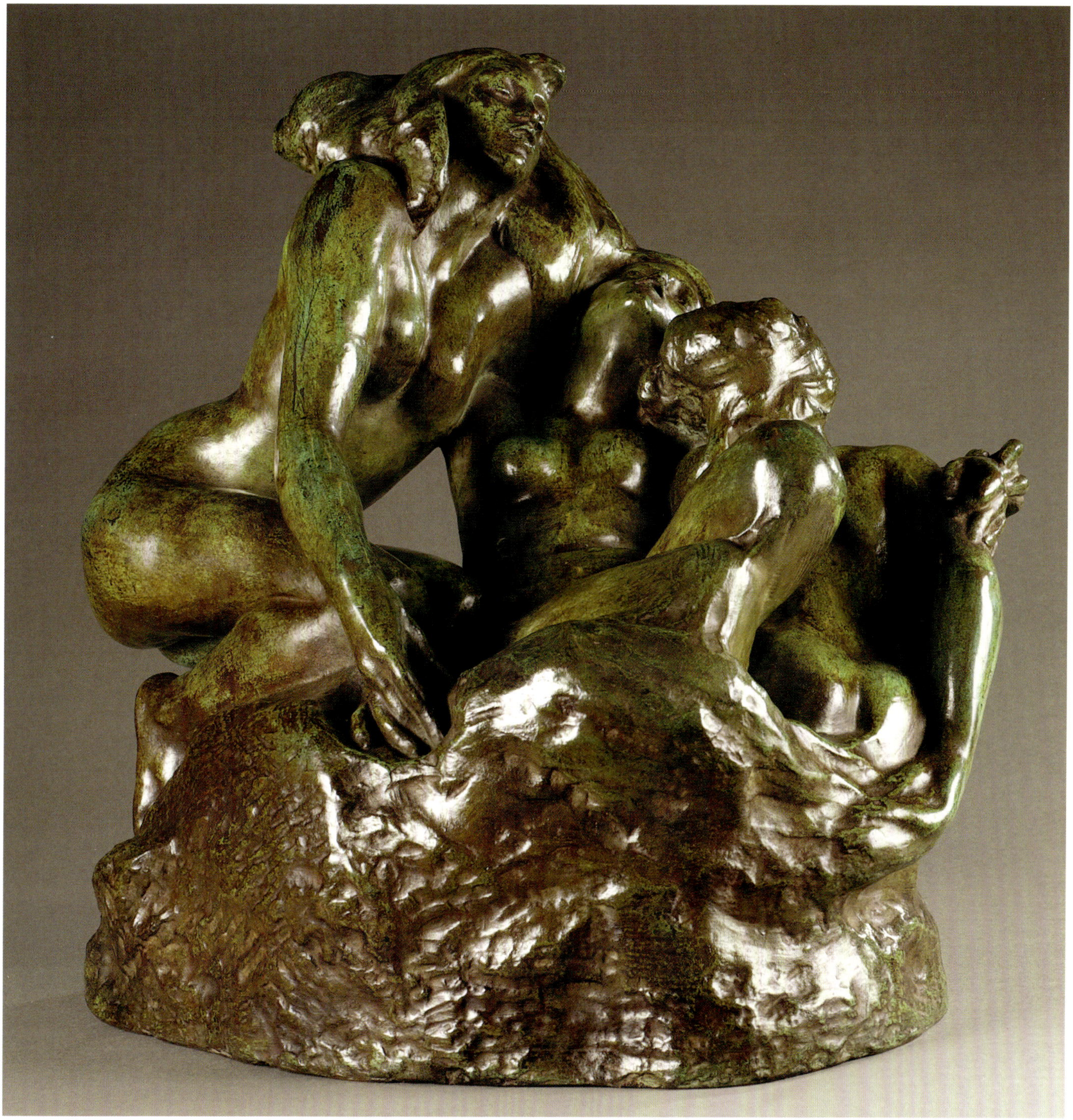

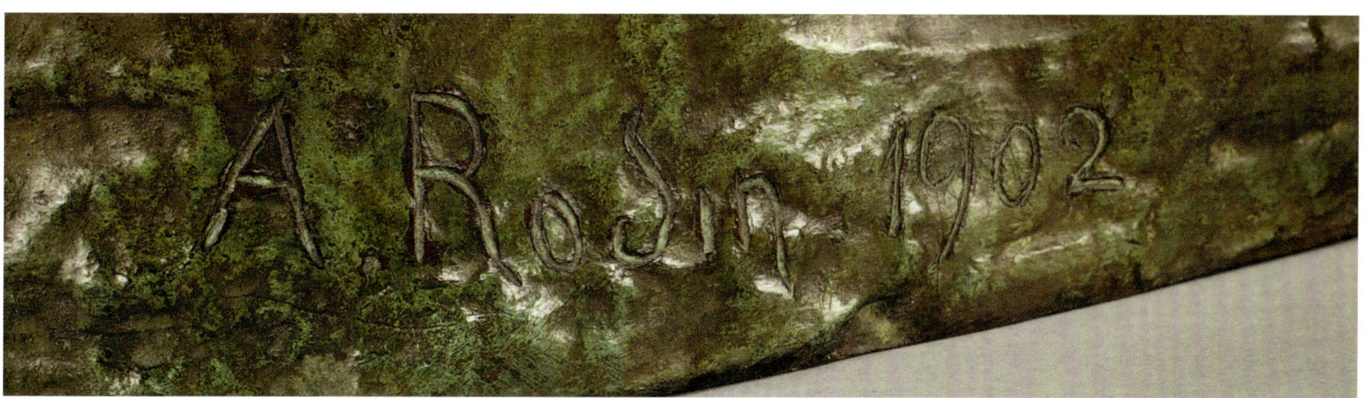

Eternal Spring, First State

L'éternal Printemps, Premier État

Signed A. Rodin with repeat raised interior signature
Inscribed © By Musée Rodin 1969 and Georges Rudier Fondeur Paris
Bronze with a dark brown and black patination
Height: 20¼ inches (51.4 cm)

Provenance:
Musée Rodin, Paris
Dominion Gallery, Montreal
Private Collection, Canada
Private Collection
Robert Bowman Gallery, 2008
Private Collection, Turkey

Conceived in 1884, this example was cast in 1969.

The present model, known as *Eternal Spring First State*, corresponds to Rodin's earliest conception of the sculpture, before the addition of the rocky structure below the man's left arm, which can be seen in the Barbedienne edition. In the present version, the man's leg is also free from the base, unlike in the Barbedienne edition.

Along with *The Kiss*, the present work was originally conceived to represent the tragic love Story of Paolo and Francesca, as told in Dante's *Inferno*. Given the predominance of the front view of the work, it is possible the model was first intended to adorn *The Gates of Hell*. An image taken by Charles Bodmer in 1886, shows an early sketch for the work displayed in front of the frame for the *Gates*, perhaps lending weight to this hypothesis. Nevertheless, there is no documentary proof that Rodin ever intended the work to adorn his great portal.

The date of conception, 1884, does however tie in with the period in which Rodin's relationship with Camille Claudel was blossoming and it has been suggested that perhaps the images of tenderly embracing lovers carried some autobiographical significance for the sculptor. Rodin himself cited the composer Beethoven as an influence, telling Jeanne Russell much later that 'it was whilst listening to it for the first time (Beethoven's Second Symphony) that I pictured *Eternal Spring*, just as I have modelled it since.'

It is also important to note that the torso of the woman was in fact taken from Rodin's earlier work *Torso of Adele*, which he sculpted between 1878 and 1872. This work depicts the torso of Rodin's favourite model Adèle Abbruzzesi, which is used without adjustment in the present work.

Whatever provided the exact genesis for the two lovers; *Eternal Spring* went on to become an icon of romantic love and one of Rodin's most well known and certainly most commercially successful models.

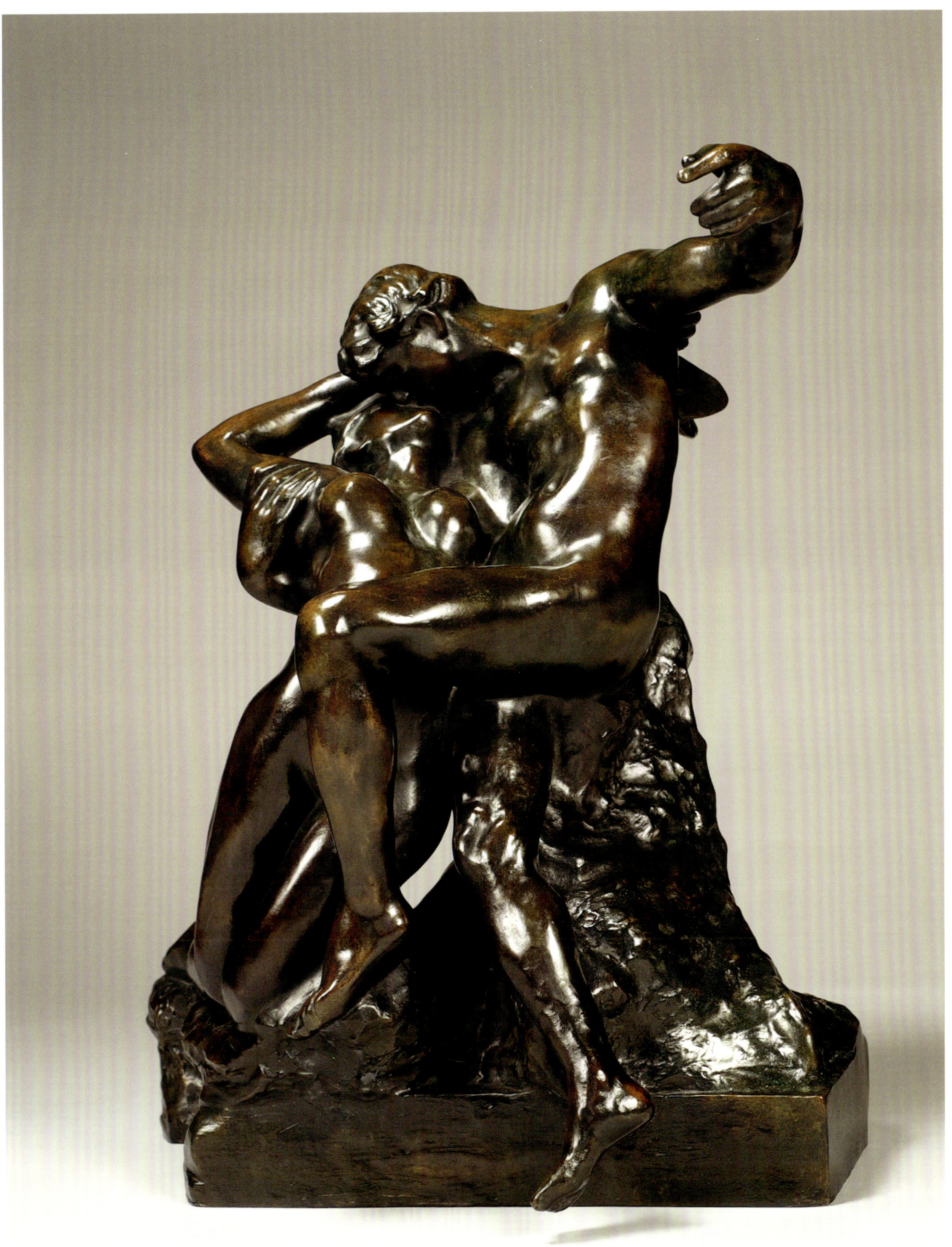

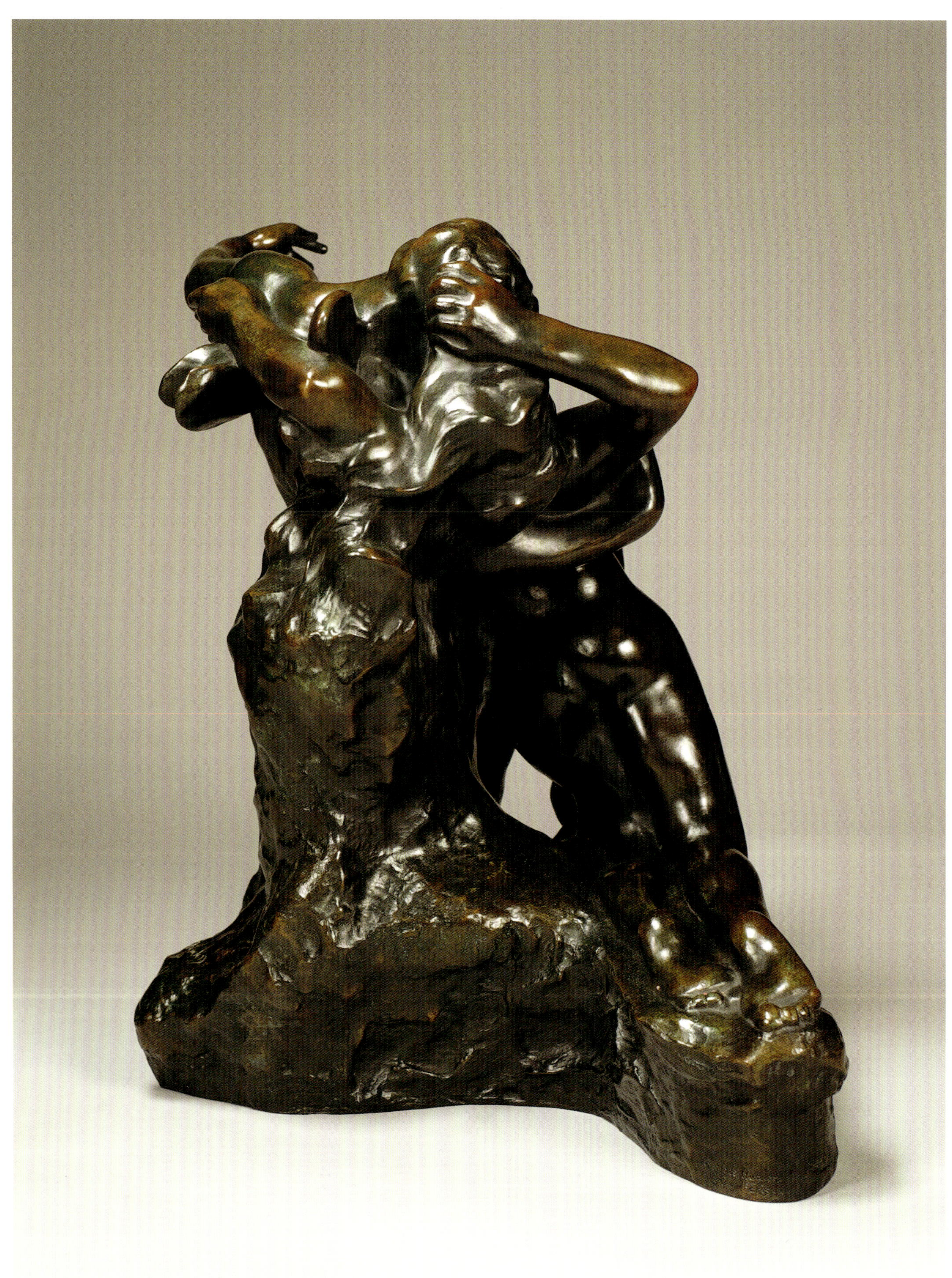

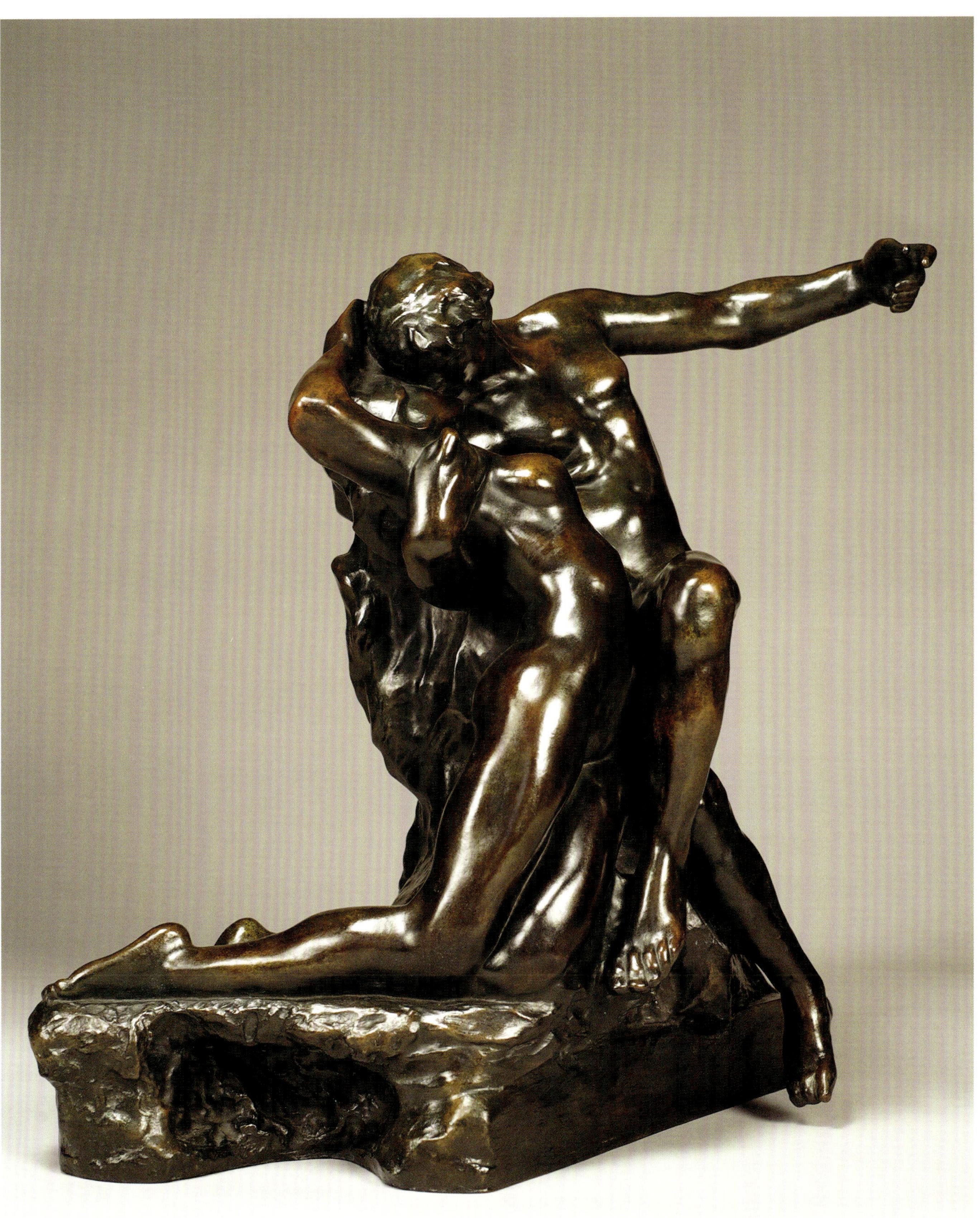

Eternal Spring, Second State, 1ˢᵗ Reduction

Éternal Printemps, Second Etat, 1ᵉʳᵉ Reduction

Signed Rodin
Inscribed F. Barbedienne Fondeur Paris
Bronze with a black and green patination
Height: 26 inches (66.5 cm)

Provenance:
Madame Leblanc-Barbedienne, Paris
Mme Jeanne T. Hill, Paris
Selected Artist Galleries, New York
Himan Brown, New York, acquired 1969
Robert Bowman Gallery, 2012
Private Collection, Norway

Conceived in 1884, this example was cast between 1898 and 1918. Between fifty and fifty-eight casts of the present model were cast in this size by the Barbedienne foundry between 1898 and 1918. Rodin agreed a ten year renewable contract for the Barbedienne foundry to produce an unlimited edition of the model in 1898. The foundry produced four sizes of this model, 66cm, 50cm, 40cm and 25cm. The Alexis Rudier then cast twelve bronzes for The Musée Rodin after 1930.

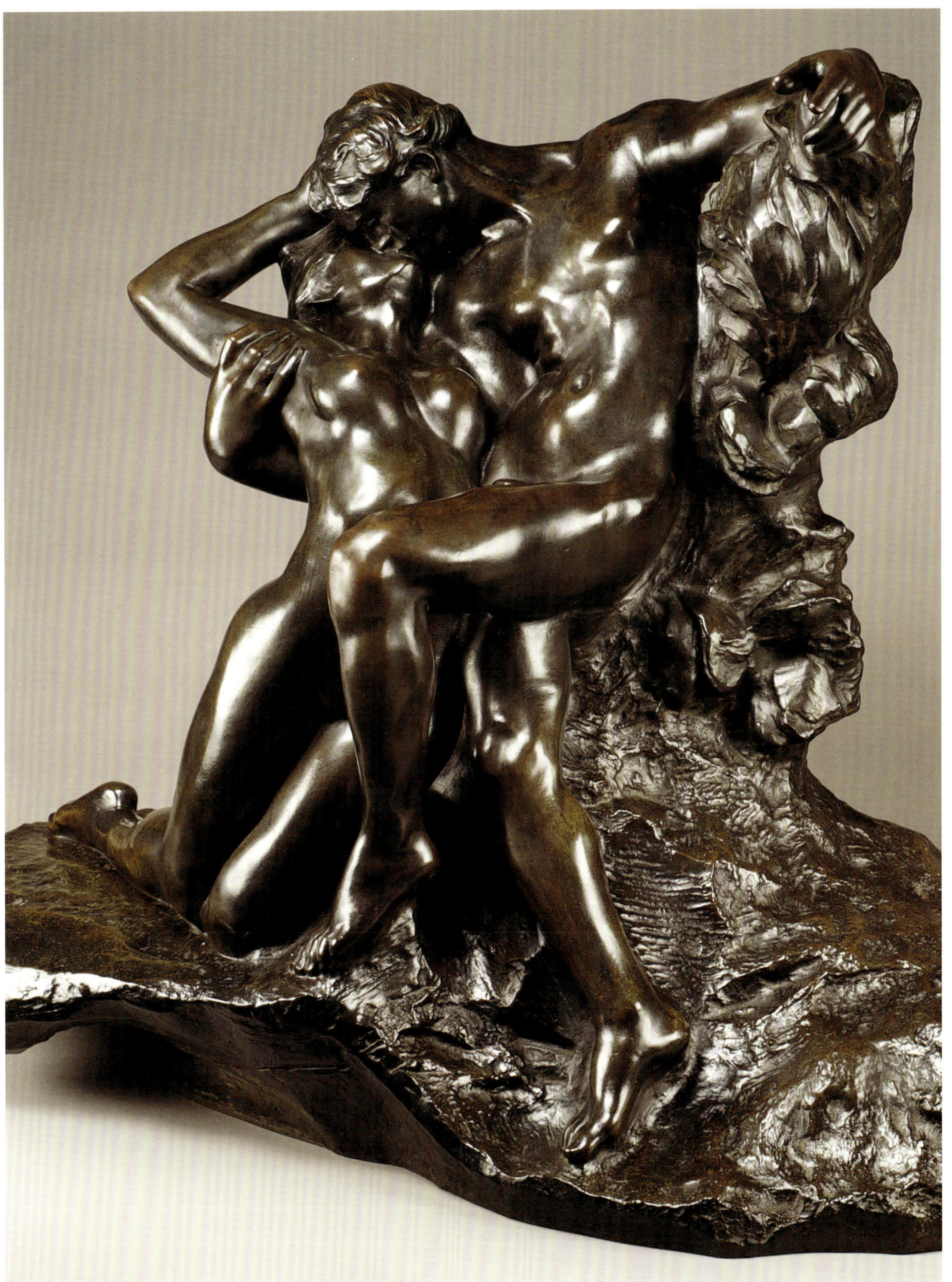

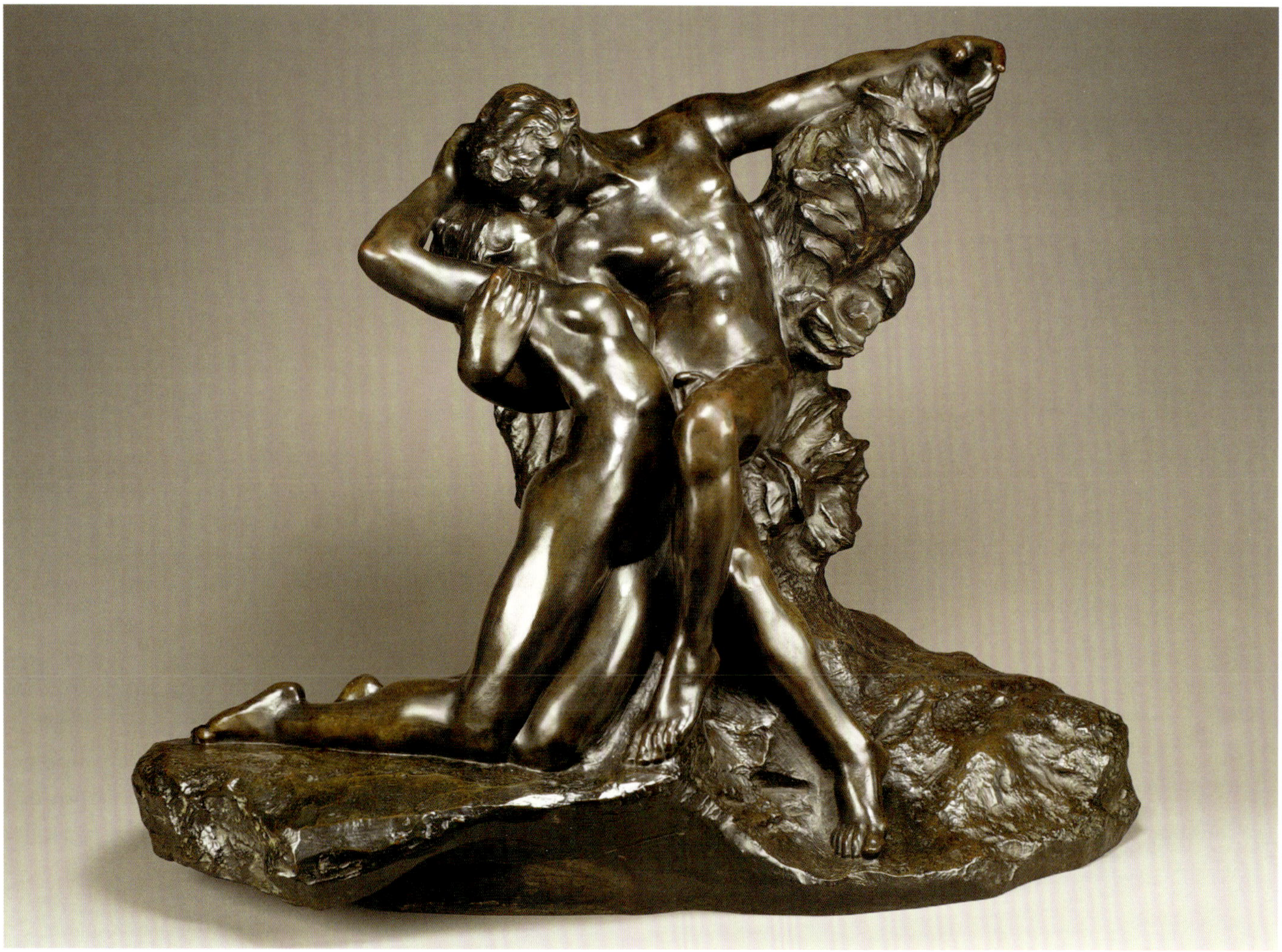

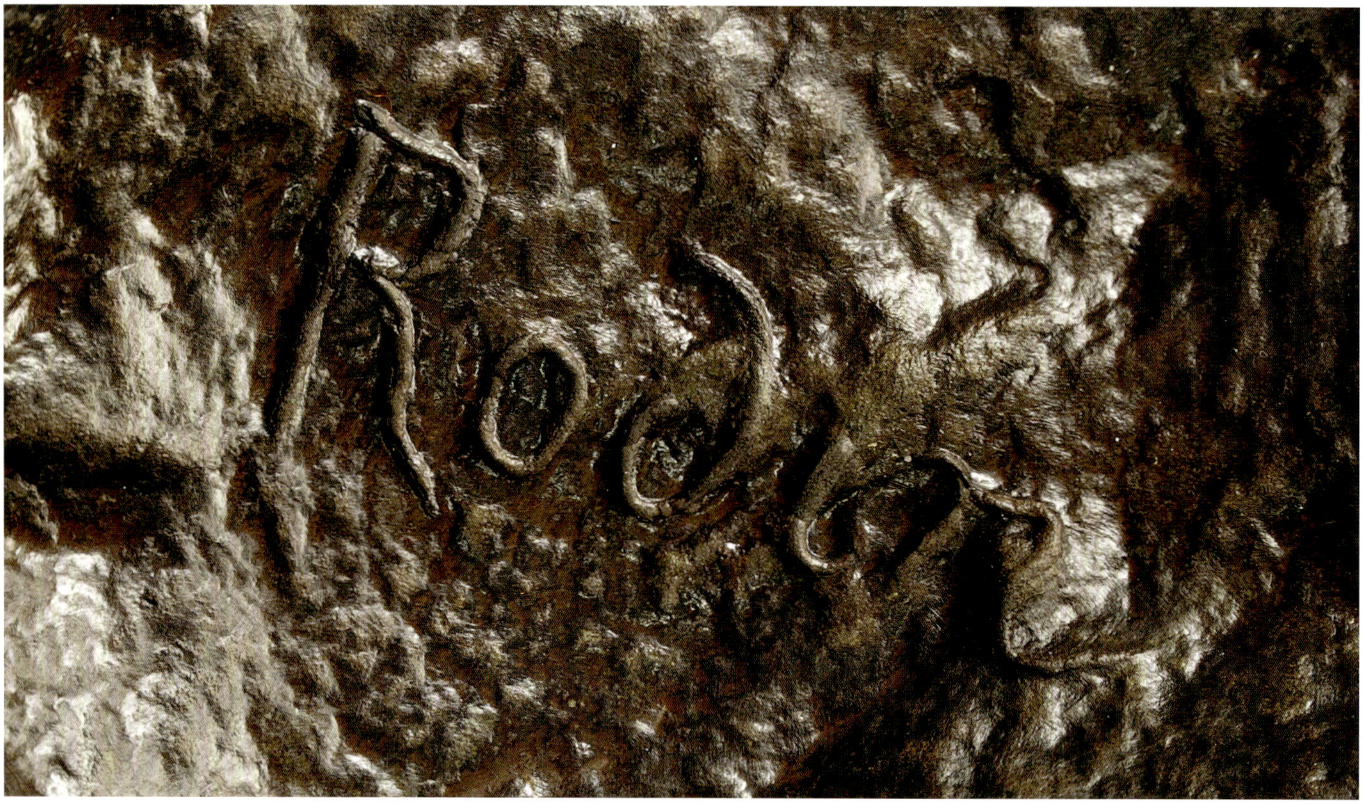

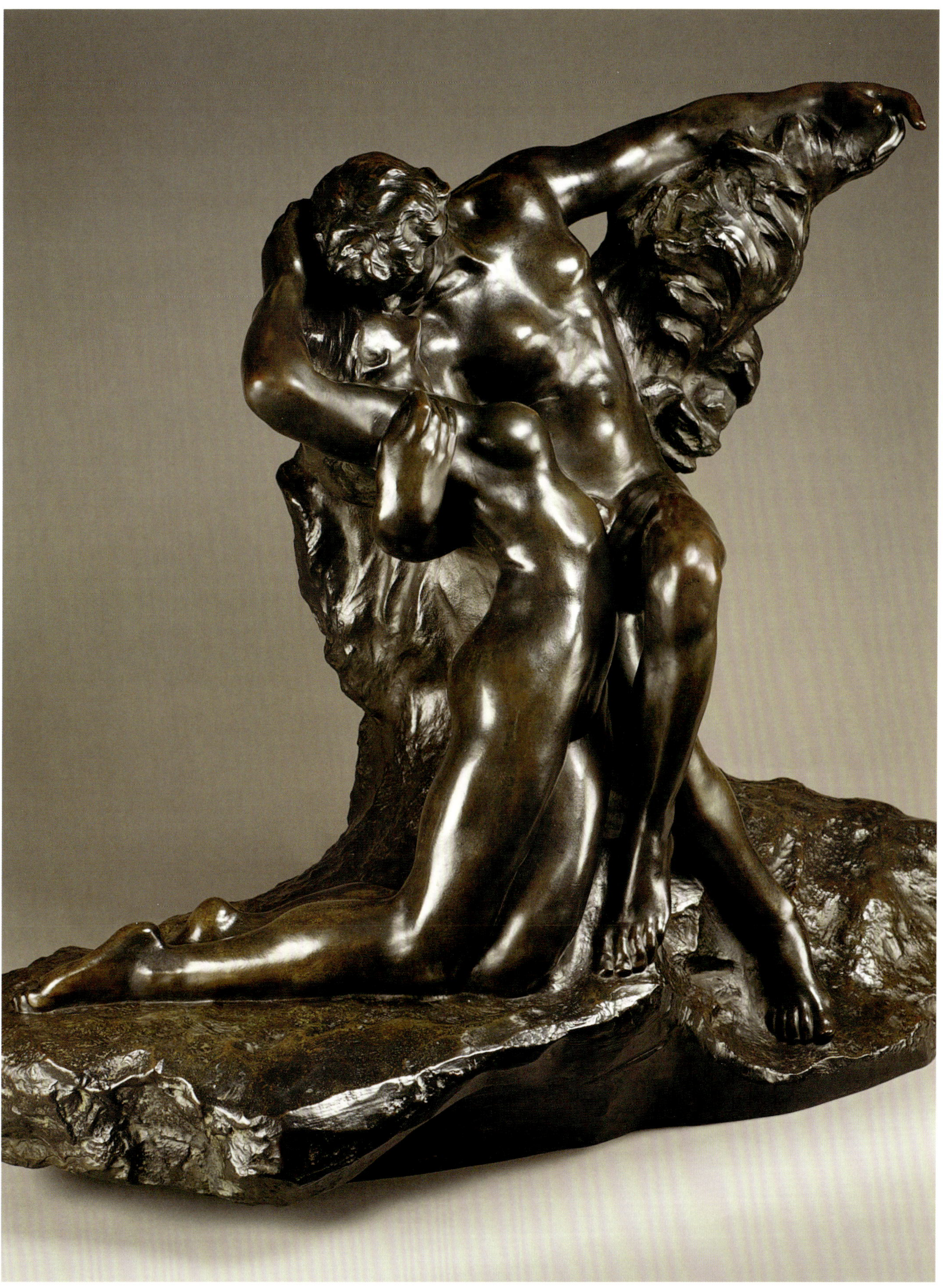

Eternal Spring, Second State, 3rd Reduction

Eternal Printemps, Second État, 3ème Réduction

Signed Rodin
Inscribed F. Barbedienne Fondeur with the letter S in the inside
Bronze with a rich dark red and brown patination
Height: 15¾ inches (40 cm)

Provenance:
Fuji Gallery, Tokyo
Mitsukoshi department store, Tokyo
Acquired from the above in 1980
Robert Bowman Gallery, 2009
Private European Collection

Conceived in 1884, this example was cast between 1898 and 1918. Between eighty and eighty-three casts of the present model were cast in this size by the Barbedienne foundry between 1898 and 1918. Rodin agreed a ten year renewable contract for the Barbedienne foundry to produce an unlimited edition of the model in 1898. The foundry produced four sizes of this model, 66cm, 50cm, 40cm and 25cm.

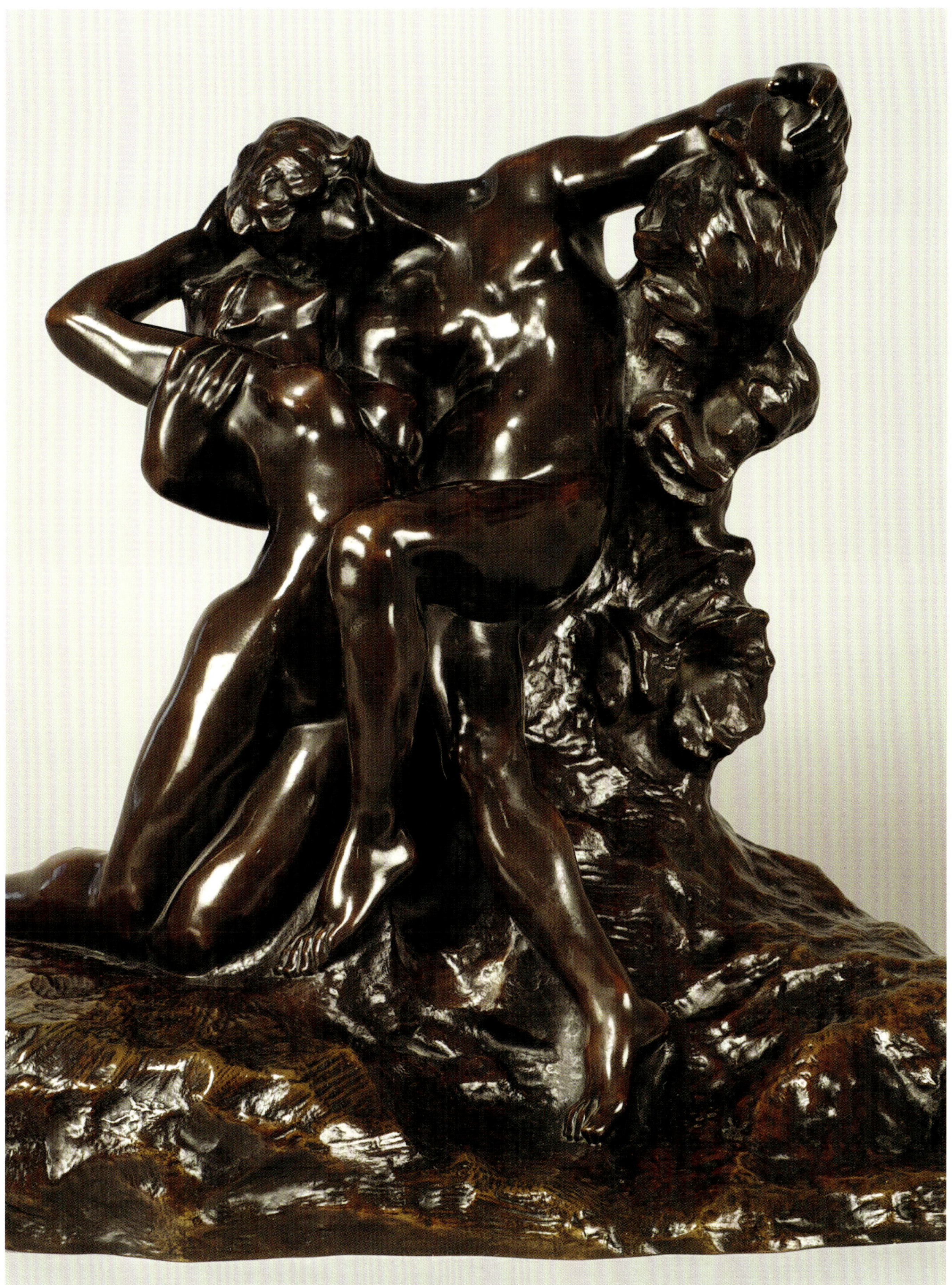

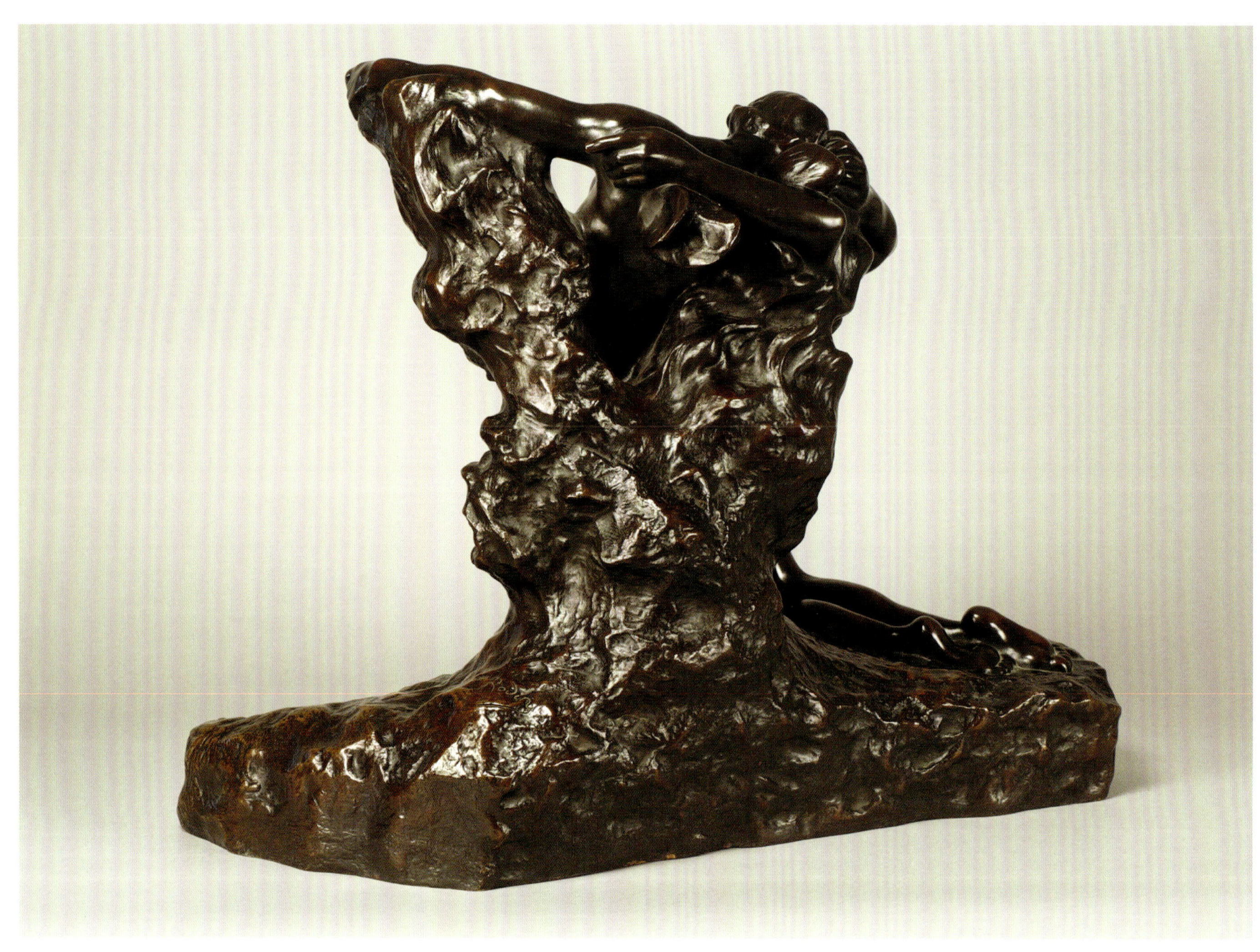

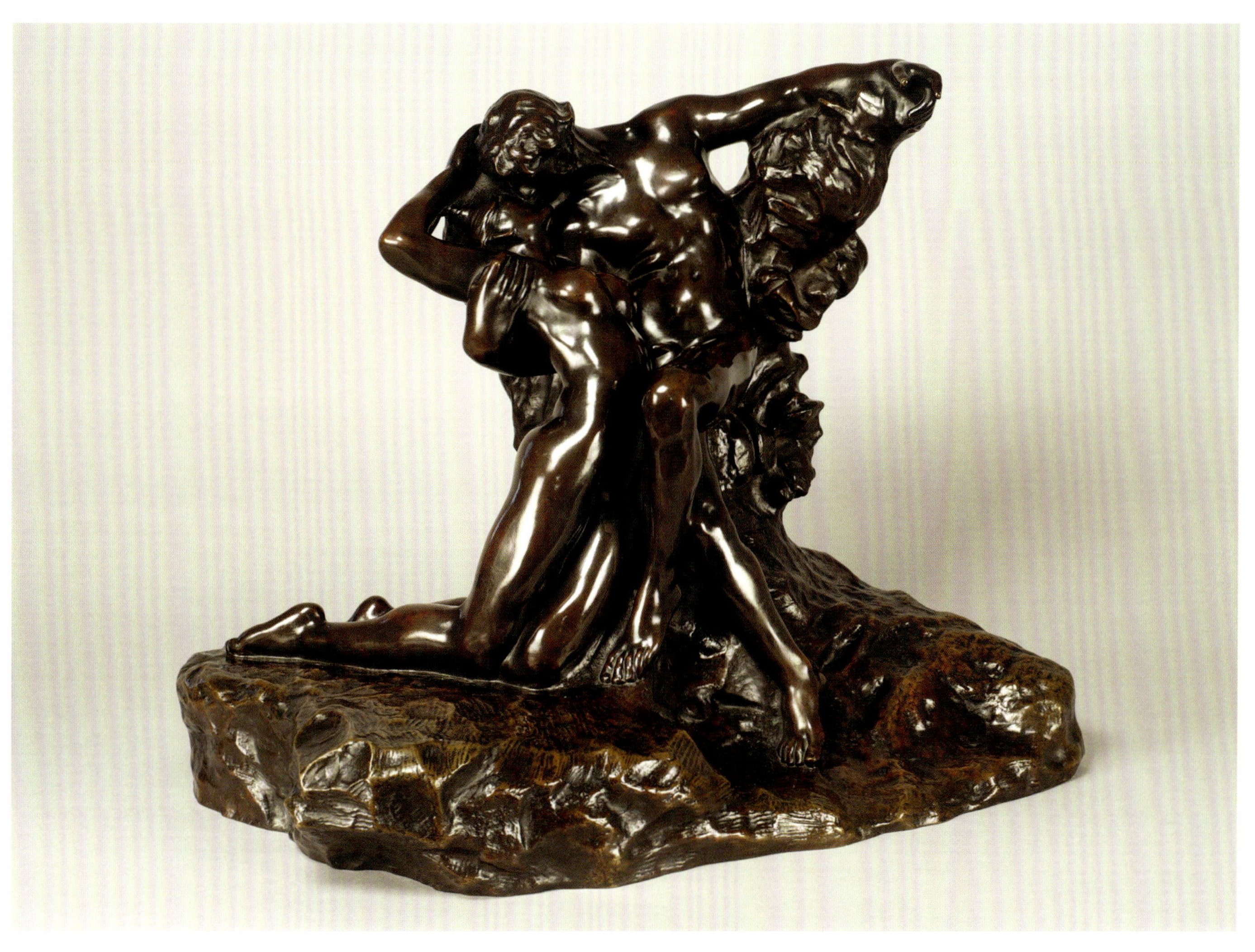

Eternal Spring, Second State, 4ᵗʰ Reduction

Eternal Printemps, Second État, 4ᵉᵐᵉ Réduction

Signed Rodin
Inscribed F. Barbedienne Fondeur with the letters VL in the interior
Bronze with a rich dark red and brown patination
Height: 9½ inches (24.8 cm)

Provenance:
Private Collection, France
By Descent

Conceived in 1884, this example was cast between 1898 and 1918. Between sixty-three and sixty-nine casts of the present model were cast in this size by the Barbedienne foundry between 1898 and 1918. Rodin agreed a ten year renewable contract for the Barbedienne foundry to produce an unlimited edition of the model in 1898. The foundry produced four sizes of this model, 66cm, 50cm, 40cm and 25cm.

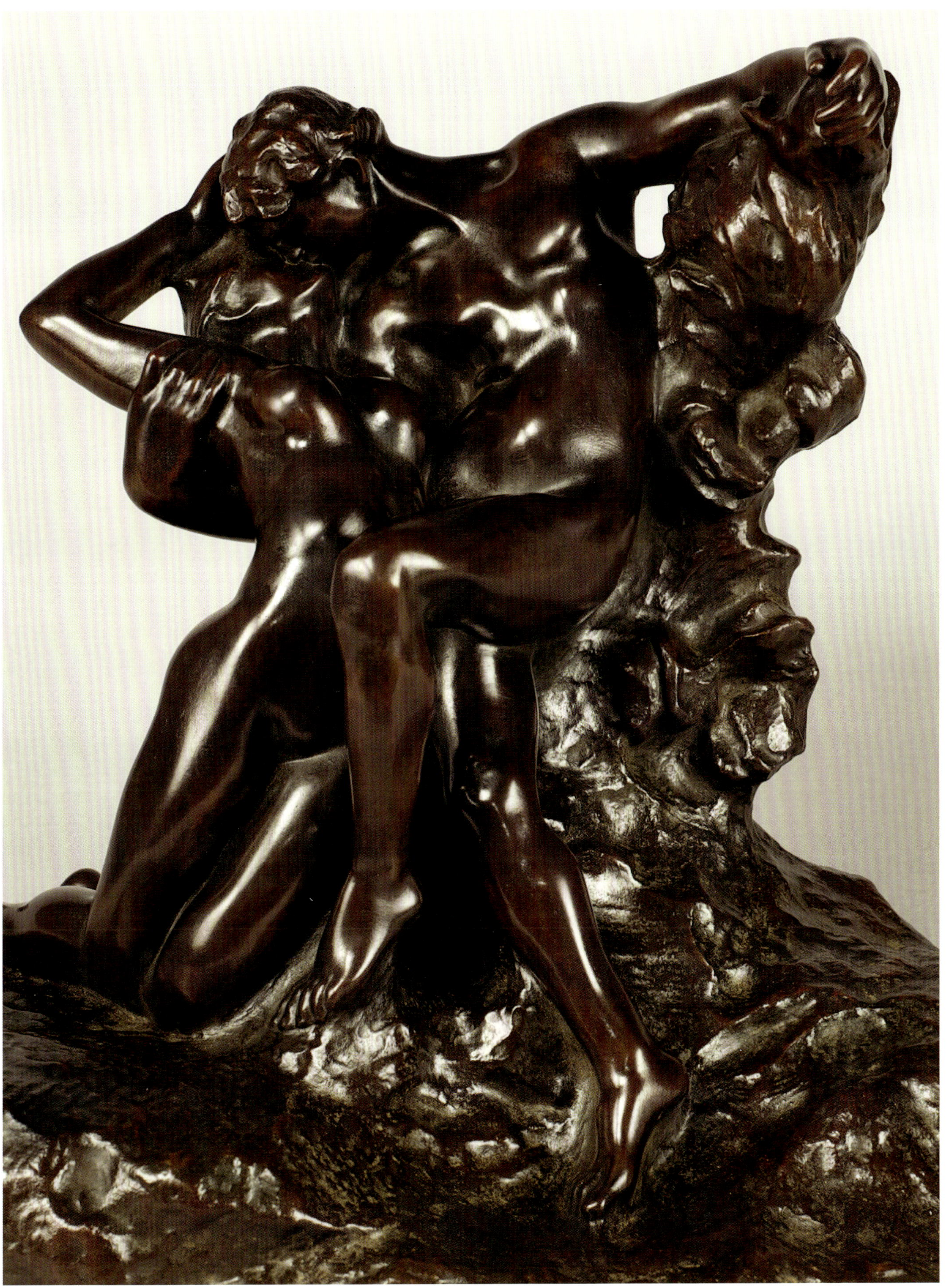

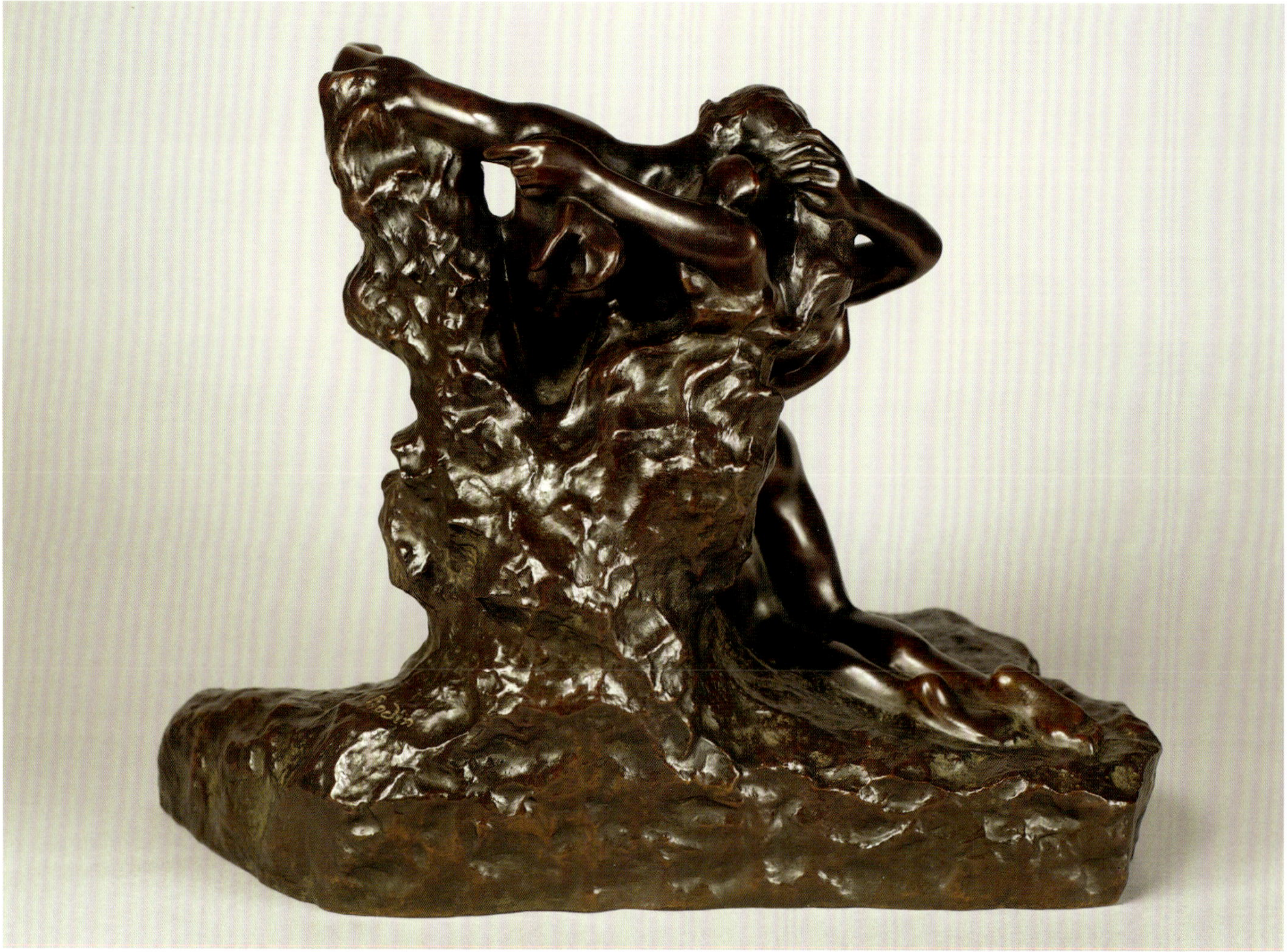

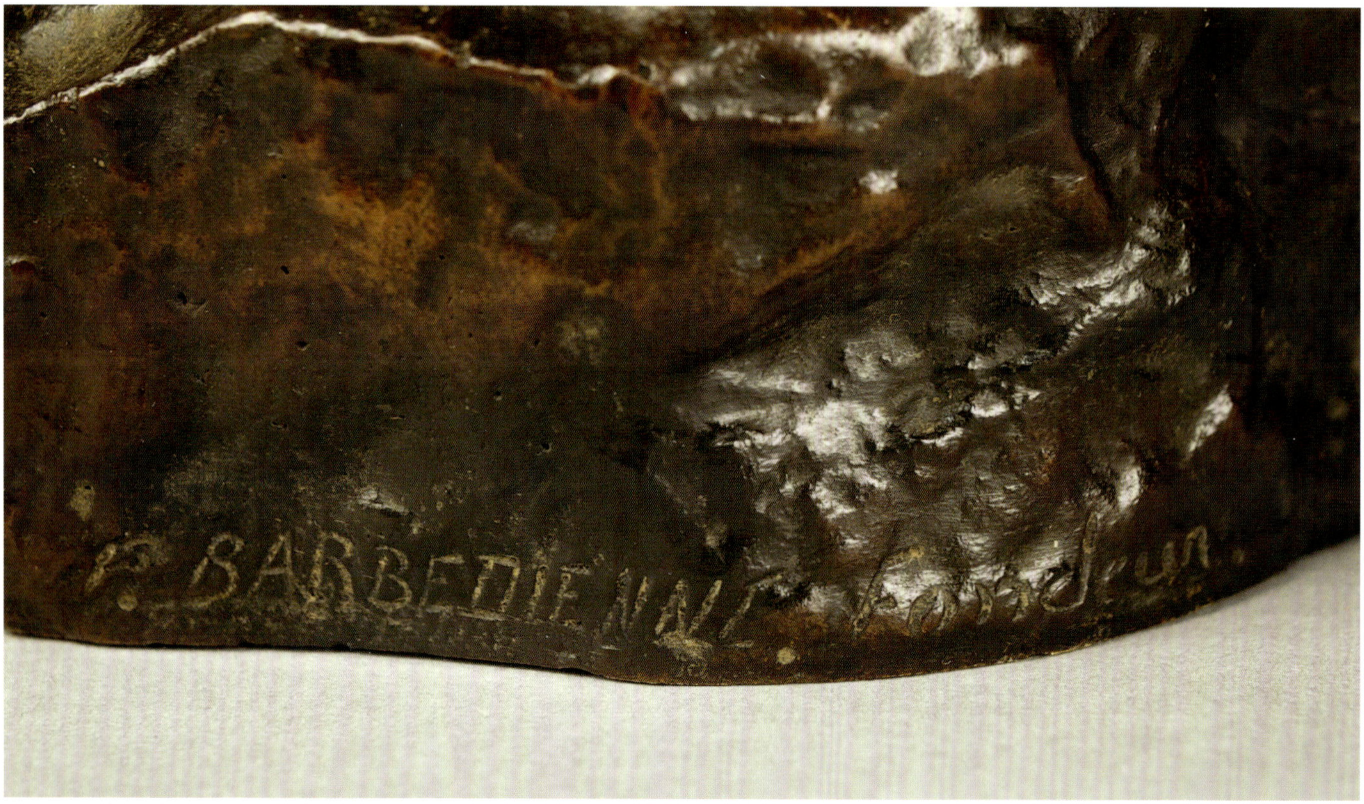

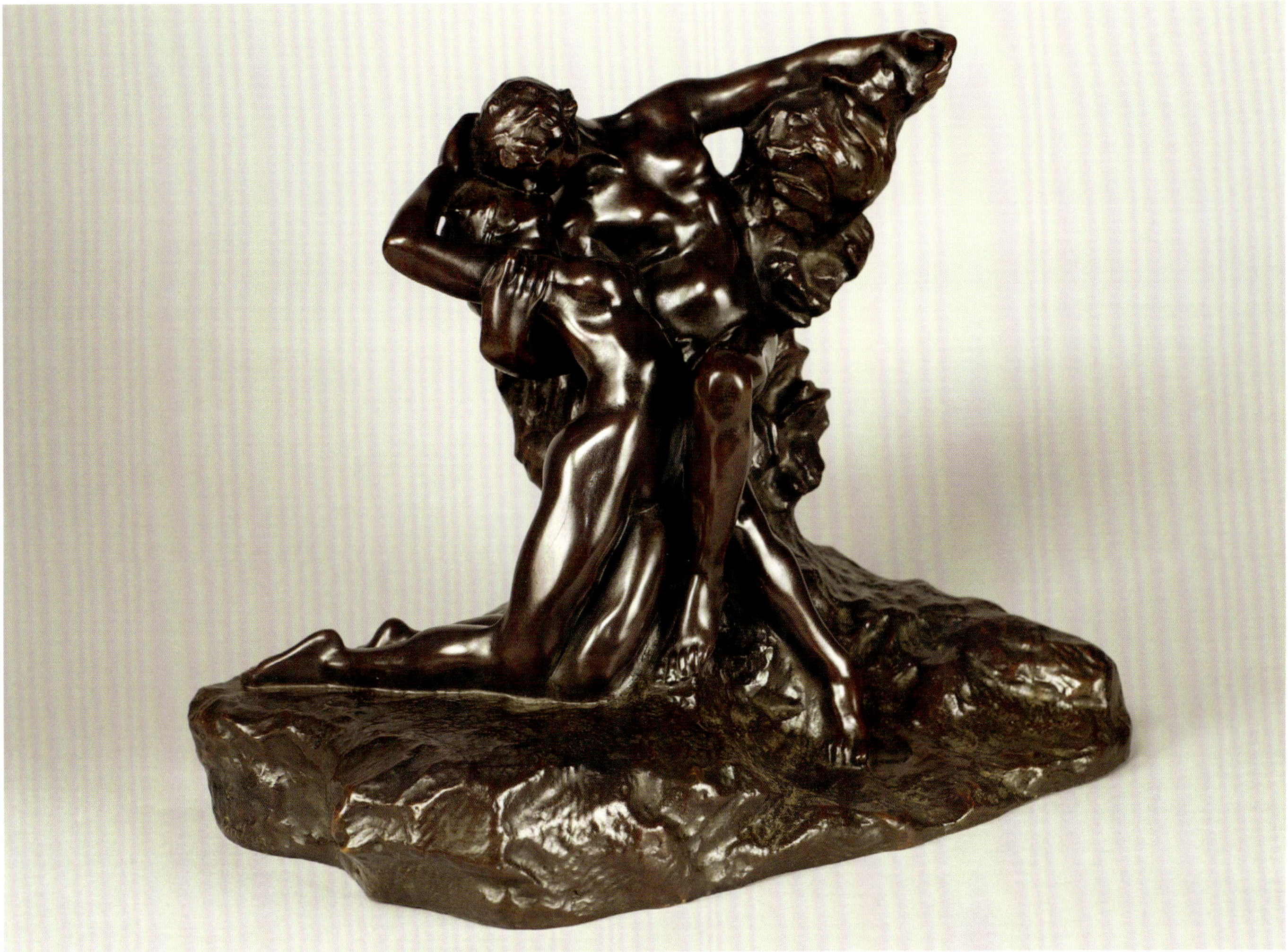

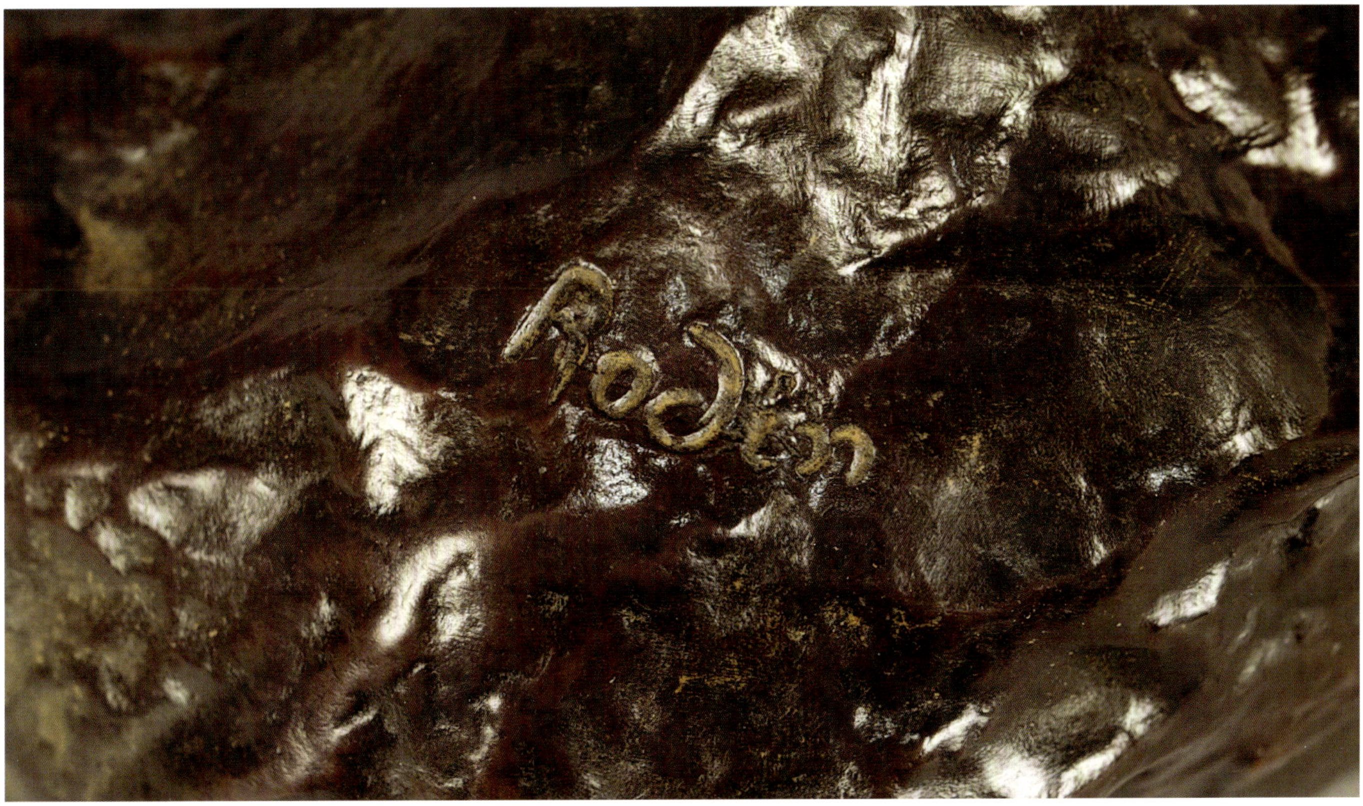

Torso of Adele

Torse d'Adèle

Signed A. Rodin with repeat raised interior signature
Inscribed © by Musée Rodin in 1956 and Georges Rudier Fondeur Paris
Bronze with a dark brown patination
Height: 17½ inches (44.2 cm)

Provenance:
Musée Rodin
World House Galleries
Samir Bawachi
Thence by descent to Marcus Willies
Robert Bowman Gallery, 2013
Private Collection, UK

Conceived circa 1878, this example was cast in 1956. This model was never cast during Rodin's lifetime. In total thirteen casts were made for the Musée Rodin. The first cast by the Alexis Rudier foundry in 1928, then three further casts by the same foundry between 1943 and 1952. Nine casts executed by the Georges Rudier foundry between 1953 and 1960.

According to Antoinette Le Normand-Romain the *Torso of Adele* was modelled as early as 1878 and survives in 10 separate plaster versions at the Musée Rodin. Much like many of Rodin's sculptures, it later appeared in *The Gates Of Hell*, where in the final version it linked the area behind *The Thinker* to the moldings that formed the frame of the *Gates*.

The present work depicts one of Rodin's favorite models Adele Abbruzzesi, and immediately calls to mind his seminal work *Eternal Spring* in which the torso is used in an almost identical pose. Here we see Rodin's masterful handling of the human form. Even in bronze, the softness of the model's skin is expertly rendered, as is the graceful arching of her back and twisting hips.

It appears that Rodin considered the work complete during the 1890s and he exhibited the plaster in both Brussels and the Netherlands during 1899.

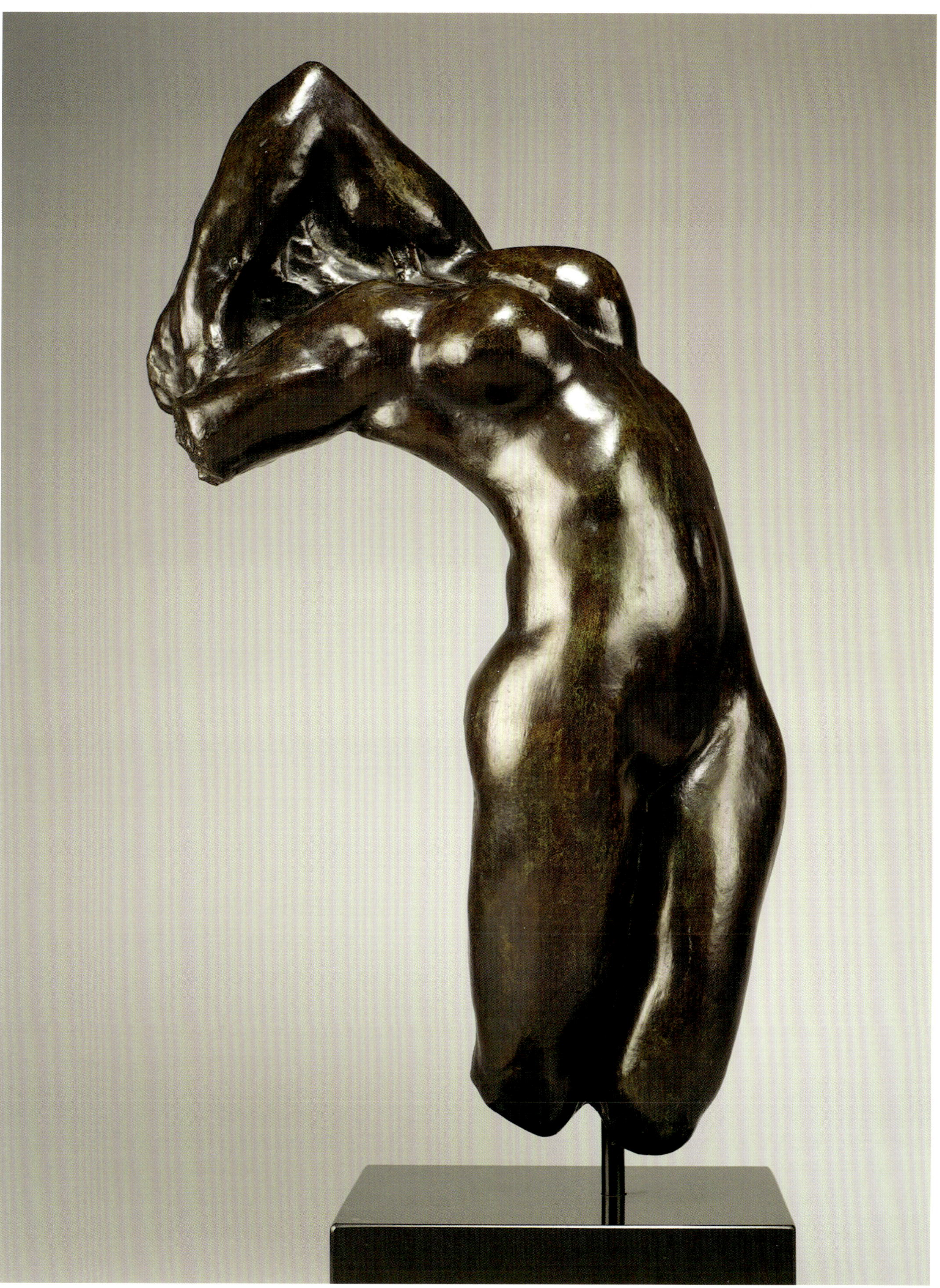

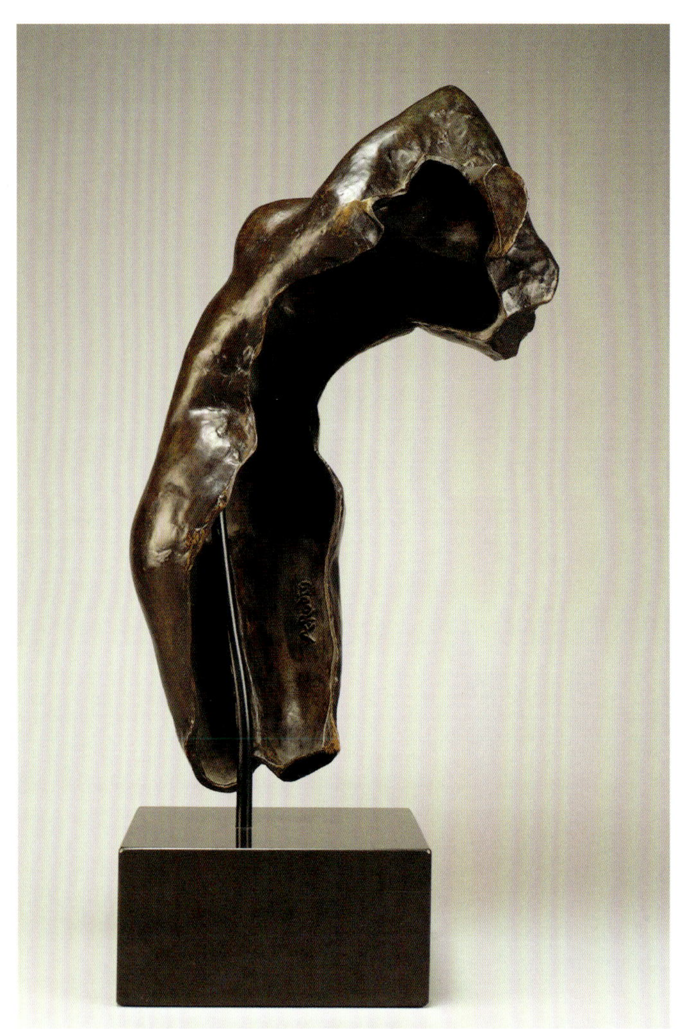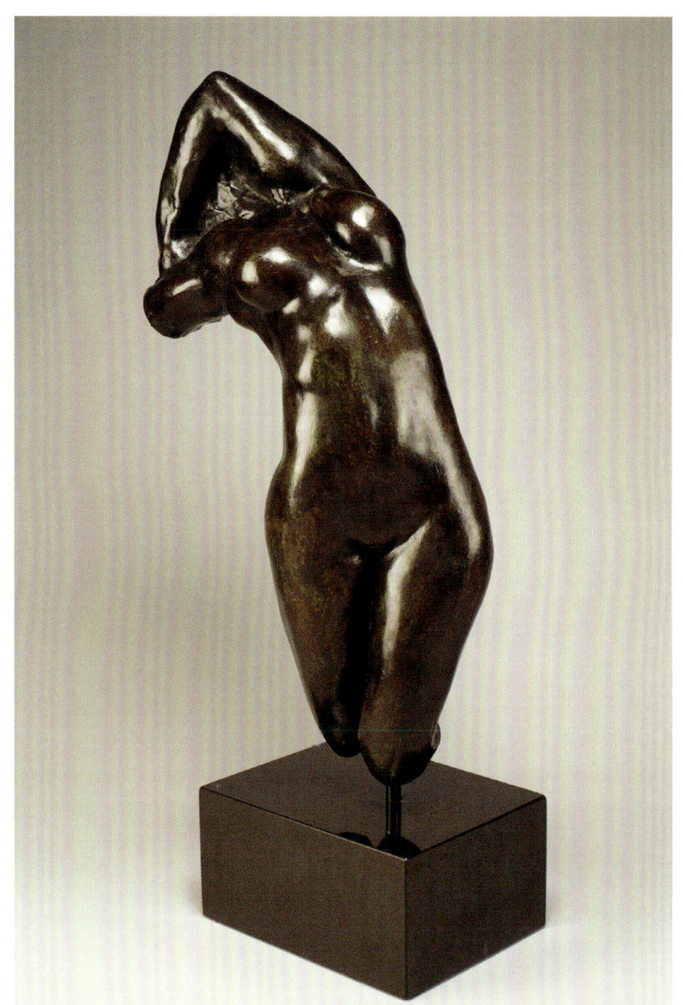

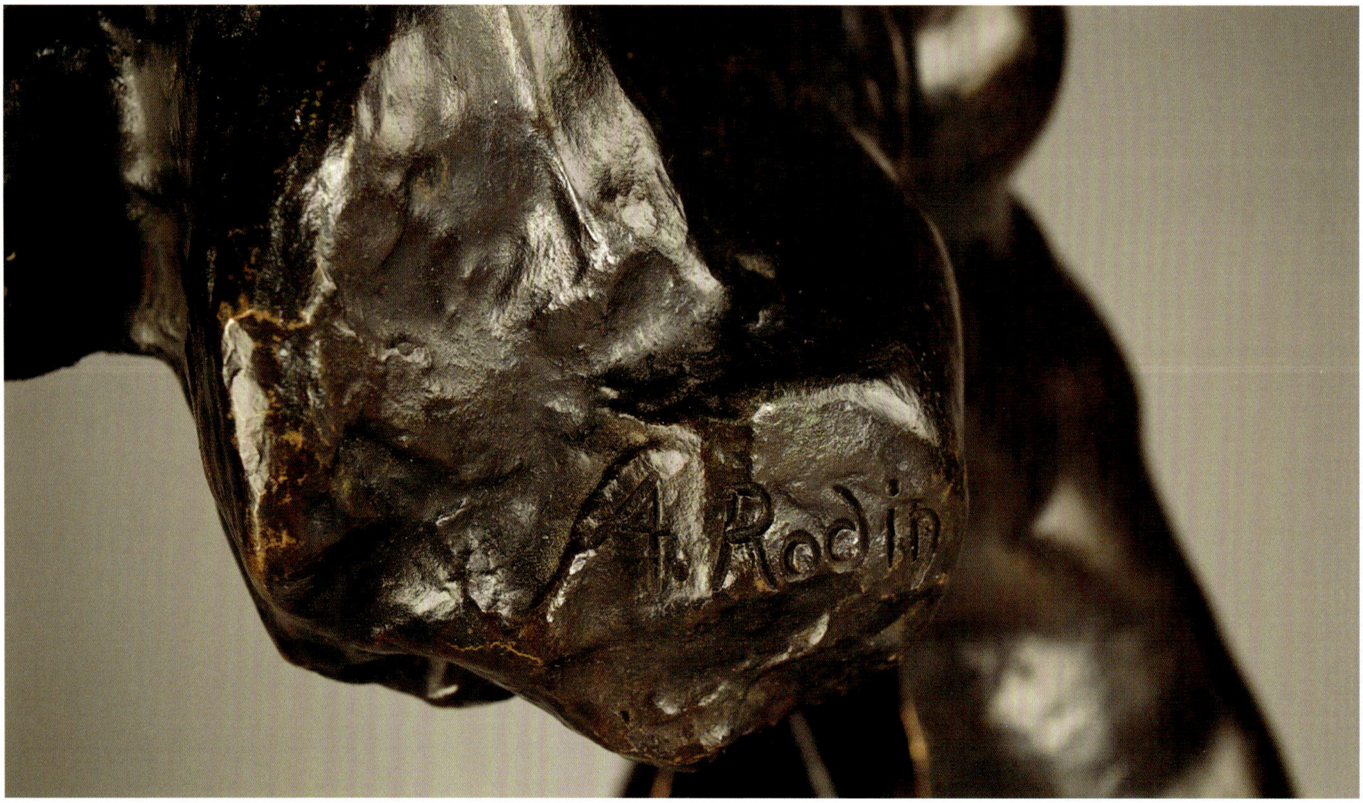

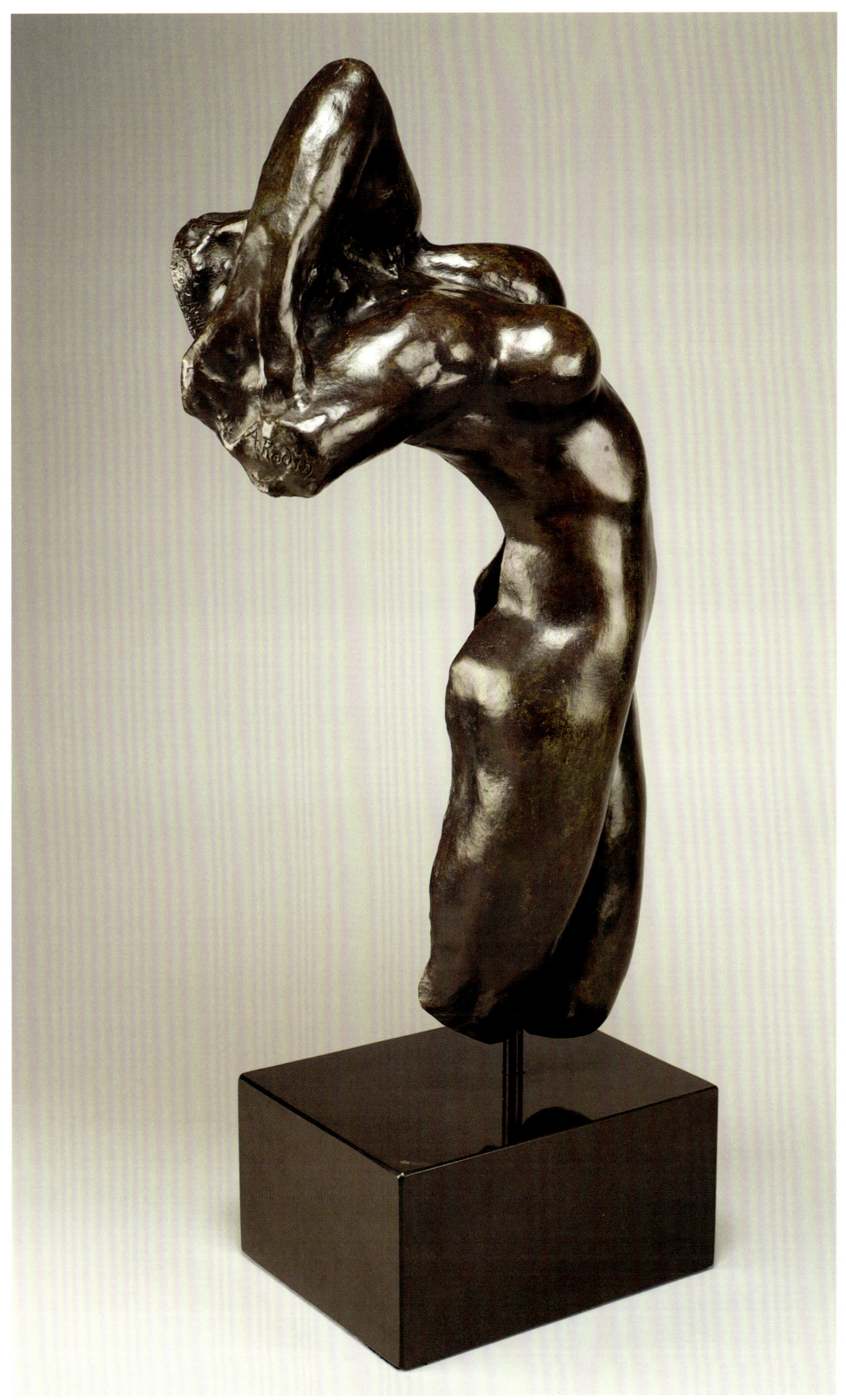

First Maquette for the Monument to the Burghers of Calais, Version Without a Pedestal

Première Maquette pour le Monument aux Burgeois de Calais, Variante sans Piédestal

Signed A. Rodin
Inscribed © by Musée Rodin and E. Godard Fond Paris
Numbered 11
Bronze with a rich dark brown patination
Height: 13 inches (33 cm)

Provenance:
Musée Rodin
M. Senda Ohmiya, Pref. de Stame, Japan acquired 1977
Exhibited:
Seibu Museum of Art, Tokyo, Japan 1976
Museum of Modern Art Monoka & Kobe, Japan, 1977

Conceived in 1884, this example was cast in 1975. The model was never cast during Rodin's lifetime. In total nine casts of this variation without the pedestal were cast for the Musée Rodin between 1971 and 1976 by the Godard foundry.

The present work is the first maquette for Rodin's iconic monument *The Burghers of Calais*. The monument was conceived as homage to the brave citizens of Calais who sacrificed themselves to the invading English forces during the 100-year war.

According to the legend, detailed in Jean Froissart's Chronicles (1360–65), the King of England Edward III laid siege to Calais during 1346. After 11 months, as starvation gripped the inhabitants of the surrounded city, Edward commanded that they send out six men holding the keys to the city as an acknowledgement of defeat. These men, all of who held high ranking positions, were then to be executed in order to save the other citizens. Although the burghers were eventually spared, after Philippa of Hainault, the Queen of England, asked her husband to pardon them, it was the original heroism of the act that so moved Rodin.

Rodin began work on an initial model for the monument in 1884, before the commission was even fully confirmed. Over the next 5 years he reworked the model a number of times, executing the figures both independently and as a full group of 6. The monument, eventually completed in 1889, represented a radical departure from traditional works of this nature. Rodin was particularly concerned with illustrating the humanity of the figures, rather than simply portraying them as exalted heroes. Even in this early study, it is clear that the sculptor has begun to conceive not only the burgher's relationships with one another, but also the different ways in which they approached what appeared to be their impending doom.

'I did not group them together in a triumphant apophasis: for such a glorification of their heroism would not in any way have corresponded to reality…. With the uncertain outcome of their final inner struggle being waged between their devotion to the city and their fear of dying, it is as if each of them has to face their conscience alone.'

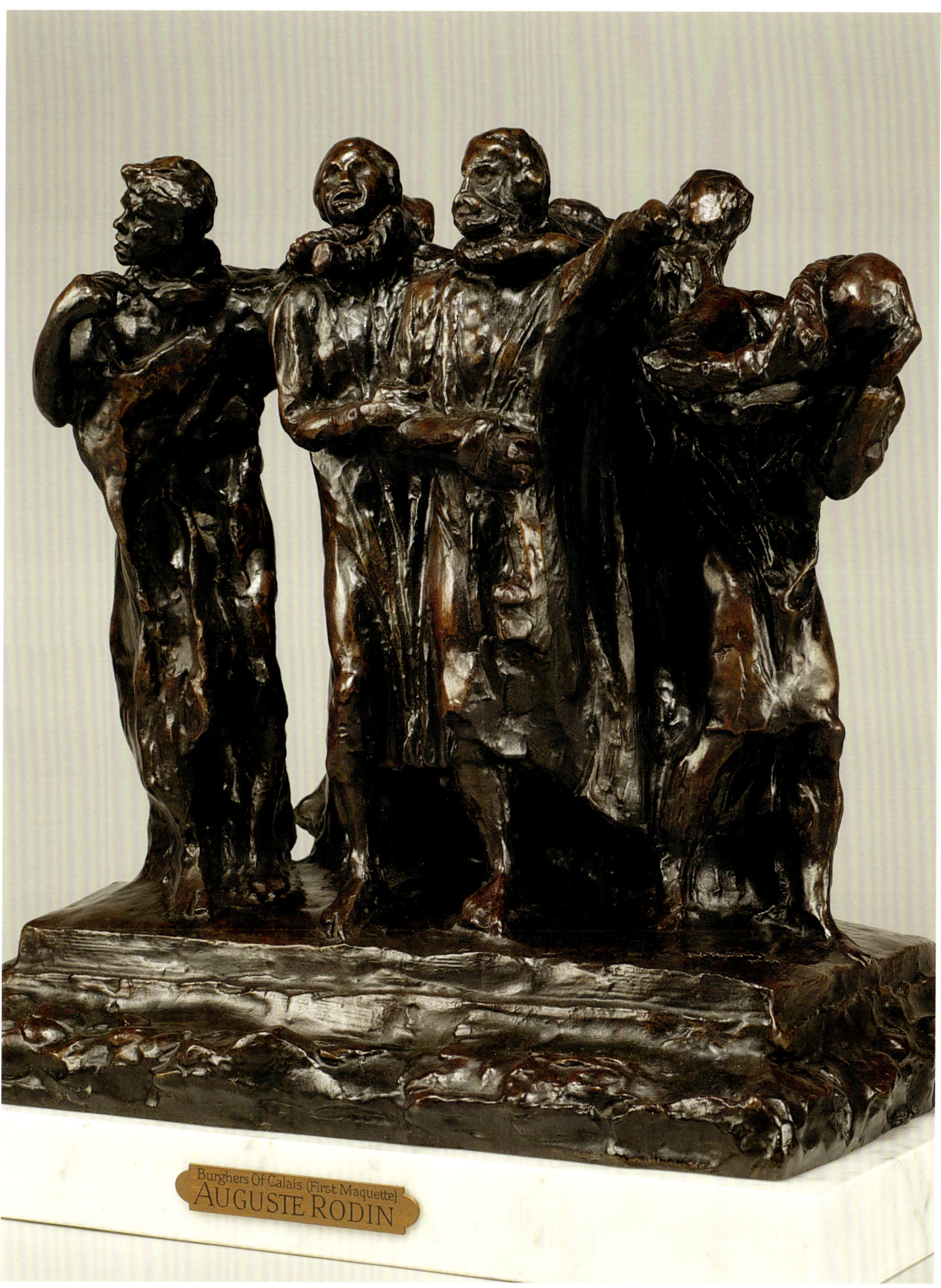

Burghers Of Calais (First Maquette)

AUGUSTE RODIN

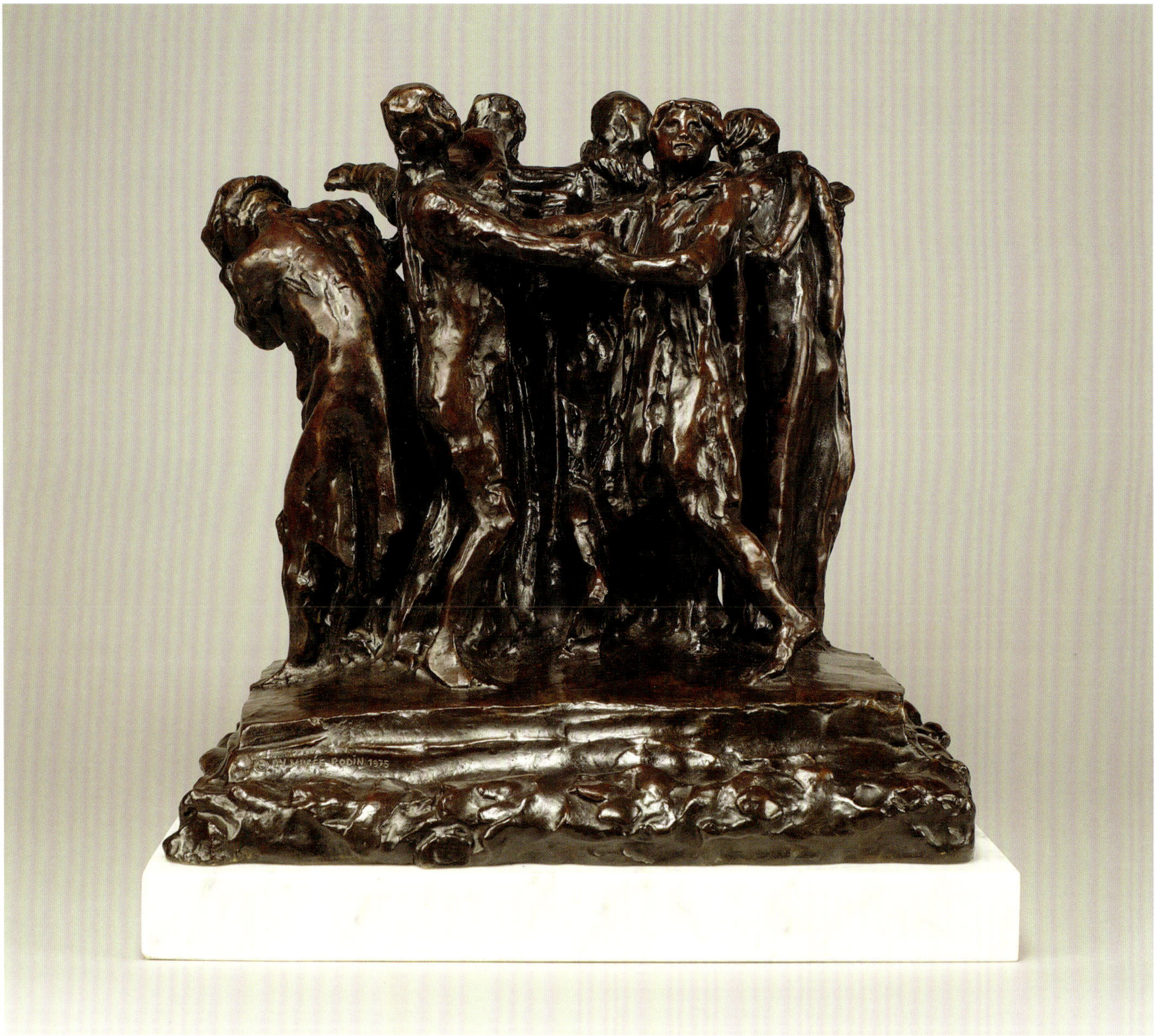

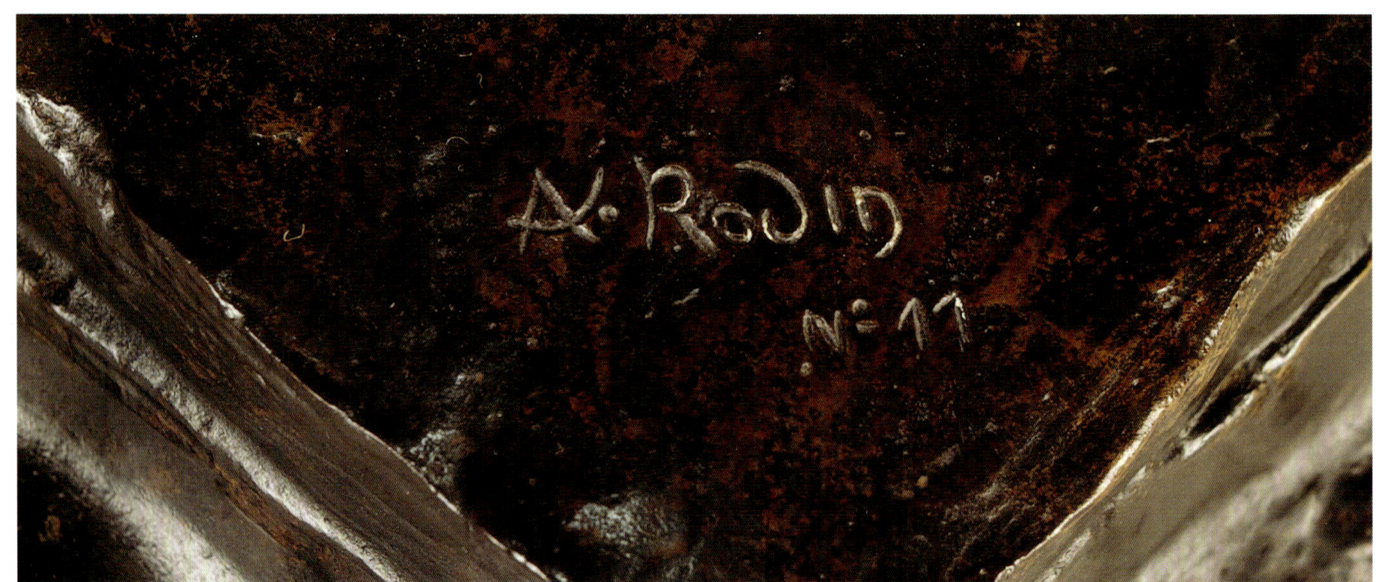

A. Rodin
N° 11

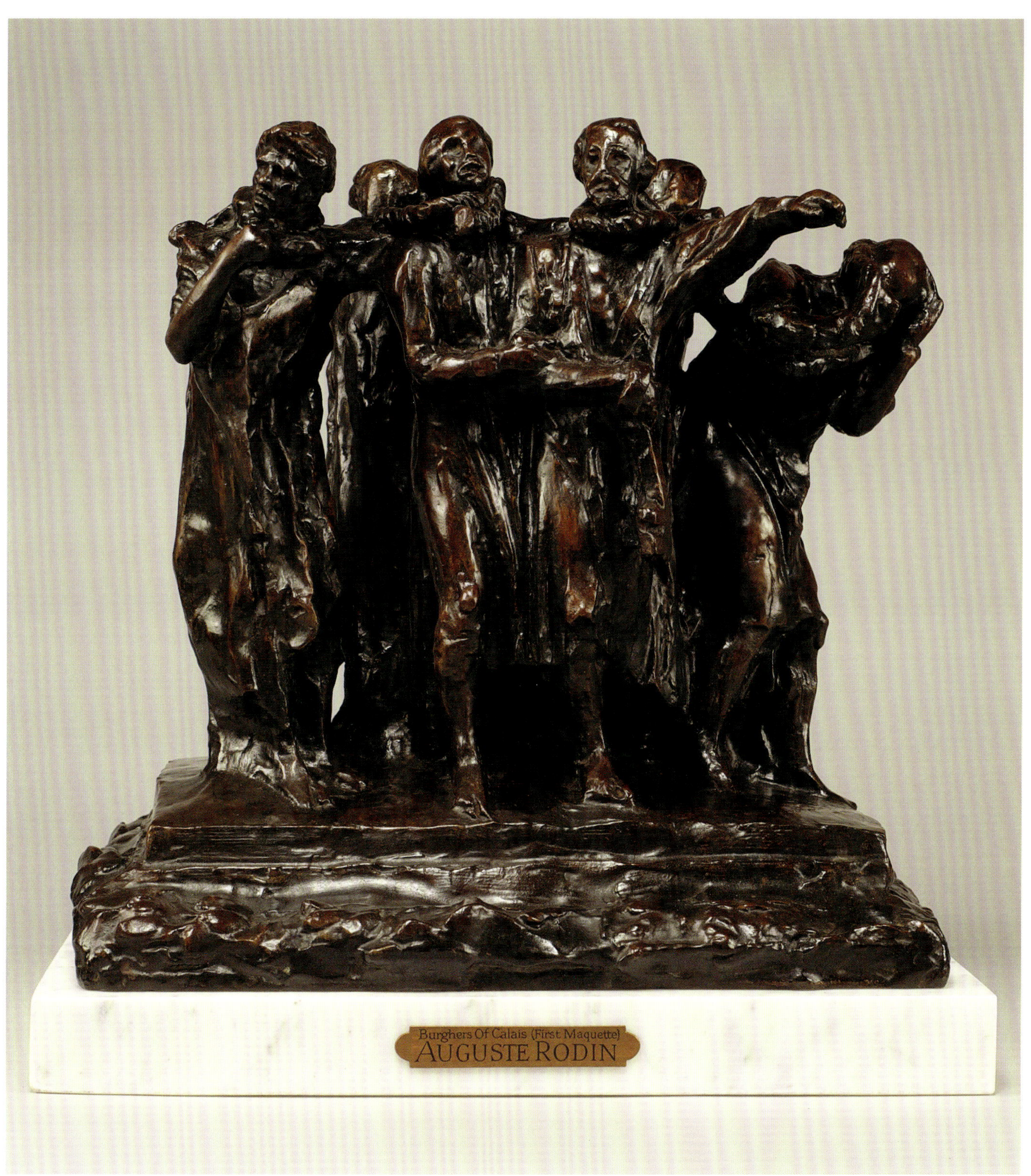

Burghers Of Calais (First Maquette)
AUGUSTE RODIN

Jean d'Aire

Jean d'Aire

Signed A. Rodin with repeat raised interior signature
Inscribed © by Musée Rodin 1958 and Georges Rudier Foundeur Paris
Bronze with a green and dark brown patination
Height: 18 inches (46.5 cm)

Provenance:
Musée Rodin
Erich Cohn, New York, acquired 1958
By 1973 acquired by Mr Kornfeld and Mr Klipstein, Berne

Conceived between 1887 and 1895, this example was cast in 1958. The Comité Rodin estimates that around fifty casts of this model in this size were made between 1899 and 1960 by the following foundries; Perzinka, Francoise Rudier, Alexis Rudier and Georges Rudier.

Jean d'Aire was the second citizen of Calais to offer himself as a sacrifice to the English forces during the siege of Calais in 1346. 'Then another greatly respected and wealthy citizen, who had two beautiful daughters, stood up and said that he would go with his friend, master Eustache de St Pierre' wrote Jean Froissart (c1337–1405) in his chronicles detailing the hundred-year war.

In the model we see Jean d'Aire carrying the key to the city. Clad in a monks robe his head is held high even in this most defeating of moments. The work is not only the most iconic of all of Rodin's burghers, but also his most popular. Rodin himself was incredibly pleased with the model, keeping a monumental version in his own possession until his death in 1917. This example is now in the Calouste Gulbenkian Foundation, Lisbon.

As with all the burghers, Rodin modelled Jean d'Aire a number of times. The present work, also executed independently as a monumental figure, is a reduction of the model used by Rodin in his final group. This differs from the study for the second maquette, which shows the burgher carrying a number of keys on a small pillow. Rodin also created a nude study of the figure.

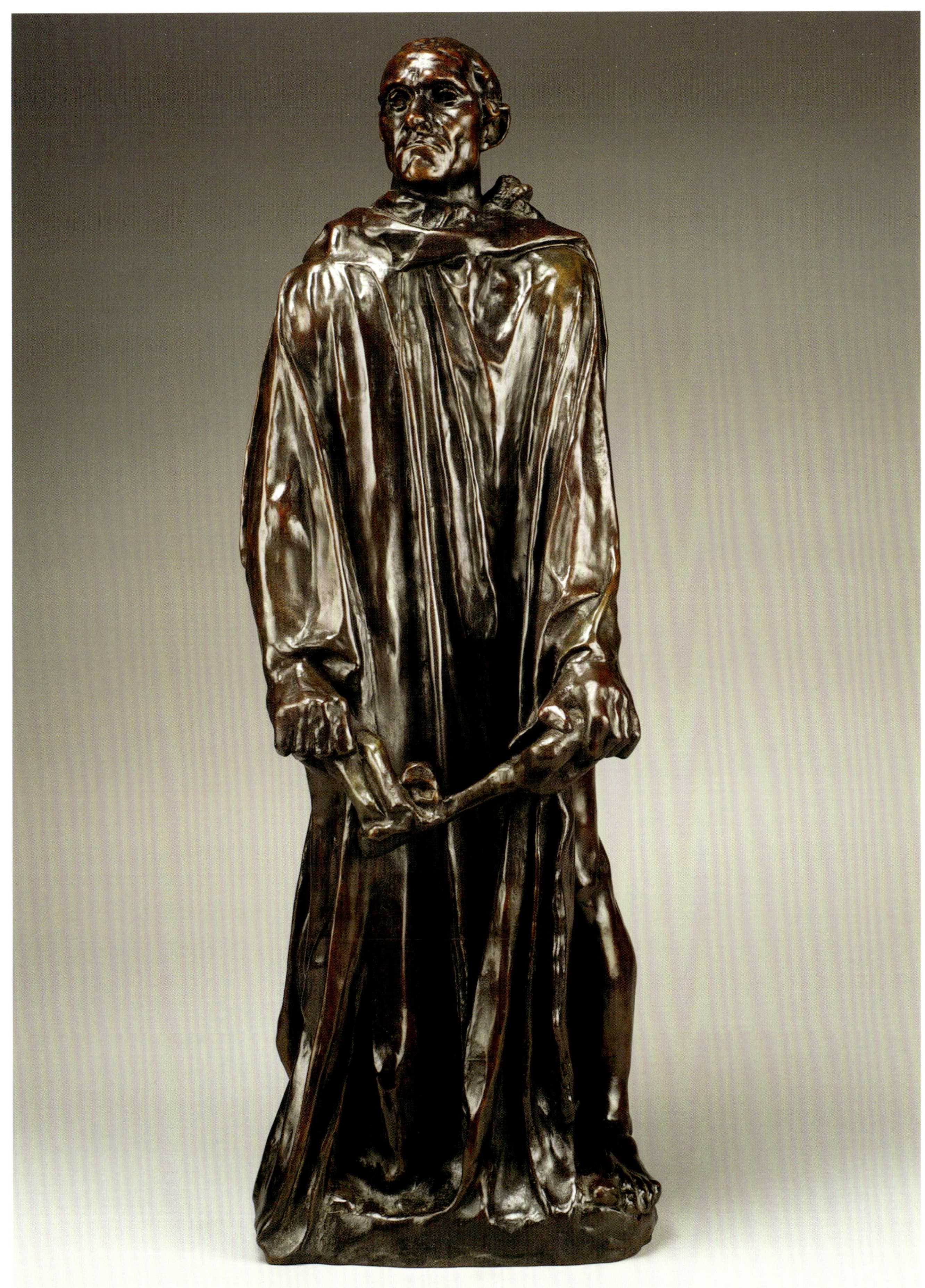

Pierre de Weissant, Second Maquette

Perre de Weissant, Deuxième Maquette

Signed A. Rodin
Inscribed © By Musée Rodin 1971 and Susse Fondeur Paris
Bronze with a dark brown patintion with light golden highlights
Height: 27 inches (69 cm)

Conceived in 1885, this example was cast in 1971. This model was never cast during Rodin's lifetime. The Susse foundry made thirteen casts for the Musée Rodin between 1969 and 1974.

As with all the burghers, Rodin modelled Pierre de Weissant a number of times. The present version, known as the version from the second maquette, differs from the model incorporated into the final *Monument to the Burghers of Calais*, particularly in the treatment of the drapery and right hand.

Nevertheless, the exaggerated contrapposto and elevation of the right arm echo the final version, as well as Rodin's nude study of the same figure. These variations illustrate Rodin's working methods at this time, where he would first model the figures naked, perfecting the pose, before later adding the drapery or clothing.

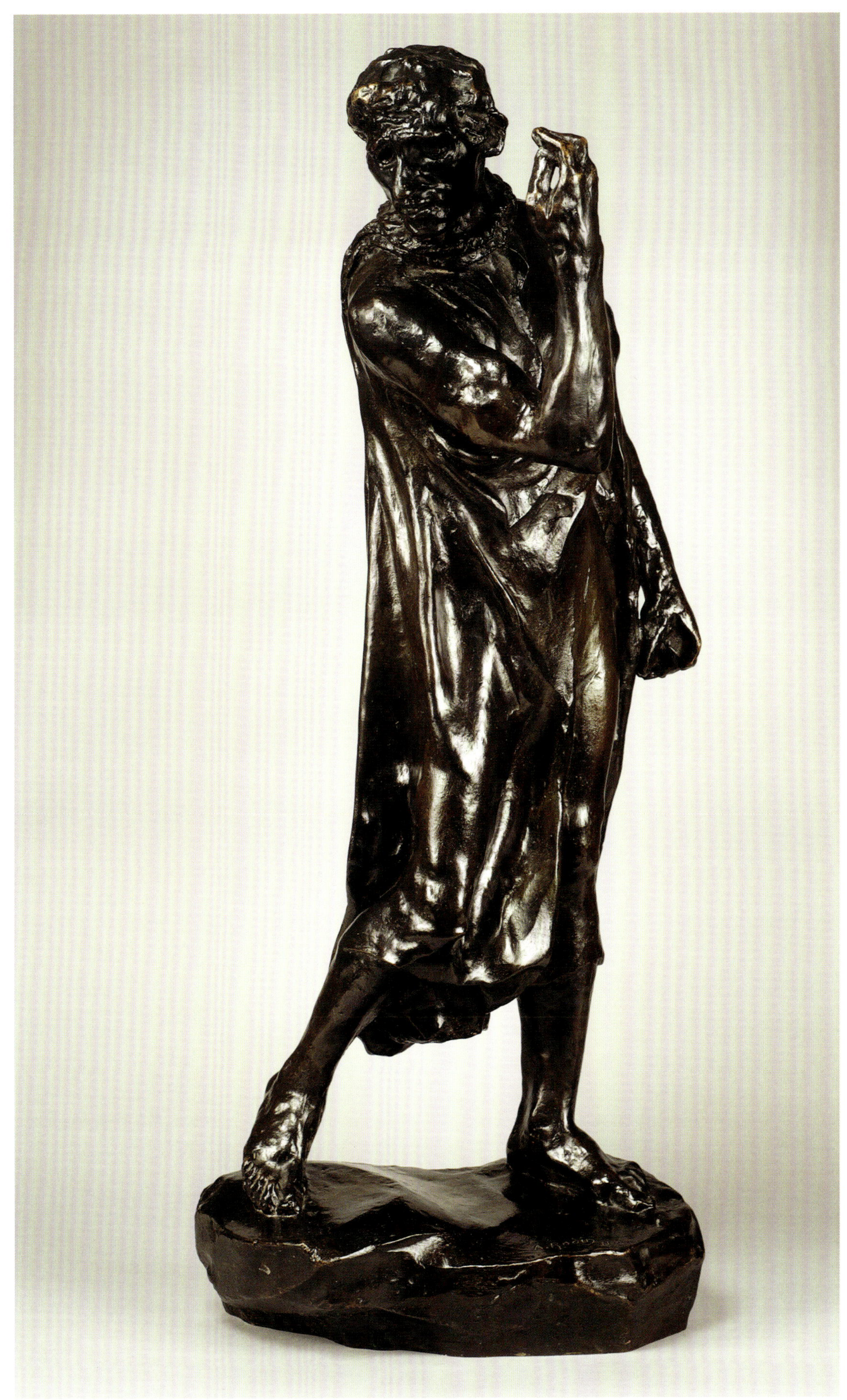

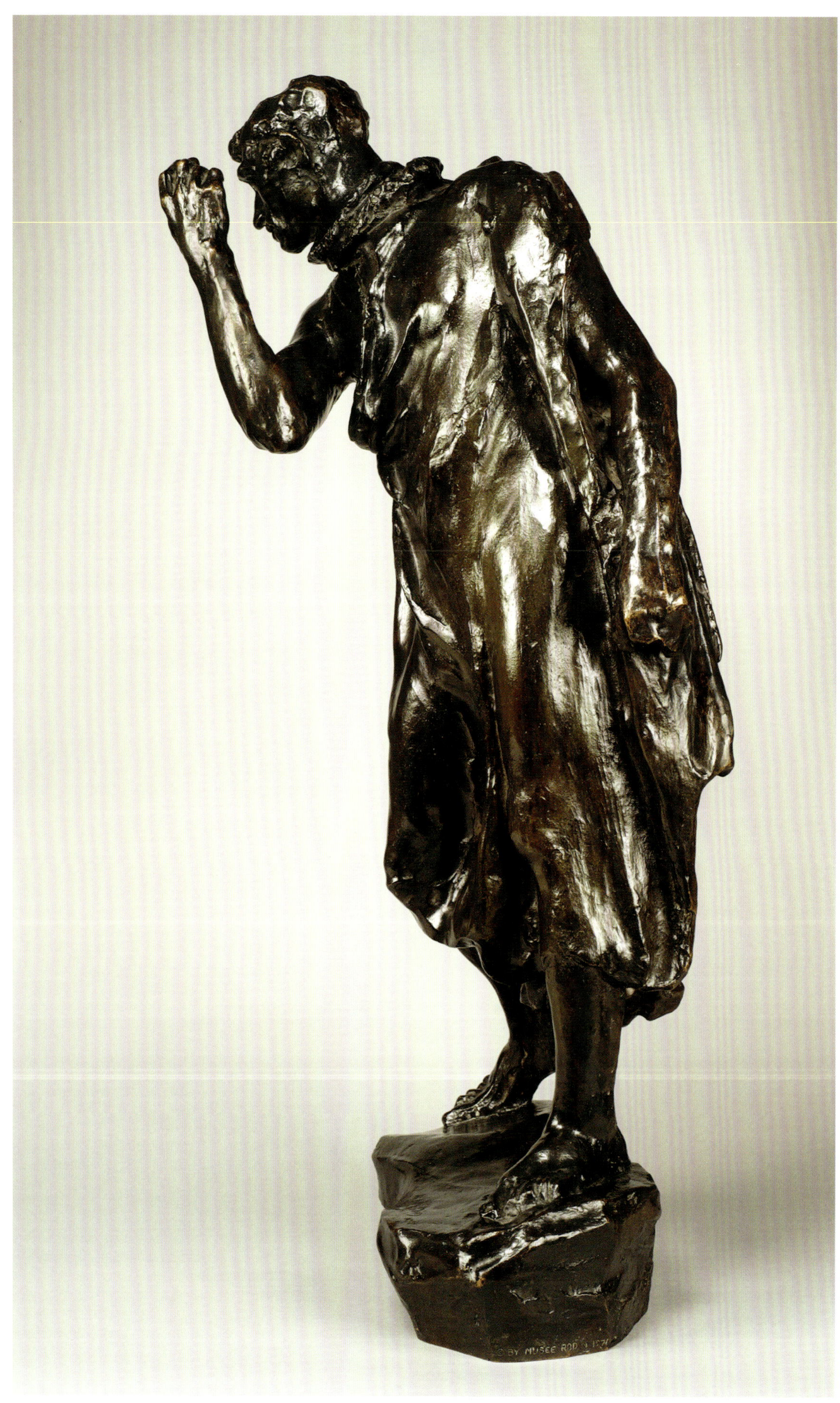

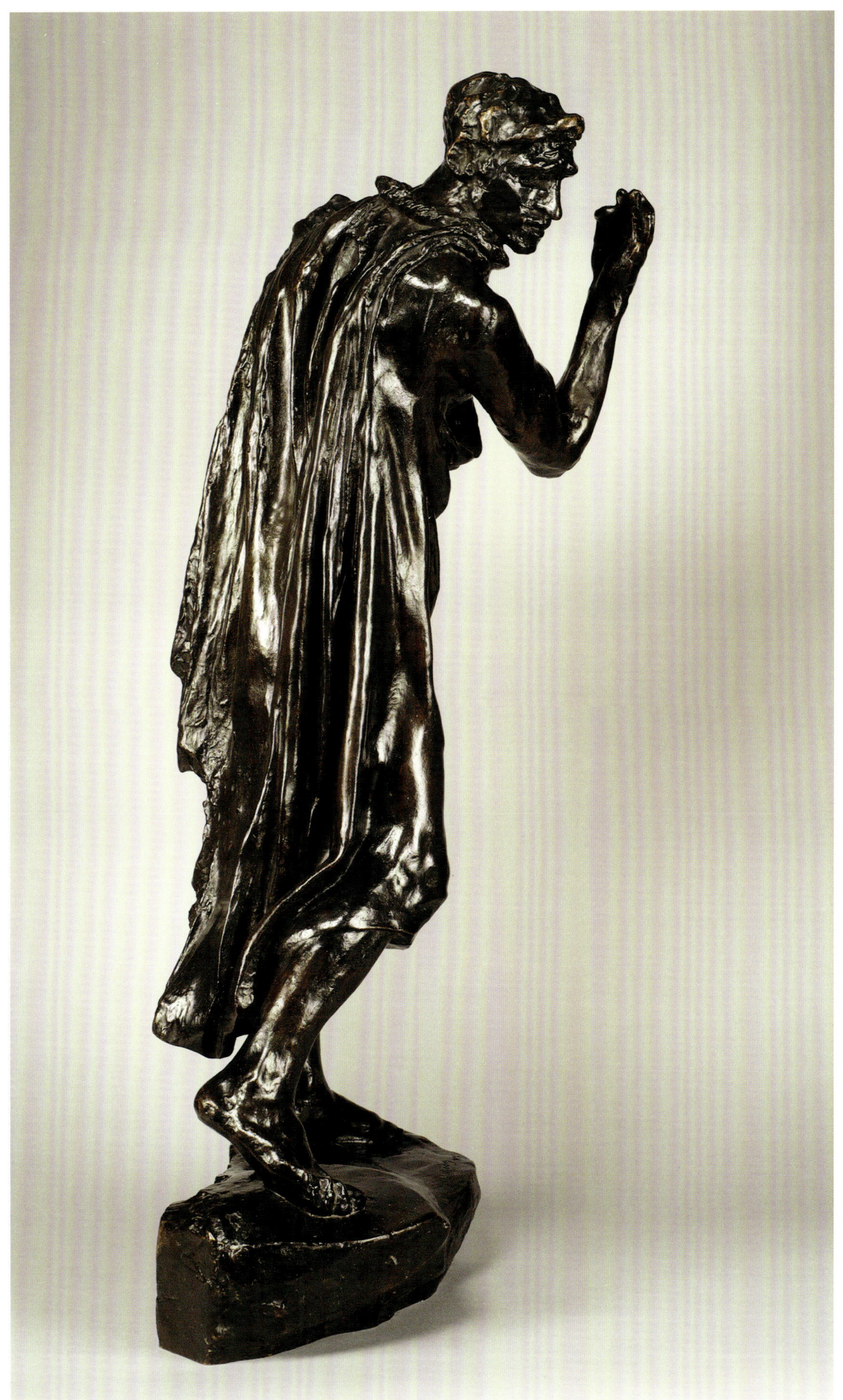

Jean De Fiennes, Variant of the Second Maquette

Jean de Fiennes, Variants de la Deuxième Maquette

Signed A. Rodin
Inscribed © By Musée Rodin 1970 and Susse Fondeur Paris
Numbered 2
Bronze with a rich dark brown patination
Height: 28 inches (71.3 cm)

Provenance:
Musée Rodin 1970
Dominion Gallery, Toronto 1973
Private Collection, USA
Robert Bowman Gallery, 2012
Private European Collection

Conceived in 1885, this example was cast in 1970. This work was never cast during Rodin's lifetime. The Susse foundry made thirteen casts for the Musée Rodin between 1969 and 1977.

Jean de Fiennes was not mentioned in Foissart's chronicles and his name only came to be known in 1863 when Baron Kervyn de Lettenhove published a manuscript found in the Vatican library identifying Jean de Fiennes and Andrieu d'Andres as the two unknown burghers. He is now considered to have been the captain of the town of Calais and the burgher who first opened the city gates to face the English.

Nevertheless, despite his bravery, here Fiennes is depicted with outstretched arms appealing to the other burghers. Rodin has captured a brief moment of doubt, as if Fiennes is questioning whether the group are making the right decision as they walk towards what appeared to be certain death. The sculptor brings to life the heroism of self sacrifice for the greater good, whilst clearly depicting emotions that such a sacrifice would invoke.

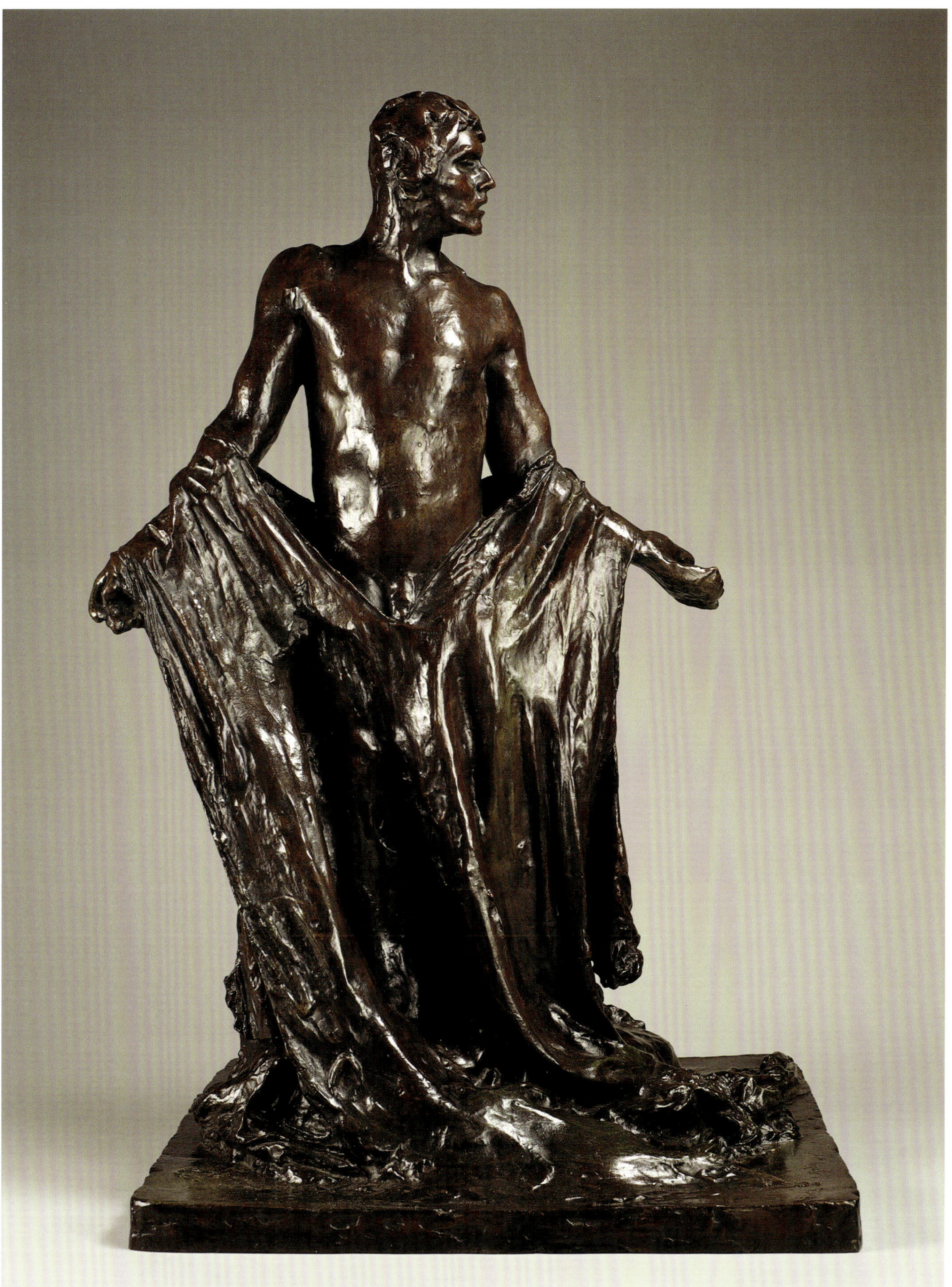

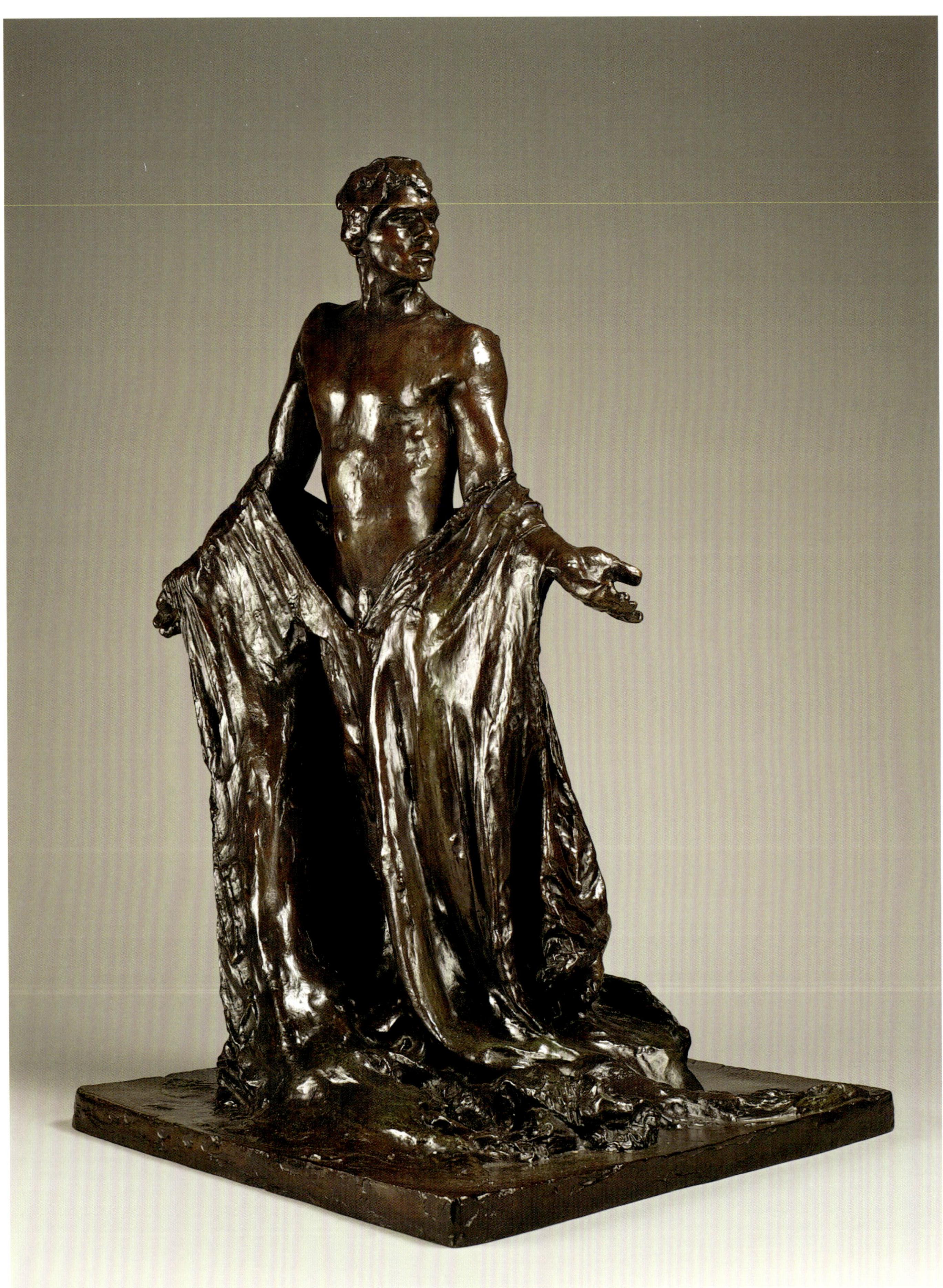

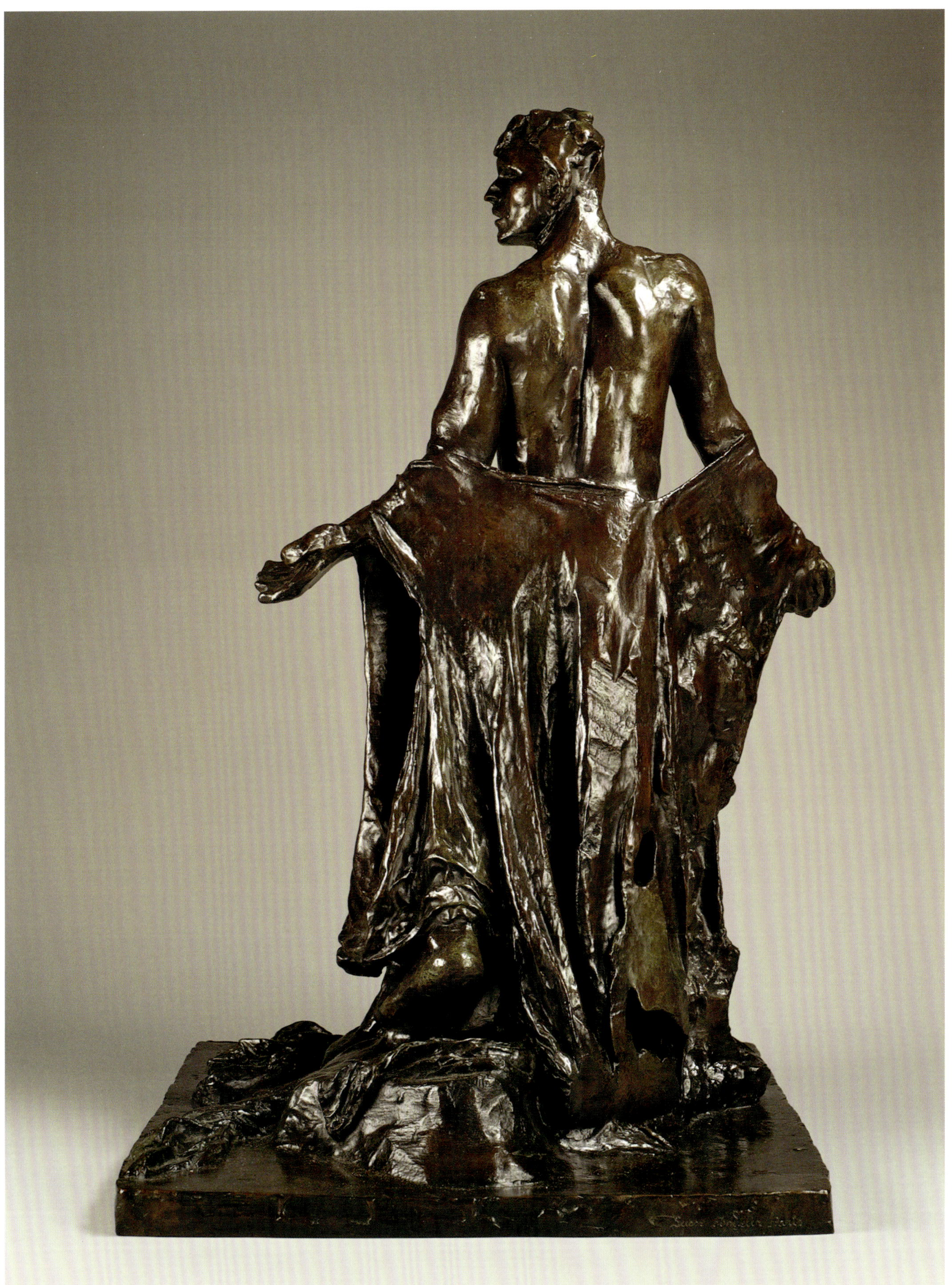

The Thinker

Le Penseur

Signed A. Rodin with repeat raised interior signature
Inscribed Alexis Rudier Fondeur Paris
Bronze with a rich black and dark brown patination
Height: 15 inches (38 cm)

Provenance:
Marcel Miguet, Paris supplier of exotic woods to Emile Ruhlmann, acquired between 1930 and 1940
Thence by Descent
Private Collection, Paris

Conceived in 1880, this cast was executed circa 1925. In total, the Comité Rodin estimate that there were forty-five casts made of the Thinker in the present size. The Alexis Rudier foundry made eight casts during Rodin's lifetime. All further casts were made for the Musée Rodin by the Alexis Rudier foundry before 1945.

The Thinker is perhaps the most iconic sculpture of all time. Since its initial conception in 1880, it has become celebrated not only as a masterpiece of artistic endeavor but also an image inscribed into popular culture and recognisable the world over.

Rodin conceived the work for the tympanum of *The Gates of Hell*. In his final design the muscular naked figure dominates the great portal, looking down over the inferno below and the viewer who looks up at him. Rodin originally saw the figure as representing Dante himself, but later amended this idea and instead created a more generalised figure, symbolising the very essence of thought and creativity.

Rodin argued in a letter published by the newspaper Gil Blas in 1904. 'Guided by my first inspiration I conceived another thinker, a naked man, seated upon a rock, his feet drawn under him, his fist against his teeth, he dreams. The fertile thought slowly elaborates itself within his brain. He is no longer dreamer, he is creator'.

The Thinker belongs to a number of works inspired by Michelangelo, which Rodin modelled in the early 1800s. Rodin had visited Italy in 1875 and here compositional references to *Il Penseroso* can be clearly seen. Rodin also looked at the masters of the 19th century and undoubtedly referenced Carpeaux's *Ugolino* (1861) in the present model. Indeed, Rodin even owned a small bronze cast of the work, where *Ugolino* is seen with his chin on his hand and elbow resting heavily on his knee.

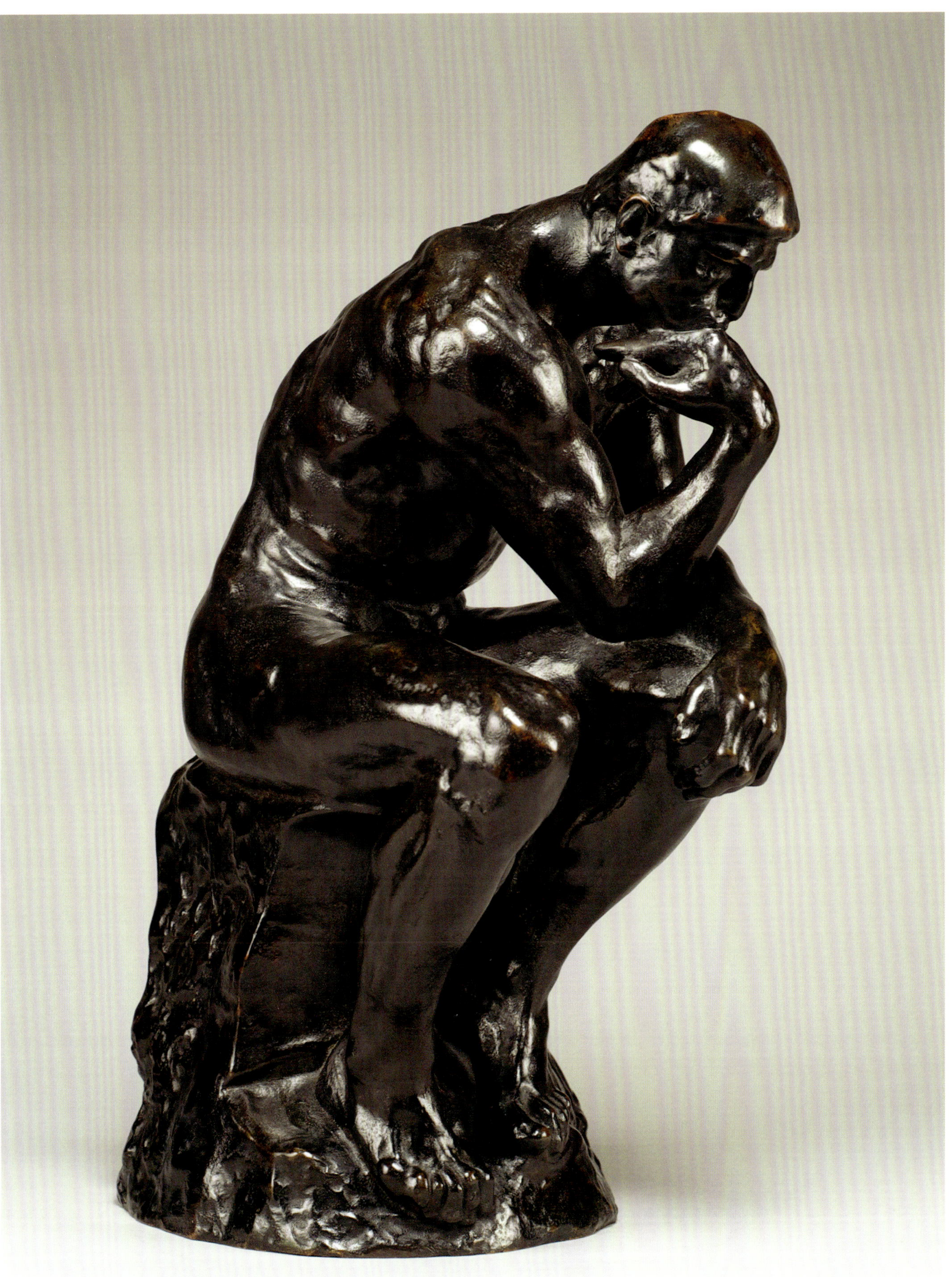

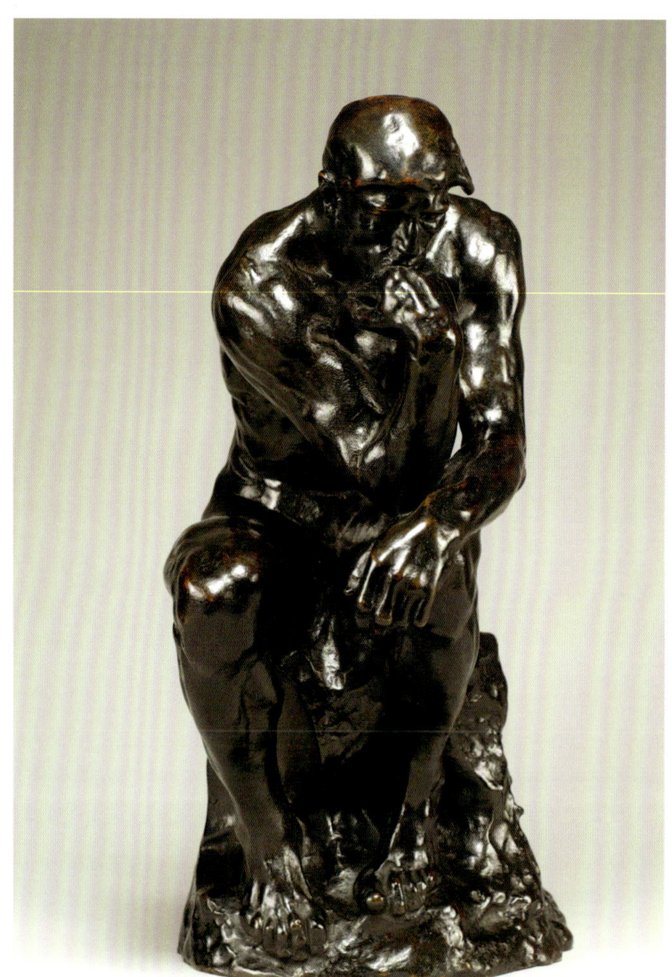 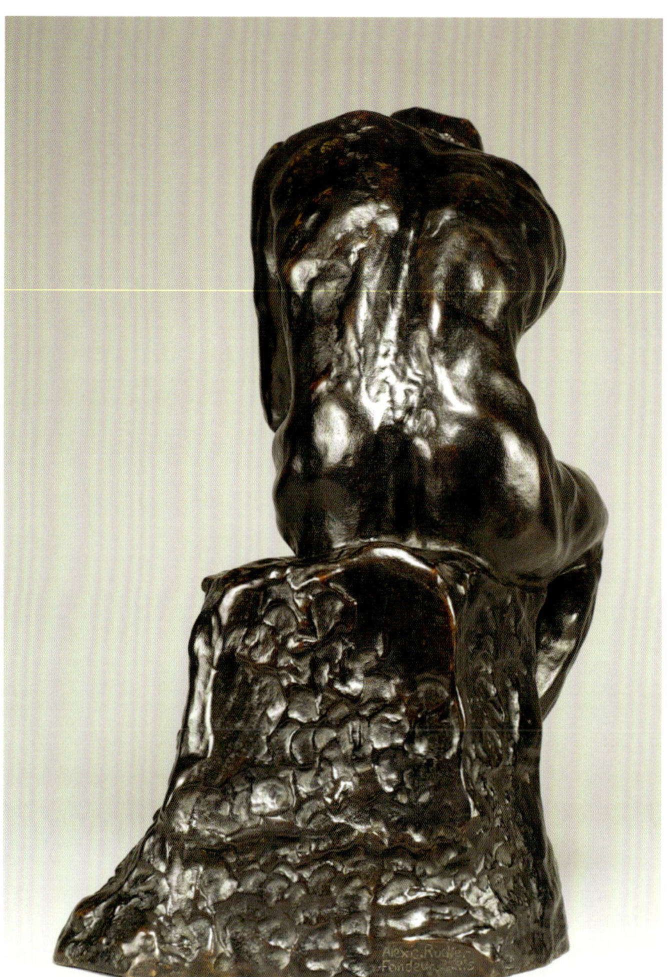

Rodin drew on the influence of both Michelangelo and Carpeaux, combining compositional elements with his own vigorous modeling to produce what would become a pure embodiment of the process of the thought.

'What makes my Thinker think is that he thinks not only with his brain, with his knitted brow, his distended nostrils and compressed lips, but with every muscle of his arms, back and legs, with his clenched fist and gripping toes' argued the sculptor.

The Thinker was much sought after during Rodin's lifetime by both collectors and museums. Rodin had the work cast in three sizes, a reduction (of which this is an example), in the original 72cm size and also a monumental size. One of the enlargements, which Rodin began working on in 1902 was presented to the City of Paris in 1904 and was first sited in front of the Pantheon. This cast is now in the collection of the Musée Rodin.

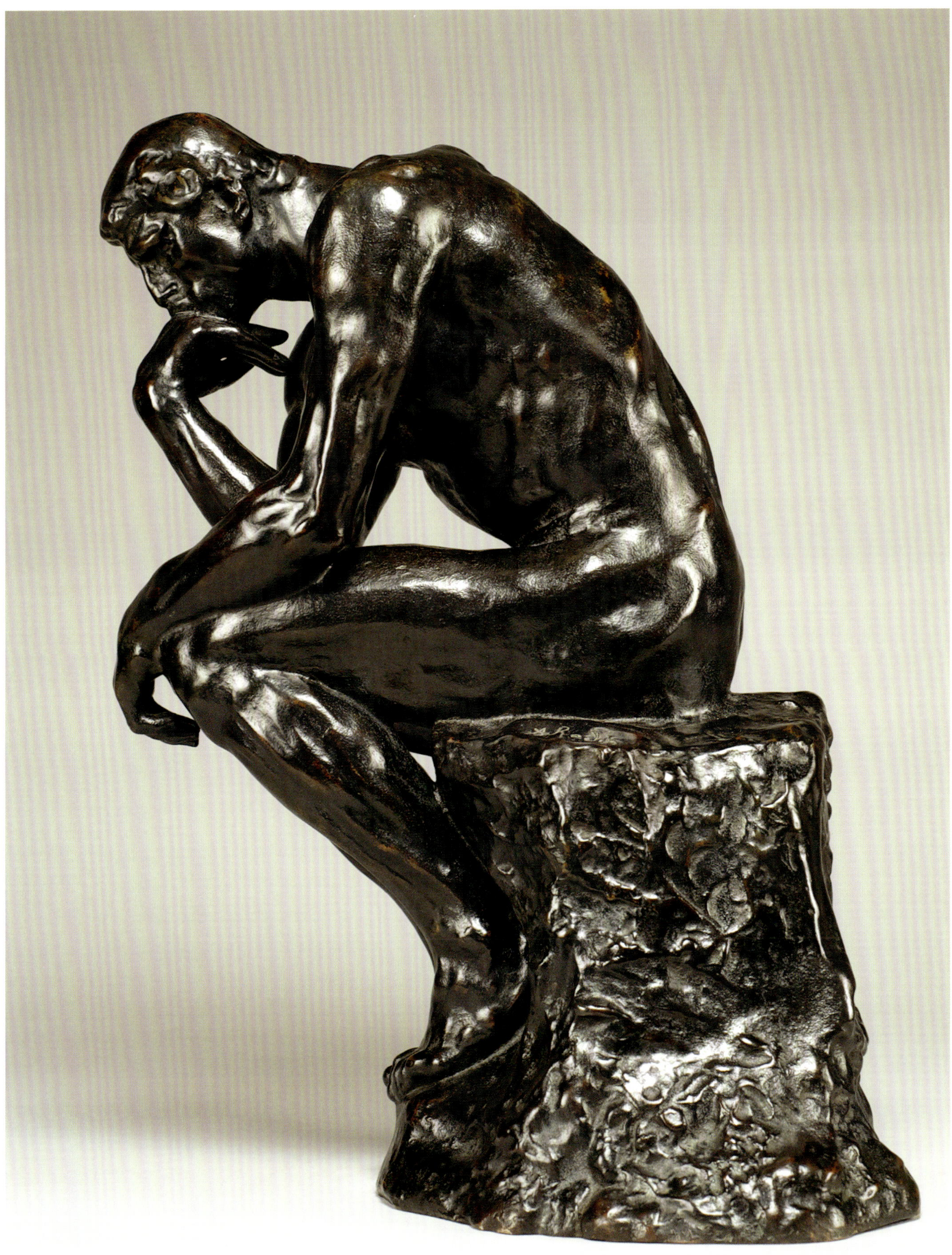

The Thinker

Le Penseur

Signed A. Rodin with repeat raised interior signature
Inscribed Alexis Rudier Fondeur Paris
Bronze with a black and dark brown patination
Height: 28¼ inches (71.8 cm)

Provenance:
Musée Rodin, Paris
Eugène Rudier, Paris
M. Friedrich Welz (acquired from the above in 1940 for the Landes Galerie in Salzburg)
Confiscated by the Allies in Austria between 1945 and 1946 and entrusted to the Commission Nationale de Récupération, Paris
Musée Rodin, Paris (entrusted by the Direction des Musées de France on Nov 17, 1949)
Janos Peter Kramer, Buenos Aires
Parke-Bernet, Inc., New York, April 5, 1967, lot 11
Acquired at the above sale by the late owner
Robert Bowman Gallery, 2008
Private Collection, Norway

Conceived in 1880, this cast was executed circa 1925. The Comité Rodin estimates that there were between forty-five and fifty casts made of The Thinker in the present size between 1902-1952. Seventeen of these were cast during Rodin's lifetime.

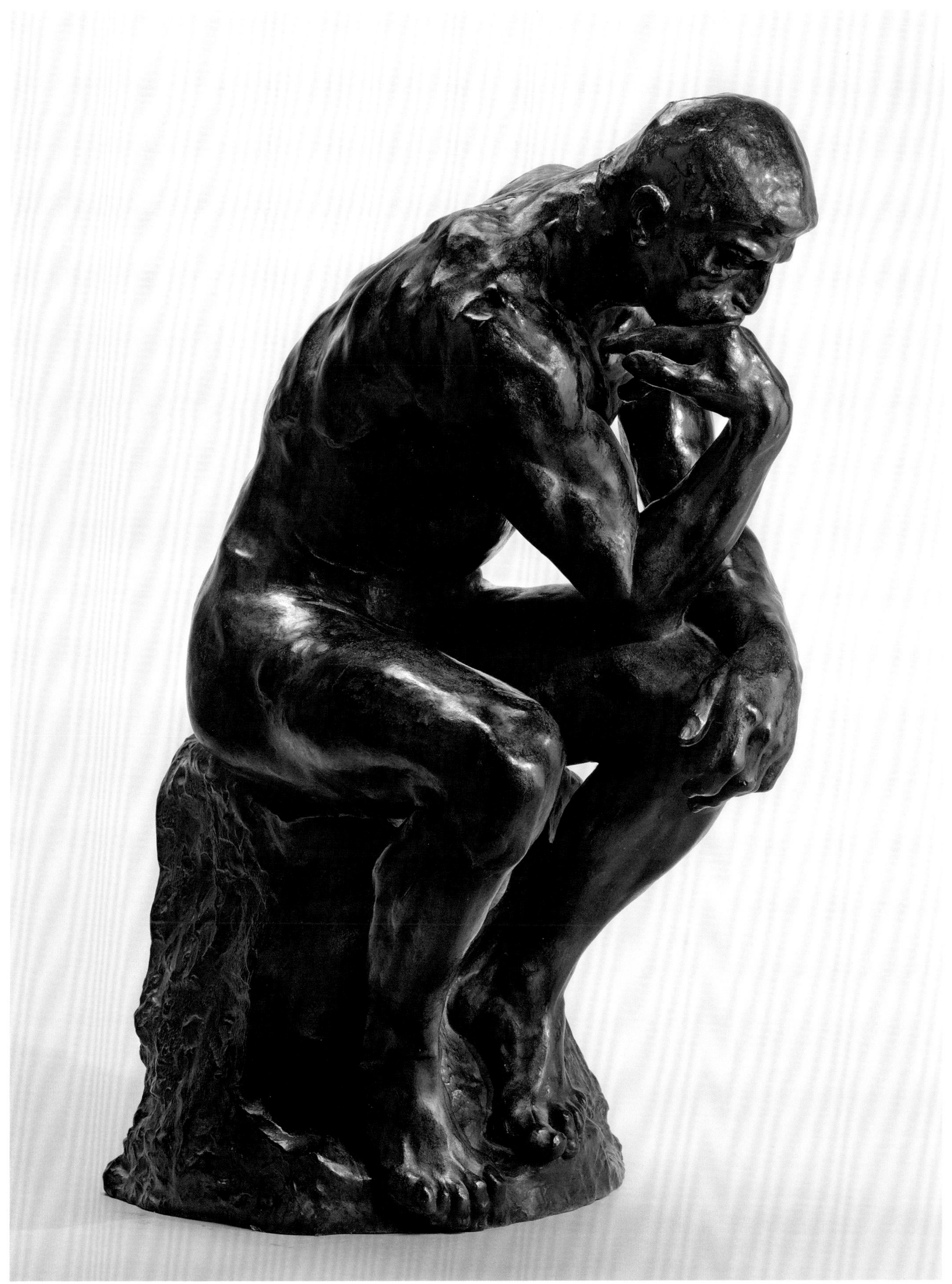

Saint John The Baptist, Reduction No. 2

Saint Jean-Baptiste, Réduction No. 2

Signed A. Rodin
Inscribed Thiebaut Fres Fumiere et Cie Suc
Bronze with a mid brown patination
Height: 19⅞ inches (50.8 cm)

Provenance:
Collection Charles Flammarion, Paris (circa 1930)
Thence by descent to Mr and Mrs Henri Flammarion
Robert Bowman Gallery, 2005
Private collection, USA

Conceived in 1880 this lifetime cast was made before 1908. At least thirteen casts were made before 1908. Eleven casts were made for Musée Rodin by the Alexis Rudier foundry then another eight by the Georges Rudier Foundry between 1955 and 1975.

Here Rodin shows us a candid observation of John The Baptist laid bare. Without the usual identifying attributes we are denied any narrative context for the figure allowing us to focus on the form and gesture.

Rodin described how the arrival of Pignatelli, an Italian peasant from the Abruzzi, offered himself as a model and gave him the idea for this figure: 'As soon as I saw him, I was filled with admiration; this rough, hairy man expressed violence in his bearing… yet also the mystical character of his race. I immediately thought of John the Baptist, in other words, a man of nature, a visionary, a believer, a precursor who came to announce one greater than himself. The peasant undressed, climbed onto the revolving stand as if he had never posed before; he planted himself firmly on his feet, head up, torso straight, at the same time putting his weight on both legs, open like a compass. The movement was so right, so straightforward and so true that I cried: 'But it's a man walking!' I immediately resolved to model what I had seen.'

A two meter high bronze of *John the Baptist* also cast by Thiébaut Frères Fondeurs, was presented to the Victoria and Albert Museum by the Committee of Subscribers in 1902. This was the first Rodin sculpture to enter a public collection in England and soon came to symbolise his dominant influence on early 20th century sculpture.

To celebrate the V&A acquisition, Rodin was honoured by a dinner hosted by George Wyndham at the Café Royal, after which he was unofficially honoured by students from the Slade and South Kensington Schools, who harnessed themselves to Rodin's carriage and driven by the American painter John Singer Sargeant pulled their hero through the streets of London.

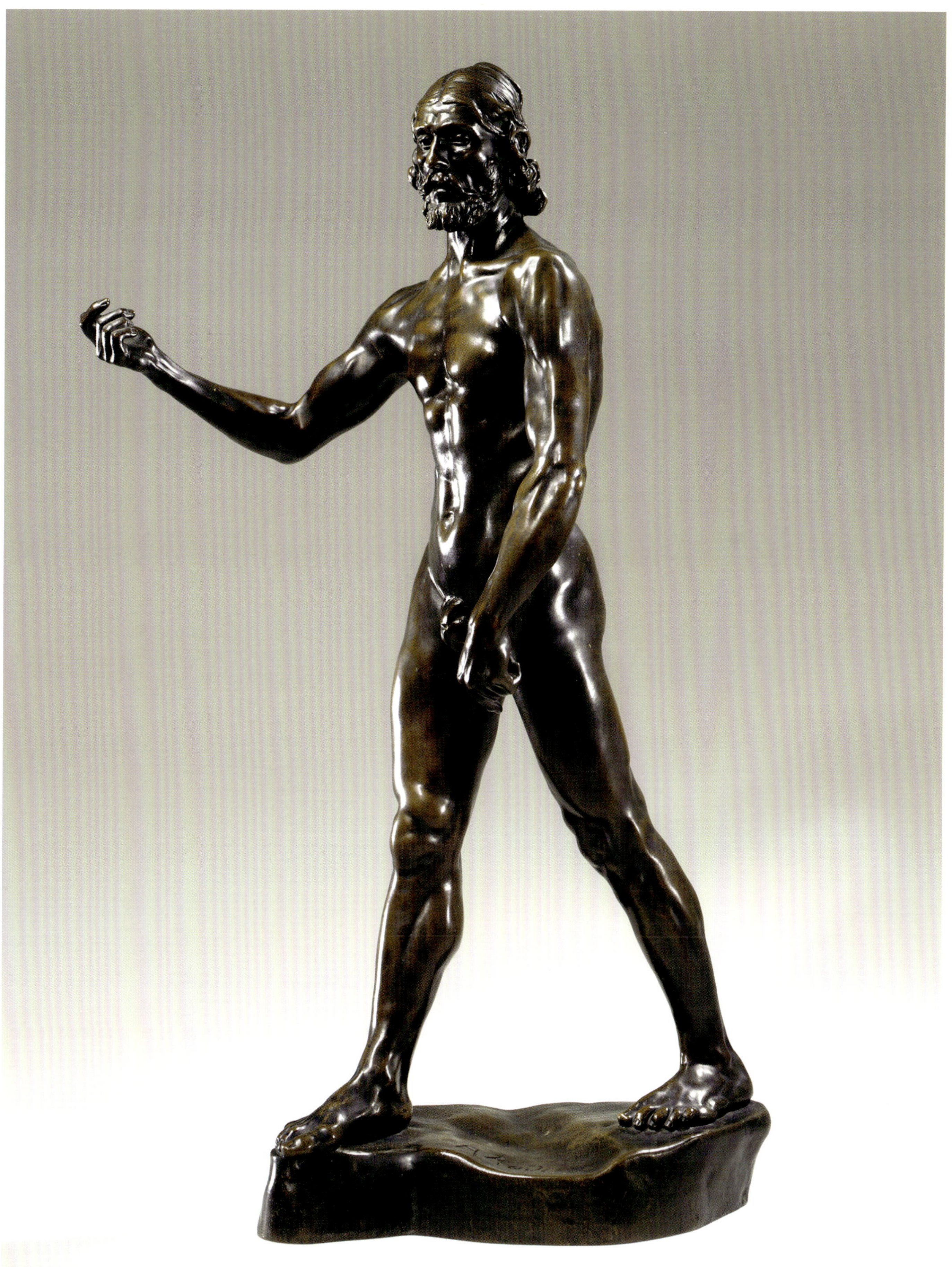

Head of St John the Baptist, Model on a Plate with Full Face

Tête de Saint-Jean Baptiste, Modèle au Plateau, Version de Face

Signed A. Rodin
Inscribed with the foundry mark A.Rudier. Fondeur. Paris
Bronze with a green and brown patination
Height: 7 inches (17.8 cm)

Provenance:
Frances Leventritt, New York
Robert Bowman Gallery, 2012
Private Collection, Australia

Conceived circa 1887, this example was cast between 1940 and 1950. Rodin, who first used the Francoise Rudier foundry and then the Alexis Rudier foundry, produced the model in an un-numbered edition. The Musée Rodin continued the edition using the Alexis Rudier foundry until 1949. The Georges Rudier foundry made four casts for the Musée Rodin between 1965 and 1974.

Rodin created his life-size figure of *St. John the Baptist* preaching in 1878. He returned to the subject ten years later in 1887, this time focusing on the end of the saint's life and here we see St John's severed head, depicted shortly after his execution.

According to Christian tradition, Salome, daughter of Herodias and stepdaughter of Herod, had danced for her stepfather, seducing him into offering her anything she desired. Following pressure from her mother, Salome asked for the head of John the Baptist, which Herod reluctantly granted her.

The subject was a popular one at the time with variations on the theme being produced by Antokolski in 1879 and Carriés in 1881.

Rodin made two versions of the subject, the first showing the severed head on its side resting on a large platter, the second with the head resting on its back. The present example is of the second type, which can also be seen at the top of *The Gates of Hell*. Versions of the work were also carved in marble and exhibited at the Monet-Rodin Exhibition in 1889 and Rodin's solo exhibition at the The Pavillon de l'Alma in 1900.

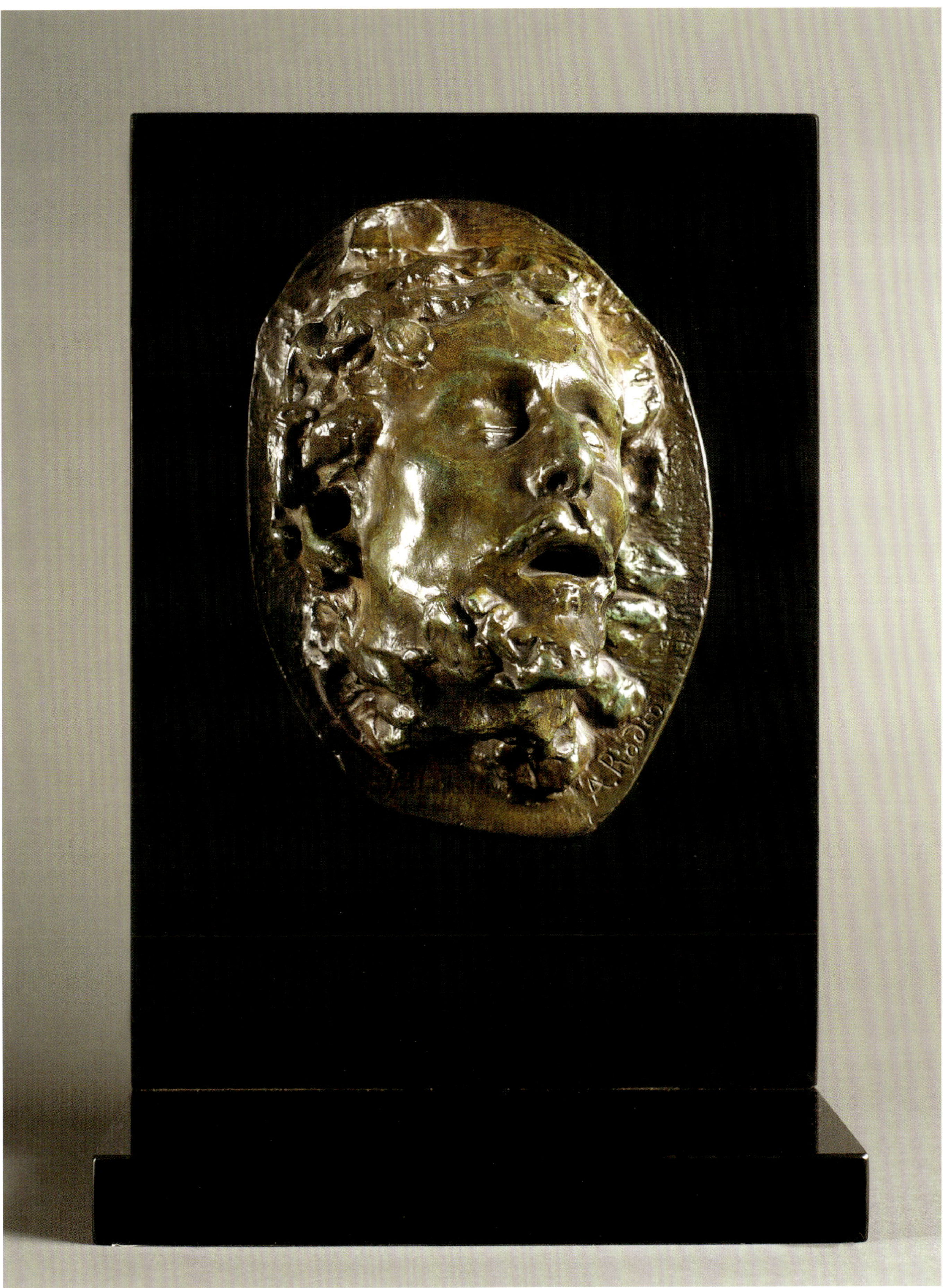

The Prodigal Son, Large Model

L'Enfant Prodigue, Grand Modèle

Signed A. Rodin with repeat raised interior signature
Inscribed Alexis Rudier / Fondeur, PARIS
Bronze with a dark brown patination
Height: 54¾ inches (139 cm)

Provenance:
Musée Rodin, Paris
Eugène Rudier
Private Collection, Lyon
Vieux Chine antiques, Paris
Private Collection, Belgium
By Descent

Conceived in 1884, this example was cast in 1942. The Alexis Rudier foundry cast six bronzes between 1913 and 1917, then a total of fifteen casts were made for the Musée Rodin. The first six of these by the Alexis Rudier foundry between 1927 and 1945, then a further nine casts by the Georges Rudier foundry between 1960 and 1974.

One of Rodin's most celebrated works, *The Prodigal Son* is derived from the larger group *Ugolino*, which was originally conceived as part of the sculptor's design for *The Gates Of Hell*. Specifically the child to the left of the main figure in *Ugolino* matches the head and torso of the present work.

The work was originally conceived in 1884 before being enlarged in stone by François Pompon in 1894. Originally titled *Child of the Century*, the model was quickly renamed *The Prodigal Son* in reference to the biblical parable (Luke 15:11-32).

According to the story a father divides his estate evenly between his two sons. One son uses his inheritance shrewdly; the other squanders his on wild living. Eventually the wayward son returns home to his father proclaiming, 'I have sinned against heaven and against you. I am no longer worthy to be called your son.' However, rather than rebuke his son, the father instead forgave him and held a great feast in honor of his return.

Rodin made a number of changes to the model between 1893 and 1913 when the first bronzes were cast. The original stone version was first exhibited publicly at the Salon des Cent in 1884. However in 1900, when Rodin erected his own pavilion at the Place de l'Alma to coincide with the Paris Exposition Universelle, he chose to exhibit a small plaster version of the model on a column. This was then exhibited again in 1902 in Prague. By 1905 Rodin had made significant adjustments to the large stone version, which he exhibited at Salon d'Automne in Paris. By this time the base had been sliced cleanly to the right of the figure, resembling the final bronze version. Indeed the mold from which bronzes were later cast was taken directly from this original stone, although early bronze castings display an opening in the base.

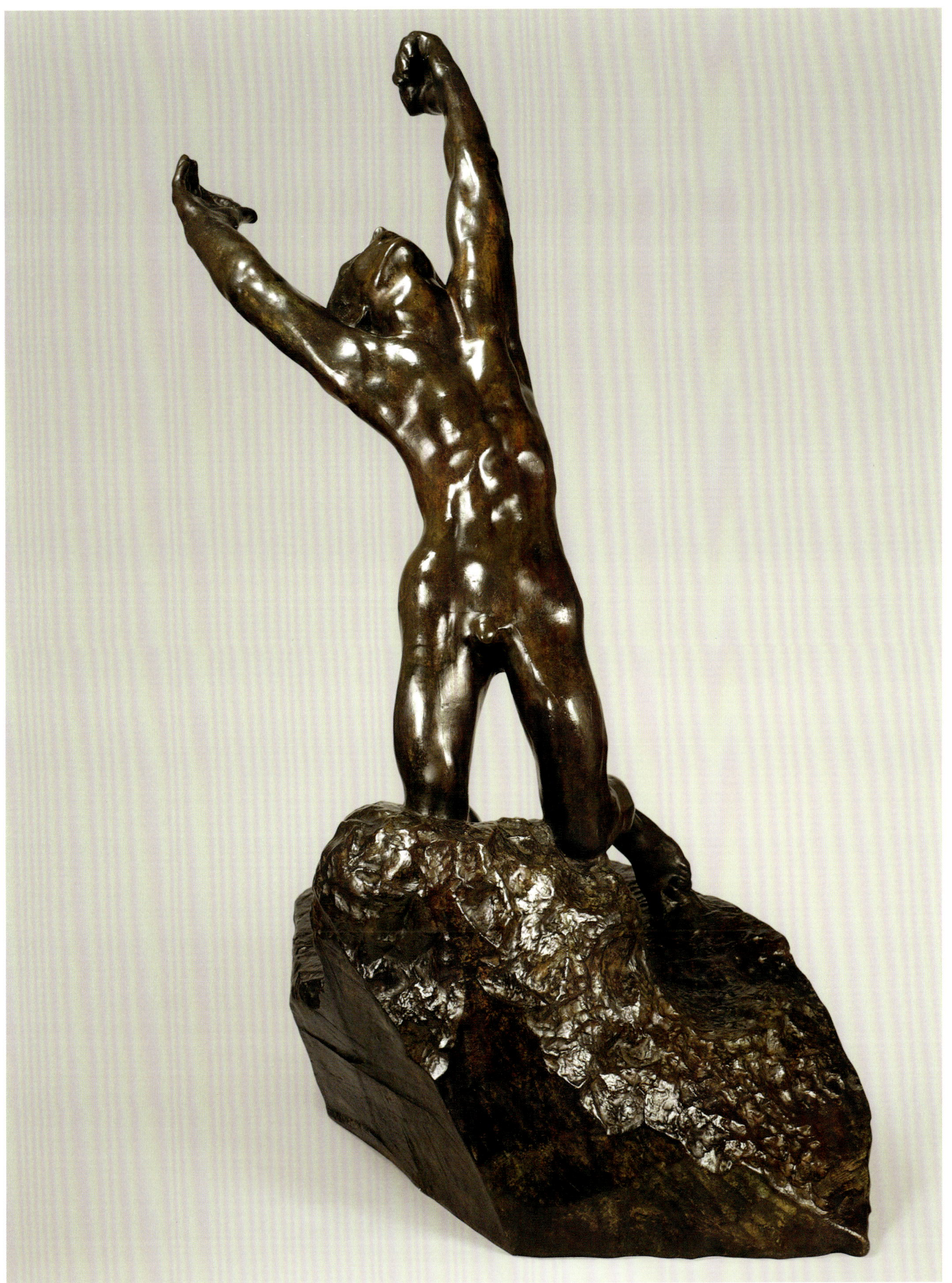

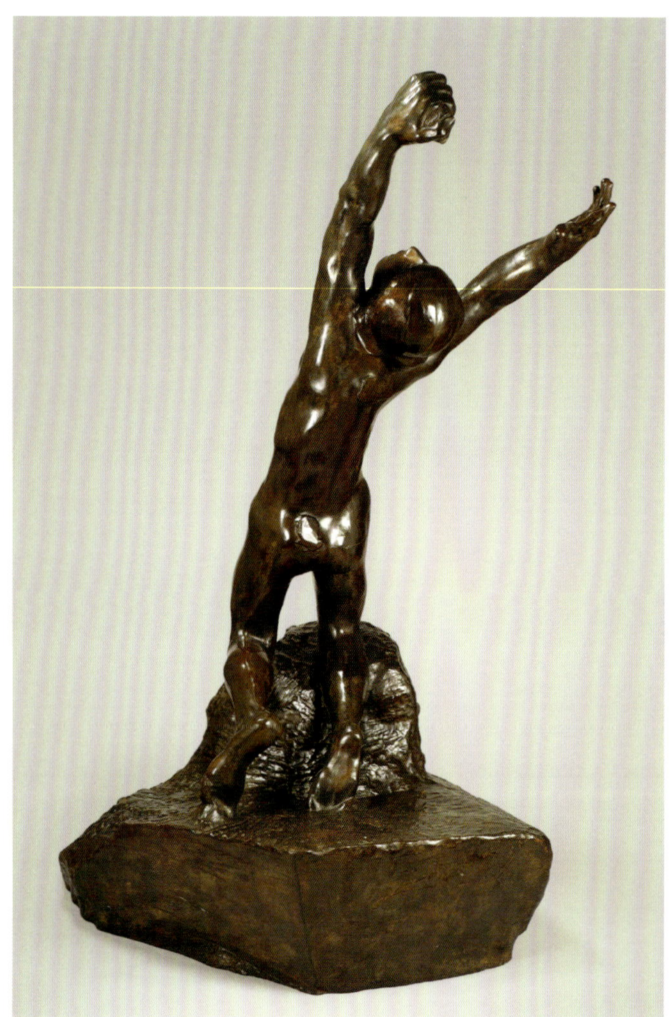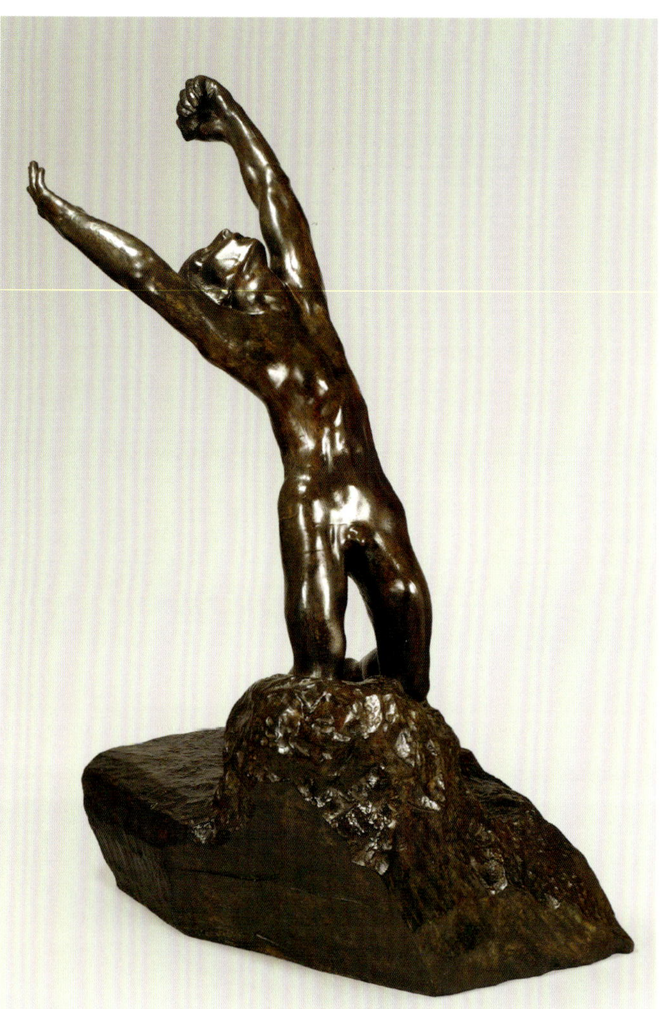

In the final version of the *Prodigal Son* we see a figure full of remorse, his outstretched arms showing his plea for forgiveness. 'I accentuate the lines that best accentuate the state of mind I am interpreting', the artist told Paul Gsell. 'I emphasised the protrusions of the muscles which conveyed distress. Here, there… I exaggerated the tendons that mark the fervor of prayer.'

Similar to the artist's famous proclamation that his *Thinker* thinks not only with his brain but also 'with every muscle of his arms, back and legs, with his clenched fist and gripping toe,' here we see a figure whose every twist, every tendon and muscle conveys that of extreme sorrow and distress.

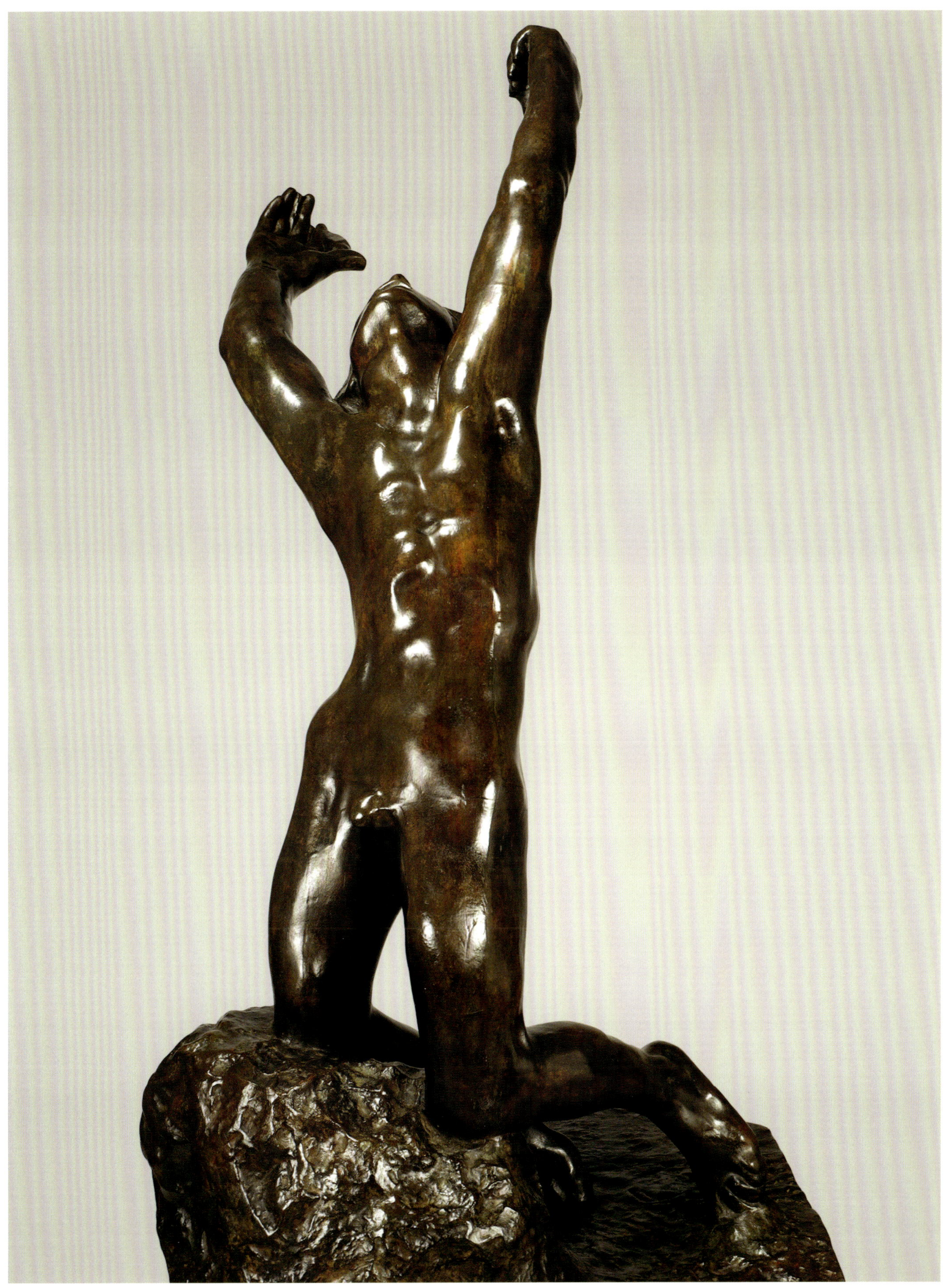

The Falling Man

L'Homme Qui Tombe

Signed A. Rodin
Inscribed © Musée Rodin 1973 and Susse Fondeur Paris
Numbered 3
Bronze with a rich dark green patination and brown highlights
Height: 23 inches (58.5 cm)

Provenance:
Musée Rodin
Private Collection, USA
Sothebys London, 21 April 2005
Robert Bowman Gallery, 2005
Private Collection, Turkey

Conceived circa 1885, this example was cast in 1973. This work was never cast during Rodin's lifetime. The Susse Foundry cast twelve bronzes for the Musée Rodin between 1972 and 1982.

The Falling Man was originally conceived to adorn the upper left door panel of *The Gates of Hell* and can be seen hanging from the lintel in the sculptor's final conception of the great portal. Indeed, it is likely that Rodin added the work after he was informed that the gates would never have a practical use, as the positioning of the figure would have made it impossible to open the door.

As was often the case when Rodin removed models from *The Gates of Hell*, he makes no attempt to hide the traces of where the model would have initially been attached to the portal. Here, the ridges on the stomach reflect those made in the original plaster and would have originally provided the rough surface for the adhesive that adhered the work to the gates.

A variation of *The Falling Man*, where the figure's feet are both on the floor (rather than with his right knee raised), was used in Rodin's model of *A Man With a Serpent*. This same figure was also combined with *The Crouching Woman* to form the freestanding group *I am Beautiful*, although in this variation, the man's arms are outstretched to hold the woman against his chest. *The Falling Man*'s torso and head were also used in the group *Avarice and Lust*, which features on the *Gates of Hell* at the lower right-hand section.

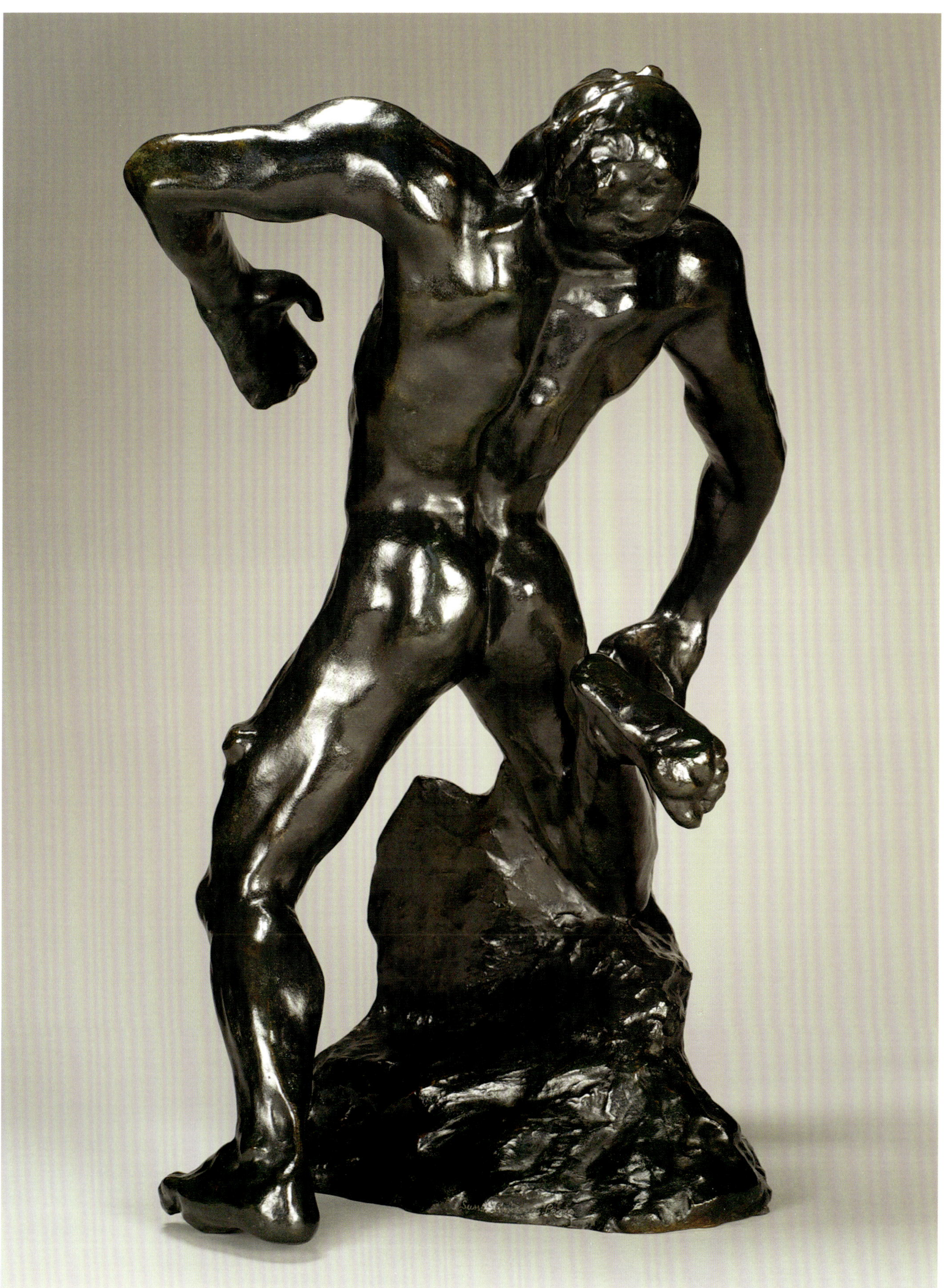

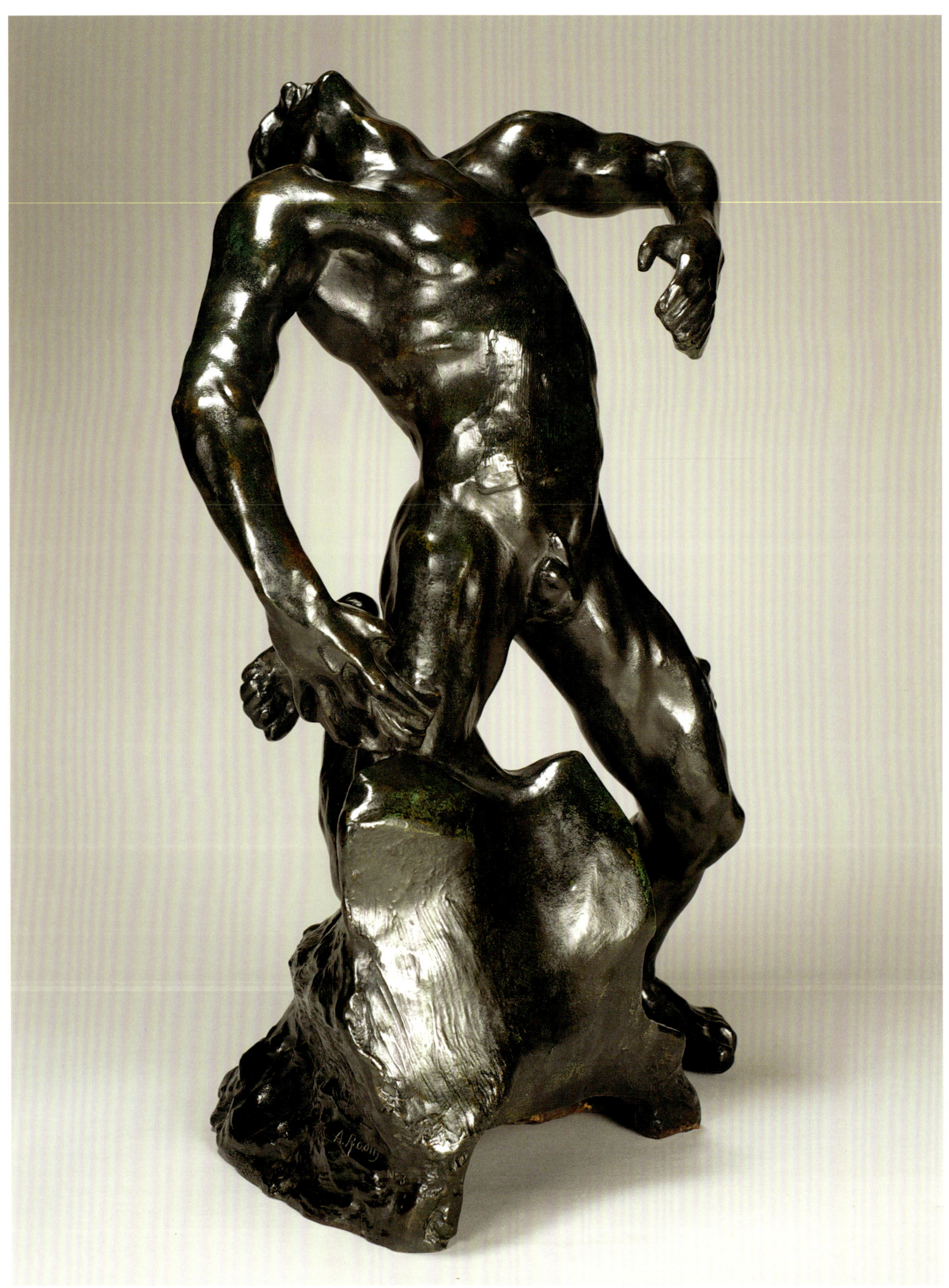

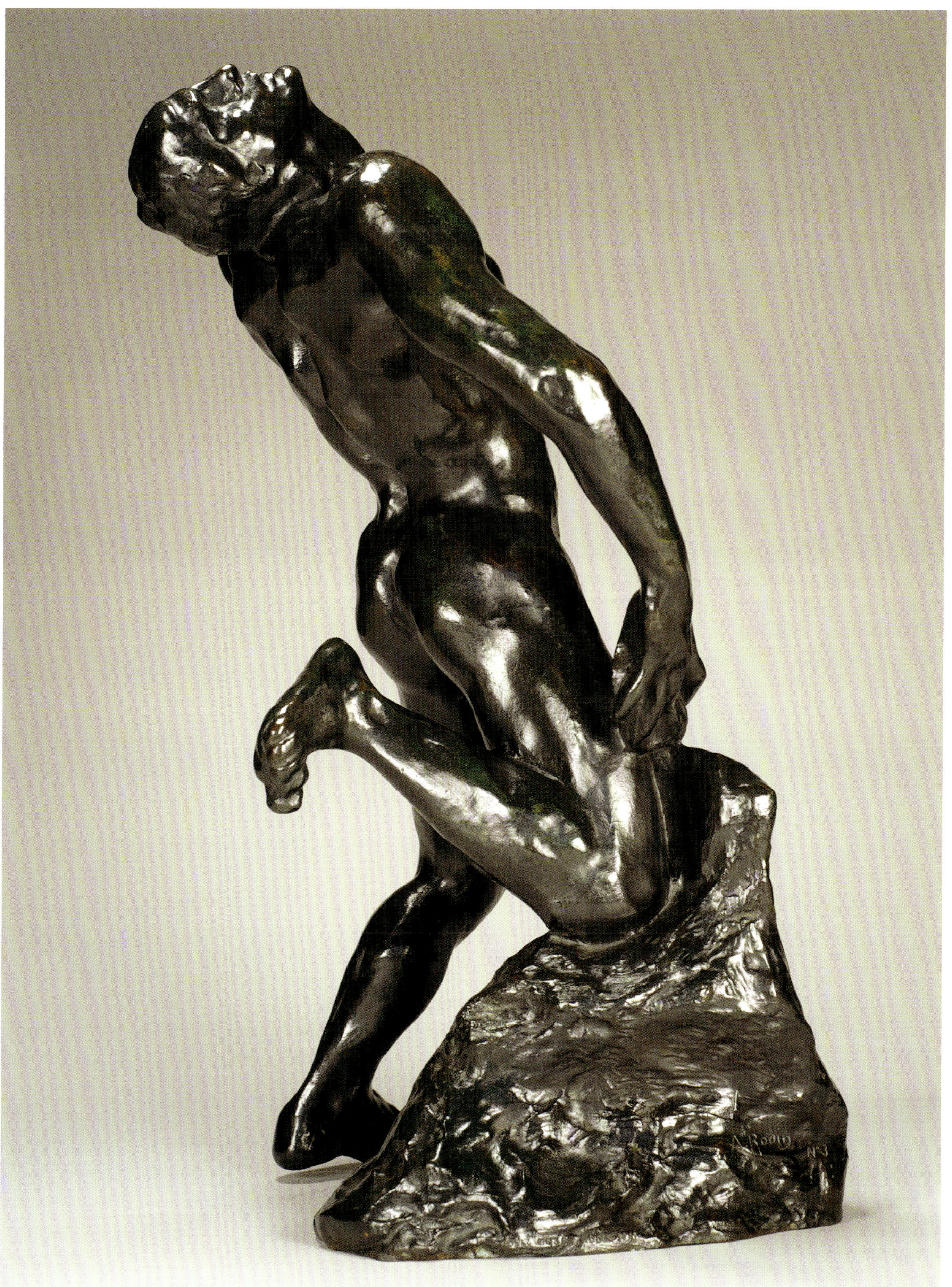

Polyphemus

Polyphème

Signed A. Rodin
Inscribed Alexis Rudier Fondeur Paris
Bronze with a rich dark brown/black patination with green and red highlights
Height: 9½ inches (24 cm)

Provenance:
Jules Mastbaum
Mrs Patrick Dinehart
Robert Bowman Gallery, 2009
Private Collection, Luxembourg

Conceived in 1888, this example was cast in the 1920s. No lifetime casts of Polyphemus were made. Three unmarked casts are known. The Alexis Rudier foundry made at least five casts for the Musée Rodin between 1922 and 1951, then seven further casts where made by the Georges Rudier foundry between 1957 and 1963.

The subject is taken from the Ovidian story of the giant Cyclops Polyphemus. He loved the sea nymph Galateia and upon discovering her together with Acis, son of Pan, in a cliff-side love nest, hurls a rock at them, killing Acis. In Rodin's depiction we see the Cyclops looking down upon the lovers tryst gripping the rock in a jealous rage.

As in so many of Rodin's sculptures the central figure of the sculpture was remodelled and worked several times and has been interpreted as both his figures of the *Milo of Croton* and *Narcissus*.

This cast was formerly in the collection of Jules Mastbaum who assembled the largest collection of Rodin's works outside Paris. His collection is now The Rodin Museum, Philadelphia and was extensively catalogued by John Tancock.

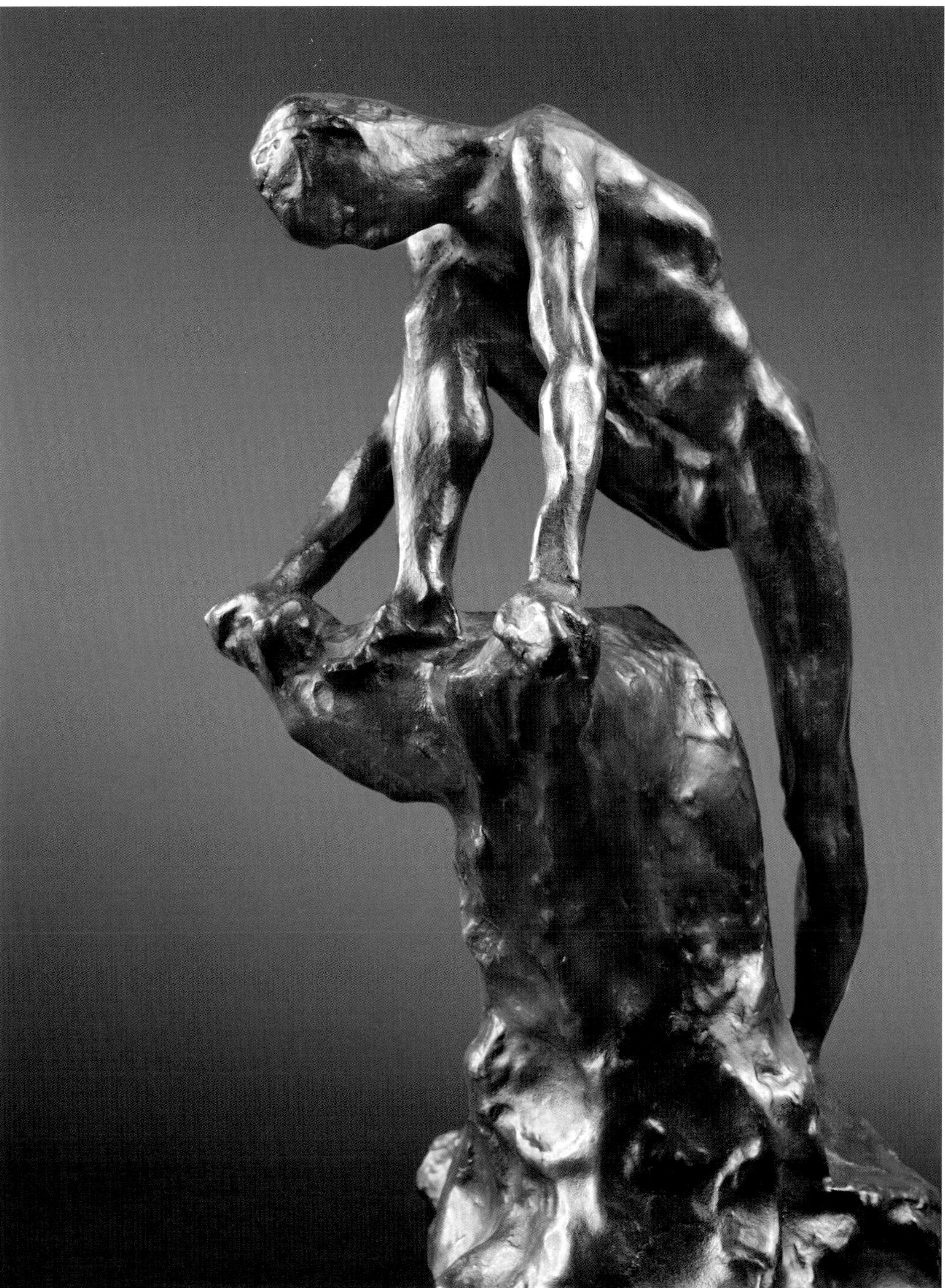

Iris, Study with Head

Iris, Étude avec Tête

Signed A. Rodin
Inscribed © by Musée Rodin 1971 and Susse Fondeurs Paris
Numbered 7
Bronze with a green and dark brown patination
Height: 20⅞ inches (53 cm)

Provenance:
Musée Rodin, Paris
Browse and Darby Ltd, London
Private Collection, UK
Sold Sotheby's London, March 24 1999. Lot 13
Acquired at above sale by Samir Bawachi
Thence by descent to Marcus Willies.

Conceived between 1890 and 1891, this example was cast in 1970. No lifetime casts of this model were made. The present example is one of twelve casts made for the Musée Rodin by the Susse foundry between 1969 and 1972.

The present model, known as *Iris, Study with Head*, is an early maquette for Rodin's *Iris*. In the later version, Rodin removes the head and further truncates the left arm, cutting it off at the shoulder.

This present work was conceived in 1891, with the headless version conceived in 1895. The model was later incorporated into Rodin's plaster maquette for his second *Monument to Victor Hugo* (also called *The Apotheosis of Victor Hugo*) in 1897. Here Iris is supported by a cloud and hangs upside-down above Hugo's head complete with a pair of wings.

An enlargement of the figure had already been made in 1894. A bronze version of this figure, which was positioned vertically and hovering above the ground, appears in photographs taken between 1896 and 1898 in front of *The Gates Of Hell*. It was at this point that the work took on the name *Iris, Messenger of the Gods*.

Rodin himself later briefly called the work *Another Voice*, when he presented it at the Place de l'Alma in Paris during a retrospective exhibition of his own work in 1900.

In Greek Mythology, Iris is known as the personification of the rainbow and a messenger who links the gods with humanity. She was described as travelling with the speed of the wind and traversed all corners of the earth as well as descending into the underworld.

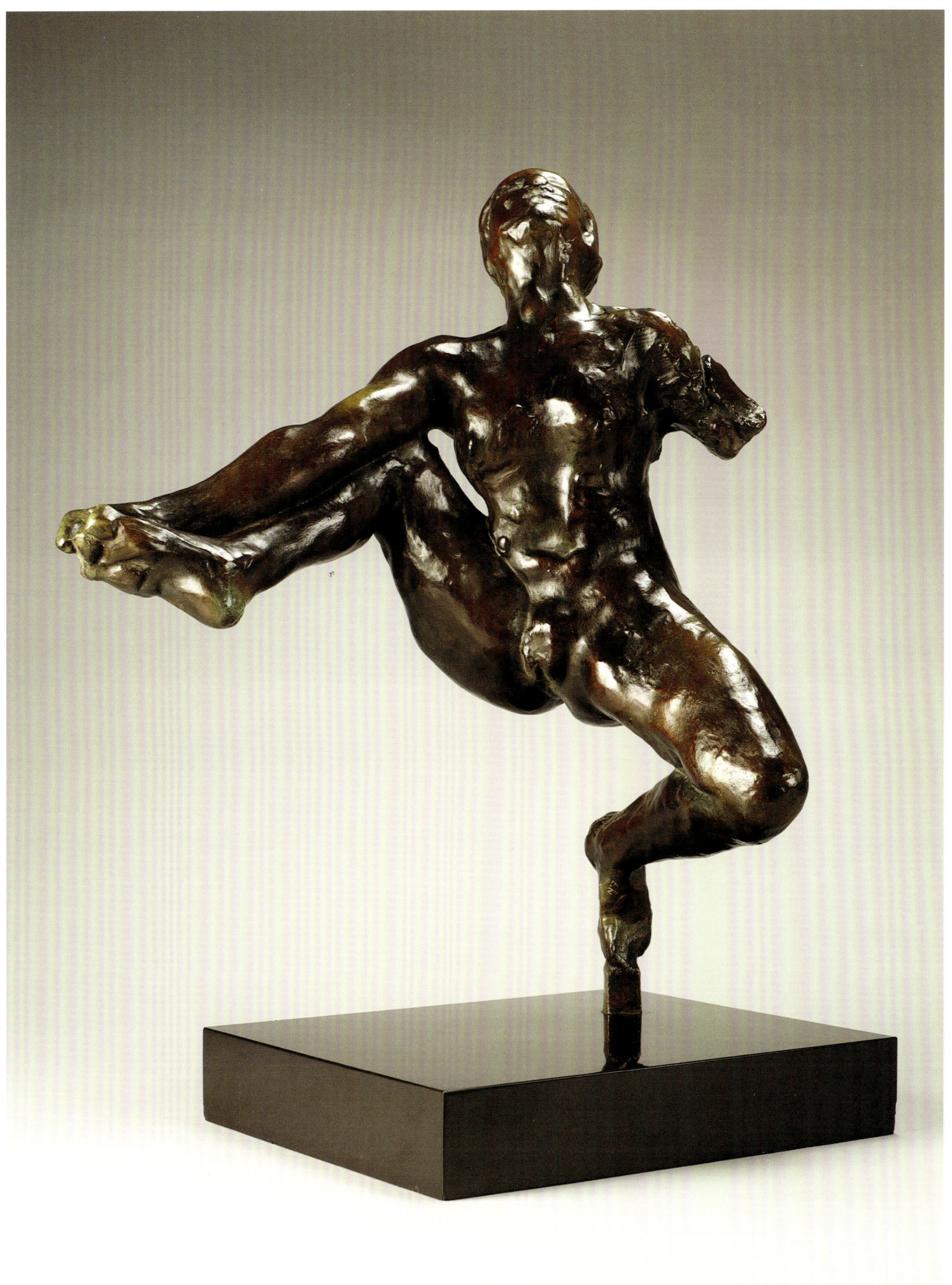

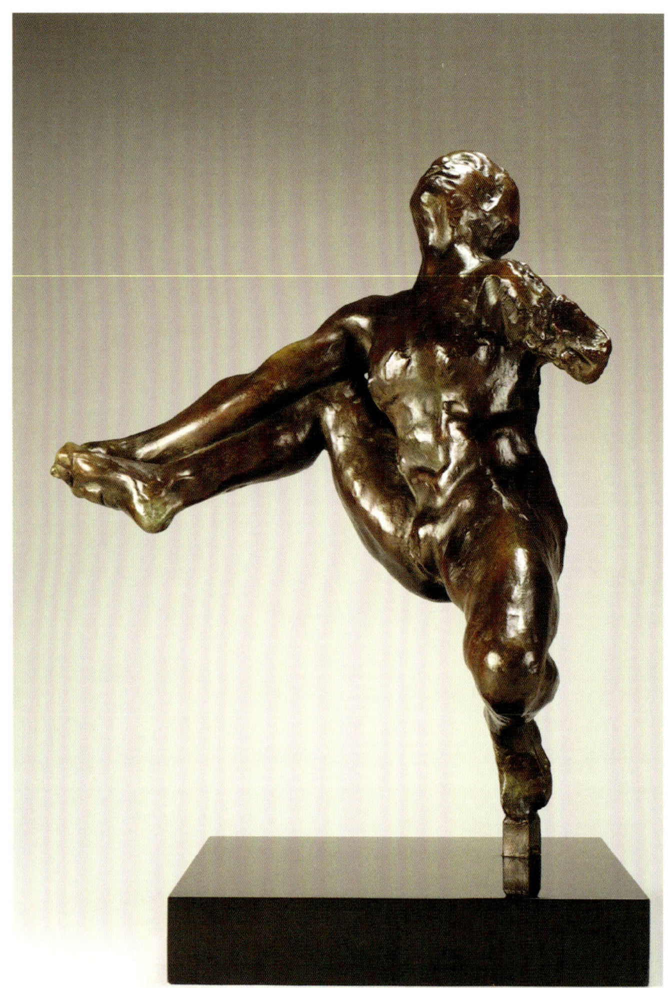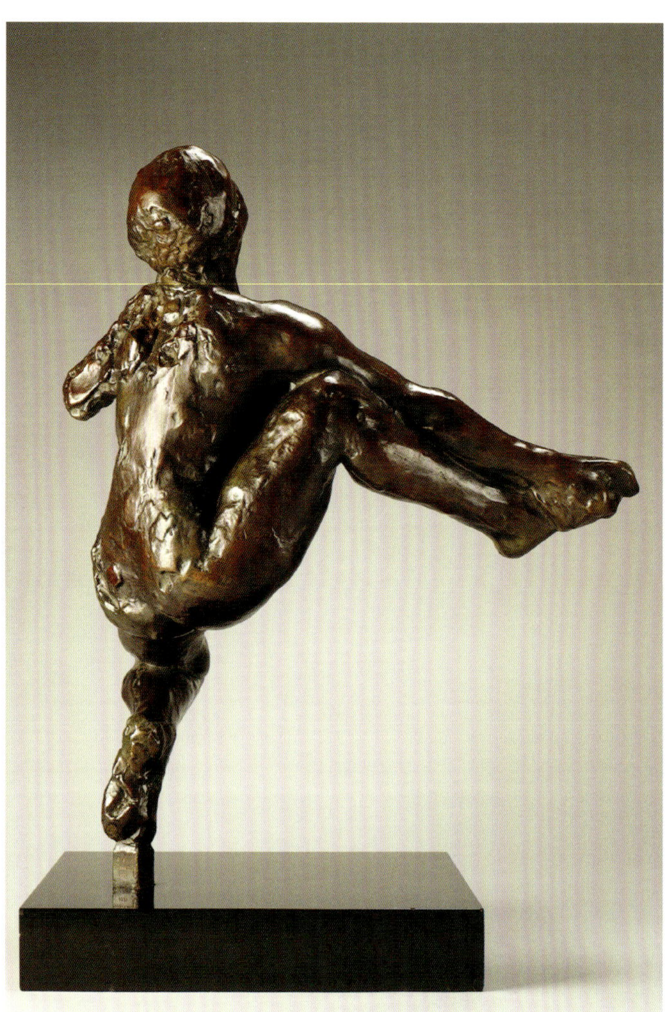

Rodin's *Iris* is therefore symbolically and mytholologically powerful as well as incredibly formally arresting. The model elicited both delight and horror from contemporary audiences who were not used to such forthright depictions of female genitalia. The works closest artistic prototype was Gustave Courbet's *The Origin of the World*, but this potentially scandalous work had been hidden in private collections since its creation in 1866, therfore was not well known to the public. It has been suggested that Rodin himself may have known the painting through Edmond de Gouncourt who saw it in 1889, but this is merely conjecture.

Rodin was well known for eschewing academic poses and encouraging his models to adopt natural stances, but here he goes much further and draws the viewers attention towards the female genitals by lifting the right leg provocatively in the air. It is likely that the model lay on her back for Rodin to sketch the work, giving the sculpture a hovering almost otherworldly appearance in its final upright position.

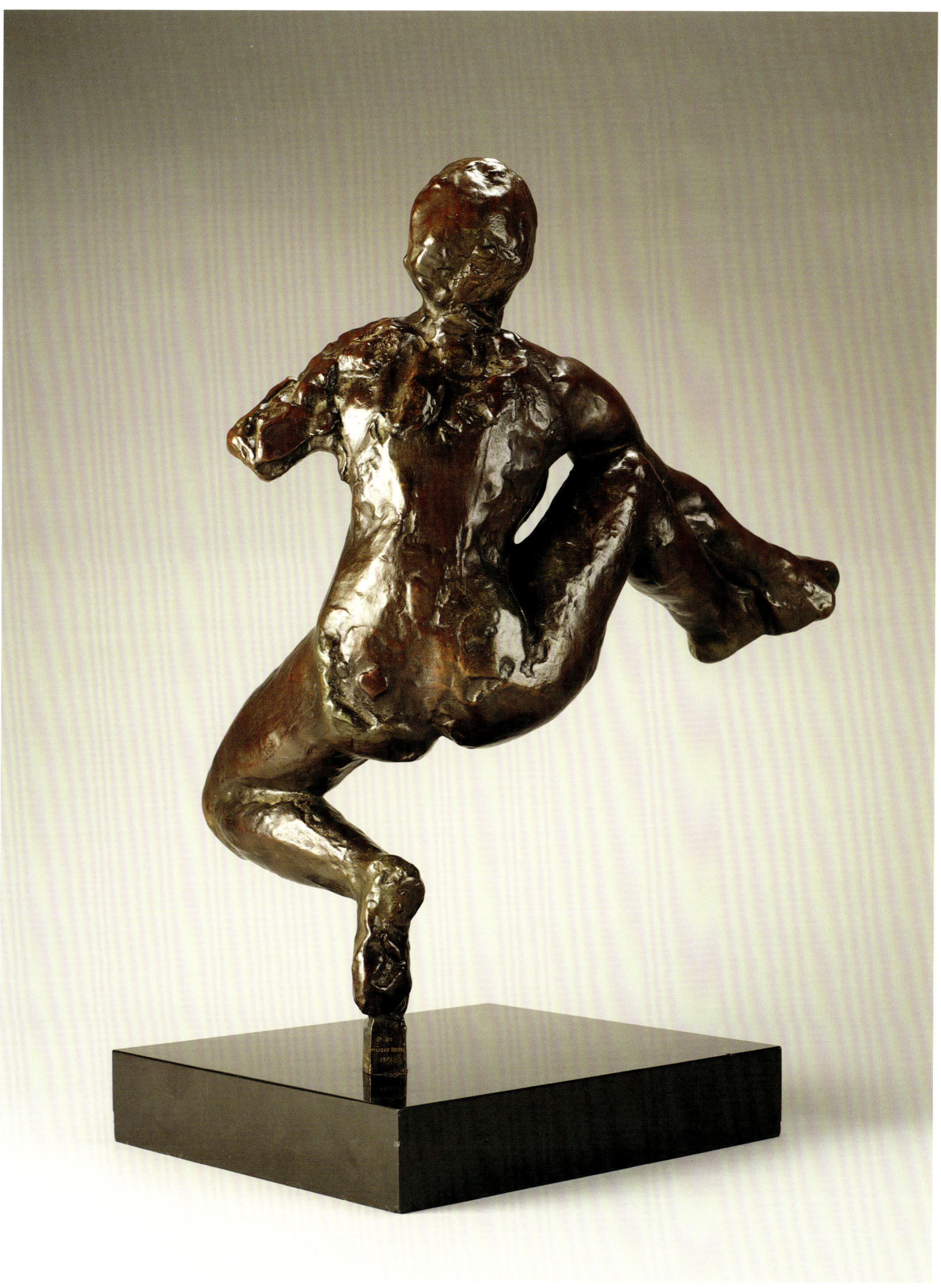

Meditation

Méditation

Signed A. Rodin with repeat raised interior signature
Inscribed Alexis Rudier Fondeur, Paris
Numbered 7
Bronze with a brown and dark brown patination
Height: 29⅛ inches (74.1 cm)

Provenance:
Musée Rodin, Paris
Private Collection, Belgium
Paul Haim, Paris
Private Collection, USA
Robert Bowman Gallery 2007
Private Collection, Turkey

Conceived in 1885, this example was cast in 1930. An edition of thirteen casts was produced for the Musée Rodin between 1921 and 1943.

Meditation was originally conceived for *The Gates of Hell* where it appeared on the far right hand side of the tympanum amongst the Judgment Group. In 1885 Rodin removed the model from the great portal and began working on it independently.

Once removed from *The Gates of Hell*, Rodin changed the model slightly, dropping the head so that it rests on the right arm and elevating the left arm so that it touches the breast.

Depicted in a dream-like state with closed eyes, the woman's strong contrapposto bears testament to the influence of Michelangelo. Rodin invites the viewer to consider the work from all angles, particularly given the complicated contours and sinuous lines created by her twisting figure.

In 1889, Rodin received the commission for a Monument to Victor Hugo. In his third project for the monument, he introduced *Meditation*, now titled *The Inner Voice*, in a composition alongside a model of Hugo himself. The monument underwent a number of transformations over the following years and by the time it was exhibited as the fourth project at the Salon of 1897, both arms of the present work had been amputated. Rodin then removed this version from the monument and began to work on it independently. The armless version was exhibited in both Dresden and Stockholm in 1897 but was poorly received, given its apparently unfinished state.

Rodin later adapted the model for further sculptures and the basic form of *Meditation* can be seen with a fishtail instead of legs in *The Siren*, seen from behind in *Christ and the Magdalen* and with another nude figure in *Constellation*.

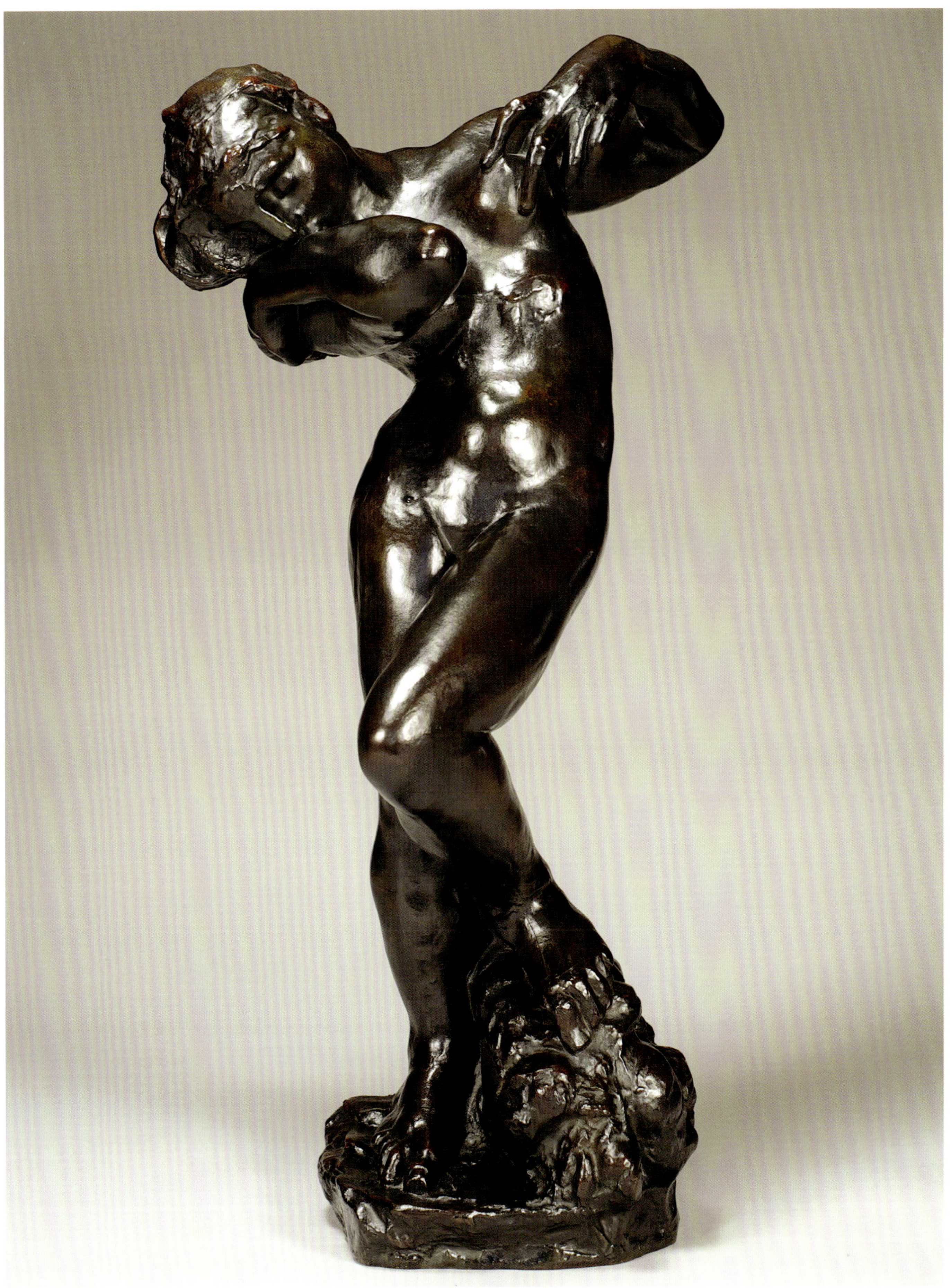

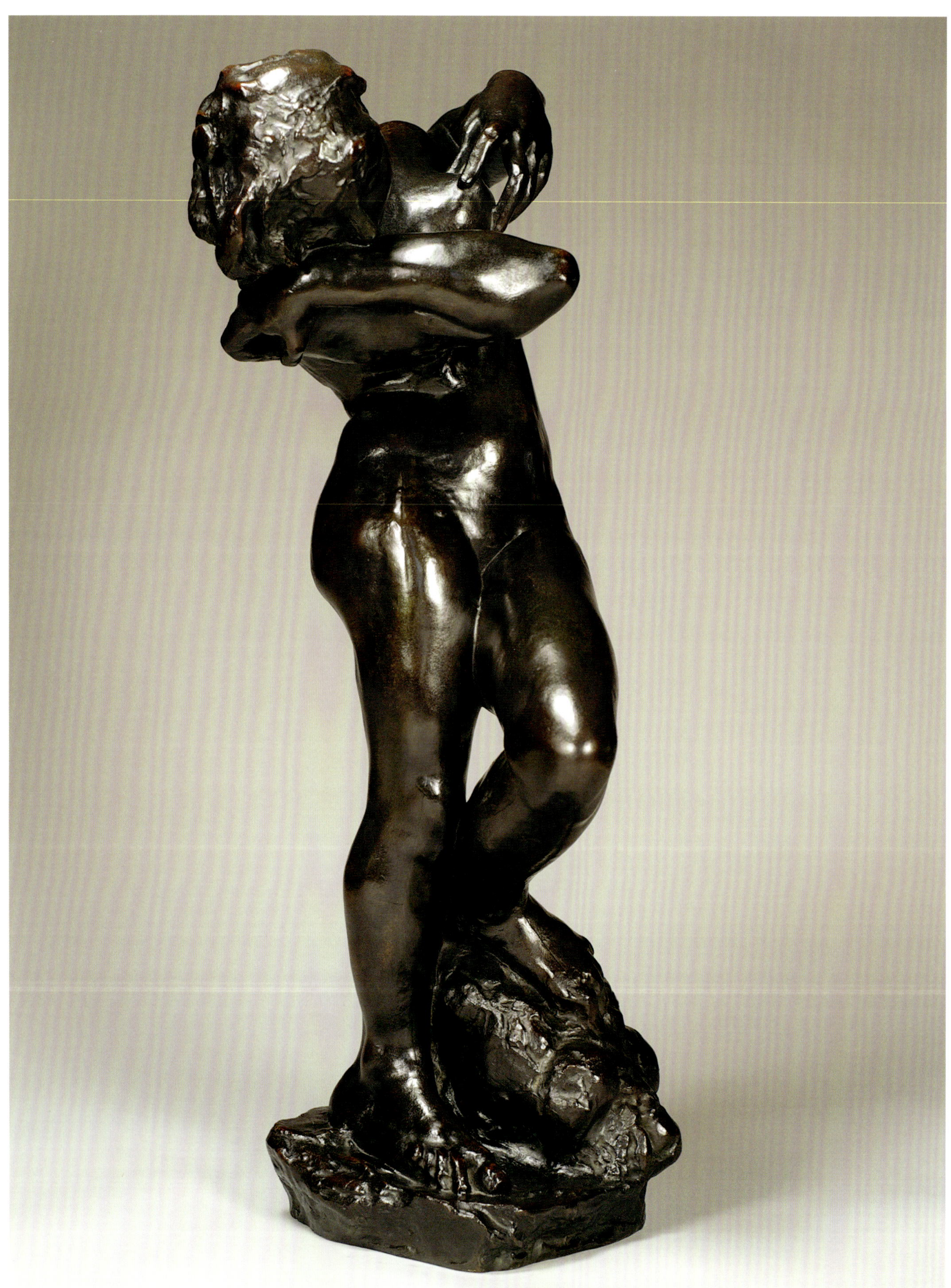

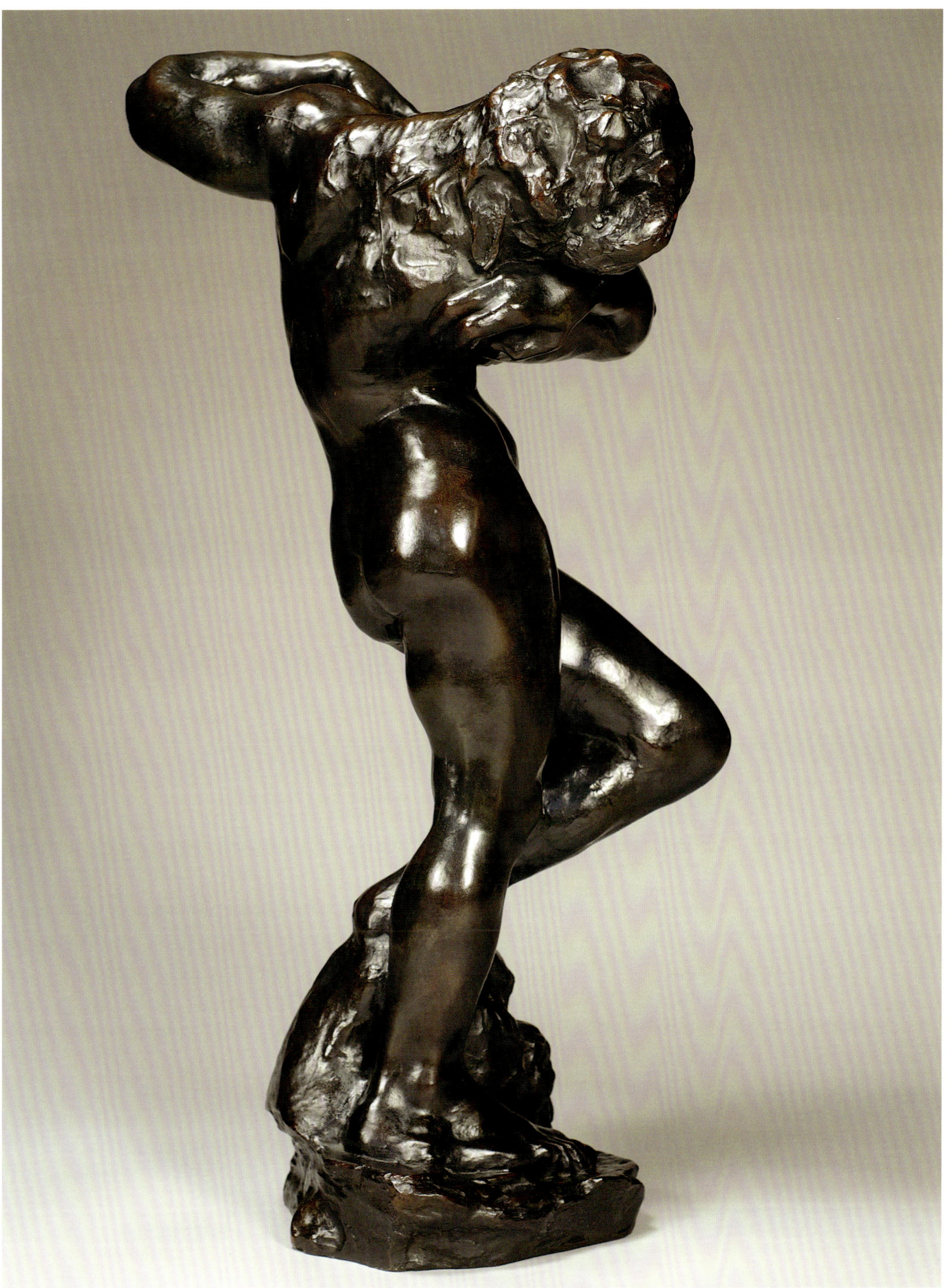

The American Athlete

Athlète Américain

Signed A. Rodin with repeat raised interior signature
Inscribed Alexis Rudier Fondeur Paris
Bronze with a black and dark green patination with light brown highlights
Height: 15¾ inches (40 cm)

Provenance:
Musée Rodin, Paris
Private Collection, Paris
Drouot, 12 December 1935
Decreux Gallery, Buenos-Aires
Private Collection, Buenos-Aires
By Descent
Robert Bowman Gallery, 2008
Private Collection, USA

Conceived in 1901, this example was cast between 1927 and 1935. The Alexis Rudier foundry made one lifetime cast of this model in 1904. Seventeen further casts were made for the Musée Rodin. The first ten by the Alexis Rudier Foundry between 1927 and 1950 and a final seven casts by the Georges Rudier foundry between 1959 and 1965.

In 1901, Samuel Stockton White III (1876–1952) offered to model for Rodin, who had previously used a fairground strongman as his model for *Adam*. White was already a famous gymnast, training with the legendary bodybuilder Eugene Sandow and winning the Sandow Prize for the strongest man in the United Kingdom in 1899. In a letter to Mrs Margery Mason, dated 25th May 1949, White wrote:

'I posed for him in 1901 and 1904 for the statuette which he called *The Athlete* [...] how I came to pose for him is rather interesting; while attending Cambridge University in England, I joined Sandow's Academy in London. During this period, I was spending some time in Paris and a friend of mine suggested that I offer myself as a model to Rodin; the idea interested me and I paid a visit to Rodin who complimented me on my development and accepted me as a model. After trying me in several standing poses, he suggested that I take a pose of my own, which I did, seated, the pose being somewhat similar to *The Thinker*.'

The single lifetime cast of this model was sent to the sitter and is now in the collection of the Philadelphia Museum, having been donated by White.

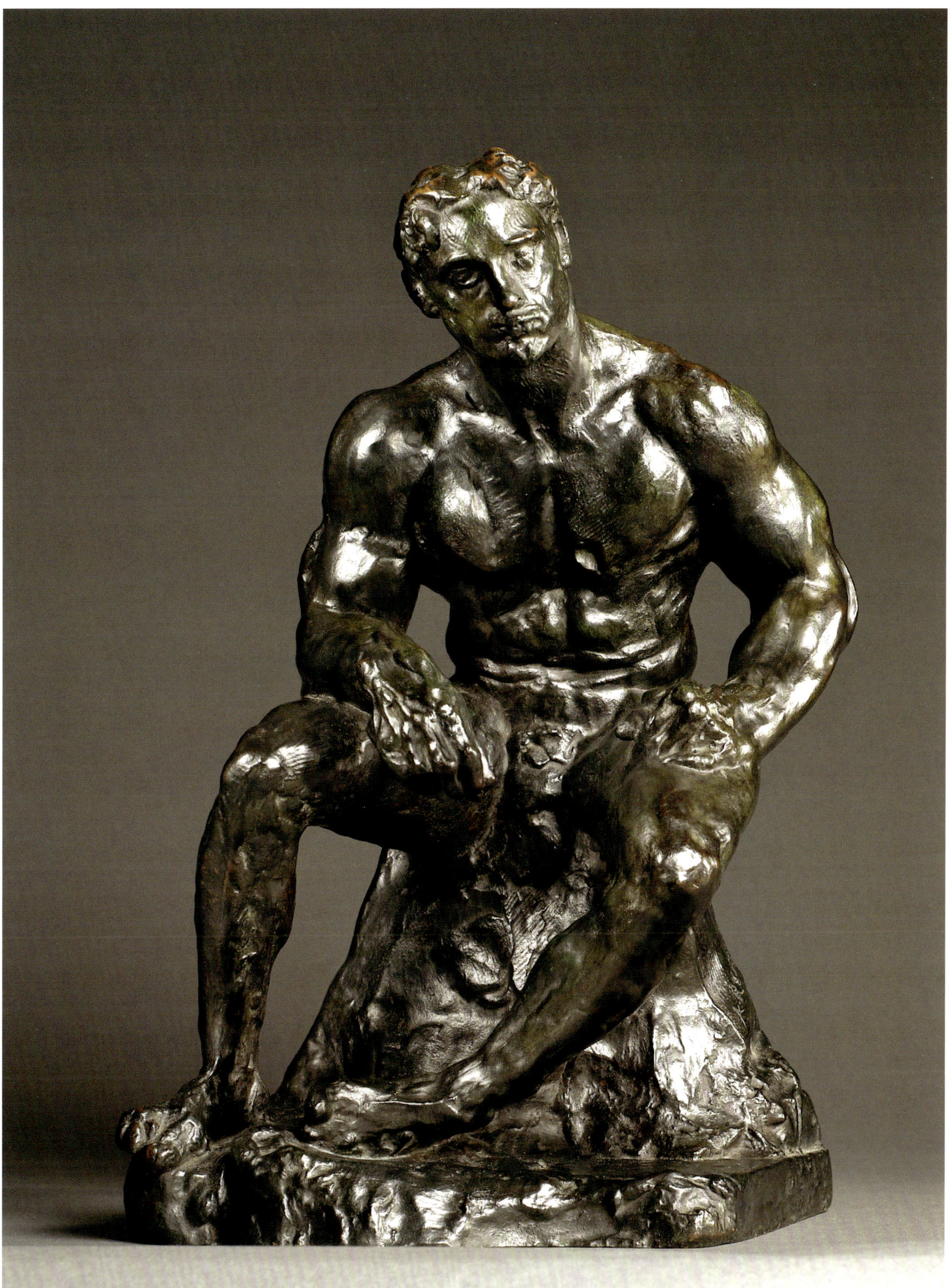

The Athlete, Second Version: Type B

L'Athlète, Deuxième Version: Type B

Signed A. Rodin with repeat raised interior signature
Inscribed Alexis Rudier Fondeur. Paris
Numbered 2
Bronze with a dark green patination with red brown highlights
Height: 17⅛ inches (43.5 cm)

Provenance:
Musée Rodin, Paris.
M. Albert Lespinasse, Paris (acquired from the above, 1955);
Auction Sale Hôtel Drouot, Paris, 23 June 1986, lot 22.
Private Collection, UK
Robert Bowman Gallery, 1993
Private European Collection
Robert Bowman Gallery, 2012
Private Collection, UK

Conceived in 1904, this bronze was cast in 1950. Two casts were made by the Alexis Rudier foundry in 1913. A further ten casts were made for the Musée Rodin. The first four by the Alexis Rudier Foundry between 1925 and 1960 and a further six casts by the Georges Rudier foundry between 1959 and 1965.

In 1904, Samuel Stockton White III (1876–1952), returned to Paris. Again he modelled for Rodin, adopting a similar pose, but this time with his head turned to the right. The second version (of which the present cast is an example) also displays a slightly less muscular physique, suggesting White had relaxed his rigorous training regime by the time this version was modelled.

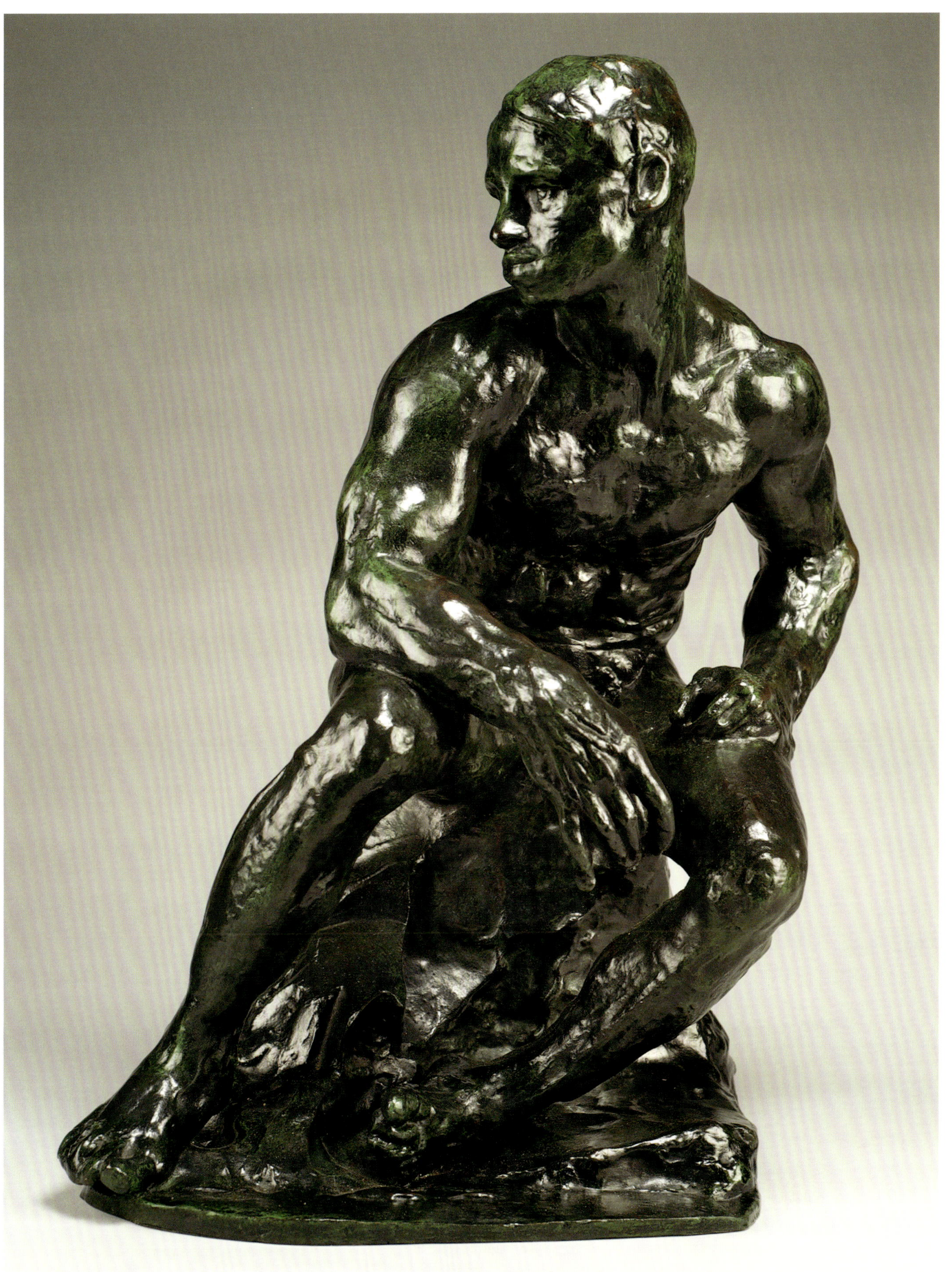

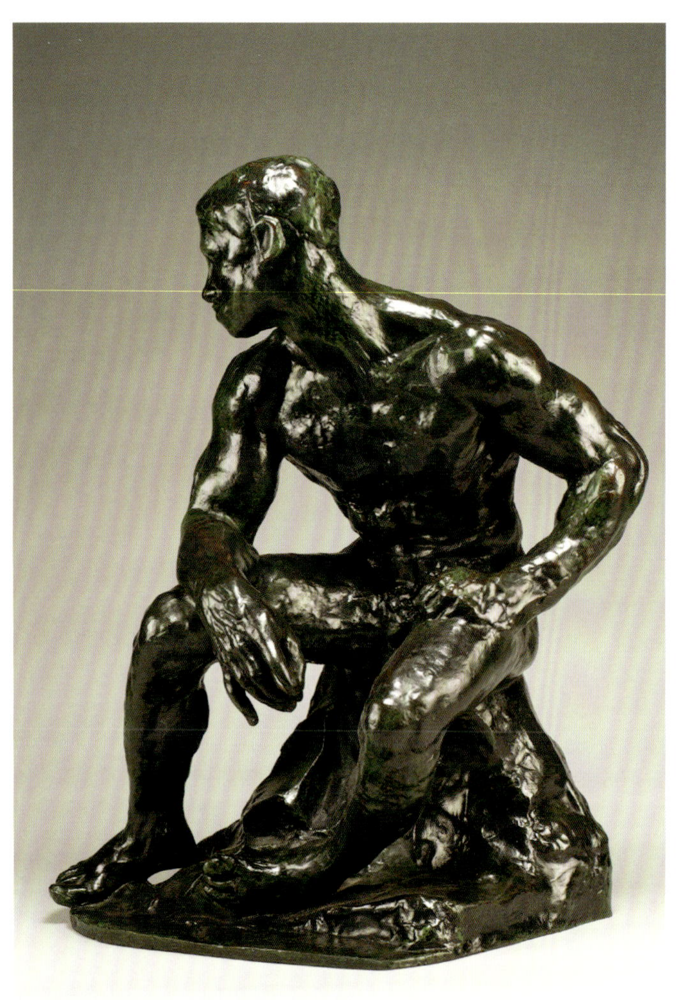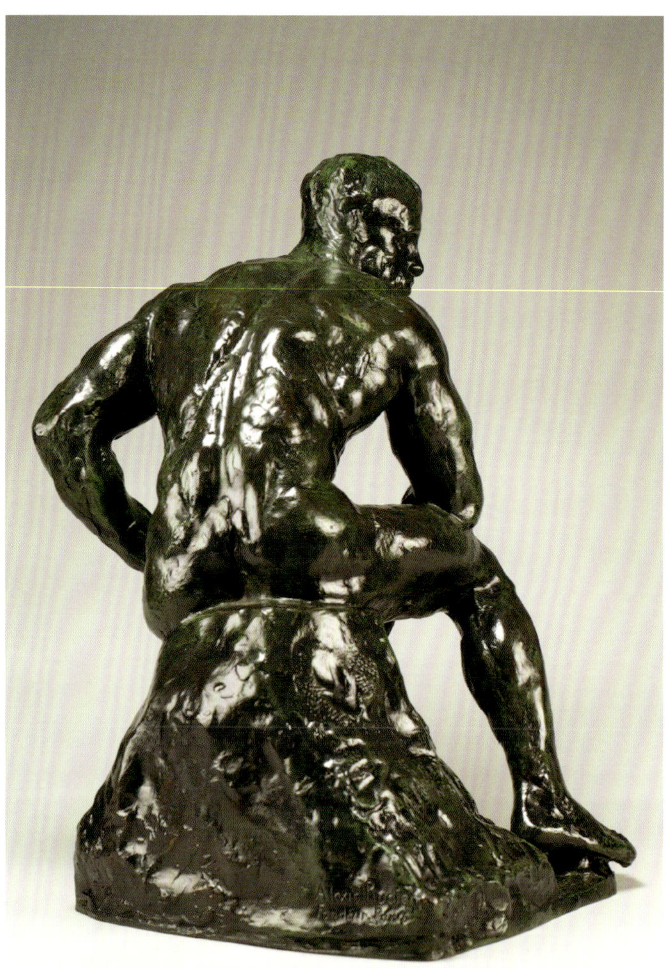

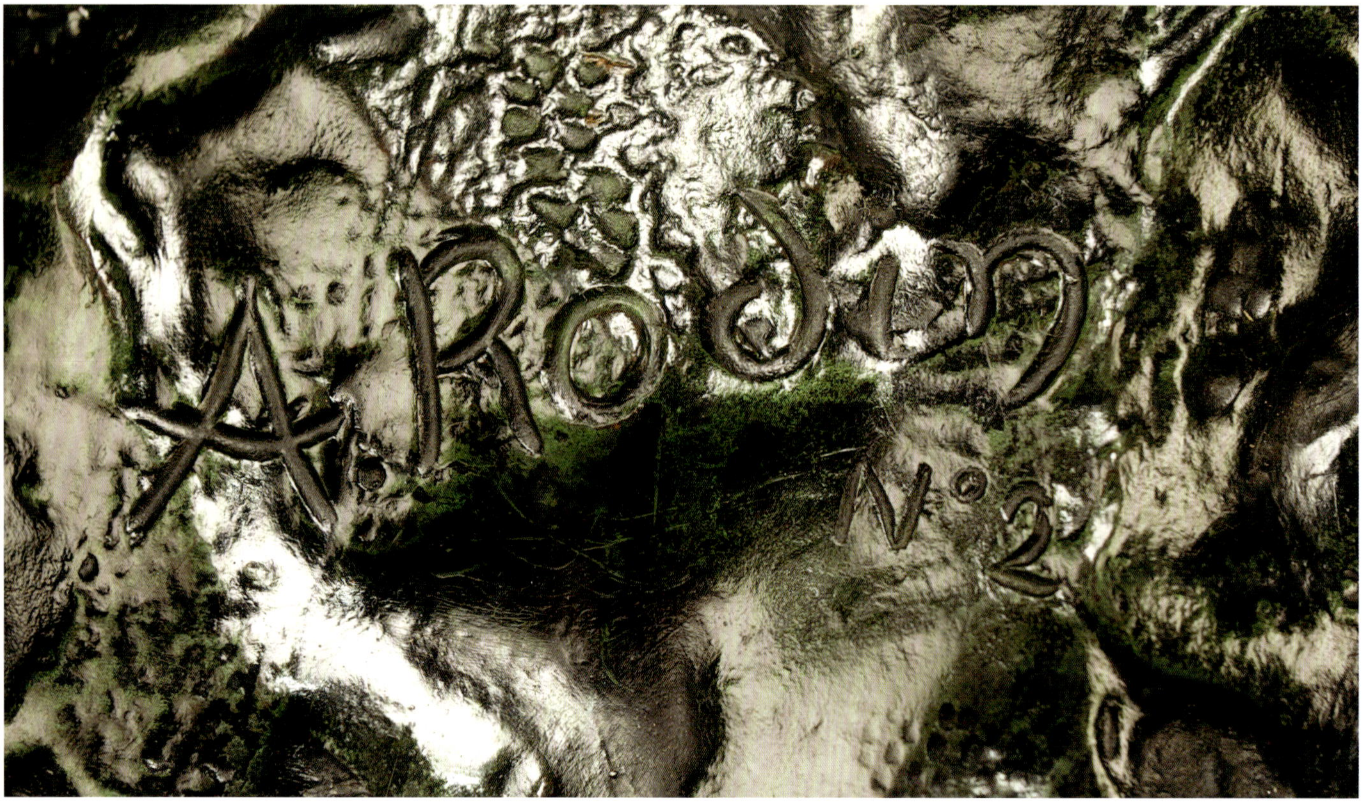

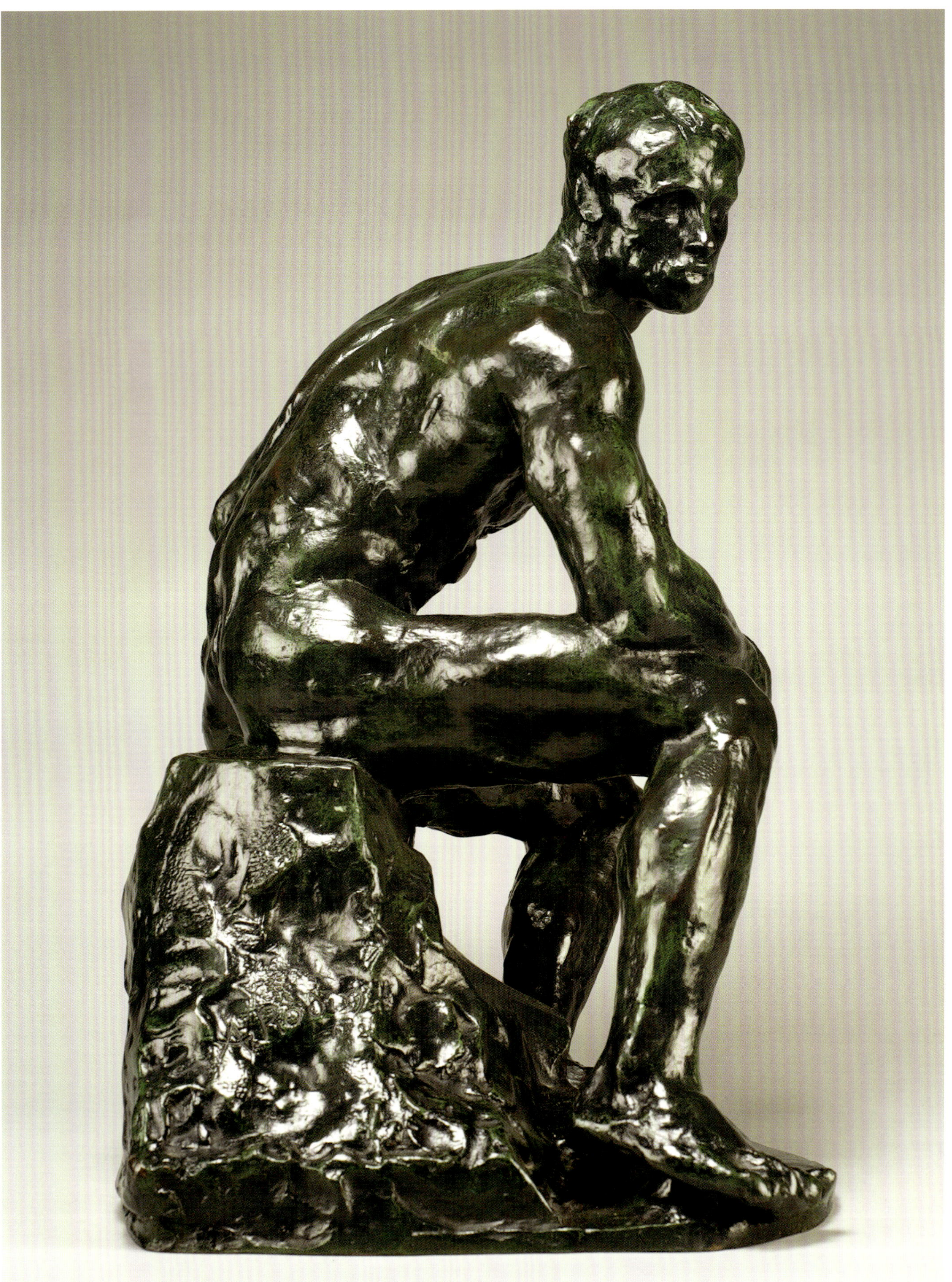

She Who Was Once the Helmet-Maker's Beautiful Wife

Celle Qui Fut La Belle Healmiere

Signed A. Rodin
Inscribed Alexis Rudier Fondeur Paris.
Bronze with a dark brown/black and blue patination
Height: 20 inches (50.6 cm)

Provenance:
Musée Rodin
Eugene Rudier, Le Vésinet (acquired from the above circa 1935–1943)
Private Collection, France (acquired from the above circa 1945)
Robert Bowman Gallery, 2013
Van Gogh Museum, Amsterdam

Conceived between 1885 and 1887, the present example was executed by the Alexis Rudier foundry in 1930 and patinated by Jean Limet (1855–1941), personal assistant of Rodin, who produced distinctive blue black patinations. Seven lifetime casts of this model in this size were cast by Gruet, Perzinka and Alexis Rudier foundries. Four casts were made by Alexis Rudier between 1918 and 1945 of which the present cast is one. A further six casts were made by Georges Rudier between 1957 and 1974.

Also known as *The Old Courtesan* and *Winter*, this sculpture first appeared in bronze on *The Gates of Hell* on the lower part of the left pilaster. Rodin created the work upon the arrival of the sitter, Maria Caira. She was the mother of one of Rodin's models and had walked all the way from Italy to Rodin's studio to see her son one last time before she died.

When Rodin met Caira he was immediately taken with her aging skin hanging from such an elegant bone structure and pressed her to stay and model for him.

It would seem this powerful work created an irresistible sculptural challenge in the artist's studio, as soon after this sculpture was created, Rodin's assistant Jules Desbois created *Misery* and Camille Claudel created *Clotho*. It would appear they too used Caira for these works, both inspired by Rodin's skill in capturing the emotion and beauty of the human body in decline.

As Rodin said regarding the similarly atypical beautiful subject *Man with a Broken Nose* 'In art, only that which has character is beautiful. Character is the essential truth of any natural object.'

The art critic and Rodin scholar Paul Gsell associated the sculpture in his 'Conversations with Rodin' with the poem *Les Regrets de la Belle Heaulmière* by François Villon (overleaf).

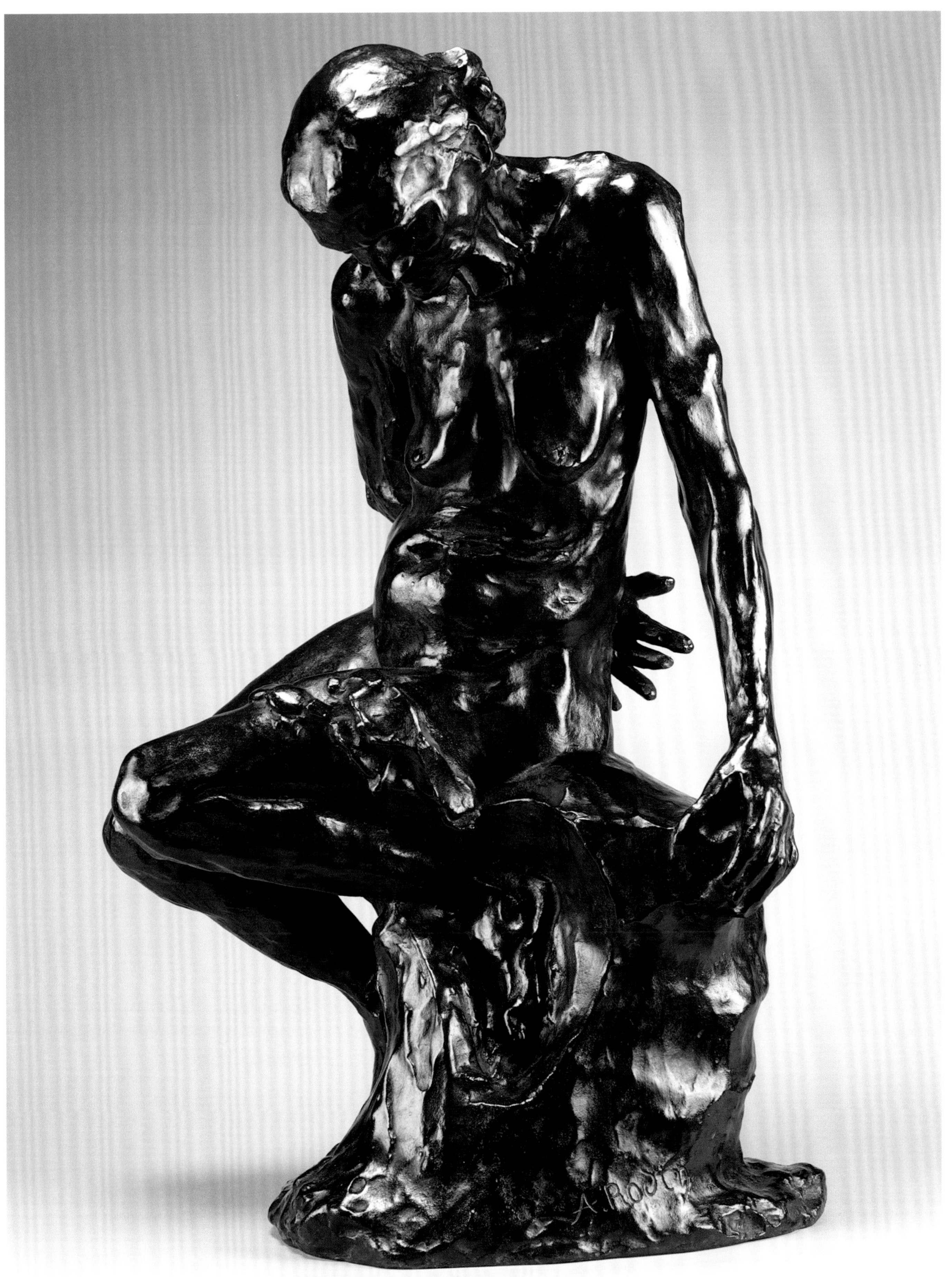

Ah, Wicked Old Age
Why have you struck me down so soon?
You have stiffened me so
That I cannot strike
And with that kill myself !

When I think Alas ! of the good times
What was, What I have become
When I look at myself, completely naked
And I see myself so changed
Poor desiccated, this shrivelled,
I nearly go mad.

What has happened to my smooth brow,
My blond hair
My slender shoulders,
Small breasts, firm thighs
High, clean, perfectly made
For love's pleasure's
This is the fate of human beauty !
Shrunken arms and clenched hands
And completely hunchbacked,
What breasts! All Wizened
Like my hips.

Les Regrets de la Belle Heaulmière - François Villon

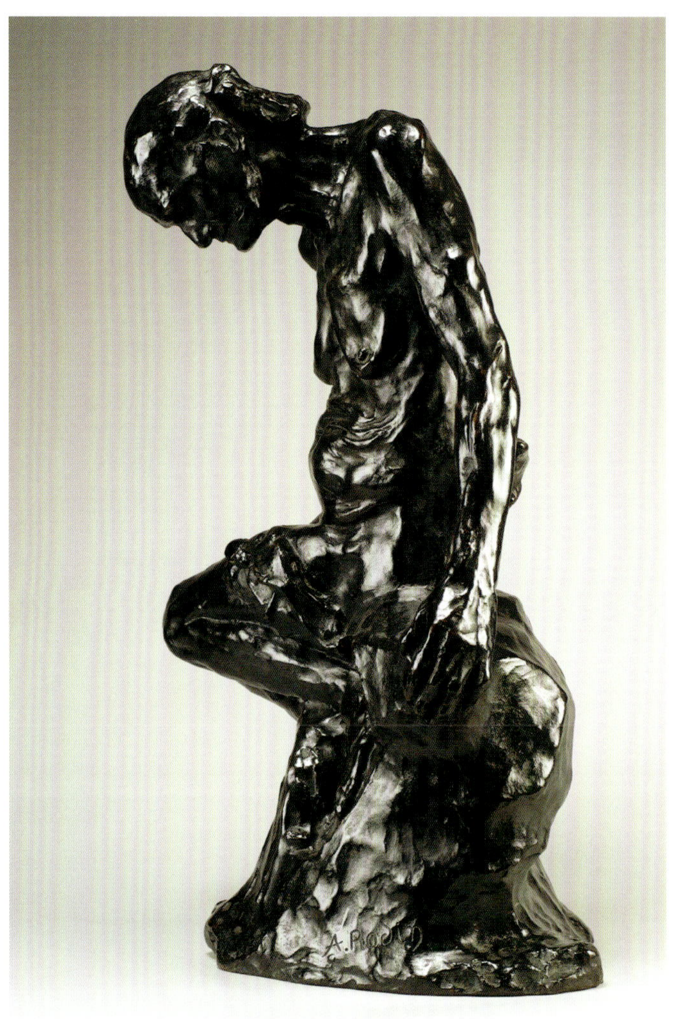

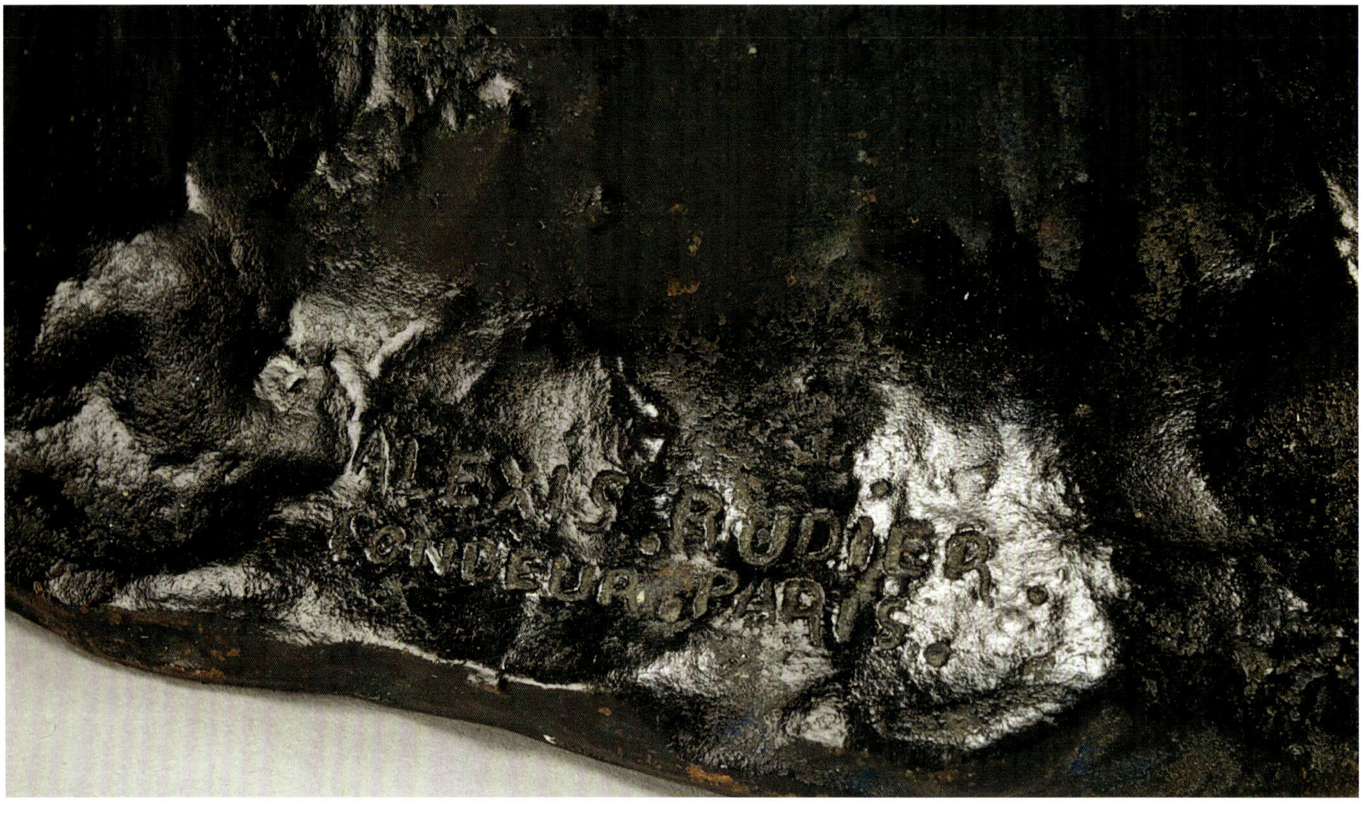

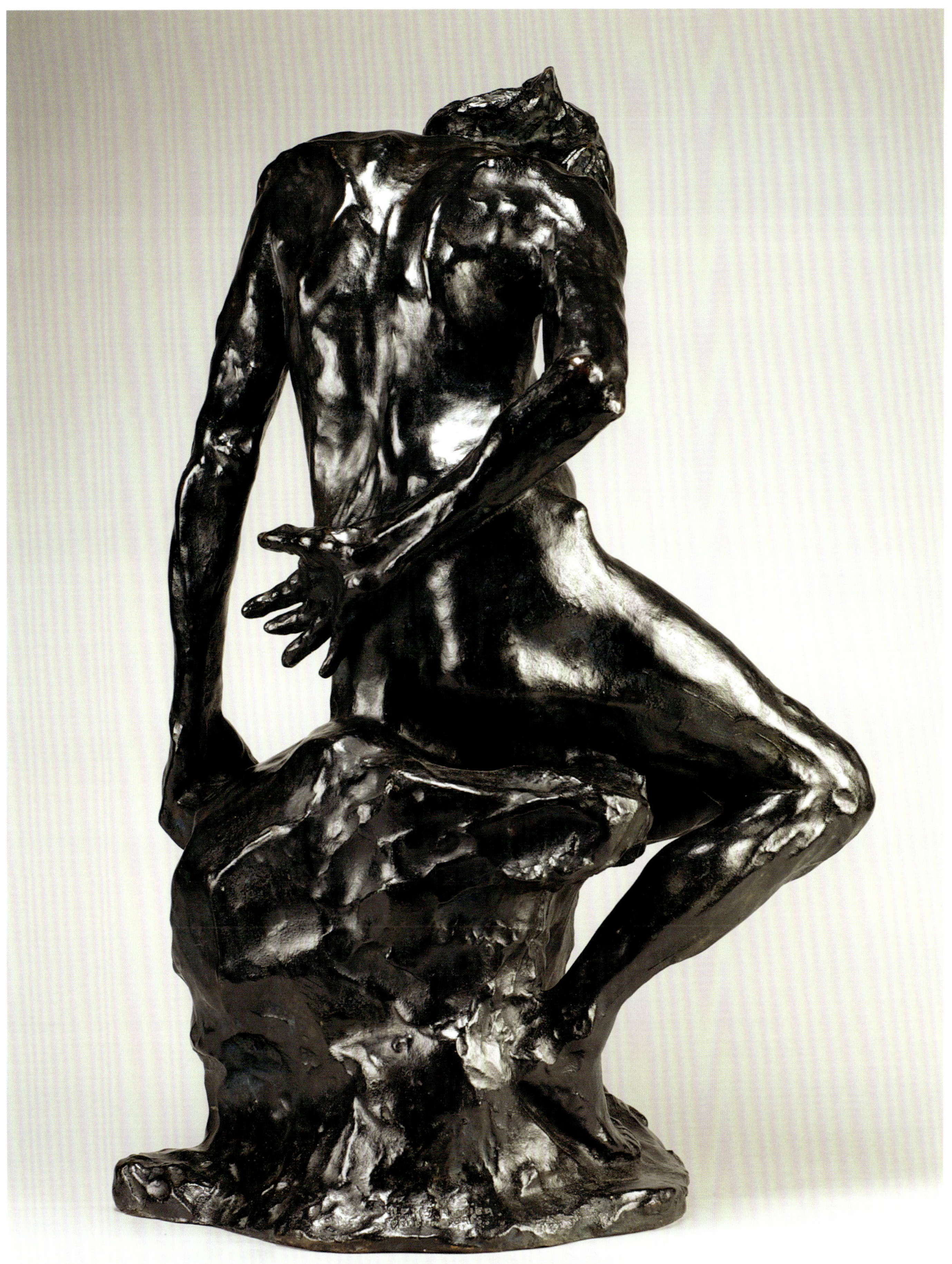

She Who Was Once the Helmet-Maker's Beautiful Wife

Celle Qui Fut La Belle Healmiere

Signed A. Rodin with repeat raised interior signature
Inscribed © by Musée Rodin 1957 and Georges Rudier Fondeur Paris
Bronze with a rich green/brown patination
Height: 20 inches (50.9 cm)

Provenance:
Musée Rodin, Paris
B. Gerald Cantor, Los Angeles acquired from the above August 1967
Mr and Mrs Malashem Riklis acquired from the above
Robert Bowman Gallery, 2010
Private Collection, Norway

Conceived by Rodin between 1885 and 1887, this cast was made in 1957. Seven lifetime casts were made by Gruet, Perzinka and Alexis Rudier. Four further Alexis Rudier casts between 1918 and 1945 and finally six further casts between 1957 and 1974 by Georges Rudier.

The philanthropist B. Gerald Cantor (1916–1996) acquired this cast from the Musée Rodin in 1967. Cantor assembled the largest private collection of Rodin sculptures in the world; he also gave four hundred and fifty sculptures public collections. He and his wife created the Iris & B. Gerald Cantor Center for Visual Arts at Stanford University to make their collection available to students and the public. The centre has the largest collection of Rodin sculptures outside the Musée Rodin in Paris.

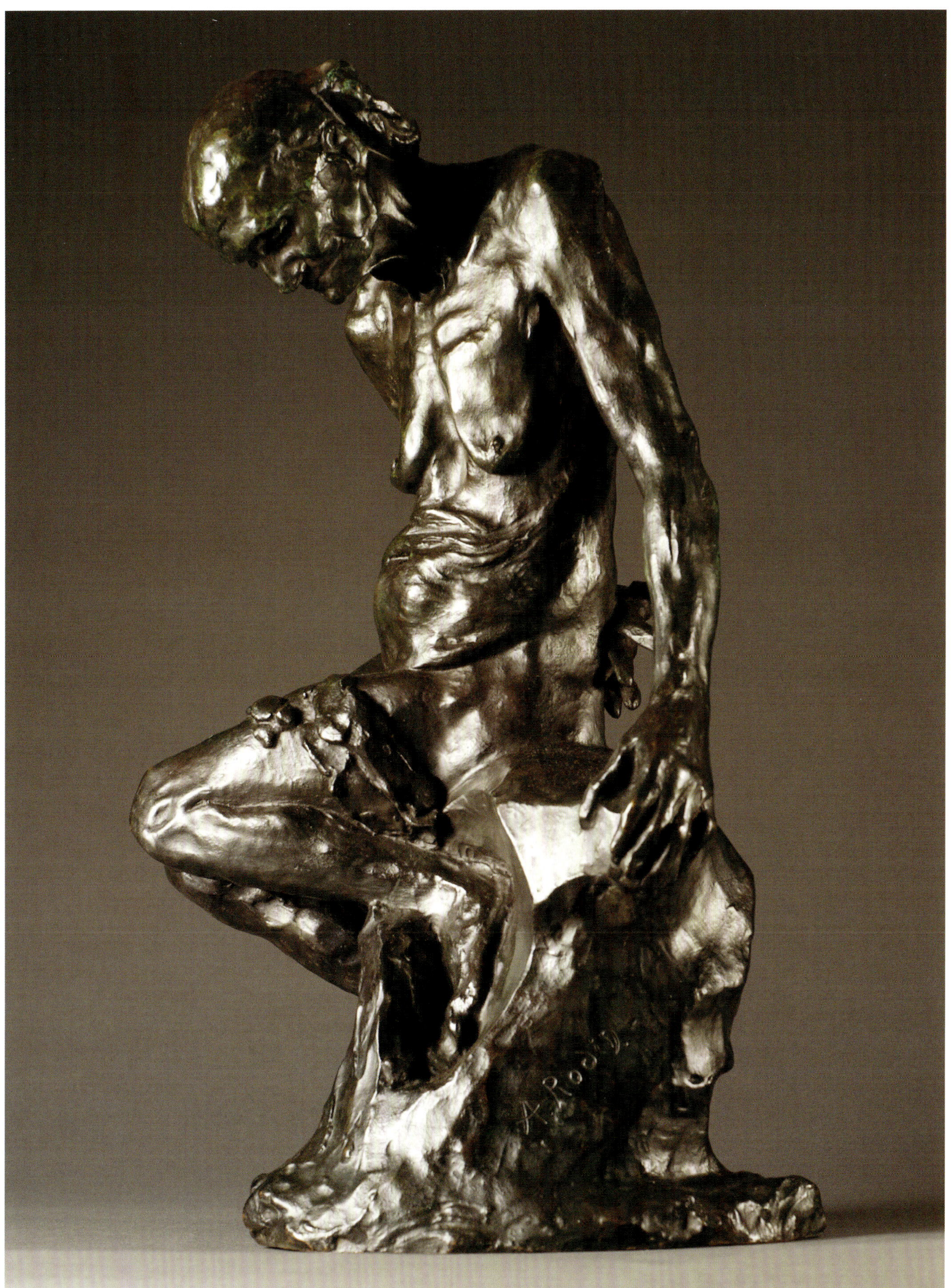

Danaide, Small Model, Type III (Choiseul Danaide)

Danaïde, Petit Modèle, Version Type III (Choiseul Danaïde)

Signed A. Rodin and with repeat interior signature
Bronze with a rich dark brown and red patination
Height: 8¾ inches (21.9 cm)

Provenance:
Claire Coudert de Choiseul, Duchesse de Choiseul, Paris, acquired directly from the artist 1907
Charles-Auguste de Choiseul-Beaupré, Duc de Choiseul, Paris
Paul Rosenberg, Paris, acquired from the above 8 February 1918
Possibly with the Hannover Gallery, London
Mme Dore Gulbenkian, Brynstone Court, London W1
The Obelisk Gallery, Jimmy G. McMullan, proprietor, 15 Crawford Street, London
Robert Strauss, Stonehurst Estate, Ardingly, West Sussex, acquired from the above 3 February 1961
Thence by descent to Derek Strauss nephew of Robert Strauss

Conceived in 1885, this version of the Danaide described as Type III, is considered to be the finest model; it was first cast in a single example by the Gruet foundry, this cast is now in the collection of the Metropolitan Museum. The second cast made is the present example executed in 1907 by the Alexis Rudier foundry, that was Rodin's preferred foundry after 1902. No other casts of the Type III were made until 1917. The Musée Rodin continued the edition with a further seven casts from the Alexis Rudier foundry between 1921 and 1942, then finally nine casts by the Georges Rudier foundry between 1961 and 1971. These casting records correspond however to all three different versions of Danaide, identified by the differing treatment of the rocky base.

The first owner of this model, the Duchesse de Choiseul, was Rodin's last great love. He entered into a romantic relationship with her in 1906, which would continue until 1912. The Duchesse de Choiseul was put in charge of all Rodin's business affairs, acting as his American agent. Gertrude Vanderbilt Whitney famously recalled her 'blocking young American sculptors from visiting with the words, 'No use disturbing him since I am here. I handle everything. I am Rodin!' In reality she exerted a powerful influence over Rodin by taking all of his business dealings in hand and raised the prices of his works substantially. The result of the tumultuous six-year affair proved immensely beneficial for Rodin. The Duchesse was credited with boosting the artist's income from 60,000 to 400,000 francs a year.

The Danaide was originally conceived as part of *The Gates of Hell*, but was eventually omitted from the final design. The work was inspired by the story of the daughters of Danaus, taken from Greek mythology.

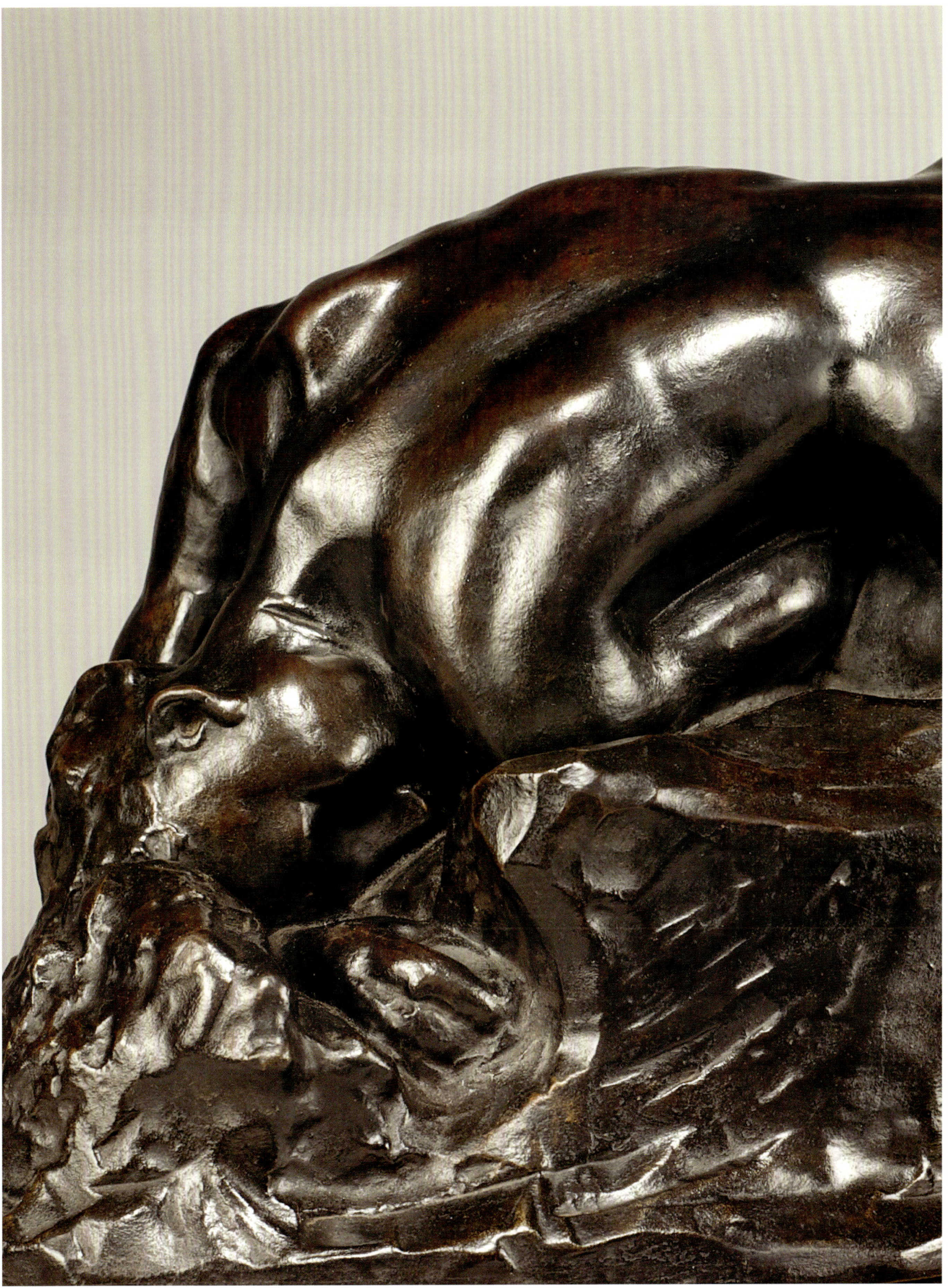

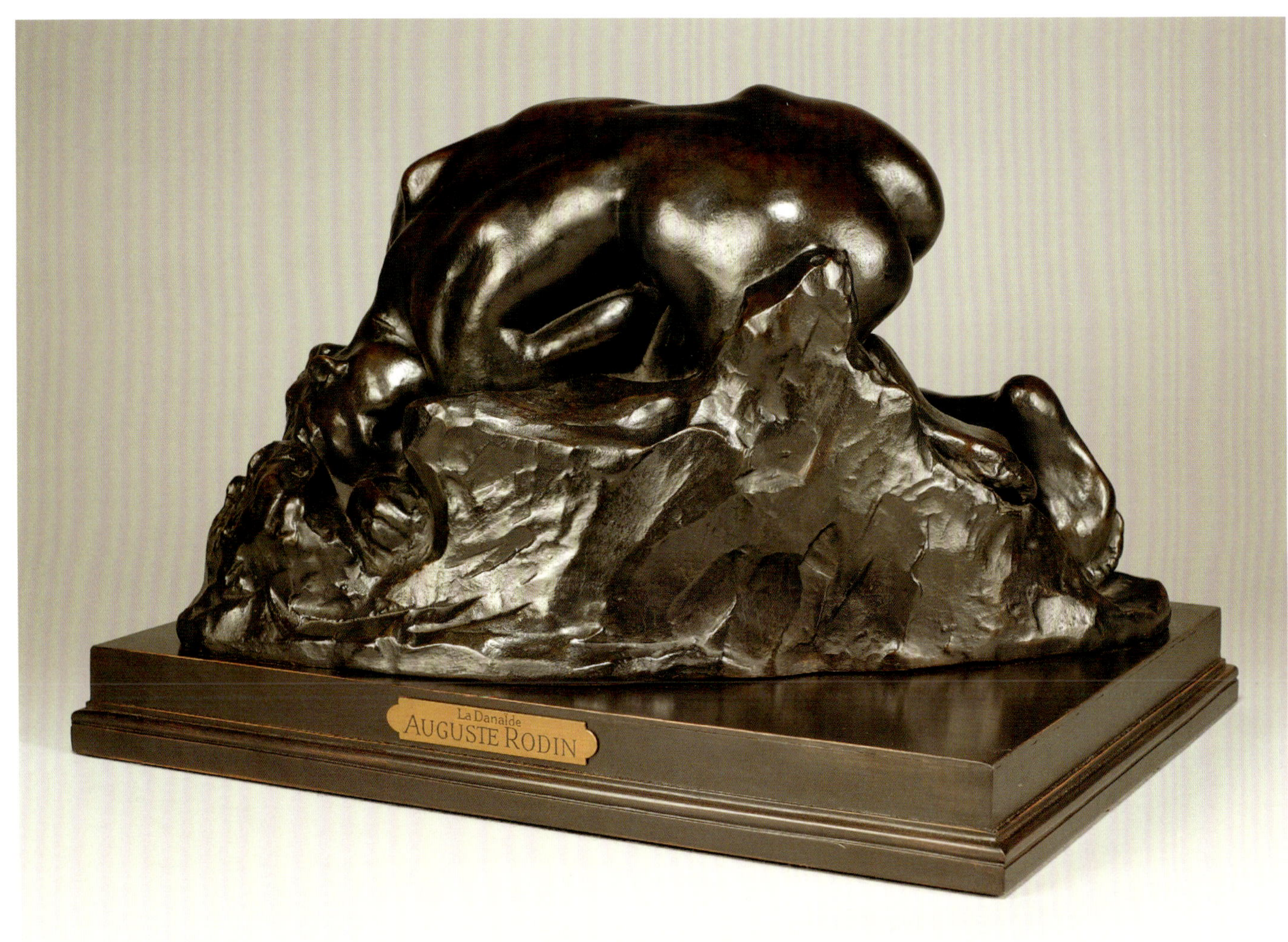

In this myth, Danaus, the son of the King of Egypt, had fifty daughters named the Danaides. His brother Aegyptus had fifty sons. Threatened by his brother, Danaus sailed to Argos with his daughters. The sons of Aegyptus pursued their cousins with the intention of marrying them and so furthering their power. The daughters were unwilling to marry but were forced to consent. Danaus therefore ordered his daughters to stab their husbands to death on their wedding night. Forty-nine obeyed their father, with only Hypermnestra sparing her beloved husband Lynceus. As a punishment for their crimes, the guilty Danaides were punished in the Underworld by having to try to fill broken vessels with water for eternity.

In the present model, Rodin portrays one of the Danaides, who has thrown herself to the ground, her water vessel by her side and her long hair flowing over the rocks. The sculptor conveys the stricken woman's despair at her absurd and inexorable task of endlessly refilling the broken vessel.

Rodin depicts the woman as youthful, sensual and vibrant despite her exhausting life in the underworld. As was common in the sculptor's work, here sensuality and pessimism go hand in hand. The sculpture is both alluring and despondent, a figure of youthful beauty and a manifestation of eternal despair.

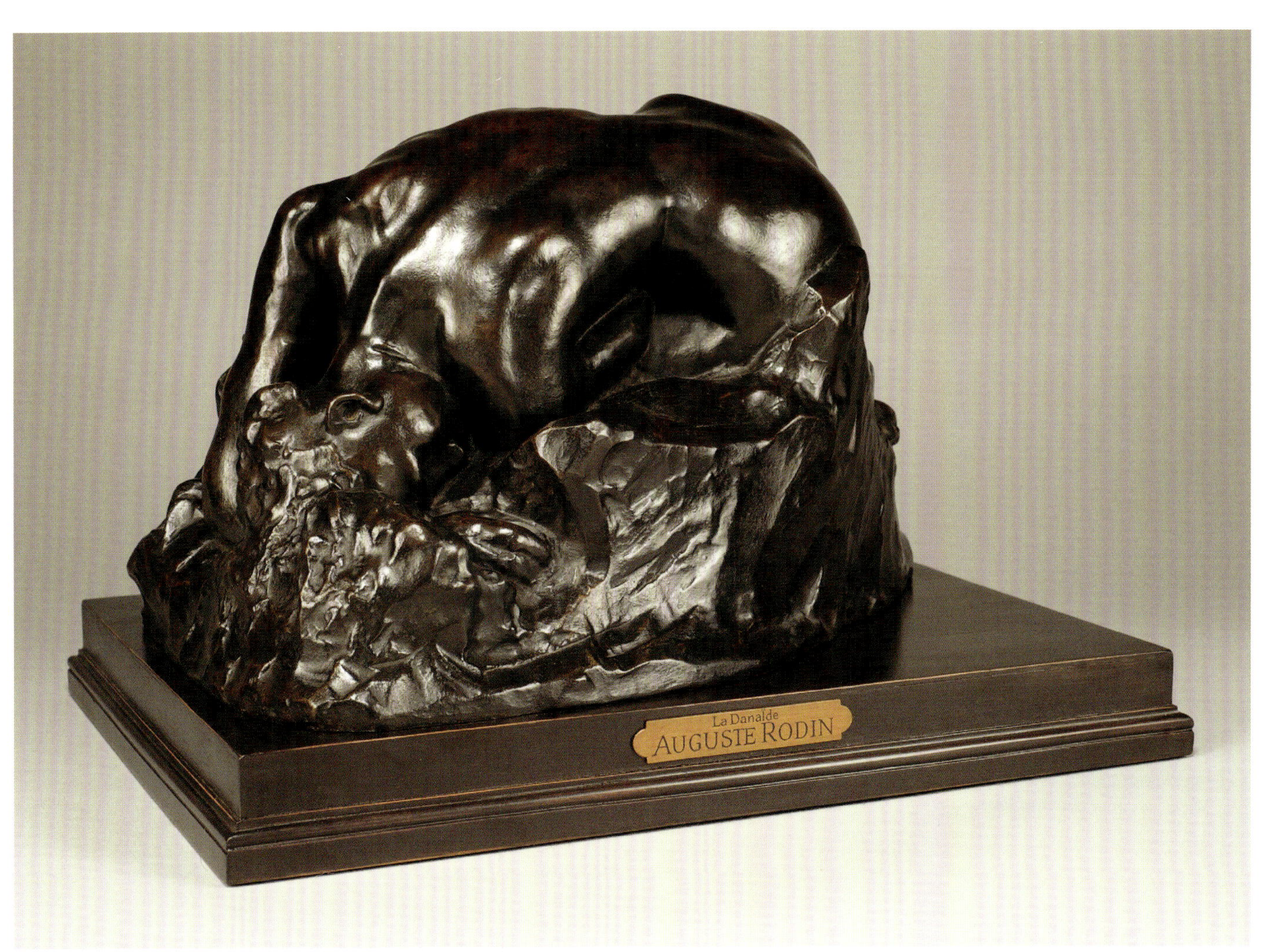

It has been suggested by Monique Laurent that the model for the work was in fact Camille Claudel, although this theory remains unproven. The theory was popularised by Bruno Nuytten's movie Camille Claudel, which merged fact and fiction by showing Camille kneeling on the floor modeling for the work.

Rodin began work on *Danaide* in 1880 and at the end of the decade the work was enlarged and transformed into marble for the Scandinavian collector, Dr. H. F. Antell. This marble was exhibited at the 1889 'Monet-Rodin' exhibition at the Galerie George Petit where it received considerable press attention. After the success of this exhibition Rodin commissioned Jean Escoula to a make a second marble of the *Danaide*, which is considered to be one of the finest marbles ever produced in his atelier. This second version was exhibited at the Salon of 1890 and was purchased by the French government. Known as the *Luxembourg Danaide* it was originally in the collection of the Musée du Luxembourg. It is now housed in the Musée Rodin collection.

Danaide, Small Model, Version Type 1

Danaïde, Petit Modéle, Version Type 1

Signed A. Rodin with repeat raised interior signature
Inscribed Alexis Rudier Fondeur, Paris
M stamped on the interior
Bronze with a light brown patination
Height: 8¾ inches (22 cm)

Provenance:
Musée Rodin
Odilon Roche, Paris
Baron Sanji Kuroki, Japan
Sothebys, New York, 11 May 2000, Lot 105
Private Collection, Oslo
Robert Bowman Gallery, 2012
Private European Collection

Conceived in 1885, this cast was executed in July 1921. The Gruet foundry executed the first cast of the Danaide. The Alexis Rudier foundry made at least nine casts between 1909 and 1917. The Musée Rodin continued the edition with seven casts from the Alexis Rudier foundry between 1921 and 1942, then nine casts by the Georges Rudier foundry between 1961 and 1971. These records however correspond to the three different versions of Danaide, which each differ slightly in the treatment of the rocky base.

The present cast can be distinguished from the lifetime casts by the addition of the 'M' stamped on the interior. The 'M' was used by the Musée Rodin between 1919 and 1922, to differentiate early posthumous casts from lifetime examples.

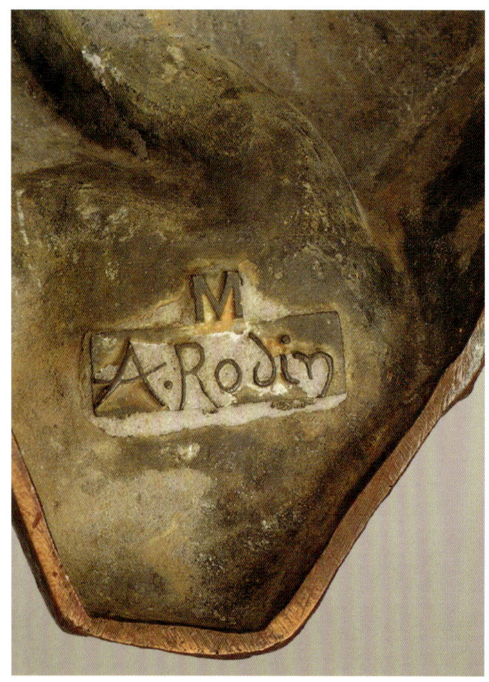

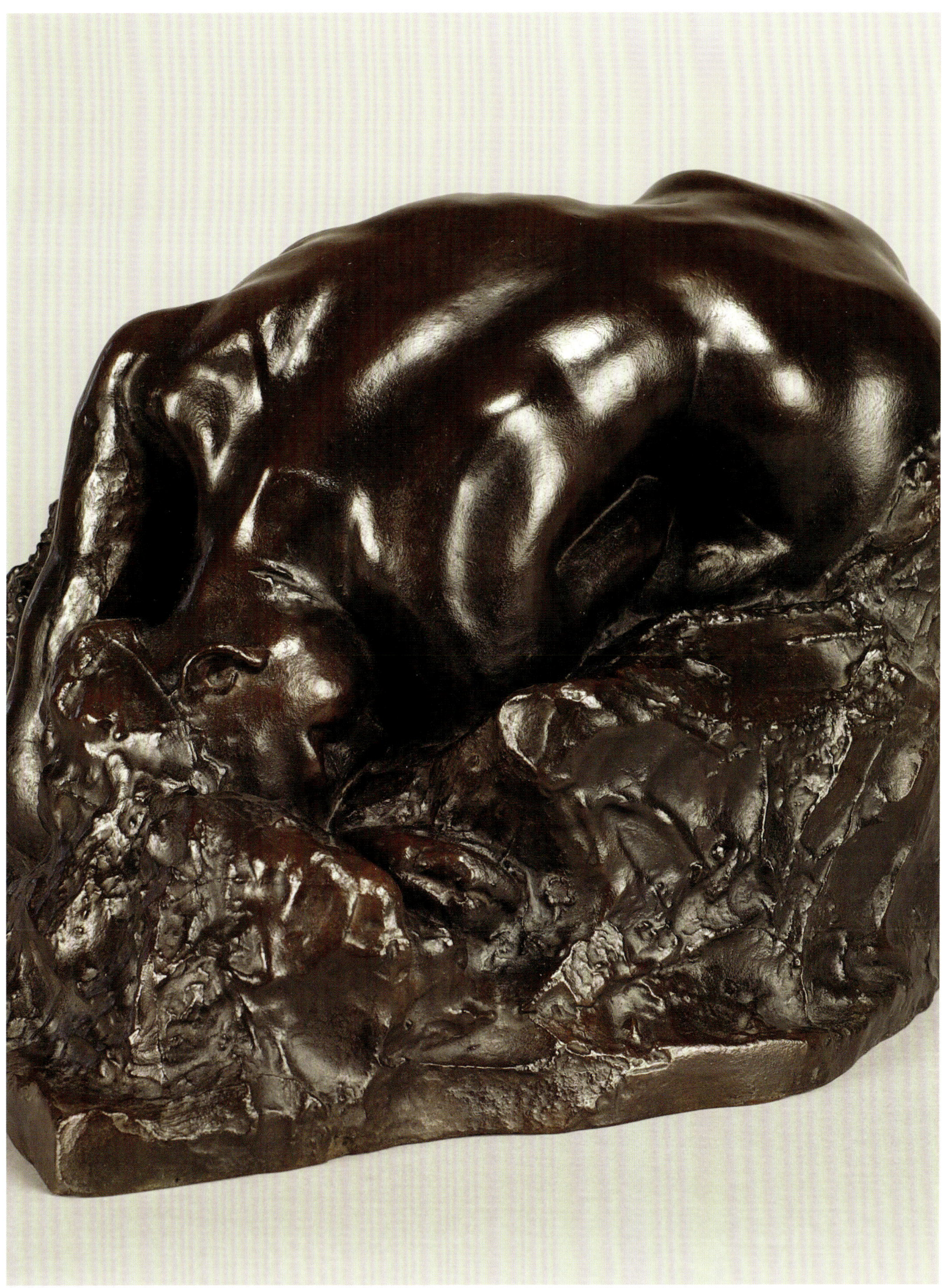

Caryatid with an Urn

Cariatide à L'urne

Signed A. Rodin and with repeat raised interior signature
Inscribed © by Musée Rodin 1966 and Georges Rudier Fondeur Paris
Bronze with a rich dark brown, red/brown and green patination
Height: 16 inches (41 cm)

Provenance:
Musée Rodin Paris
Dominion Gallery Montreal acquired 1967. This cast exhibited at the 50th anniversary of the death of Rodin Exhibition at the gallery.
Private Collection, Washington

Conceived in this format with the urn in 1900, this example was cast in 1966. Only one lifetime cast of this model was made in 1917. Three casts were made for the Musée Rodin by the Alexis Rudier Foundry between 1925 and 1942, six casts by Georges Rudier between 1966 and 1969 and three casts by Emile Godard between 1973 and 1977.

A Caryatid is a sculptural female form that serves as a support for a heavy architectural load. Caryatids normally take the form of a pillar or column, and are usually topped with a molding below the supported structure. The term comes from the Greek Karyatides, meaning woman of Karyai, who were known for their ability to carry heavy reed baskets on their heads. The use of caryatids in architectural design goes back to ancient Greece and one of the earliest and most accomplished examples can be seen at the Temple of Erechtheum on the Acropolis.

Rodin originally modelled his *Caryatid* in 1881 and in this early version the woman is seen supporting a large stone. Unusually, particularly given the appropriateness of the subject for *The Gates of Hell*, the model was conceived independently and later incorporated into the portal, adorning the top left hand pilaster in Rodin's final design.

The work was shown in 1886 at the Georges Petit Gallery alongside *Andromeda* and *Crouching Woman* in an exhibition titled *Weary Woman*. Unlike classical Caryatids, Rodin's model was recognised as a departure from the serene structures of antiquity, which appeared to carry their heavy loads both without pain or effort.

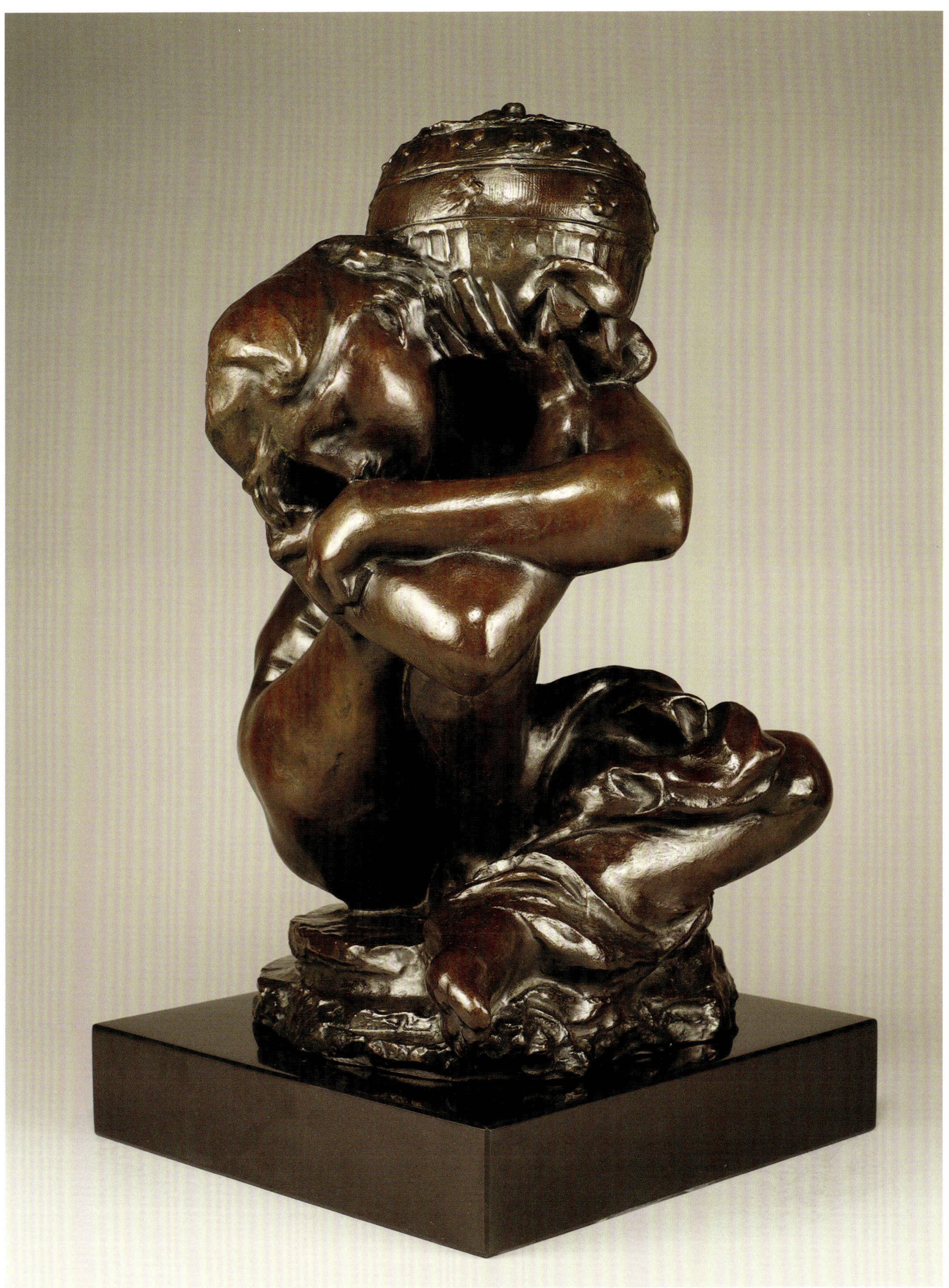

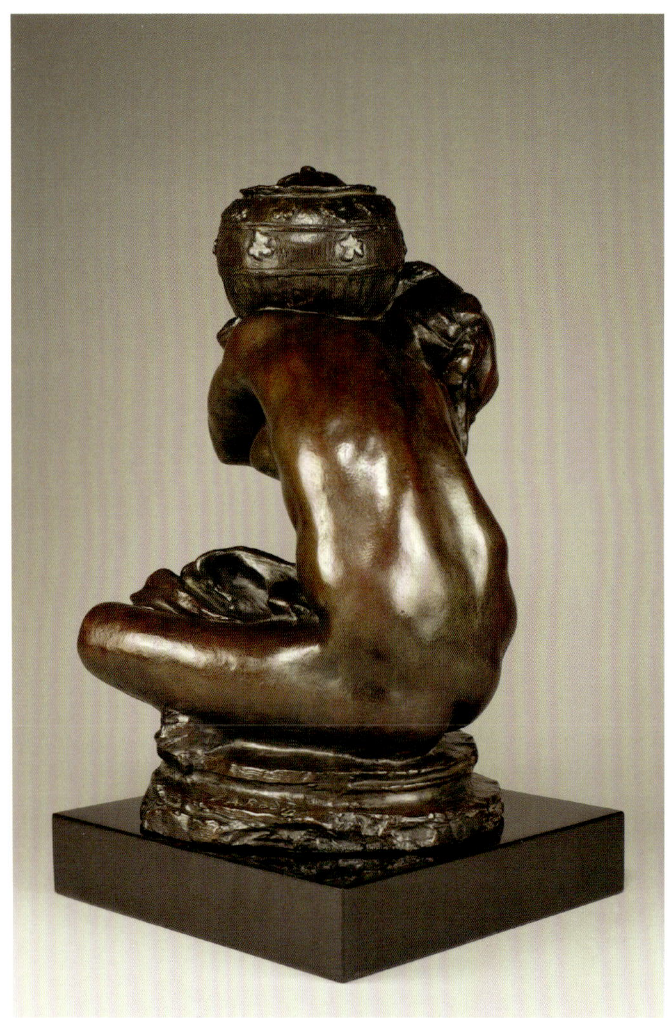 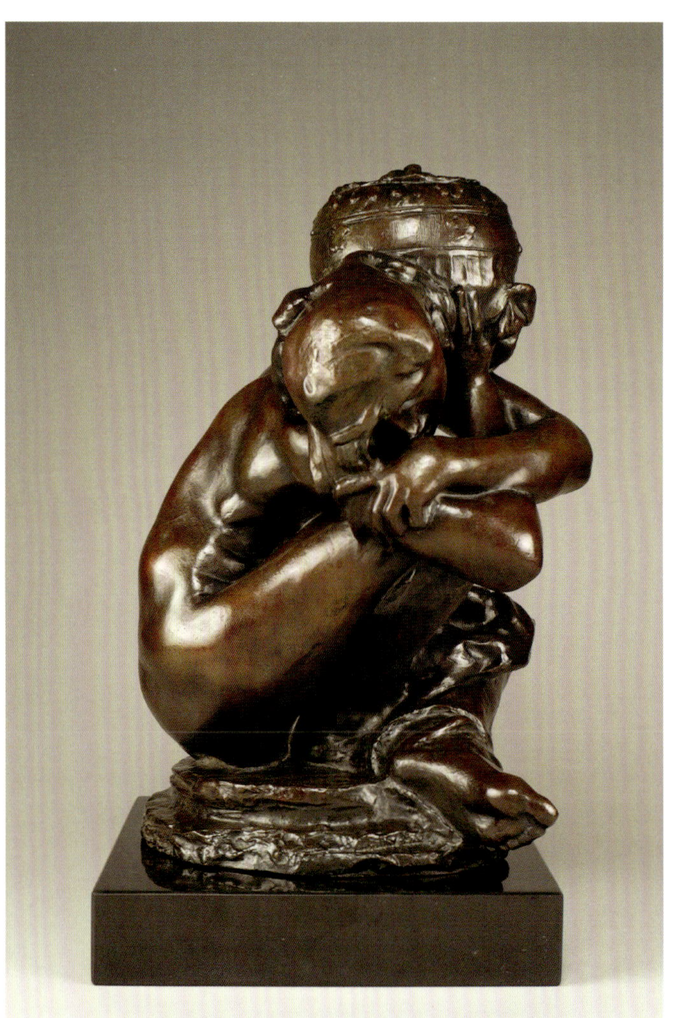

Rodin presented the work at the Salon of 1897 and explained in the catalogue that year: 'On each part of this body, the entire rock rests like a will that was greater, more ancient and more powerful, and yet its destiny, which was to carry, has not stopped. It carries, as one carries the impossible in a dream, and cannot find a way out. And despite its collapse, its weakness, the act of carrying continues, and when exhaustion strikes again, forcing the body to recline, even when reclining, it will still carry, will go on carrying forever.'

The present variant of the model was conceived around 1900 and incorporates an urn rather than a stone, a substitution probably requested by a collector or admirer of Rodin's work. The first cast of this model by Alexis Rudier (1917), was acquired by Jules Mastbaum.

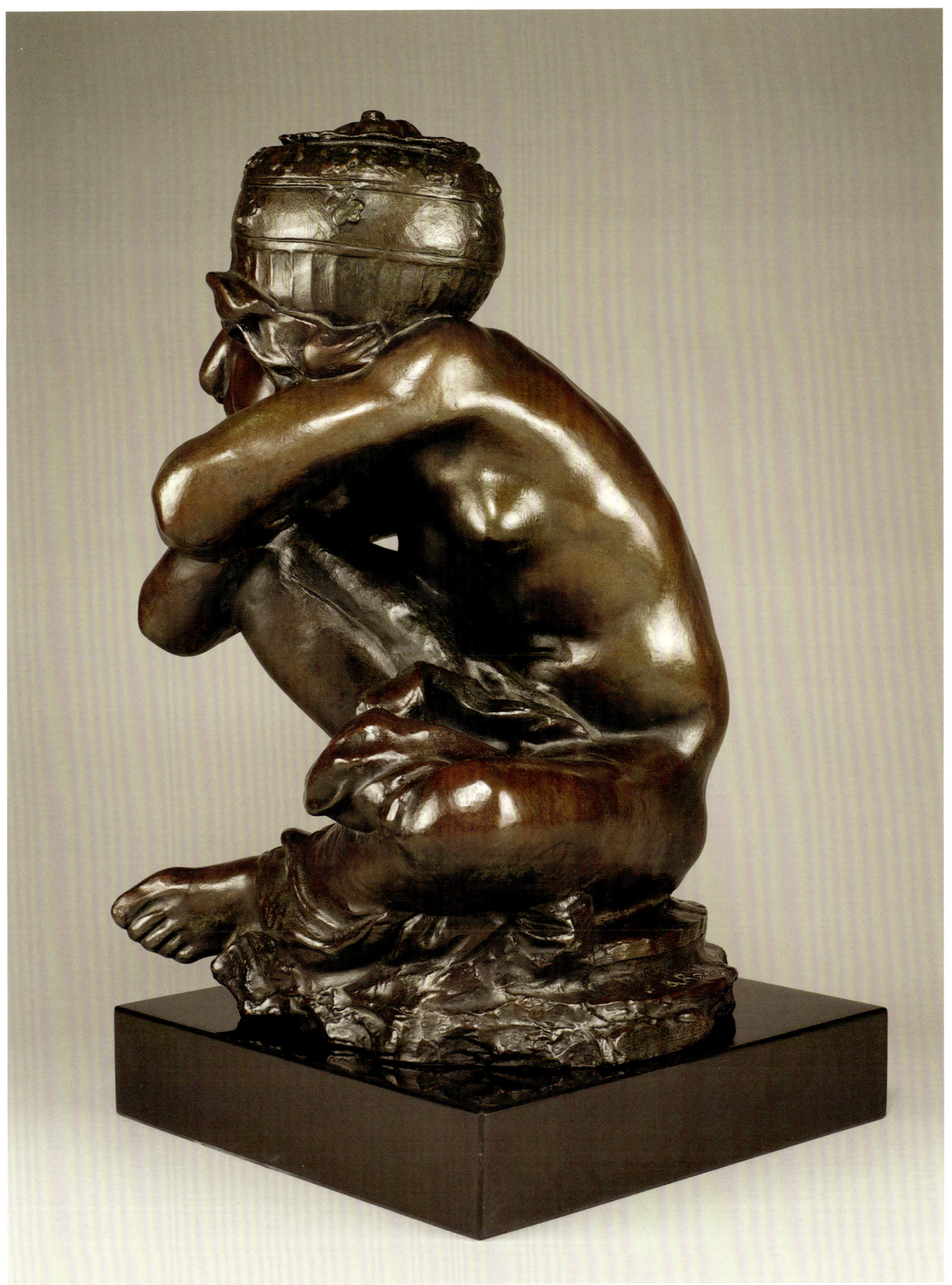

Despair Taken From The Gates

Désespoir de la Porte

Signed A. Rodin with repeat raised internal signature
Inscribed Alexis Rudier Fondeur Paris
Bronze with a rich mid and dark brown patination
Height: 7 inches (17.6 cm)

Provenance:
Musée Rodin, Paris
Private Collection, France
Drouot, Paris, 14 May 2003, Lot 77
Private Collection, France
Robert Bowman Gallery, 2010
Private Collection, USA

Conceived in 1890, this example was cast between 1930 and 1950. According to the Comité Rodin, the work was cast frequently in both plaster and bronze after 1890. The exact number of lifetime casts is unknown. The Musée Rodin continued the edition in 1920 with at least eight casts by the Alexis Rudier Foundry and six casts by the Georges Rudier foundry between 1956 and 1960.

The present version of *Despair*, known as the version from *The Gates of Hell*, is the earliest conception of this model. It can be identified a number of times on the right hand door of *The Gates of Hell* and depicts an elegant nude figure, stretching her left leg above her head whilst clasping her foot with her hand. The figure's face leans forward and her nose almost touches her knee as she hangs her head in despair.

The model, which Rodin later reworked a number of times, gives an insight into his working methods during this period and particularly the way in which he would rework certain models a number of times. Indeed, a revised version of the present model, where the figure's foot is held out in front of her, was modelled independently then re-incorporated into the *The Gates of Hell* (on the left hand door).

The present version proved immensely popular and differed from traditional depictions of Sorrow or Despair, which tended to show figures with their faces buried in their hands or entirely hidden from the viewers gaze. Here the unusual and compact composition clearly delighted both collectors and connoisseurs alike. The work was given a full page spread in a 1904 edition of Julius Meier-Graefe's *Modern Art: Being a Contribution to a New System of Aesthetics*.

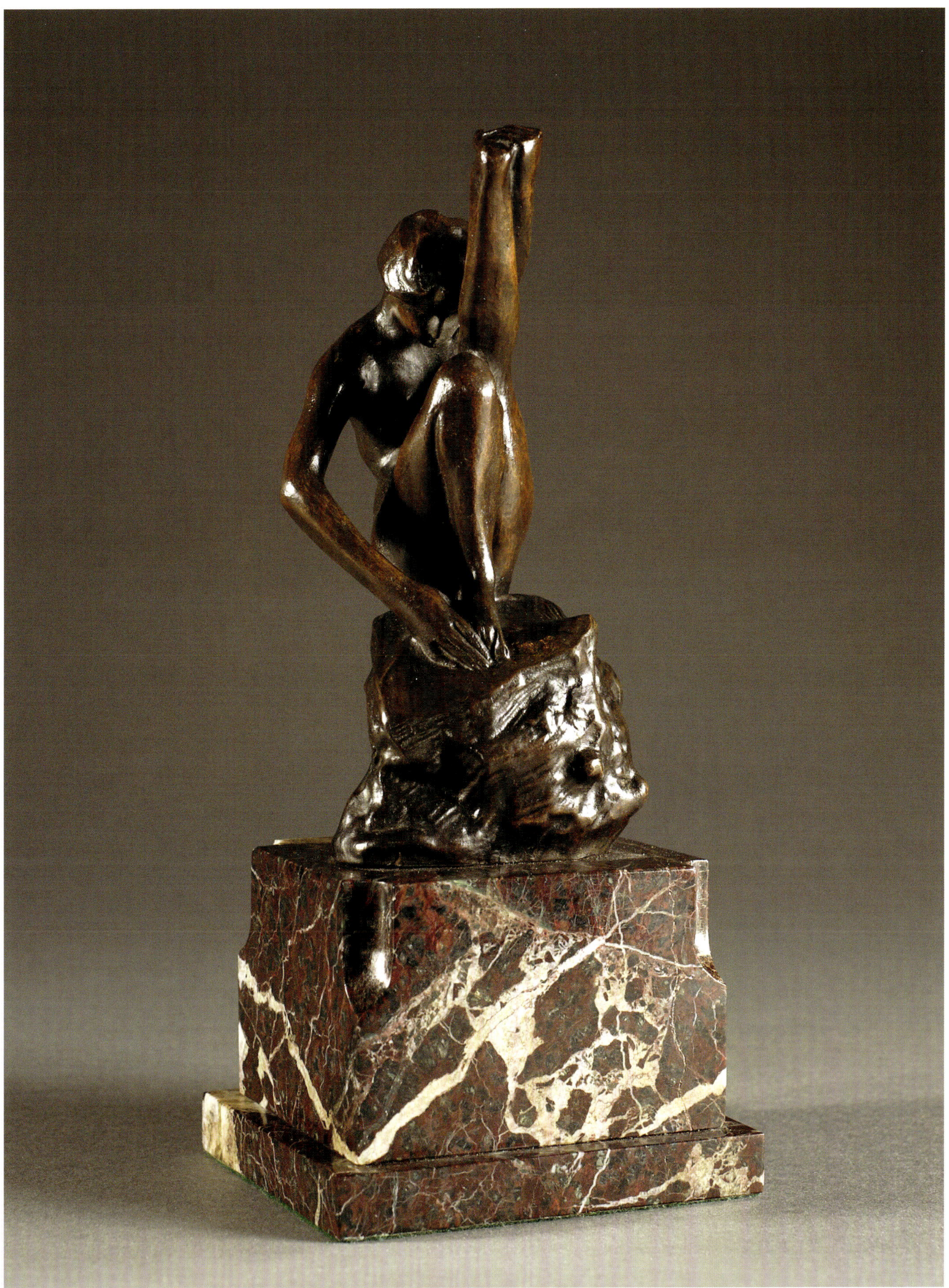

Despair from the Gates (Plaster)

Désespoir de la Porte (Plâtre)

Signed A. Rodin
Plaster with a red and brown patination
Height: 7¼ inches (18.5 cm)

Provenance:
Charles Delanglade, Marseille (gift from the artist, circa 1900)
Thence by Descent
Robert Bowman Gallery, 2011
Private Collection, UK

Conceived circa 1886, this plaster was executed circa 1900.

The Rodin Museum archives hold a letter from André Delanglade, nephew of the sculptor Charles Delanglade, dated January 2, 1927 to Georges Grappe, curator of the Rodin Museum. The letter mentions the numerous works acquired from Rodin by the Marseilles collector Antoni Roux. These works were later given by Roux to Delanglade on the death of his son. The letter states that André's 'uncle Delanglade' also acquired two plasters directly from Rodin. These were a figure of *Despair* (the present example) and *Little Mermaids*, with a dedication to Paul Arene.

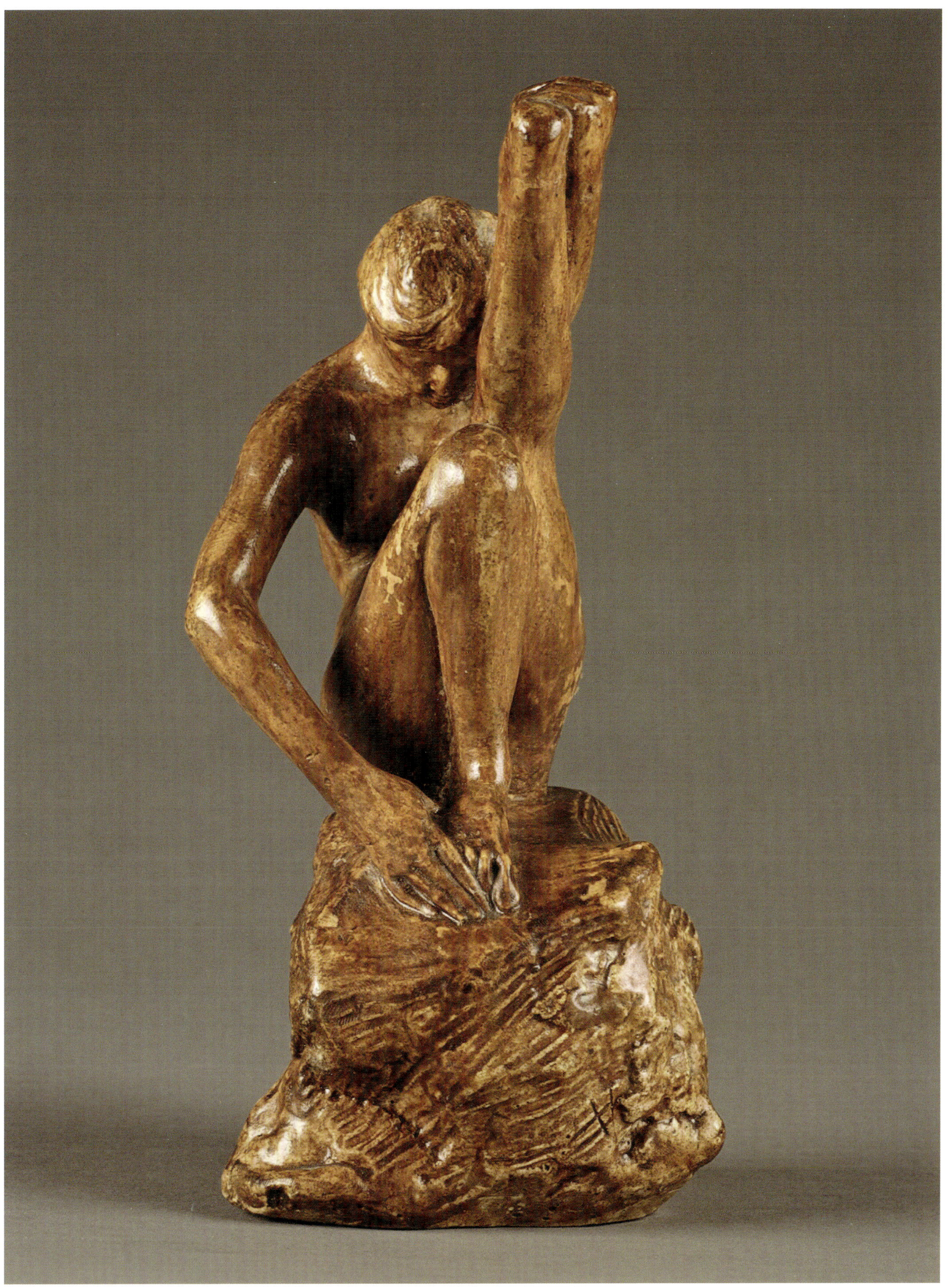

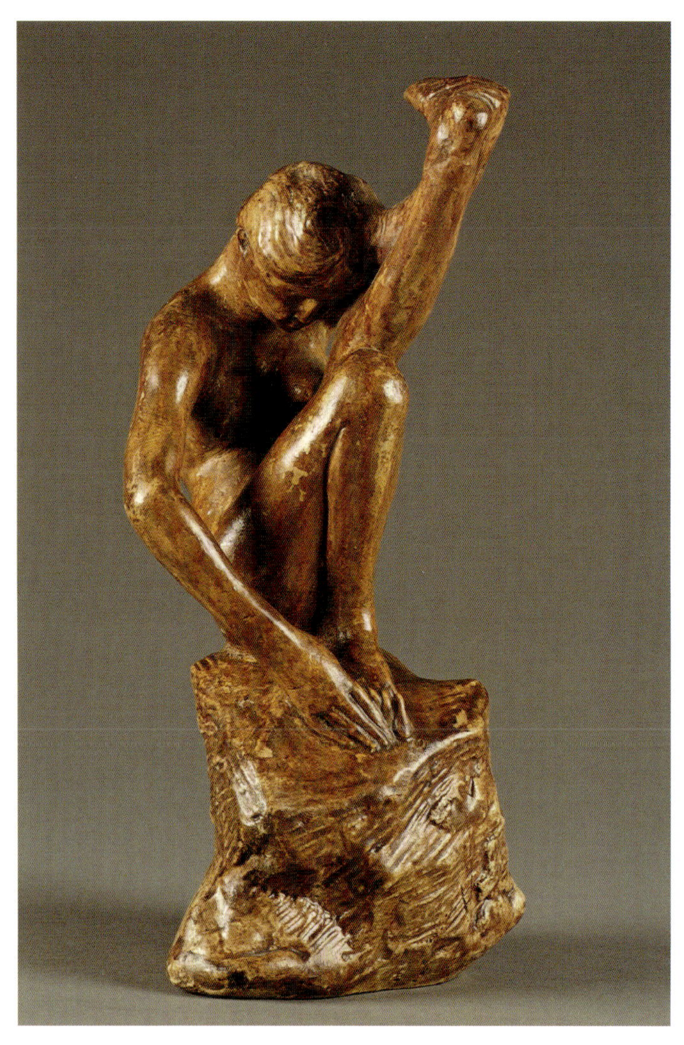
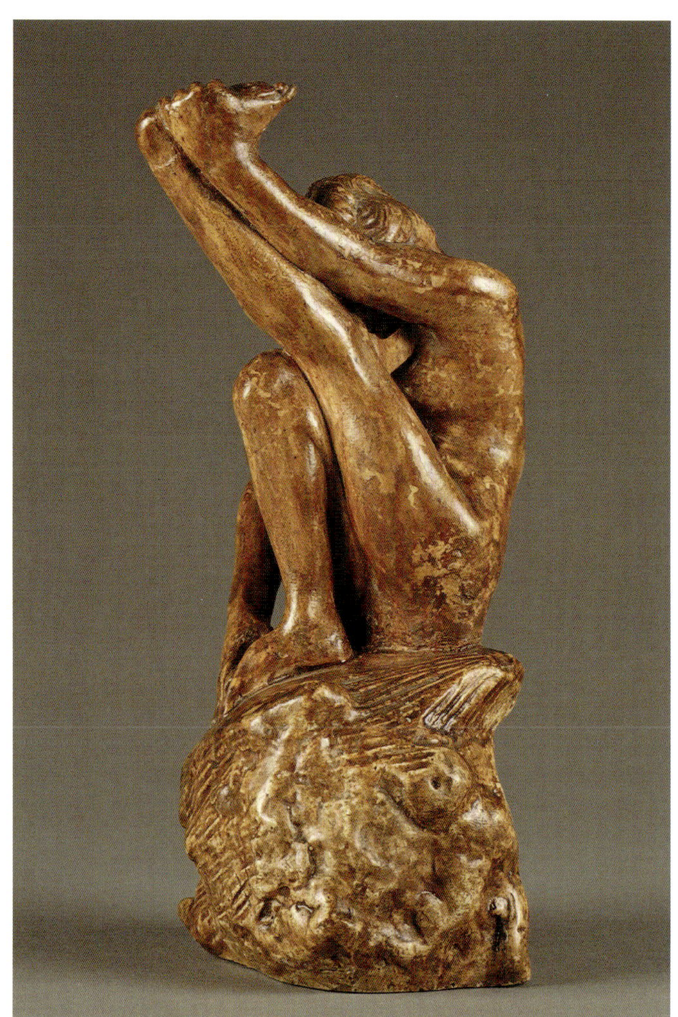

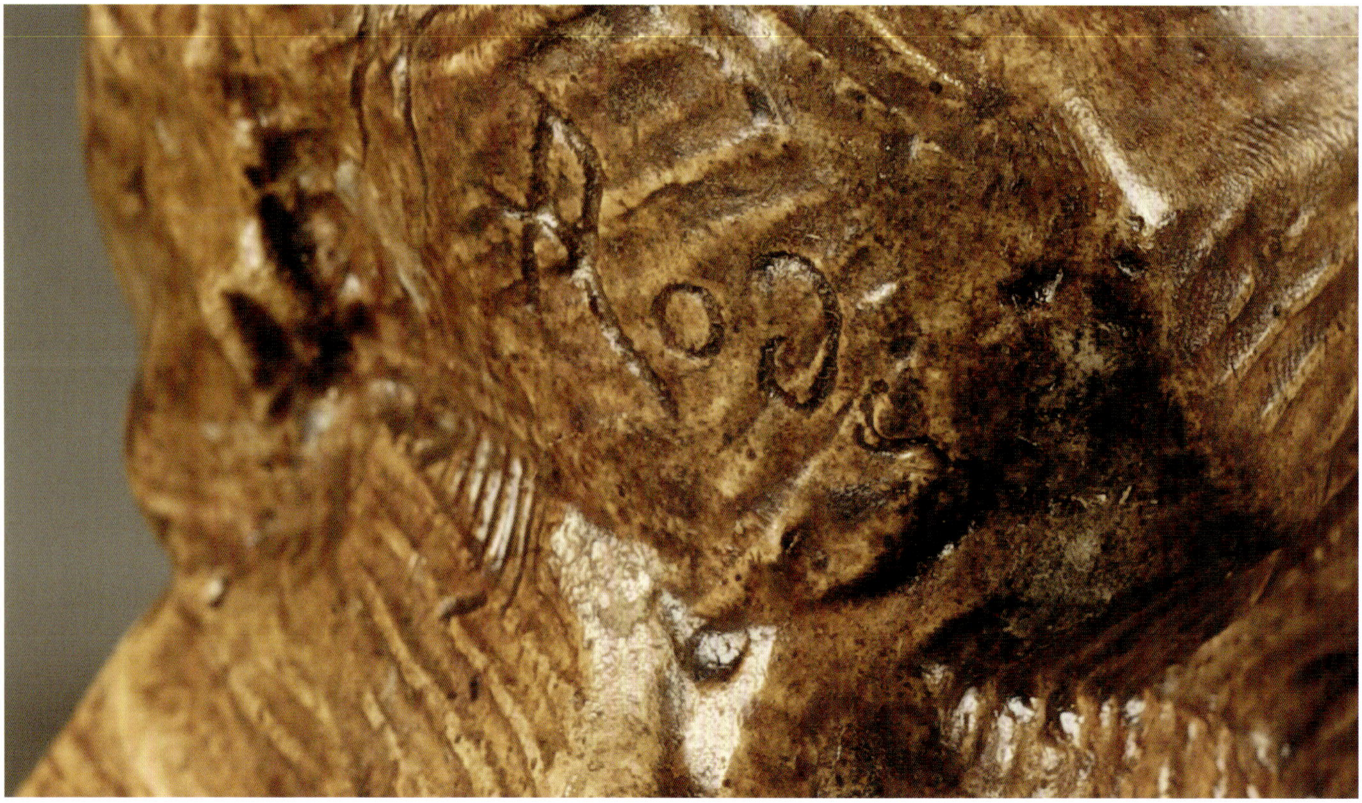

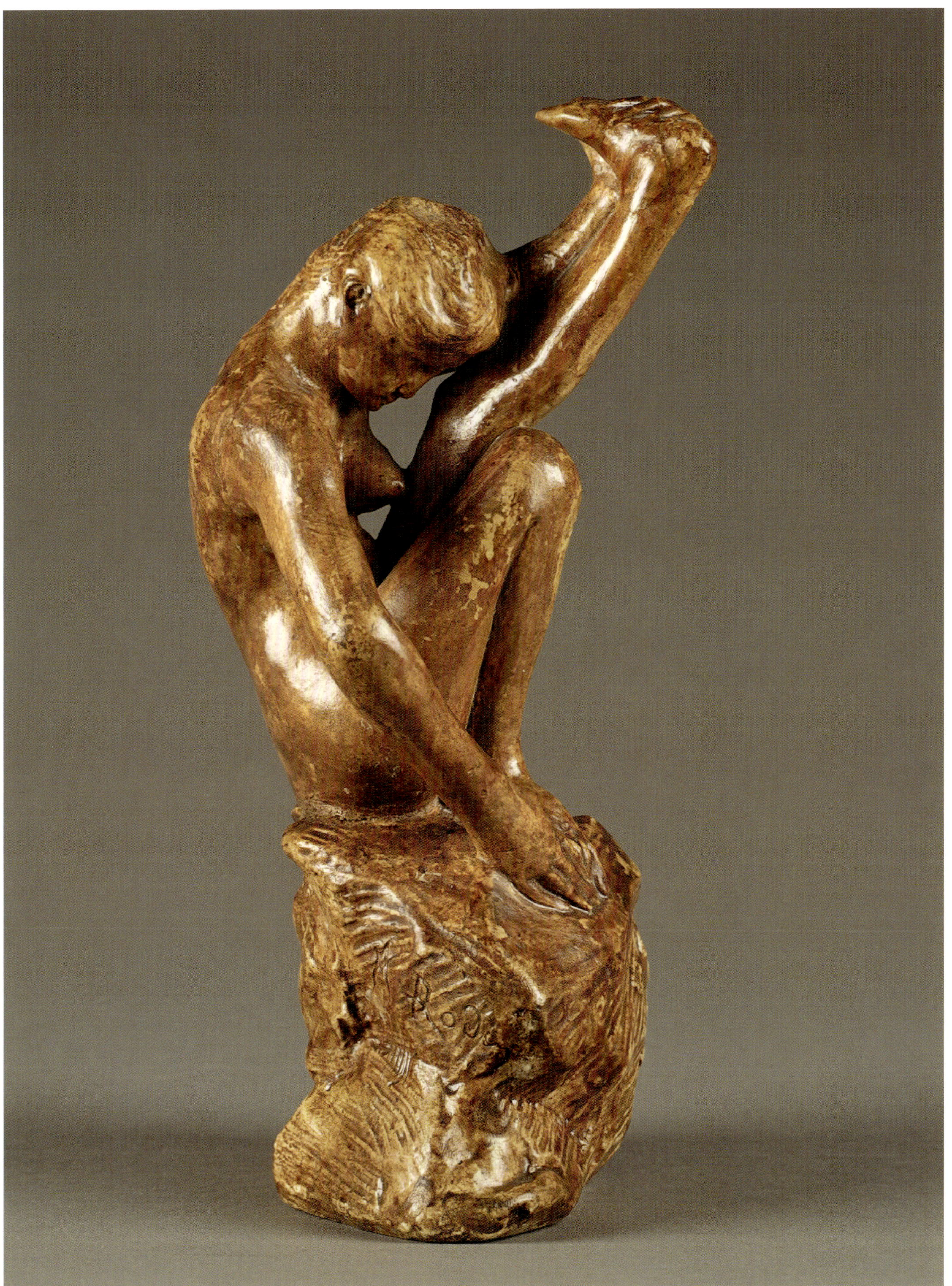

Eve, Small Model – Model with a Square Base and Flat Feet

Eve, Petit Modèle - Modèle à la Base Carrée et aux Pieds Plats

Signed A. Rodin with repeat raised interior signature
Inscribed Alexis Rudier Fondeur Paris
Bronze with a light brown patination
Height: 29⅞ inches (76 cm)

Provenance:
Musée Rodin, Paris
Edmond Courty, Paris
M. Lichenbach, Zürich (acquired from the above in October 1955)
Arthur Stoll, Arlesheim and Corseaux (acquired from the above in October 1955)
Kornfeld, Bern, June 24, 1994, lot 128
Sotheby's, New York, May 9, 1995, lot 98
Private Collection, USA
Robert Bowman Gallery, 2009
Private Collection, Turkey

Conceived in 1881, this example was cast in April 1947. The small version of Eve with a square base and flat feet was immensely popular during Rodin's lifetime. According to the Comité Rodin, it is impossible to know the exact number of casts that were made. However, the Comité estimate that around forty casts were ordered by Rodin and then the Musée Rodin by the following foundries; Froincoise Rudier, Griffoul & Lorge, Perzinka, Alexis Rudier and Georges Rudier. The last cast was made in 1967.

Eve is one of Rodin's most well-known and celebrated sculptures. He began working on a life-size study in 1881, later claiming that he was forced to rework the pelvis of the figure each day, only finally becoming aware that the model was in fact pregnant. According to the sculptor, the model eventually became too tired to pose for long periods in the studio and Rodin abandoned the work, originally perceiving it as unfinished.

Here we see the figure of Eve after her temptation by the Devil, turning inwards to protect her body, aware of her own sin and nudity. The work contrasted with other contemporary depictions of Eve, which tended towards representations of a figure in all of her innocent beauty and before her fall from grace.

After abandoning the life-size model in 1881, Rodin began work on a smaller version of the sculpture. This version, which he modelled both with a round base and square base, differed from the life-size version in the hair, position of the hands and feet. A clay model of this reduction was exhibited in 1883, first in Paris and then London. The work was incredibly well received and Rodin began to commission a series of marbles to be carved. These marbles incorporated minor variations, including the addition of a rocky structure behind Eve.

Following the enthusiasm for the model, Rodin returned to his original life-size plaster in 1899 and exhibited this without any amendments in Belgium and the Netherlands. The same year a life-size bronze cast of this plaster was displayed at the Paris Salon. Between 1901 and 1906 the sculptor commissioned Antoine Bourdelle to carve a colossal stone version of Eve, which was later bought by Carl Jacobsen.

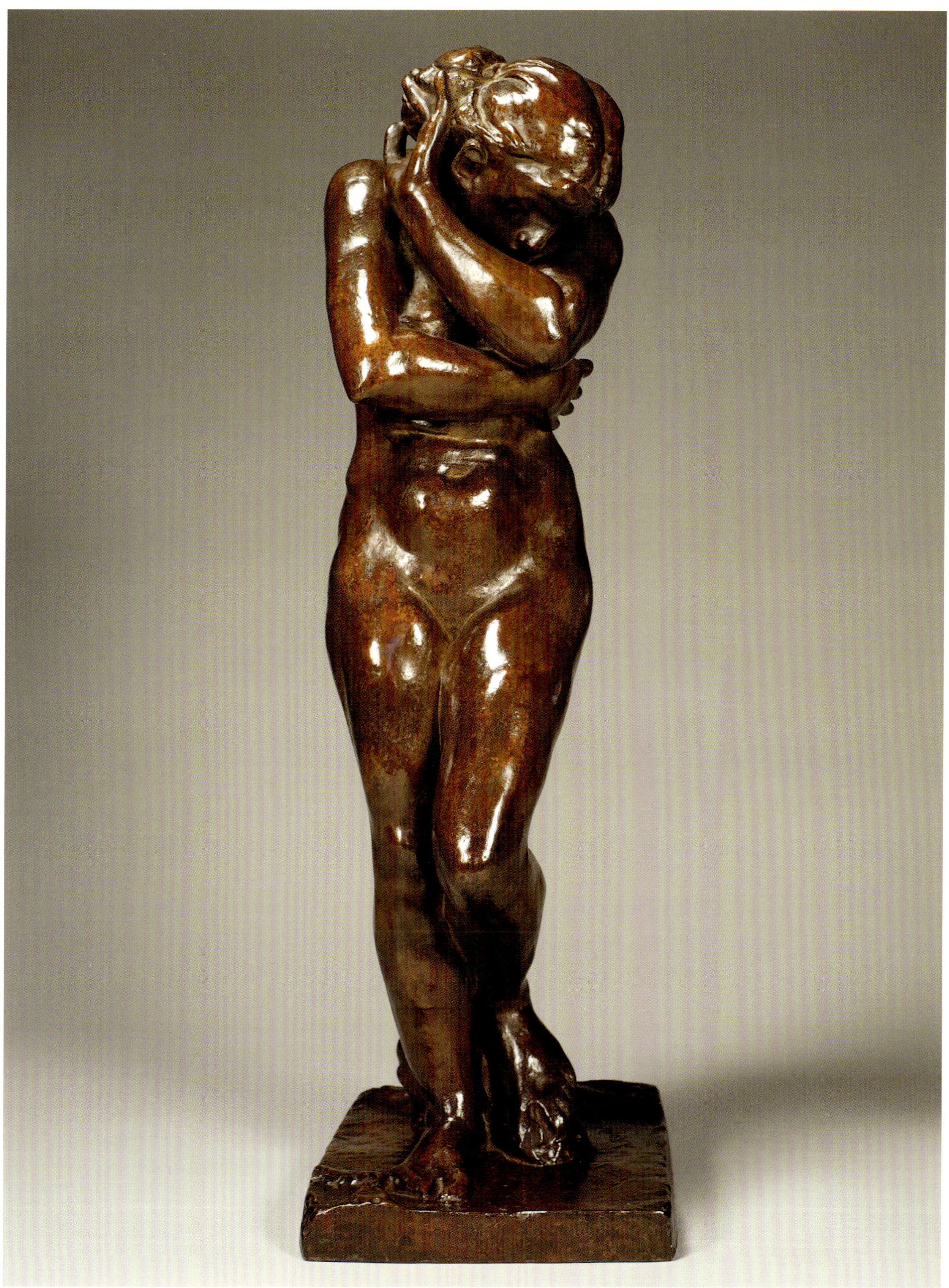

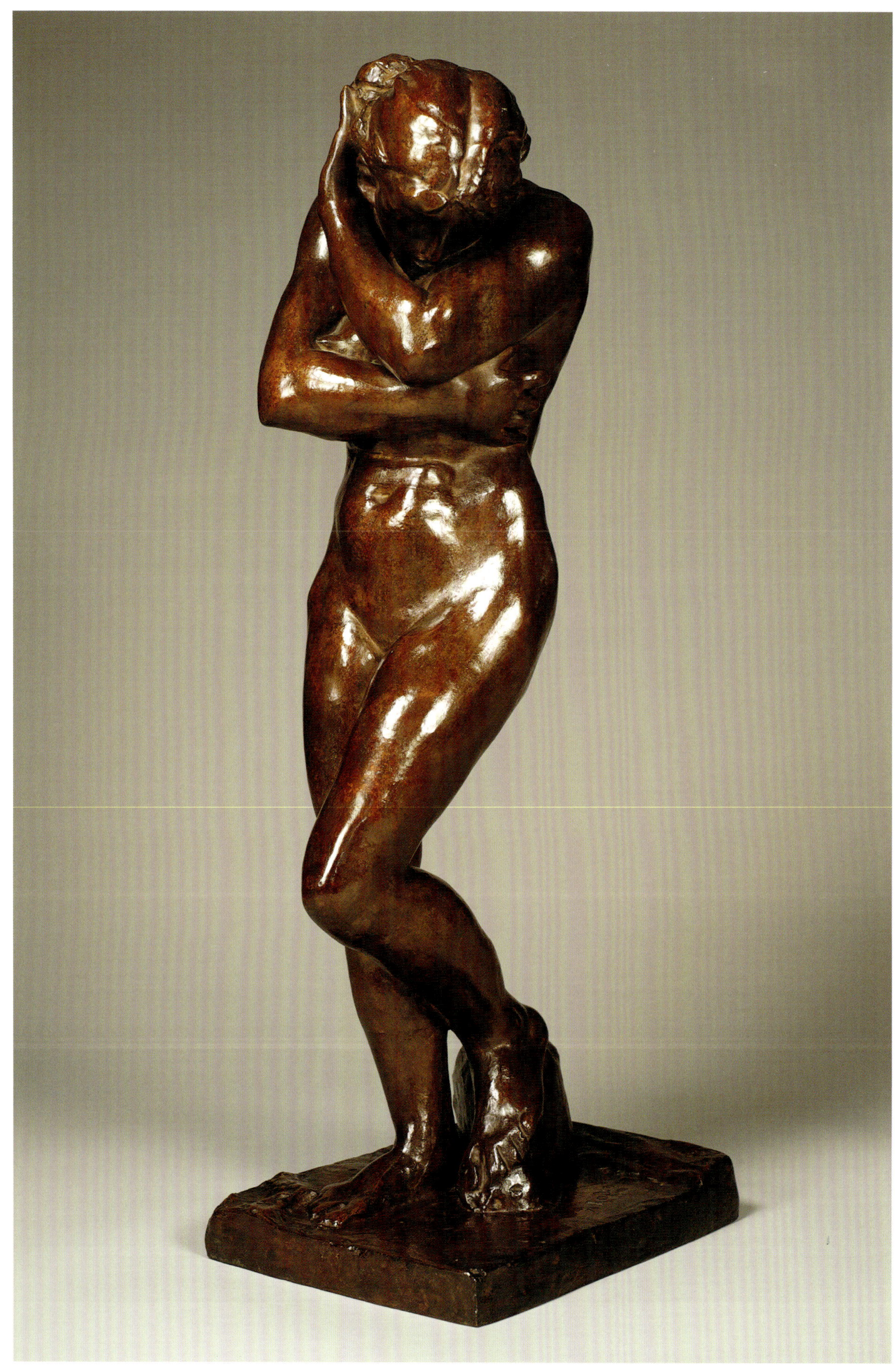

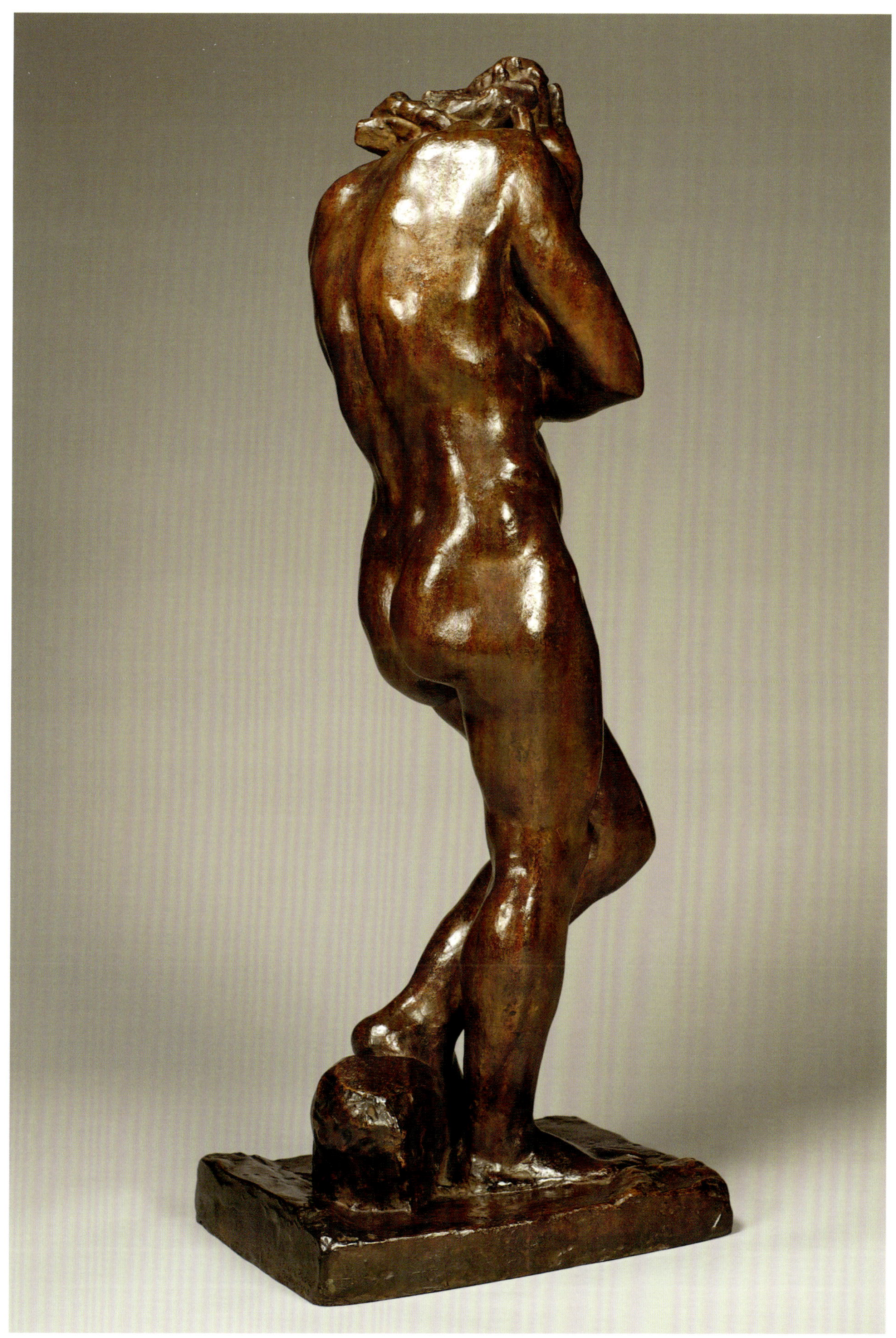

Eve, Small Model, Version with a Round Base

Eve, Petit Modèle, Version à la Base Ronde

Signed A. Rodin
Inscribed Alexis Rudier, Fondeur Paris
Numbered 1
Bronze with a rich dark brown and green patination
Height: 28 inches (71.2 cm)

Provenance:
Musée Rodin, Paris
Collection Saul Rosen, USA
By Descent
Robert Bowman Gallery, 2012
Private Collection, UK

Conceived in 1883, this example was cast in 1927. A single cast of this model was made in 1887. The Alexis Rudier foundry then made four casts for the Musée Rodin. The first two of these casts were made in 1927 (numbered 0 and 1) two further casts were made before 1949.

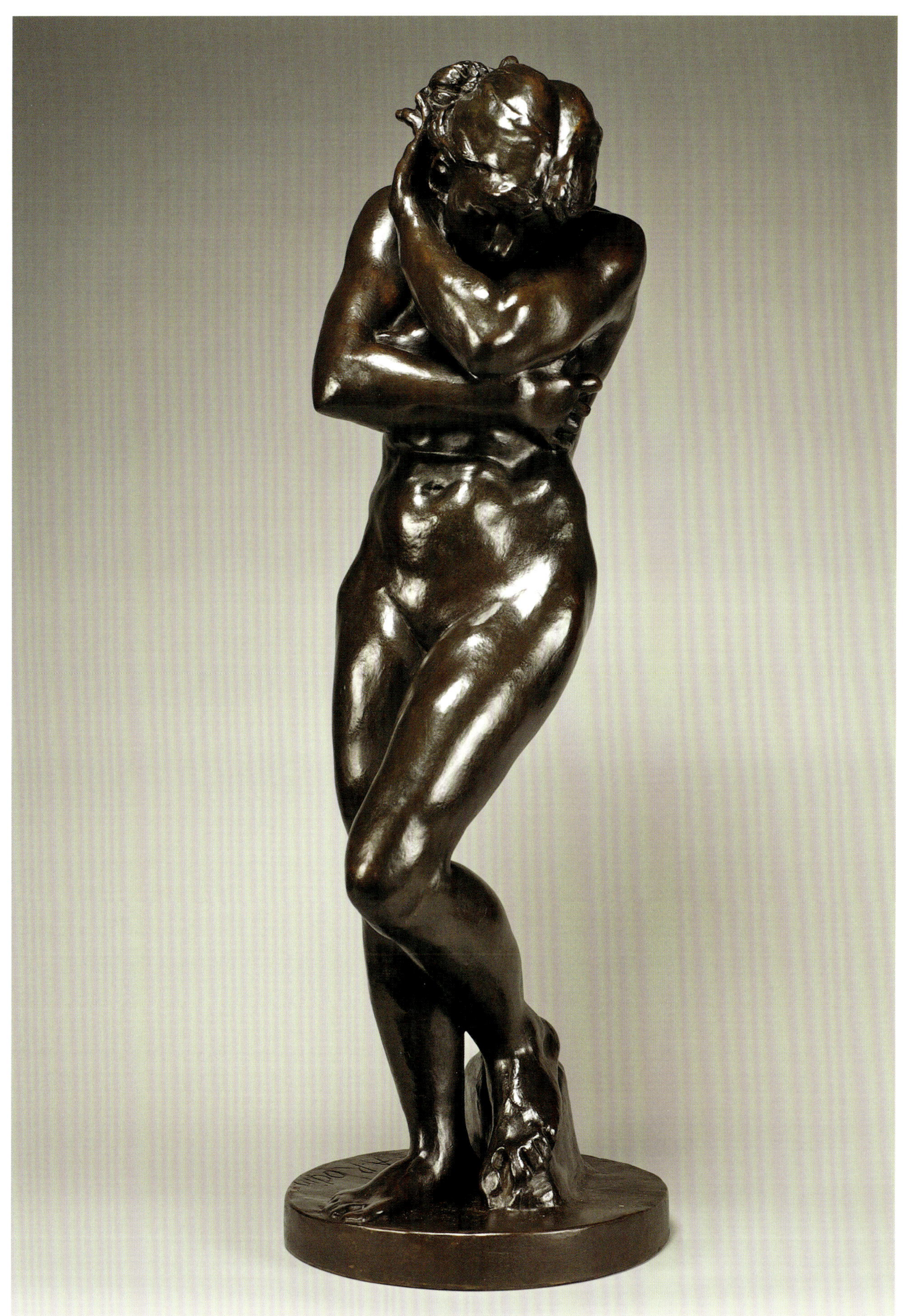

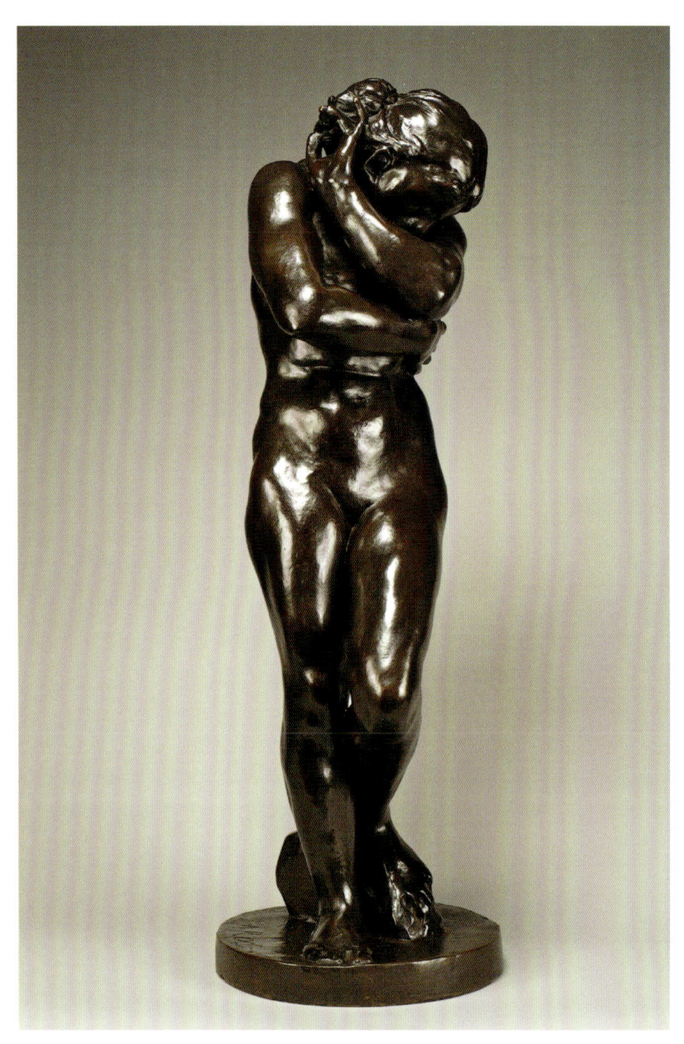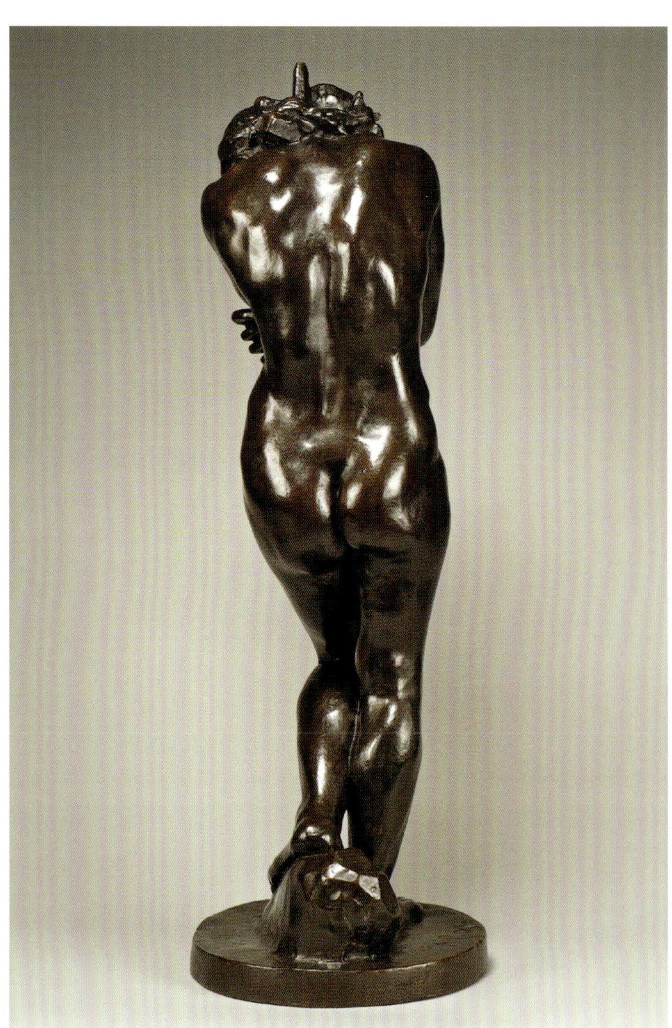

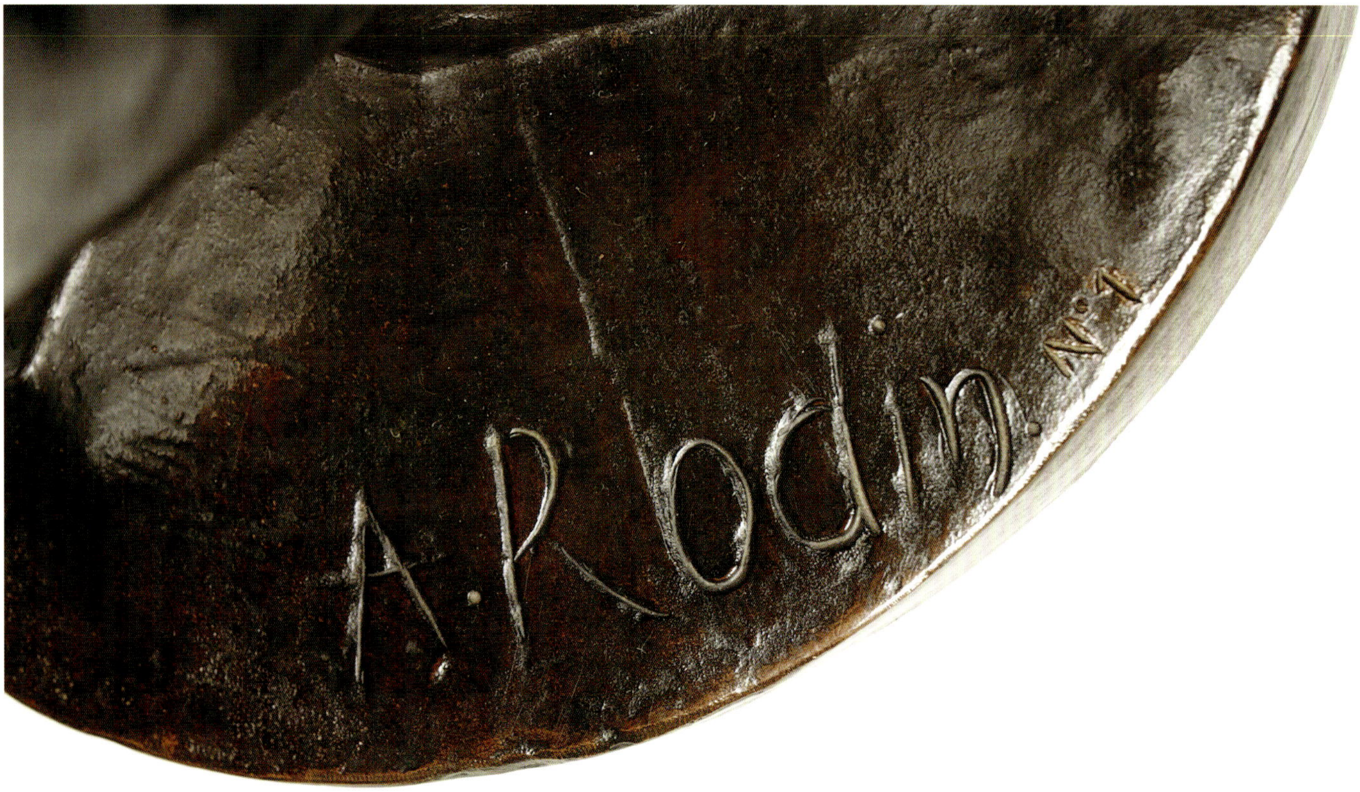

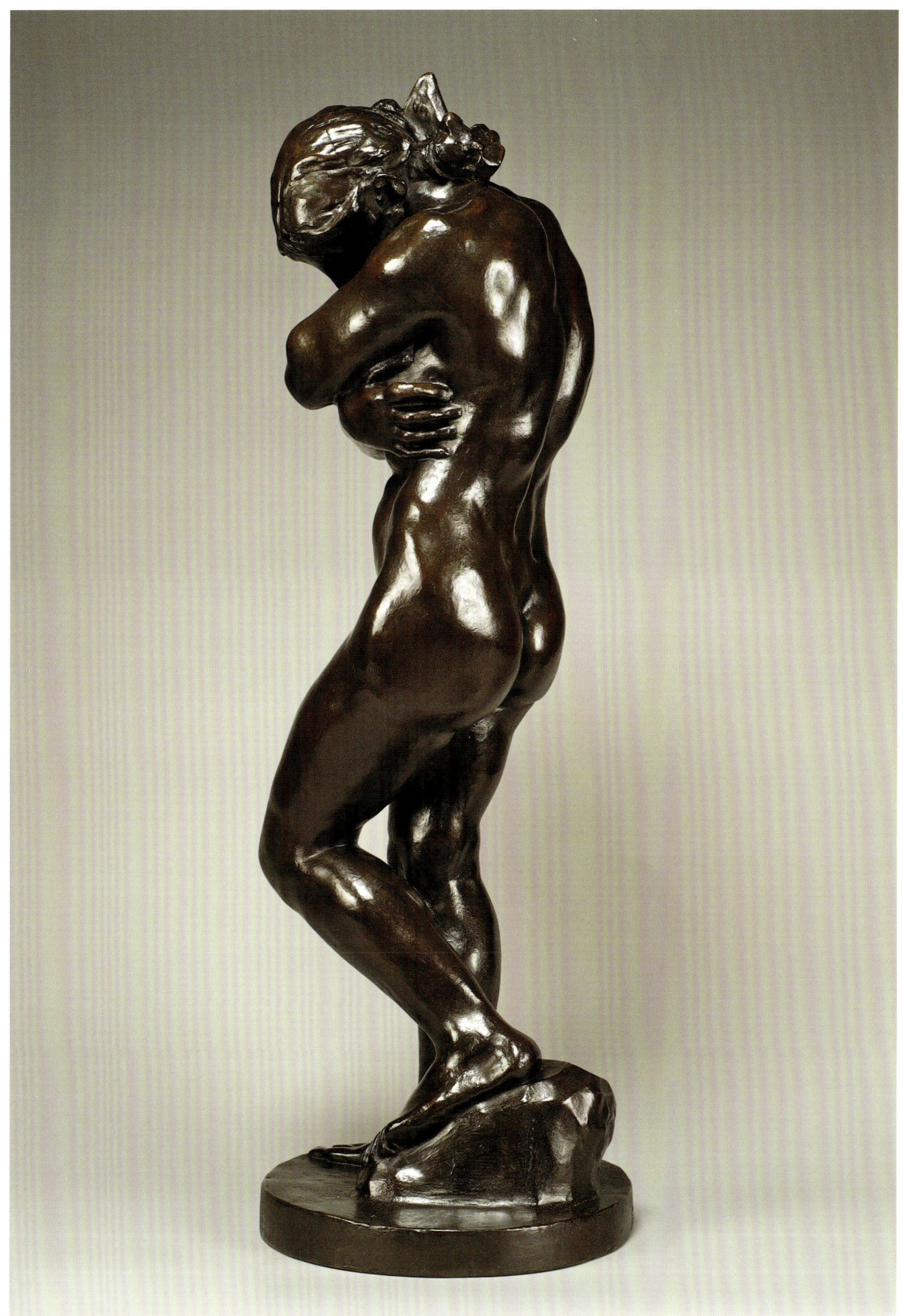

Bather with Sandals

Baigneuse aux Sandals

Signed A. Rodin
Inscribed © by Musée Rodin 1968 and Georges Rudier Fondeur Paris
Bronze with a rich dark green patination
Height: 16½ inches (42 cm)

Provenance:
Musée Rodin
David Jones' Art Gallery Sydney
Dr and Mrs. D.R. Sheumack, Sydney, 1969
Sotheby's Melbourne, 23 November 2008, Lot 27
Private Collection, Melbourne

Conceived in 1898, the present example was cast in 1968. A single lifetime cast was made by the Griffoul foundry in 1898. In total of twelve casts were made for the Musée Rodin. The first three casts by the Alexis Rudier foundry between 1931 and 1954 and then a further nine casts by the Georges Rudier foundry between 1965 and 1981.

In 1898 Rodin sculpted four terracotta female bathers to decorate the niches around the indoor swimming pool at Maurice Fenaille's villa in Neuilly. A pioneer in the oil industry, Fenaille was also an avid collector and a member of the Académie des Beaux-Arts.

After meeting Rodin in 1885, Fenaille became one of the sculptors most supportive patrons and in addition to the four finished works, Rodin also gave Fenaille the study for *Bather with a Tripod*. The present work is a study for one of the finished terracottas that later adorned the niches around Fenaille's pool.

The four of the large terracottas, now in the collection of the Musée Rodin, form part of a series of bathers that begins with the Zoubaloff *Bather*. This much earlier work, modelled before 1888, shows a seated female nude, having apparently just emerged from the water.

In *Baigneuse aux Sandales* Rodin captures the bather wearing sandals, drying herself, after swimming. Much like his other bathers, each of which has a different pose, this loosely modelled work not only highlights the soft sensuality of the female form, but also perfectly captures the movement of the model.

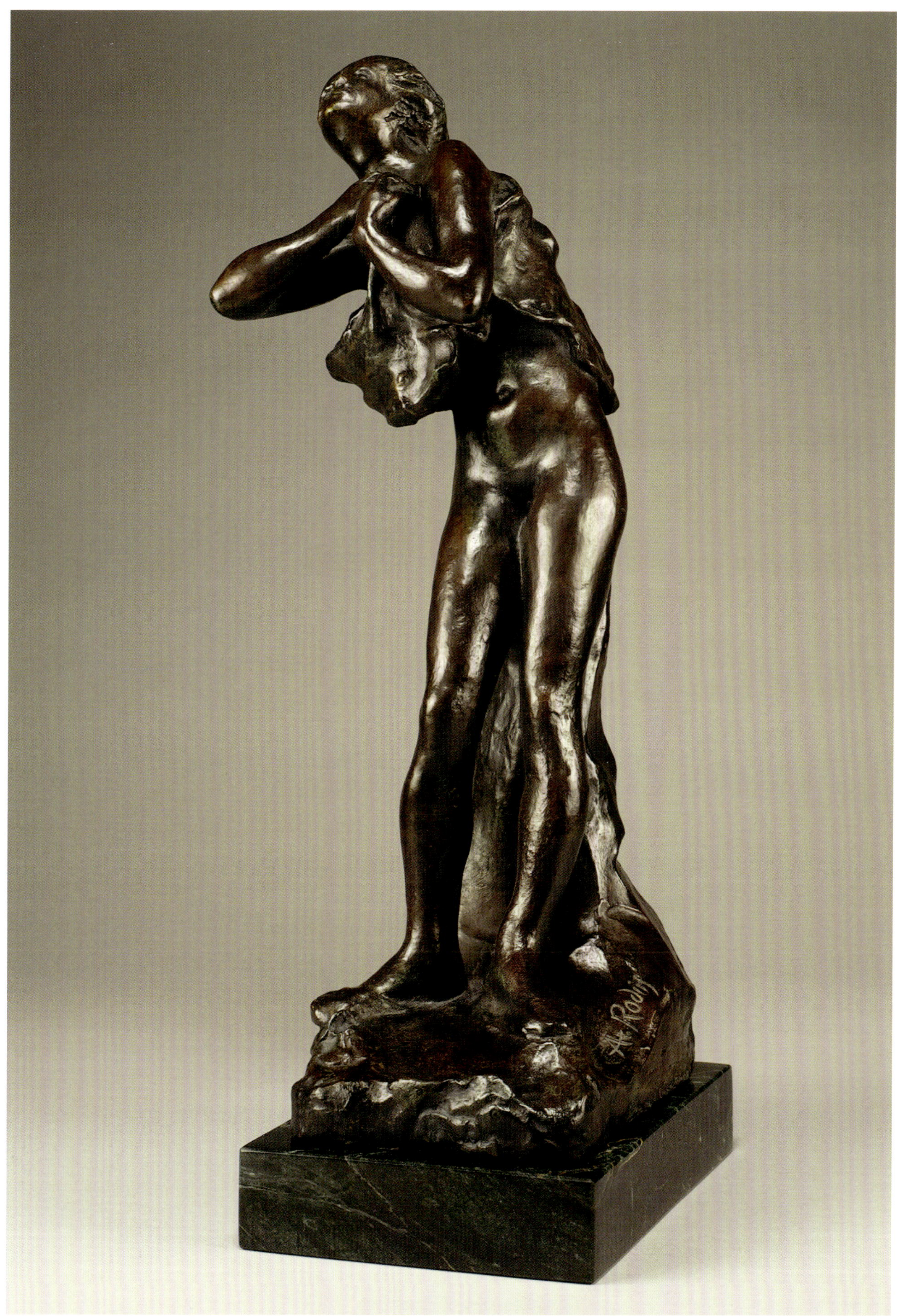

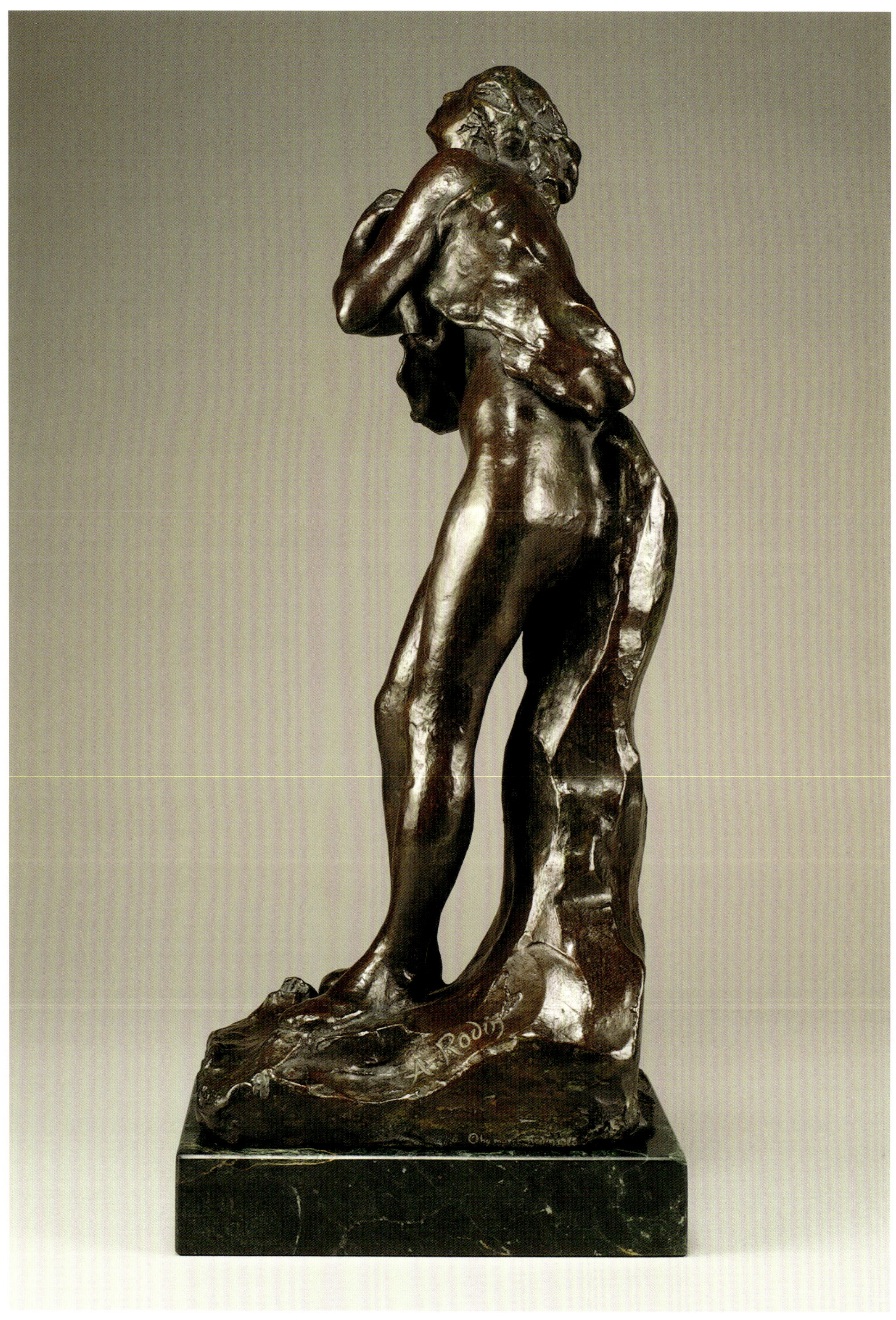

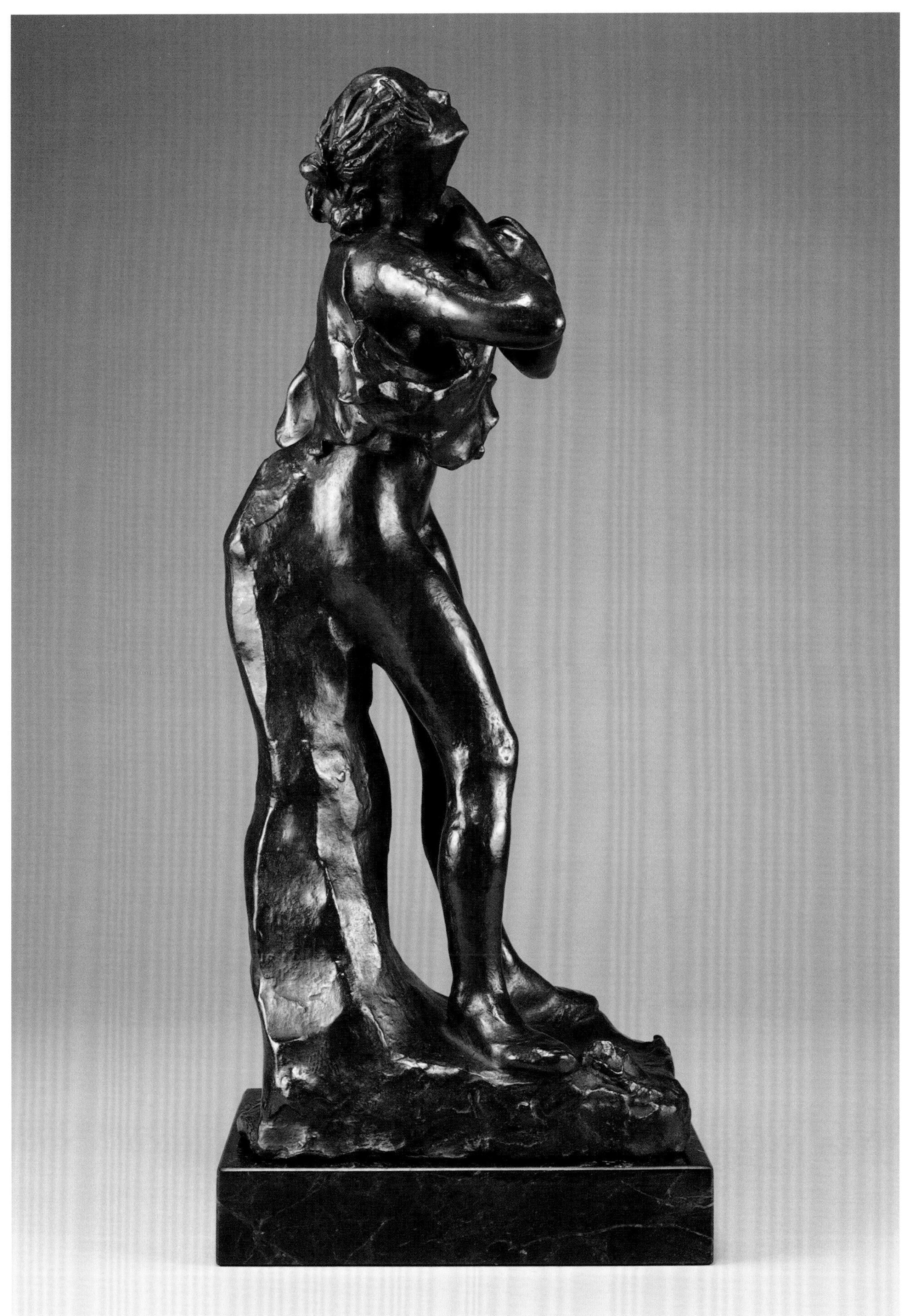

Standing Faunesse

Faunesse Debout

Signed A. Rodin
Inscribed © by Musée Rodin 1956 and Georges Rudier Fondeur Paris
Bronze with a dark brown patination
Height: 23¼ inches (59 cm)

Provenance:
Musée Rodin, Paris
Galerie Vomel, Dusseldorf
Kunsthaus Lempertz, Köln
B. G. Cantor, Beverly Hills, CA
Private Collection, New York, NY
By Descent

Conceived in 1884, this cast was executed in 1956. This model was cast eight times during Rodin's lifetime. The Alexis Rudier foundry made five casts for the Musée Rodin between 1927 and 1945 then the Georges Rudier foundry made eight casts after 1952.

The figure of the fauness, or female faun, can be traced back to the mythology of ancient Rome where the creatures were normally depicted as half woman and half goat. Here Rodin's *Fauness* appears almost entirely human and it is only the somewhat otherworldly facial features that subtly allude to her mythical nature.

In ancient mythology, both fauns and faunesses were known for their love of music and wine as well as their lustful nature. Much like the sculptor's other models depicting Faunesses, here the veiled eroticism of the model and its allusion to female sexuality would not have been lost on his contemporary audience.

Rodin conceived the present model for *The Gates of Hell*. Another similar model, *Kneeling Fauness*, which itself was a variation on *The Awakening*, was also conceived for Rodin's great portal and displays a similar figure in a kneeling position. Rodin included the model in *The Gates of Hell* before 1887, where it appeared to the right of the *Thinker* and next to *Meditation*. In this configuration it acted as the centrepiece of a group of figures known as *The Judgement* in the left part of the tympanum.

The Standing Fauness was first exhibited as an independent work in 1899, when a plaster version was shown in both Belgium and the Netherlands. The work received a rapturous response and the critic Ray Nyst described the model as a 'charming little standing Fauness, stretching her flesh and looking at her body…. She is life like a fresh morning rain'.

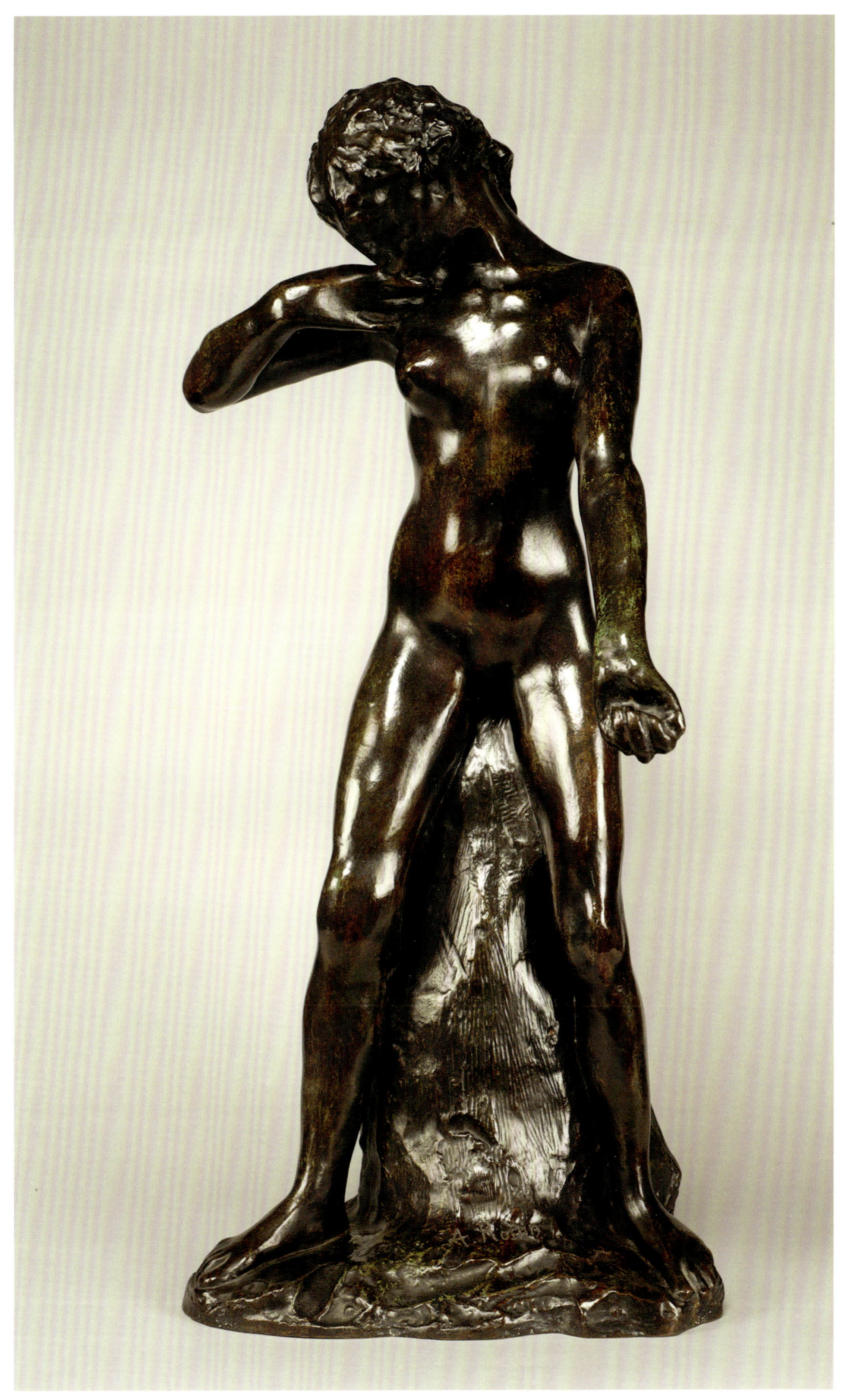

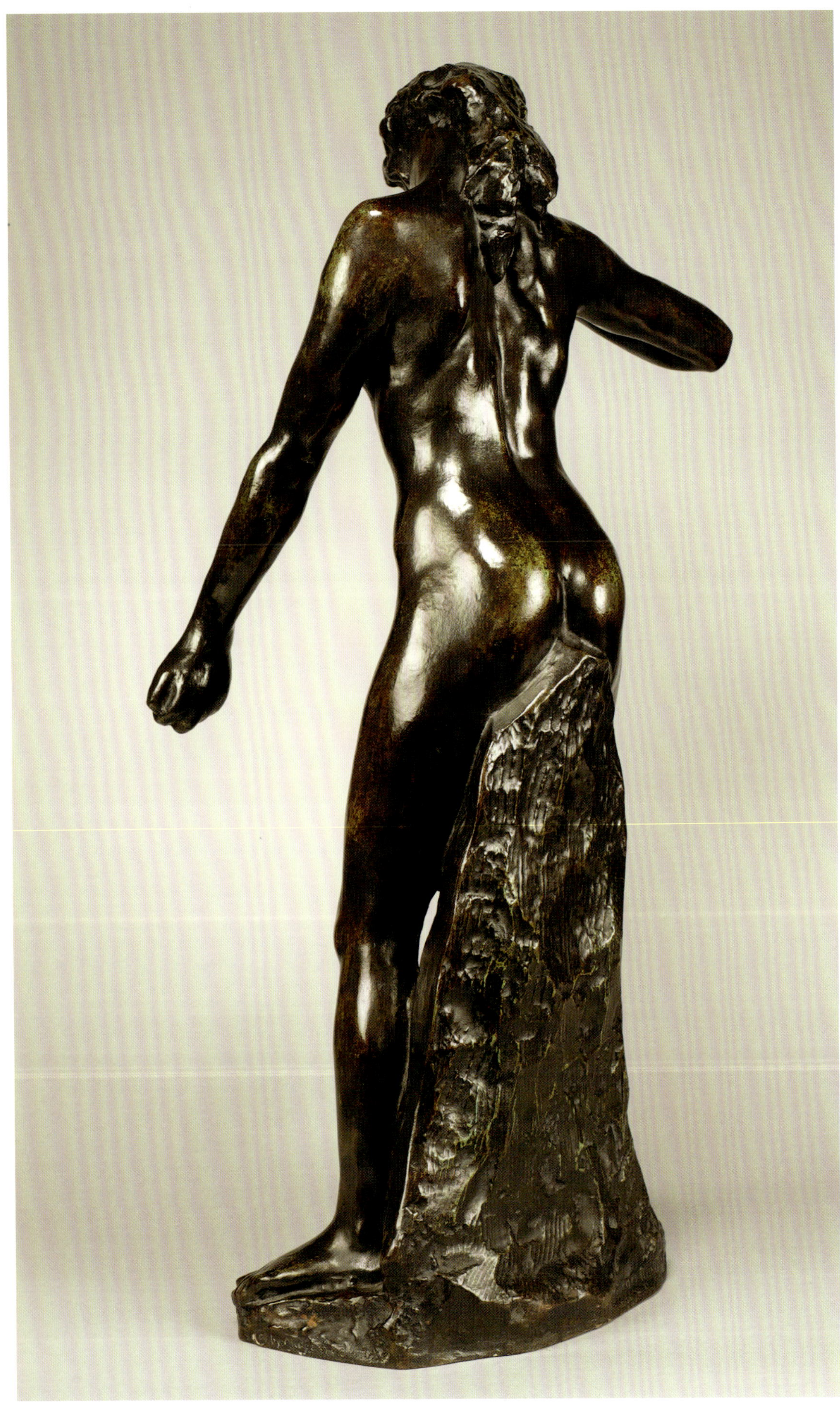

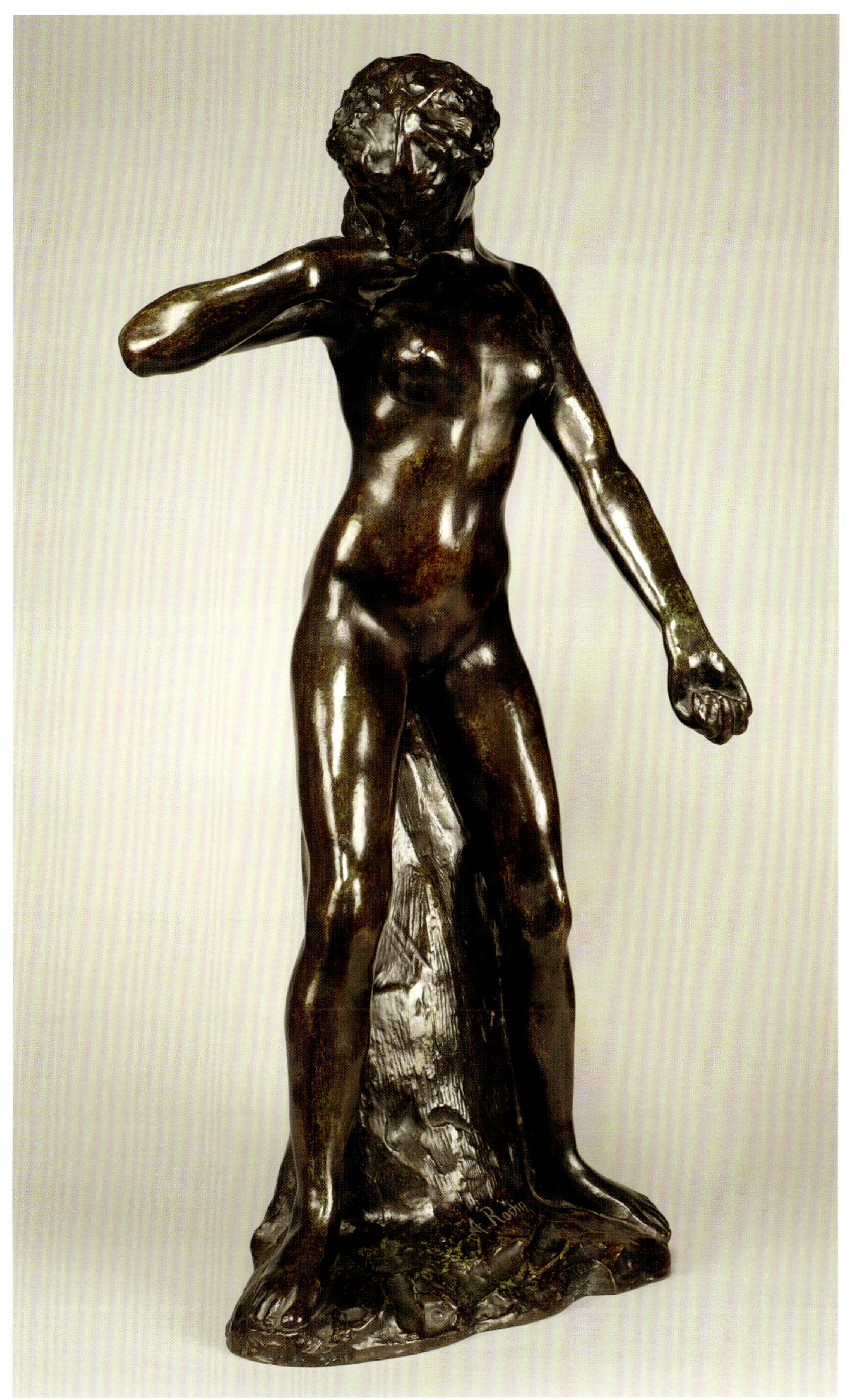

Nijinsky

Nijinsky

Signed A. Rodin
Inscribed © by Musée Rodin 1959
Numbered 8
Bronze with a rich dark brown patination
Height: 7 inches (18 cm)

Provenance:
Musée Rodin, Paris
Roland, Browse & Delbanco, London (acquired from the above, 1959)
Private Collection, USA
By Descent

Conceived in 1912, this example cast in 1959. A single edition of thirteen casts were made for the Musée Rodin by the Georges Rudier foundry between 1958 and 1959.

Vaslav Nijinsky (1889–1950), propelled ballet into the age of modernity with his performances in *Le Pavillon d'Armide*, *Le Spectre de la Rose*, and *Petrouchka*. Celebrated for his virtuosity and for the intensity of his characterizations, he was the subject of many contemporary artists such as Modigliani, Max Jacob, Marc Chagall and of course Rodin.

In 1912, at the Ballets Russes in Paris, Nijinsky choreographed and danced in Debussy's *L'Apres-midi d'un Faune* at the Theatre du Chatelet. Sadly, the performance received negative press and it was said that the 'bewildered public did not applaud'. Gaston Calmette, owner and editor of Le Figaro published a negative article in his newspaper describing the performance as 'erotic bestiality and shameless gestures… the pantomime from the body of a misshapen beast, hideous of face and even more hideous of profile…' which was '…justifiably booed'. Rodin, outraged at this article, attended the show the following night and rushed on stage to congratulate Nijinsky for his performance. In response to Calmette's article, Rodin signed an article written by Roger Marx published in Le Matin in support of the dancer. The very same day, Nijinsky travelled to Meudon to thank Rodin for his support.

In July 1912, before the Ballets Russes left for England, Rodin modelled a sketch of Nijinsky, successfully depicting his distinctive features, highlighting his broad muscular shoulders, prominent cheekbones, and elongated ears.

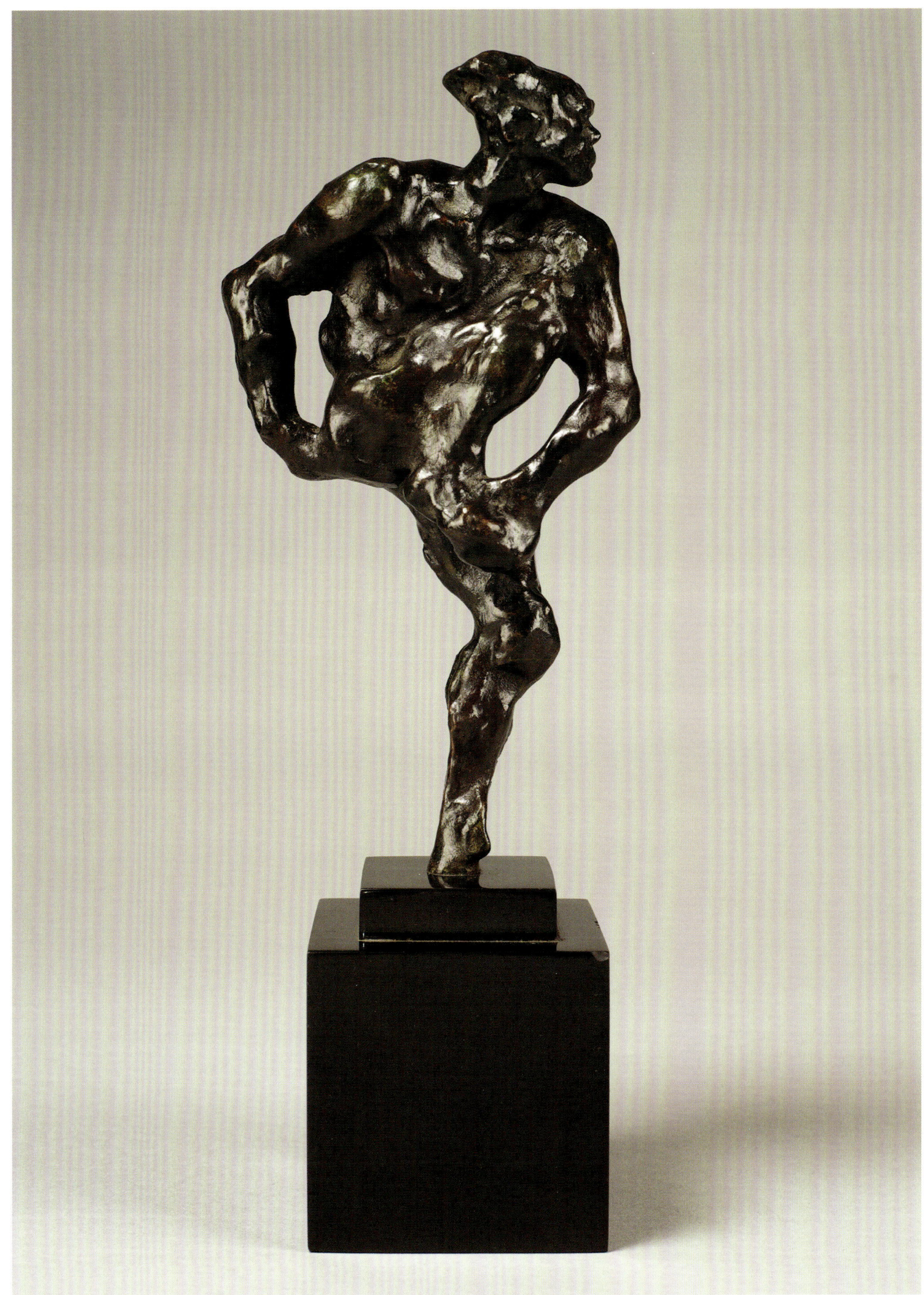

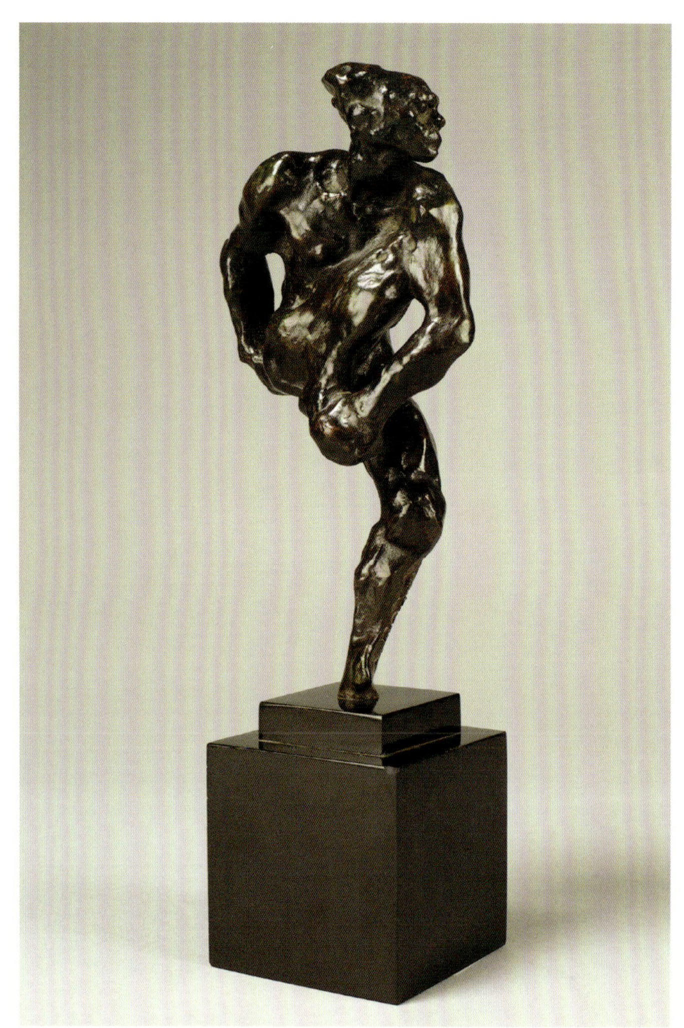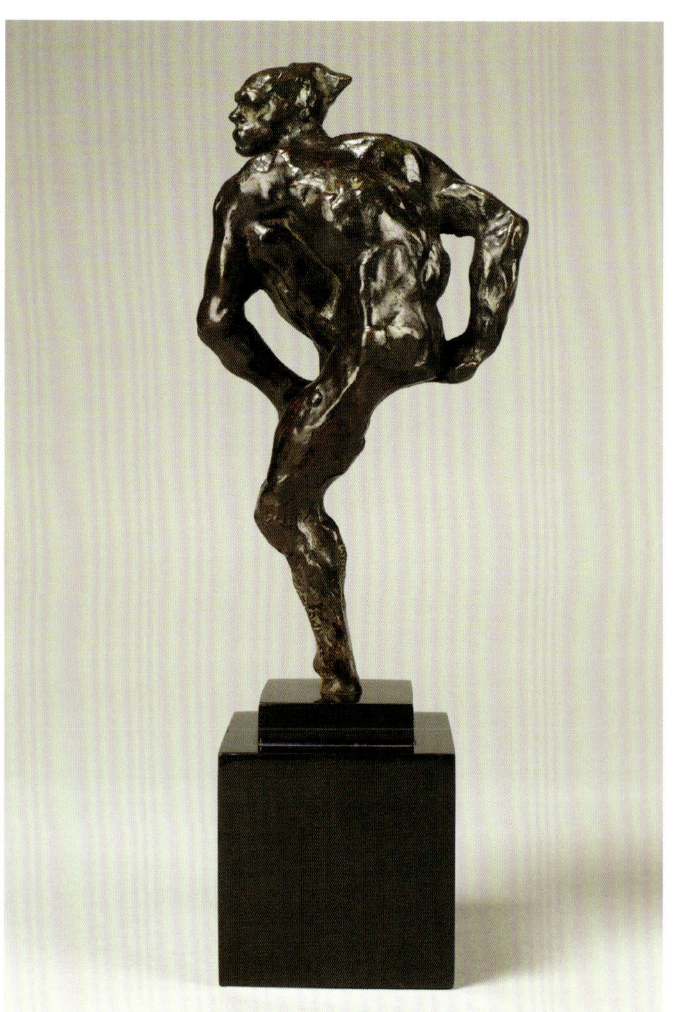

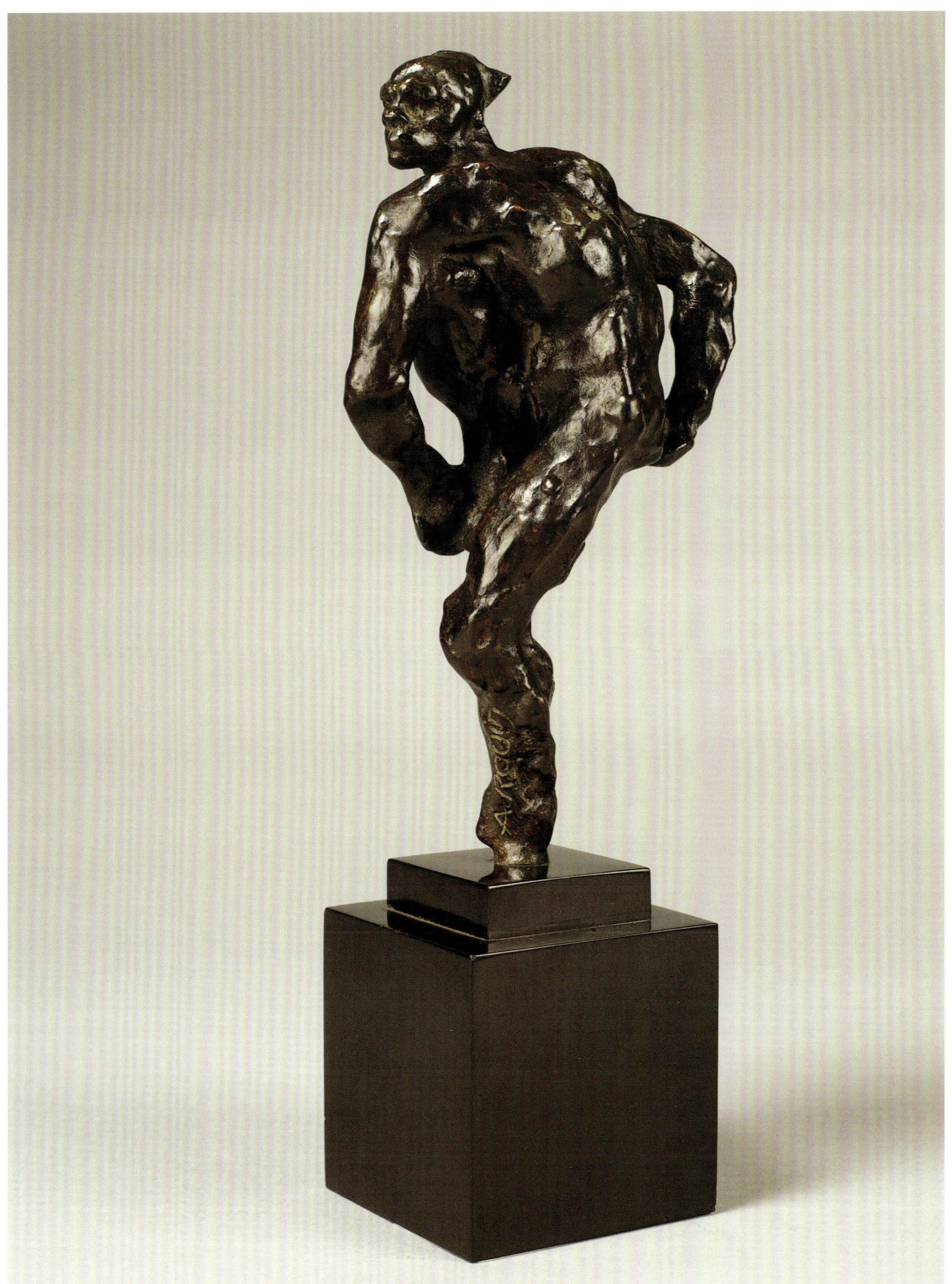

Balzac, Final Study

Balzac, Dernier État

Signed A. Rodin
Inscribed © Musée Rodin 1975 and Georges Rudier Fondeur Paris
Numbered 9
Bronze with a green and dark brown patination
Height: 42¾ inches (108 cm)

Provenance:
Musée Rodin, Paris
Private Collection, NYC (acquired from above)
Robert Bowman Gallery, 2011
Private European Collection

Conceived in 1898, this cast executed in 1975. This work was never cast during Rodin's lifetime. An edition of twelve casts in this size were made for Musée Rodin by the Georges Rudier foundry between 1972 and 1976.

The monument to Balzac was the most controversial sculpture of the 19th century. Rodin was given the commission for the monument by Emile Zola in 1891 and made an intensive study of Balzac iconography and literature before producing over fifty different studies of the bust alone.

Rodin used an unusual technique for the sculpture, modeling the work nude, based on a model called Estager and then draping the sculpture with cloth. In what became this, the final study, Rodin decided to exaggerate Balzac's features to suit the monumental scale of the figure as well as the simplicity of the modeling of the garment.

After seven years of working on the model, Rodin exhibited his final study at the Salon of 1898. In a century accustomed to scandals and public outcries the reception of the work was unparalleled in its violence. The work was rejected by the Société des Gens de Lettres, and Rodin withdrew the work from the Salon. The strength of opinion on the work was such that it divided France into pro- and anti Rodin members.

The commission was given instead to Jean Joseph Falguiere. Rodin's Balzac remained at his studio in Meudon until 1930 when it was cast for the Koninklijk Museum in Antwerp. Then finally in 1939 the Société des Gens de Lettres relented and had the work cast and erected on the corner of the Boulevards Raspail and Montparnasse in Paris.

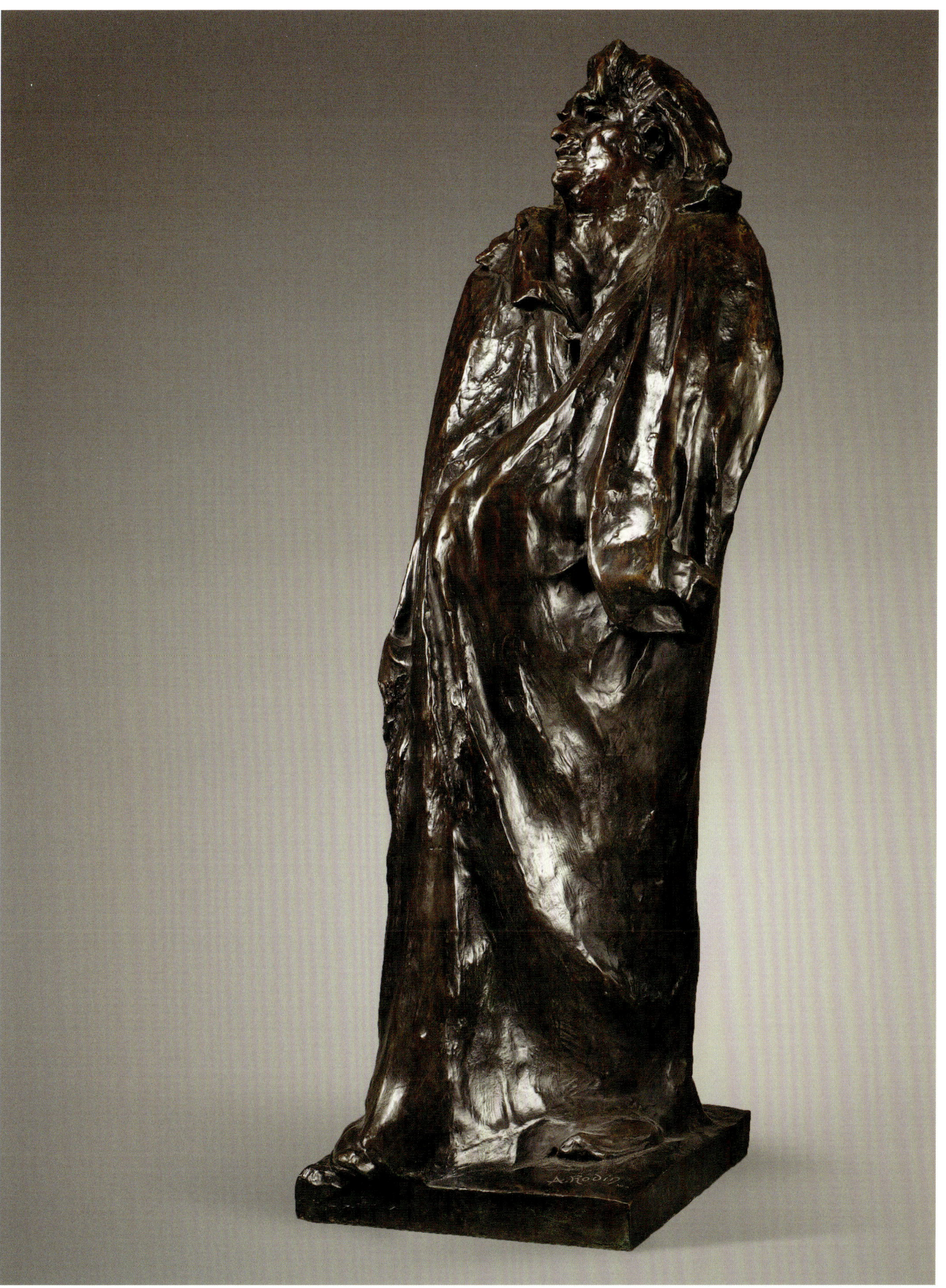

Balzac, Study Type C (Bust), 3rd Version, Large Model

Balzac, Étude Type C (Buste), 3ème Version, Grand Modèle

Signed A. Rodin with repeat raised interior signature
Inscribed Alexis Rudier Fondeur Paris
Bronze with a dark brown patination
Height: 10¾ inches (27.6 cm)

Provenance:
Gallerie Haussmann, Paris
Private Collection, France
By Descent
Robert Bowman Gallery, 2013
Private European Collection

Conceived in 1892, this example was cast between 1918 and 1927. According to the Comité Rodin, at least ten casts of the present work were executed.

Rodin worked on the model for *Balzac* for seven years, creating a number of busts, masks and full figures of the novelist and playwright. The present bust was cast under the direction of the dealer Gustave Danthon between 1918 and 1927. Danthon entered into an agreement with the Musée Rodin in 1918 to produce an edition of the model which had been donated in plaster by Rodin to Dr Joseph Charles Mardrus.

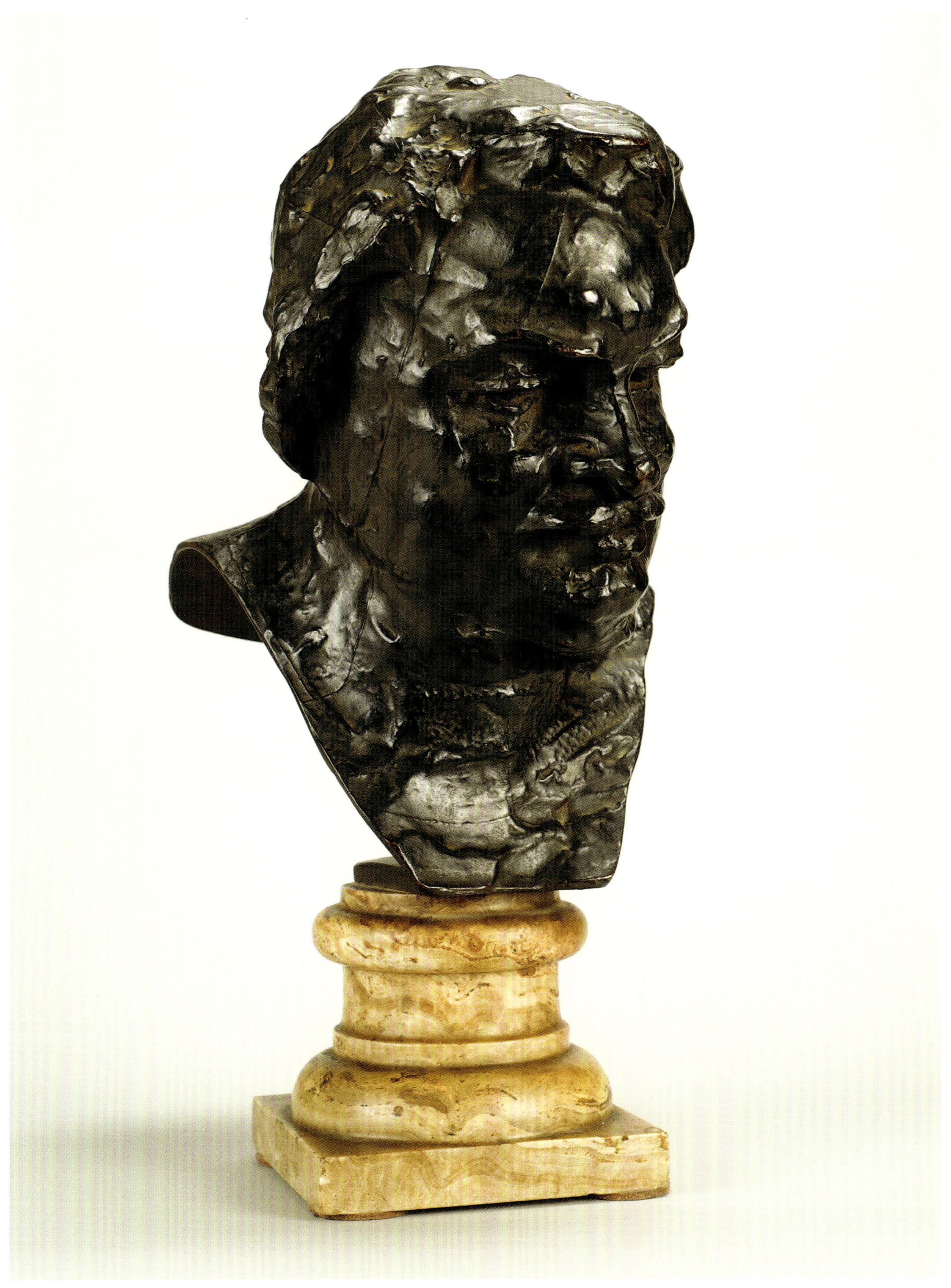

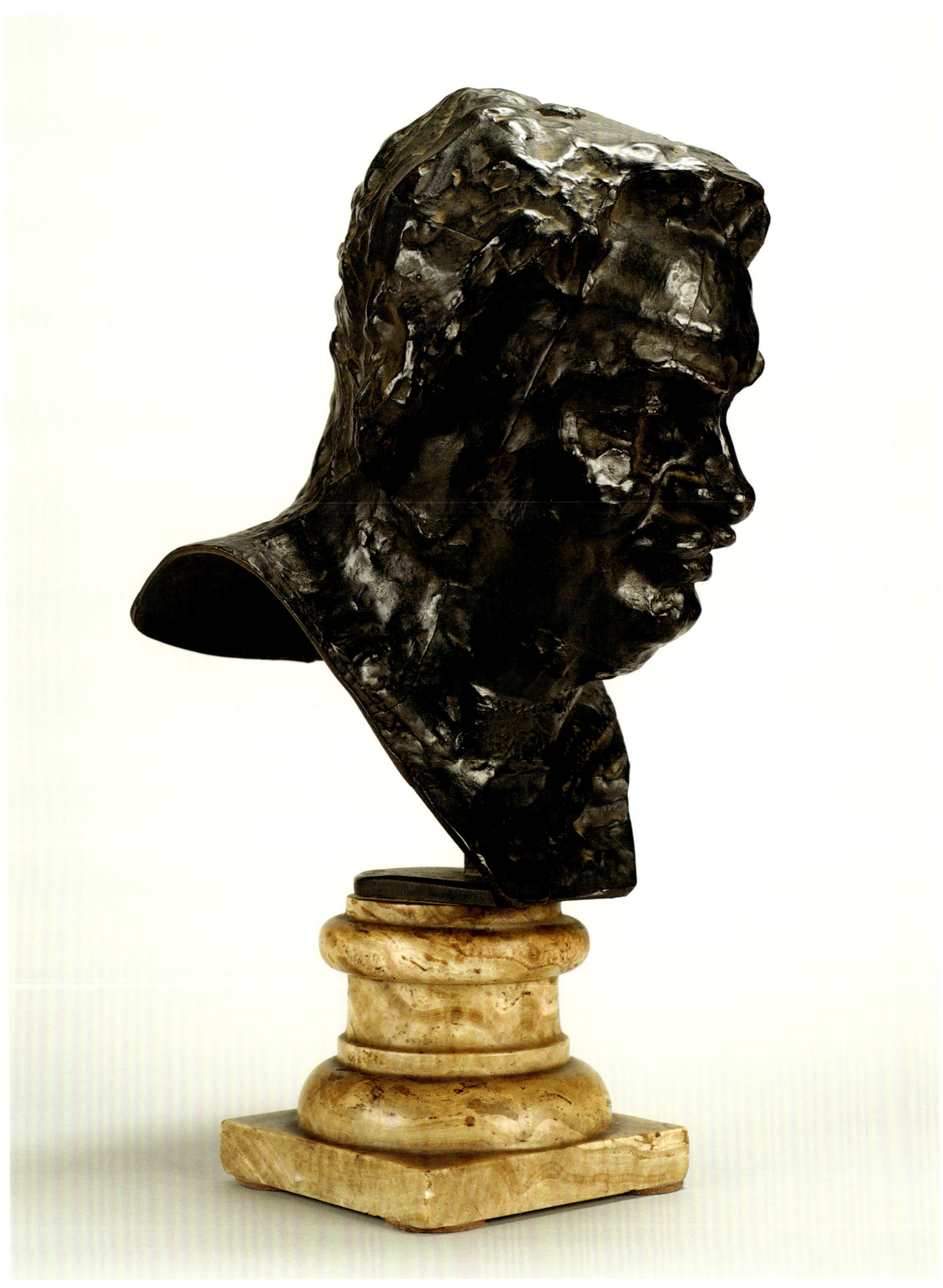

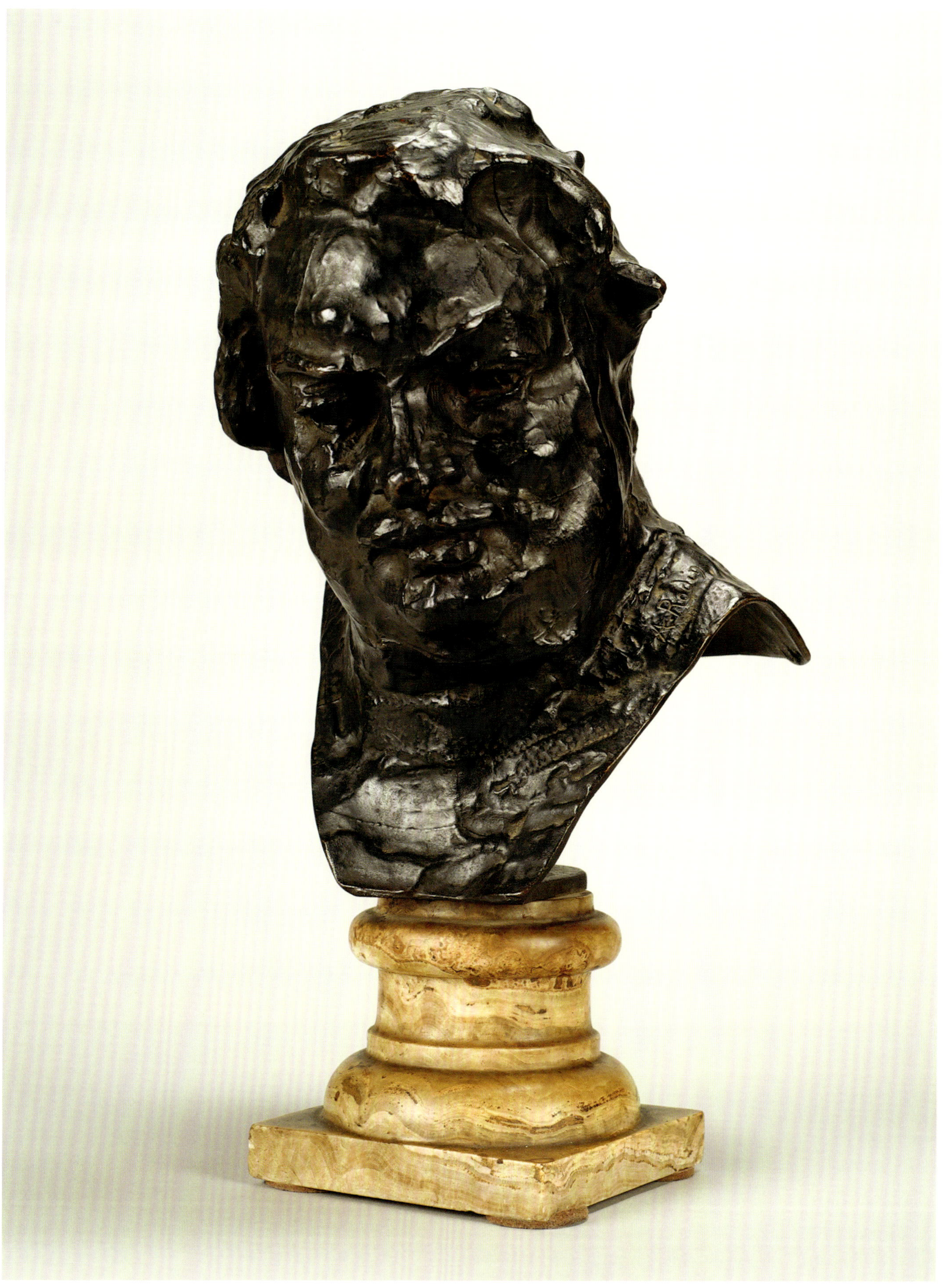

Mask of A Man With A Broken Nose, Type 2 First Model

Masque de l'Homme au Nez Cassé, Version Dite Type II Premier Modèle

Signed A. Rodin twice with repeat raised interior signature
Bronze with a rich dark brown and green patination
Height: 10½ inches (27 cm)

Provenance:
Private Collection, USA
Robert Bowman Gallery, 2010
Private Collection, UK

Originally conceived between 1863 and 1864, this variant was conceived in 1903. The present example was cast in 1910. According to Comité Rodin due to the number of variations of the present work it is impossible to know the exact number of casts that were made.

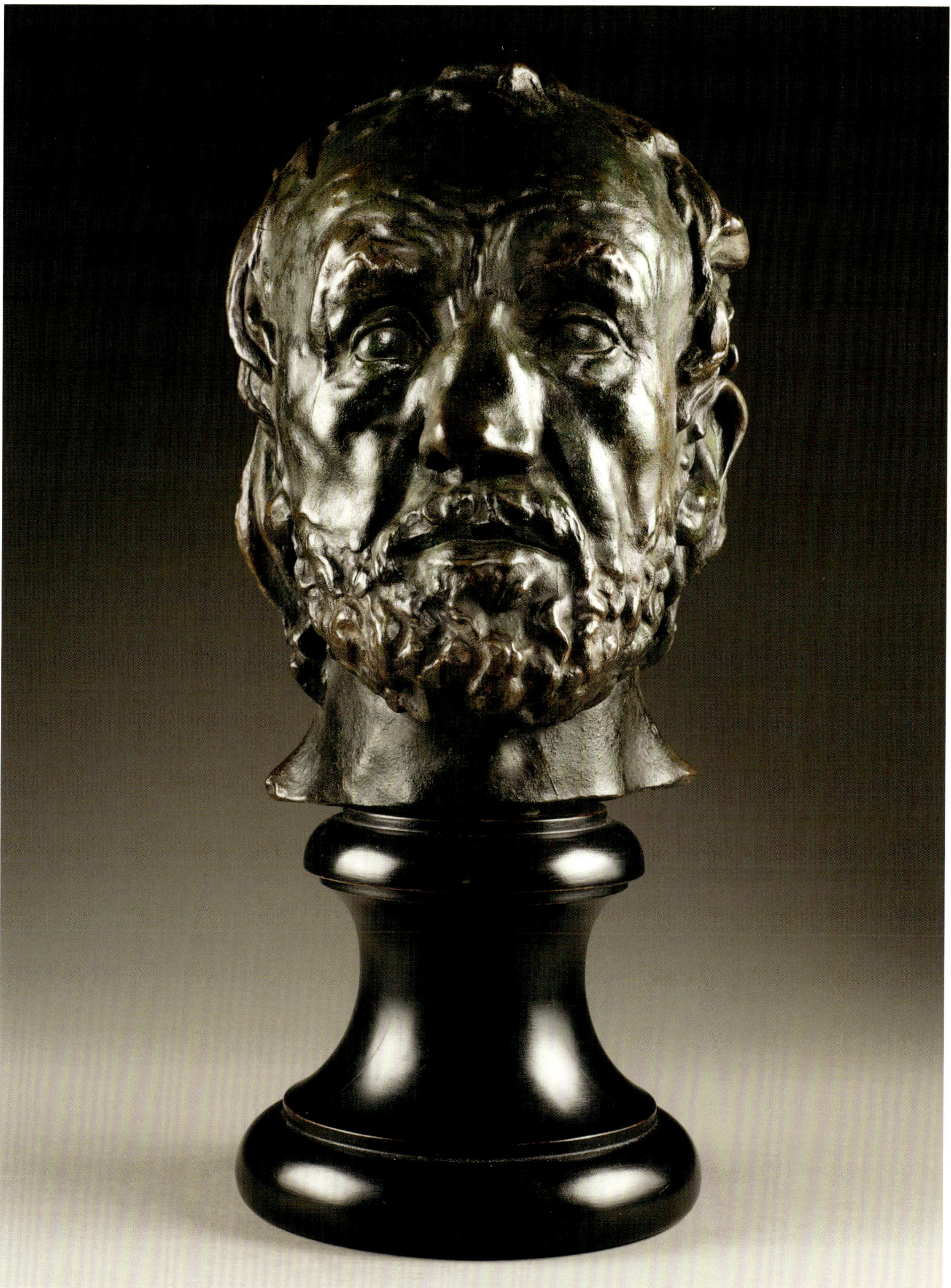

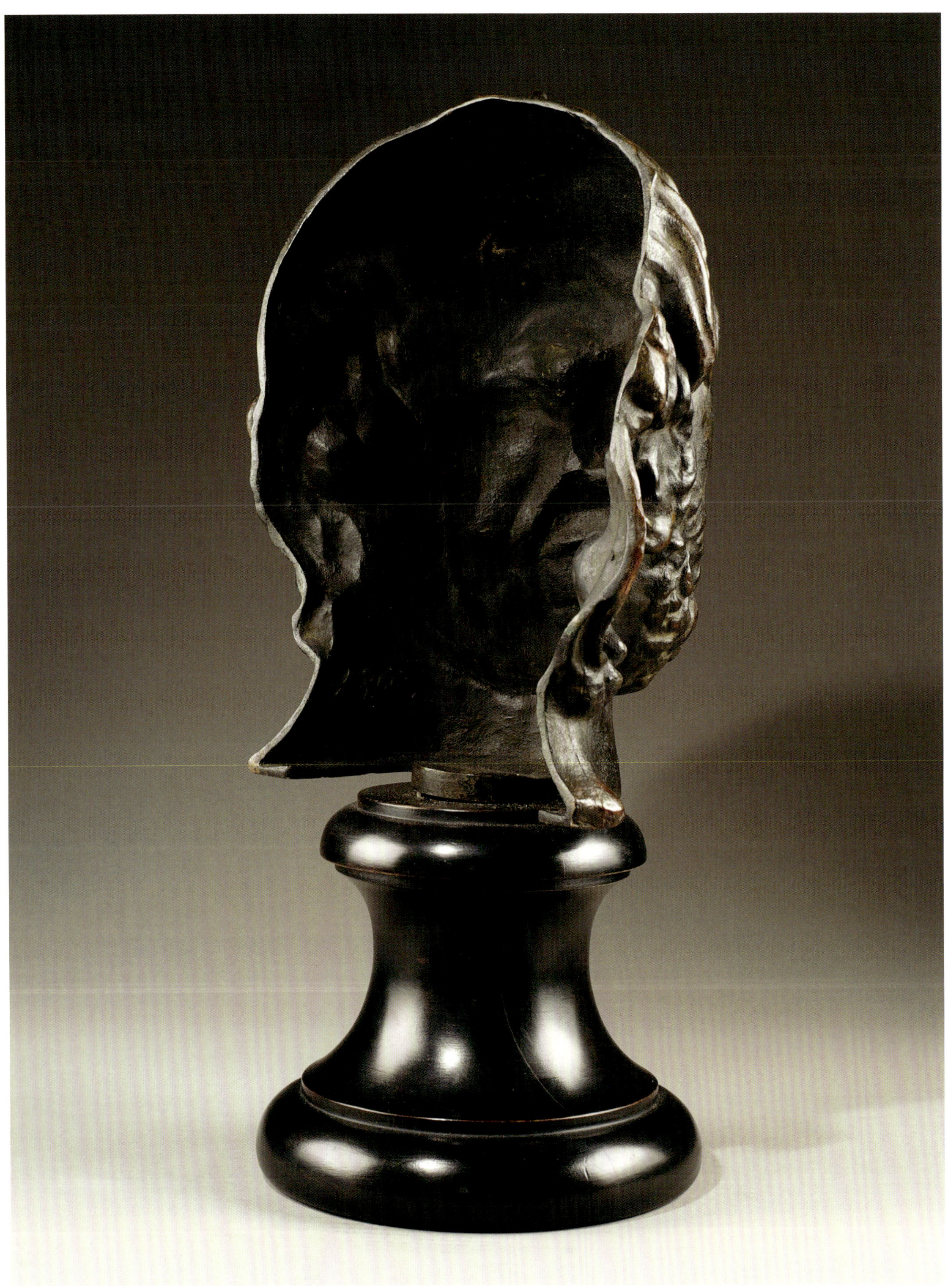

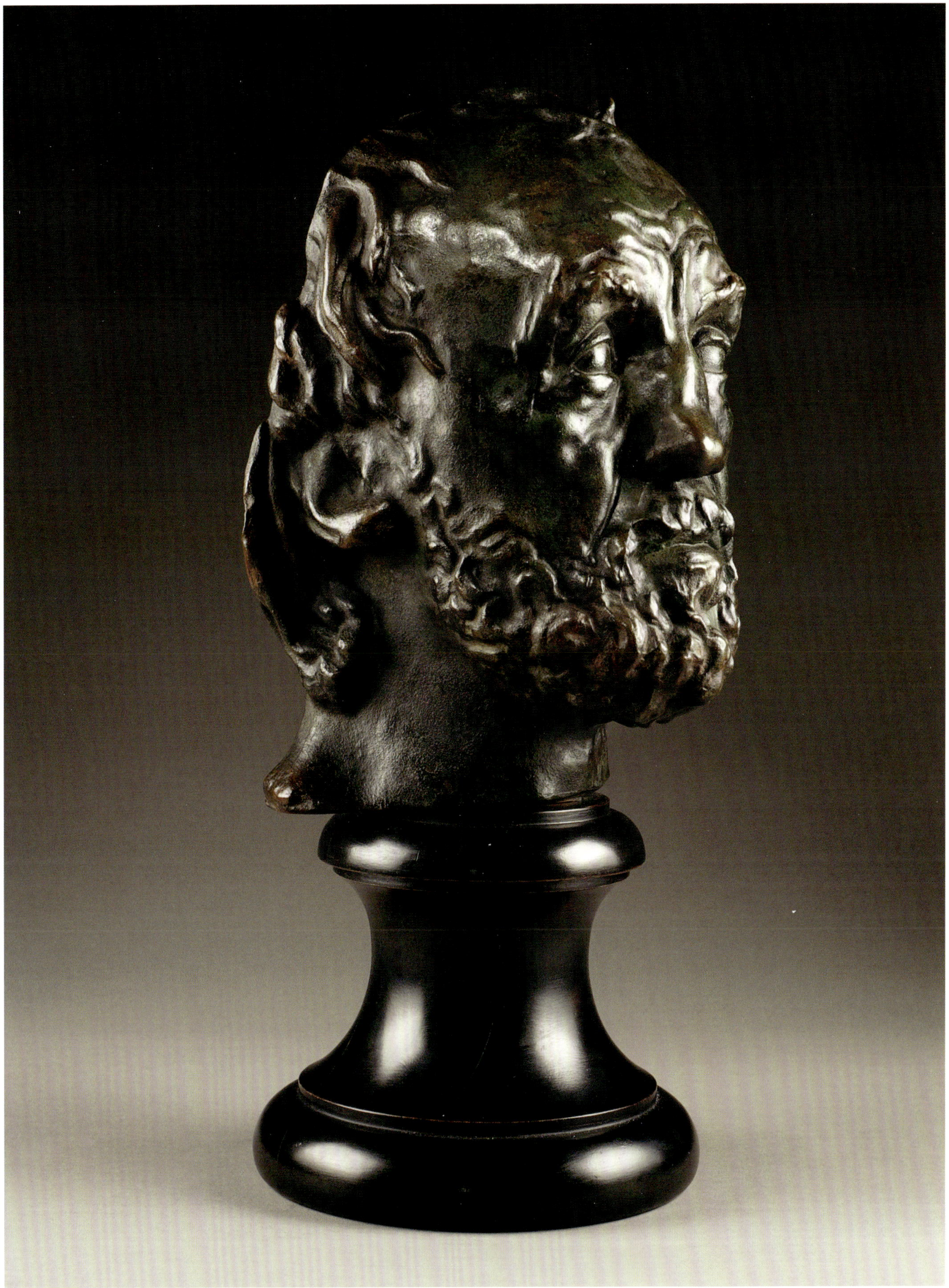

Head of A Man With A Broken Nose, Type 2 First Model

Tête de l'Homme au Nez Cassé, Version Dite Type II Premier Modèle

Signed A. Rodin
Inscribed © by Musée Rodin 1967 and Georges Rudier Fondeur Paris
Bronze with a rich green and brown patination
Height: 10 inches (27 cm)

Provenance:
Musée Rodin, Paris
B.G. Cantor, New York
Higgins Harte International Galleries, Lahaina, Maui, Hawai
Collection Thomas Thomas

Originally conceived between 1863 and 1864, this variant was conceived in 1885. The present example was cast in 1967. According to Comité Rodin, due to the number of variations of the present work, it is impossible to know the exact number of casts that were made.

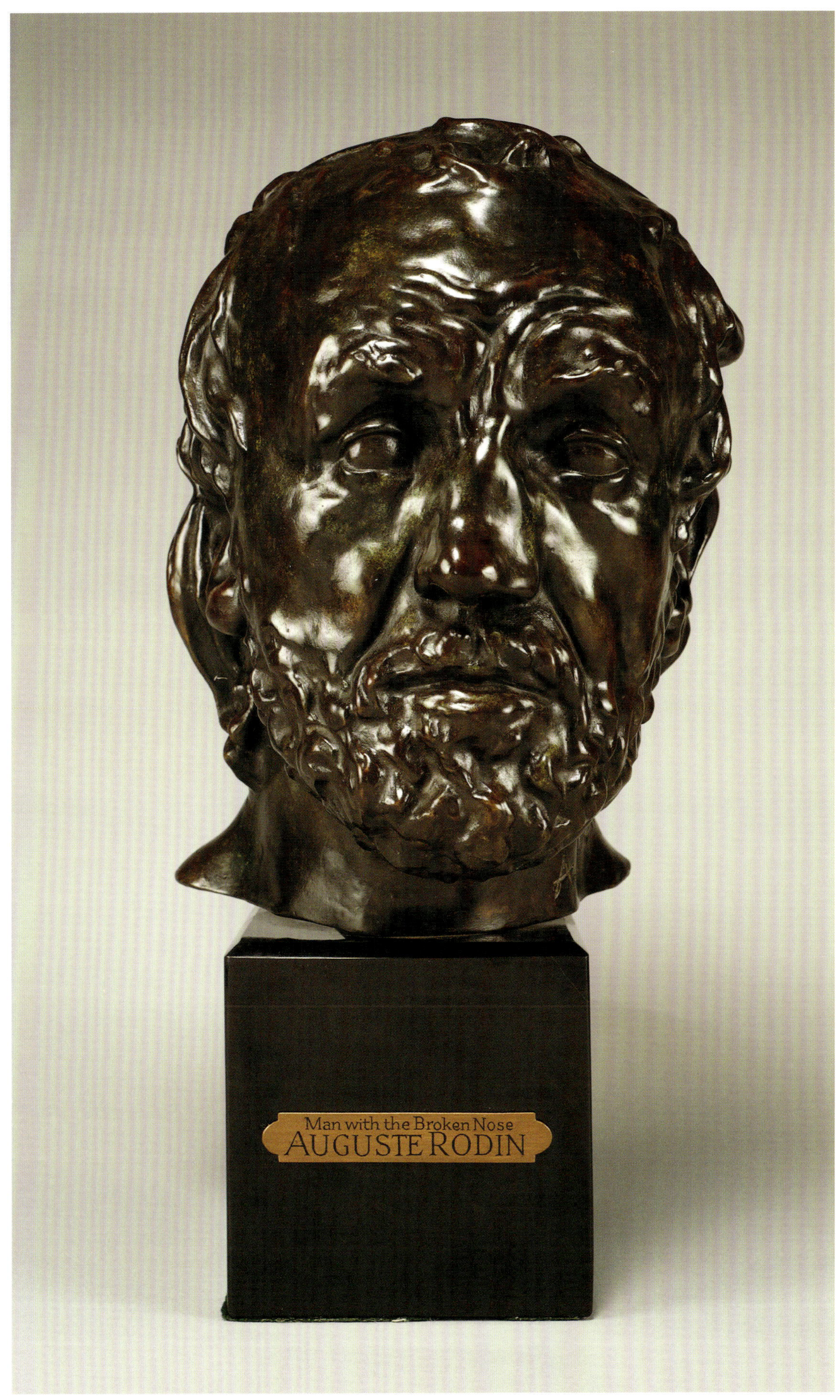

Man with the Broken Nose
AUGUSTE RODIN

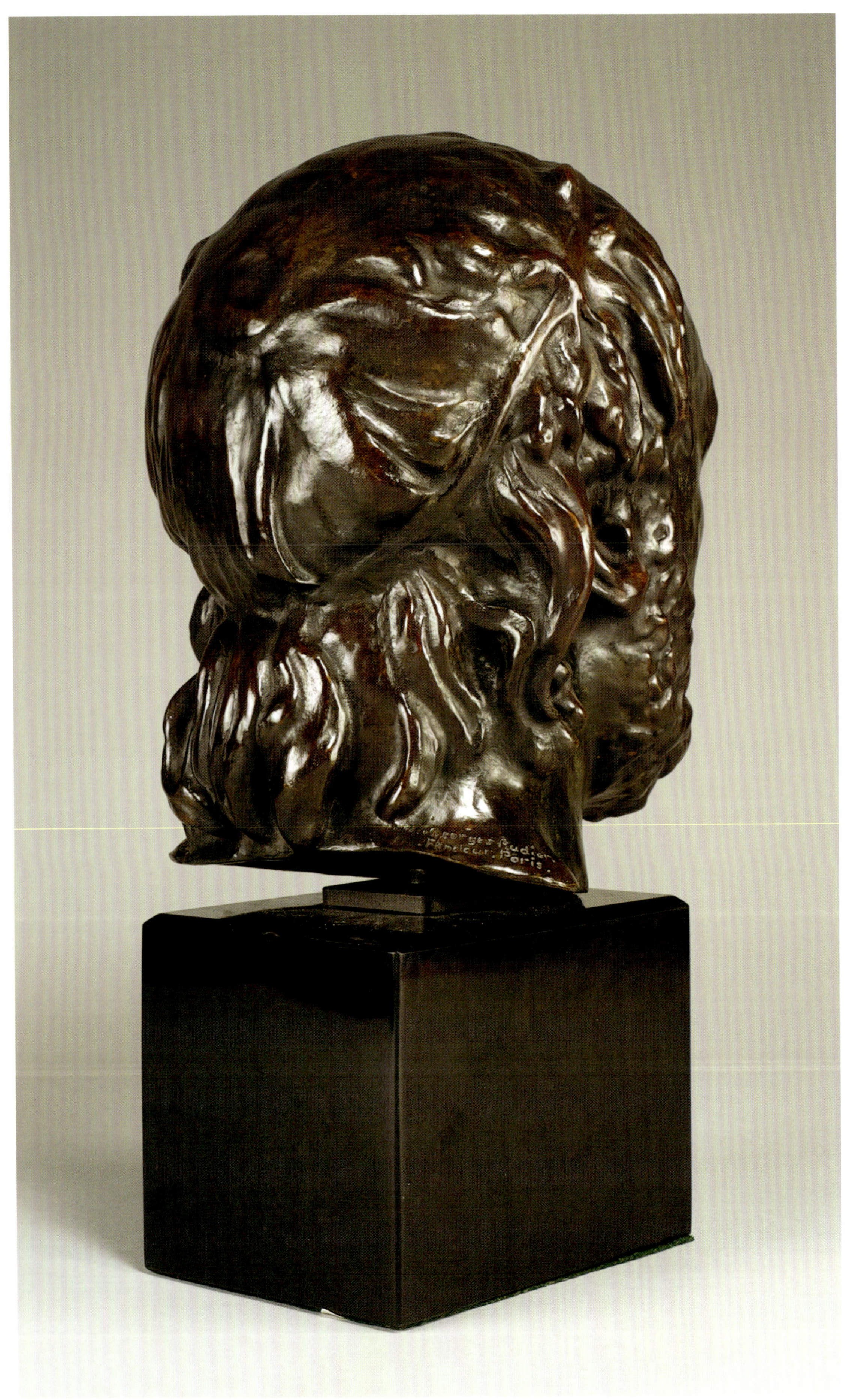

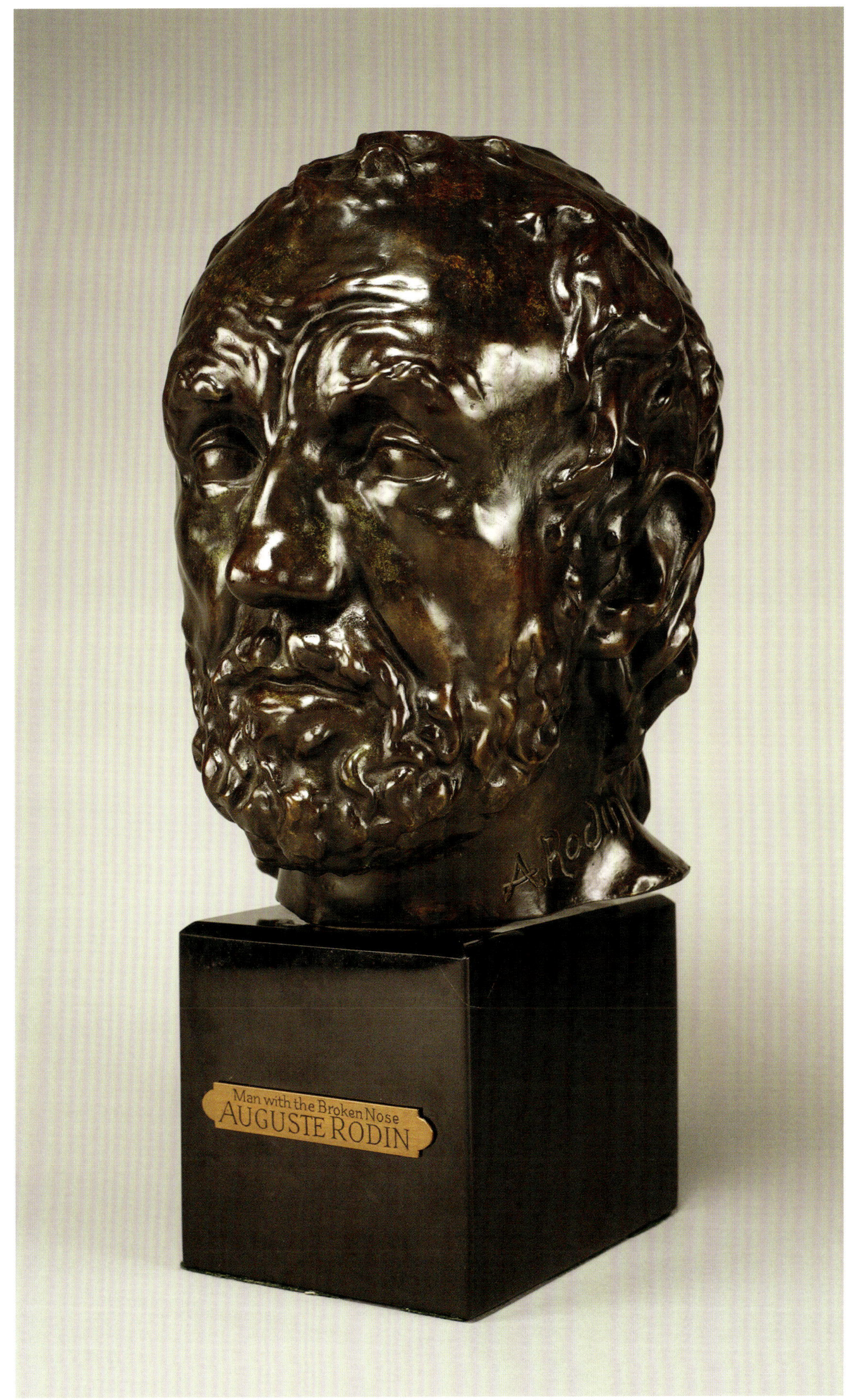
Man with the Broken Nose
AUGUSTE RODIN

Mask of A Man With A Broken Nose, Type 2 Second Model

Masque de l'homme au Nez Cassé, Version Dite Type II 2ème Modèle

Signed A. Rodin with repeat raised interior signature
Inscribed Alexis Rudier Fondeur Paris
Bronze with a brown patination
Height: 10 inches (25.5 cm)

Provenance:
Musée Rodin, Paris
Probably Henri d'Oelsnitz, Tokyo (acquired between 1919–1927)
Private Collection, Japan
By Descent

Originally conceived between 1863 and 1864, this variant was conceived in 1903. The present example was cast between 1919 and 1923. According to the Comité Rodin due to the number of variations of the present work it is impossible to know the exact number of casts that were made.

Rodin considered this portrait to be his earliest major work and described it as his first exceptional piece of modeling. He began the portrait in 1863 intending to submit it to the Paris Salon as his debut sculpture. The following year, *The Man with the Broken Nose* became *The Mask of the Man with the Broken Nose* when the cold conditions in Rodin's studio caused the back of the head to freeze and break off. Rodin, favoring the element of chance, wanted to exhibit the portrait bust as it was. He continued to work on it for over a year before submitting it to the Salon. Much to his disappointment, the Salon rejected the work in 1864 and again in 1865, unable to accept what they considered to be a fragmentary model by an unknown sculptor.

Rodin however persisted and in 1874 he commissioned Léon Fourquet to carve a marble of the model. By this point Rodin had extended the work down to the shoulders and replaced the back of the head, which had frozen off ten years previously. The work was finally accepted to the Salon and was Rodin's first work to be exhibited there. Soon after, Rodin had the mask cast in bronze and this earlier version was finally exhibited at the Salon in 1878.

The model's debt to classical antiquity is clear and the blank eyes and thick strands of hair allude to the busts of ancient Greece or Rome, an effect that would not have been lost on its contemporary audience. Nevertheless, Rodin's approach was revolutionary in that he combined this element of classicism with an expressive naturalism, the portrait being clearly modelled from life.

The work was based on a local handyman nicknamed Bibi, who modelled for Rodin in the Saint-Marcel district outside Paris. Rodin depicted Bibi without flattery, broken nose and all, beginning what would become an ongoing exploration of unconventional beauty. Indeed, Rodin was fascinated by the inevitable decline of the human body, a process that he thought imbued personality, rather than ugliness.

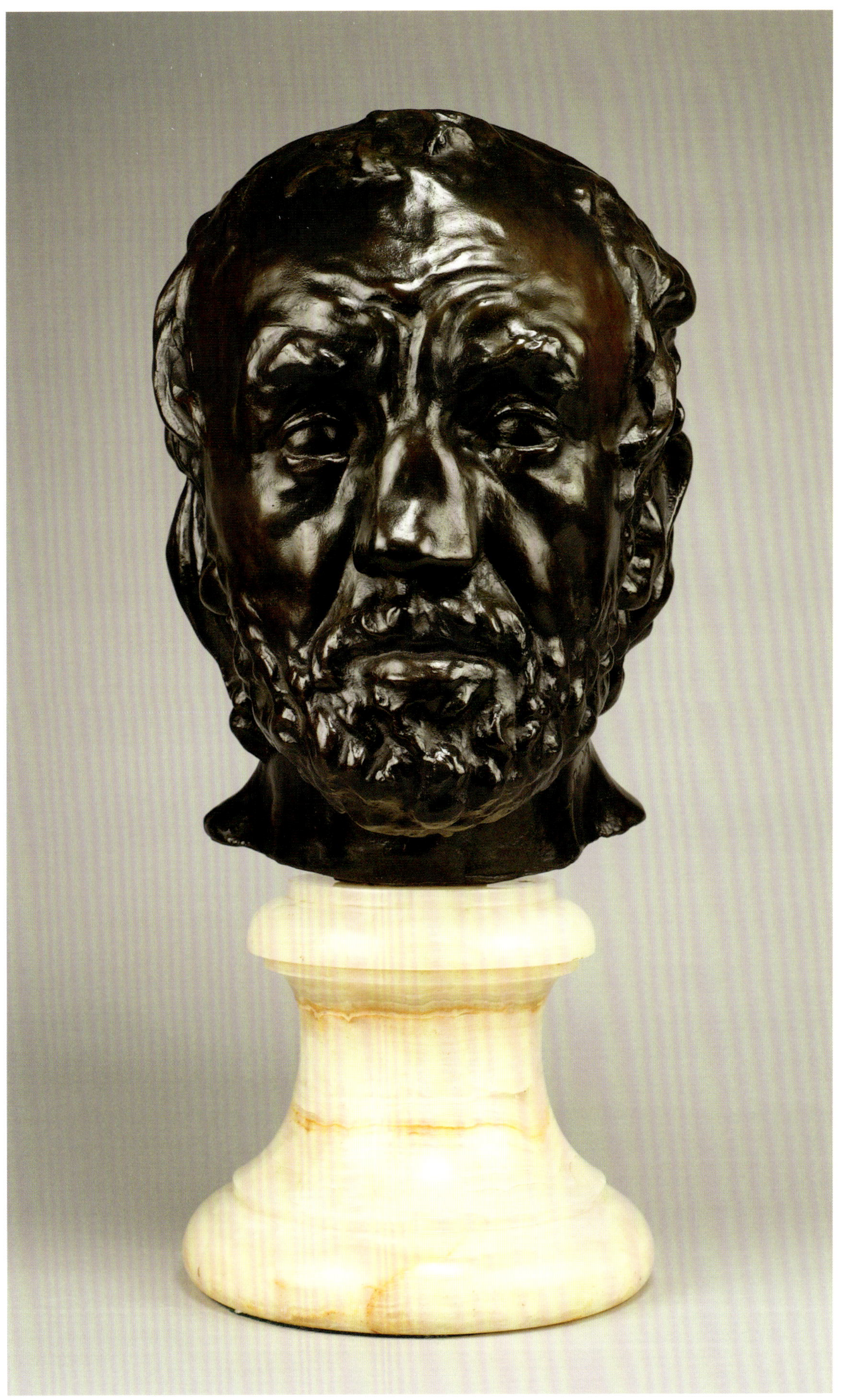

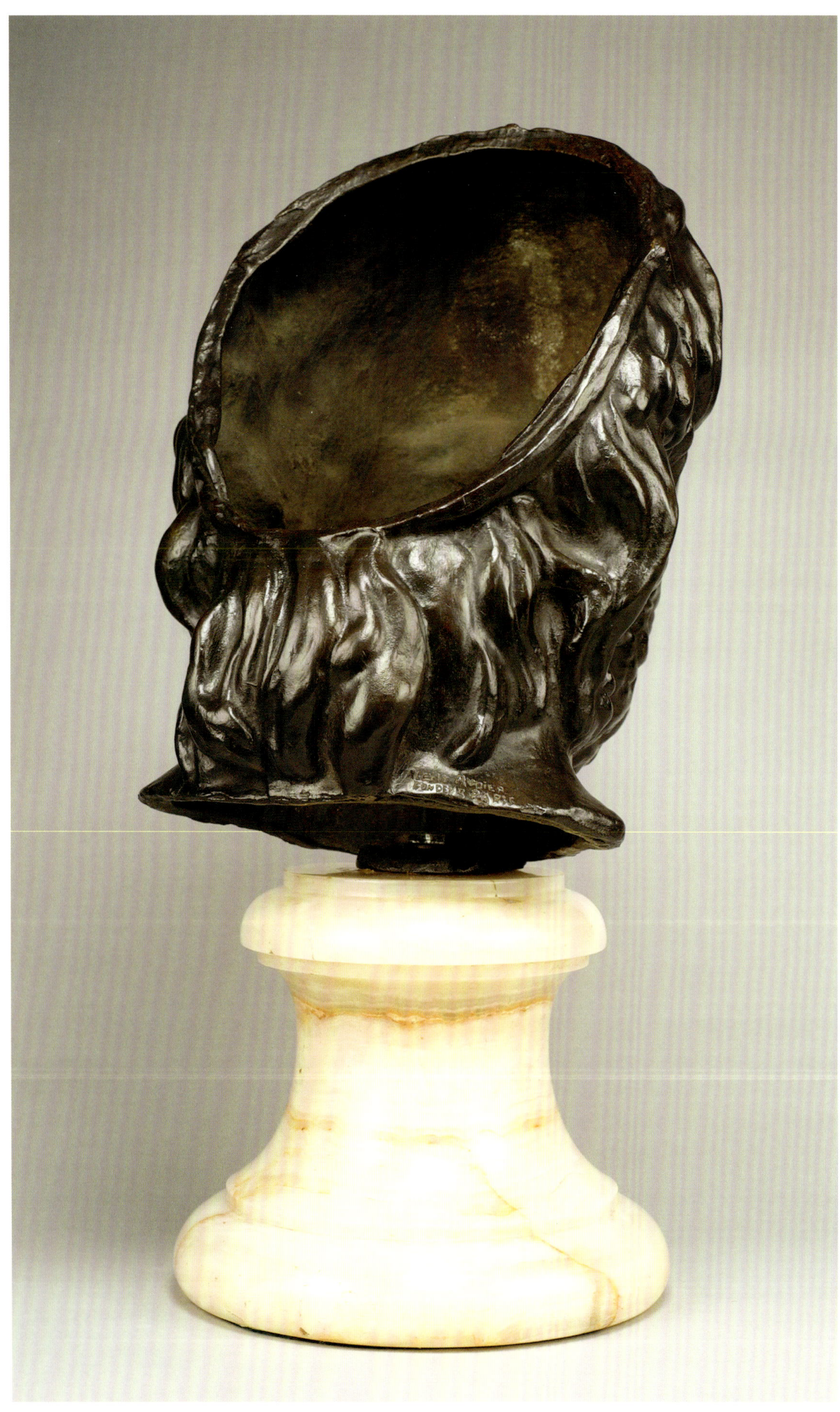

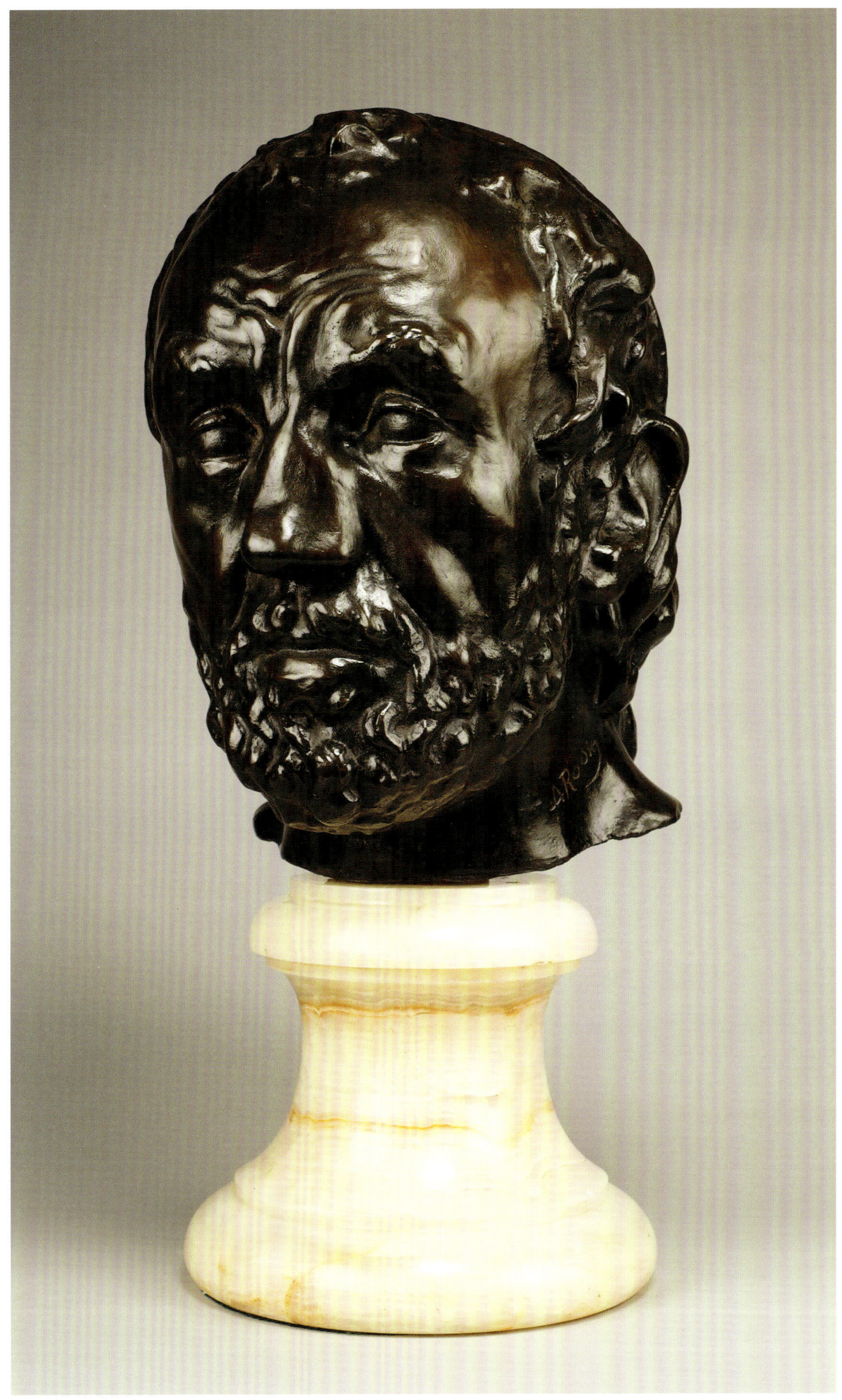

Head of George Bernard Shaw

Tête de Bernard Shaw

Signed A. Rodin with repeat raised internal signature
Inscribed © by Musée Rodin Paris 1985 and E. Godard Fond
Numbered No. I/II
Bronze with a black patination on a black marble base
Height: 11½ inches (28.5 cm)

Provenance:
Musée Rodin
Cantor Foundation
Robert Bowman Gallery, 2008
Private European Collection

Conceived in 1906, this example was executed in 1985. A total of fourteen casts were made. The first six casts by the Alexis Rudier foundry between 1914 and 1934. Georges Rudier made four casts between 1961 and 1975 and Emile Godard made four casts between 1981 and 1986.

Every sculptor of note had created their portrait of George Bernard Shaw but as the great Irish wit, playwright, essayist, journalist and critic said, 'any man who, being a contemporary of Rodin, deliberately allowed his bust to be made by anyone else, must go down in posterity (if he went down at all) as a stupendous nincompoop'.

Giving insight to the artists technique, Shaw said 'He was the most painstaking sculptor I have ever met. I gave something like thirty sittings, in as many consecutive days, at his studio in Meudon. Rodin took a large number of profiles, adjusting my face by a fraction of an inch for each—spinning my head round by degrees. He took an immense number of measurements and made so many pencil marks on the clay that he used up three pencils before the sittings were over.

'To judge by his bust of me, Rodin saw me as a French petit bourgeois. Of course, all the other sculptors who have made busts of me have endowed me with some of their own national characteristics. For instance, Prince Troubetzkoy, the Russian sculptor, saw me as a Russian intellectual Prince. Troubetzkoy's method of work was the exact opposite to that of Rodin's, Troubetzkoy worked very fast. He took hardly any measurements, relying almost entirely on his vision and inspiration. Davidson, the American sculptor, apparently saw me as a profound philosopher.'

Shaw posed for Rodin in April 1906 in Meudon. It was Shaw's wife Charlotte who commissioned a marble bust and a bronze cast of the final version for the sum of 25,100FF. Ren Chruy, who worked for Rodin at the time recalled that when Shaw sat for the artist 'Suddenly, Rodin interrupted his work and said, 'Do you know, you look like--like the devil!' And Bernard Shaw, with a smile, replied, 'But I *am* the devil!'

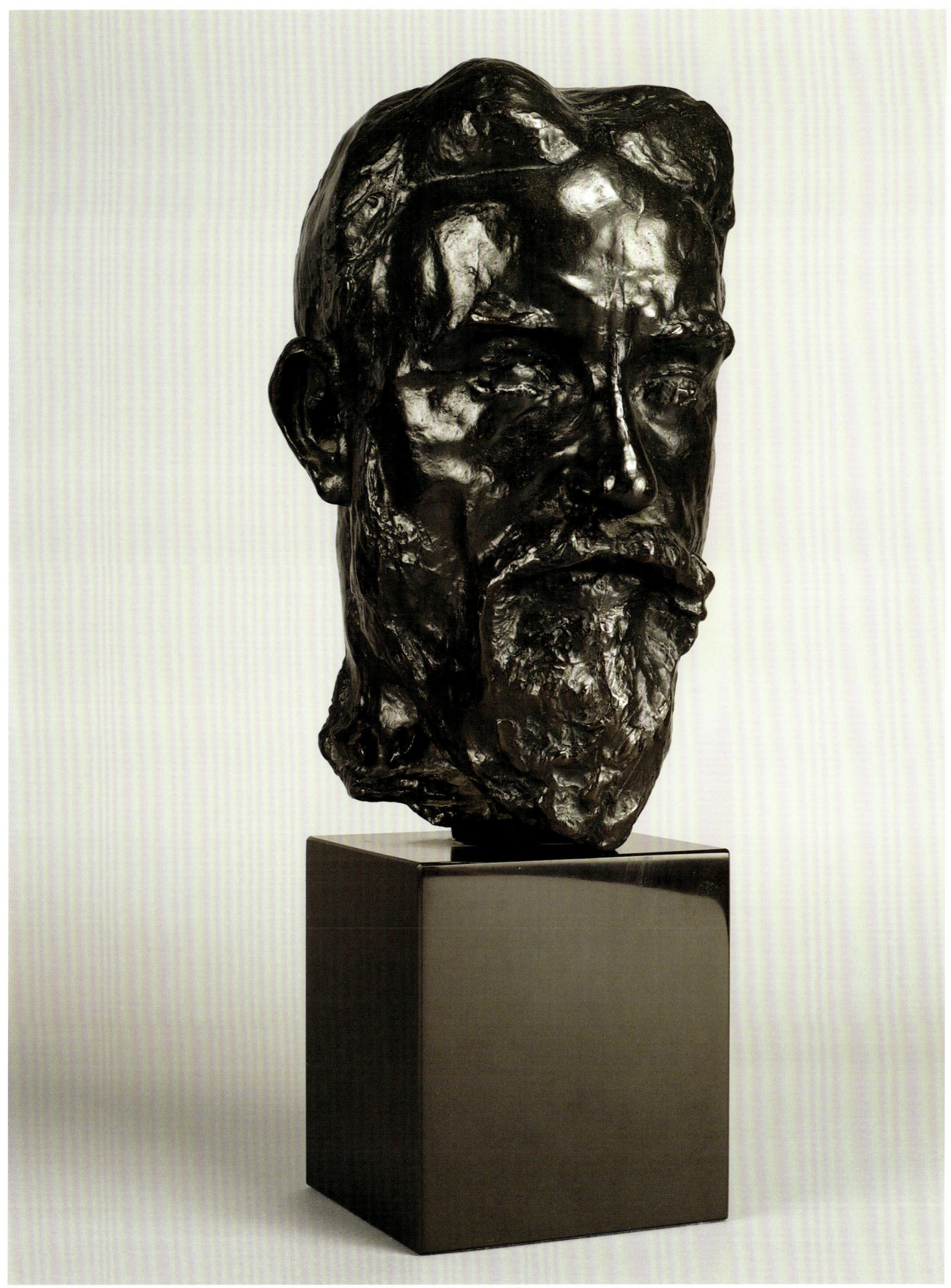

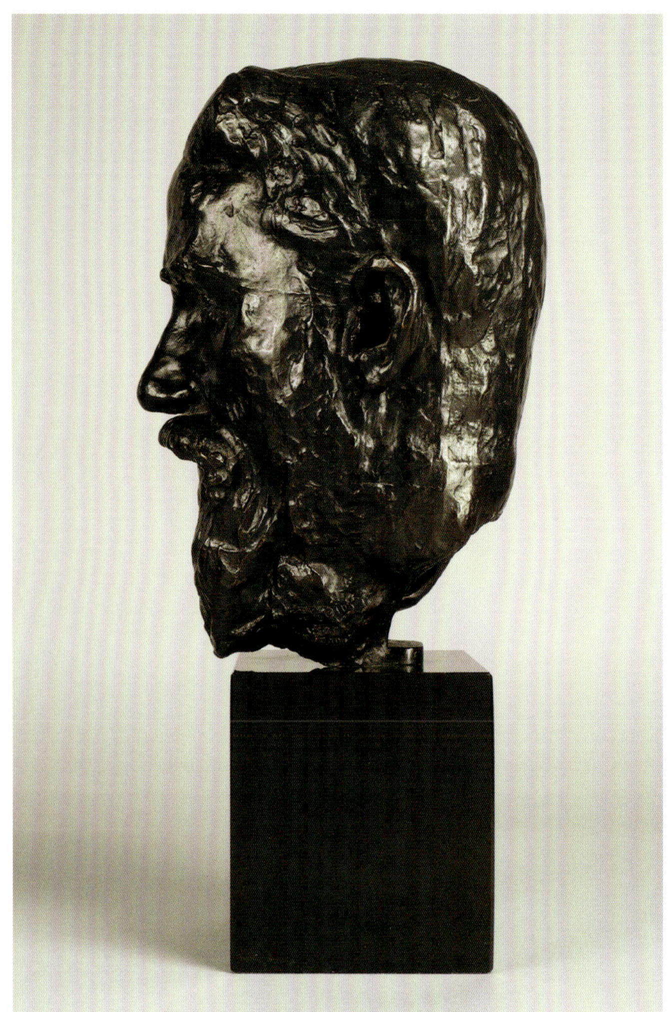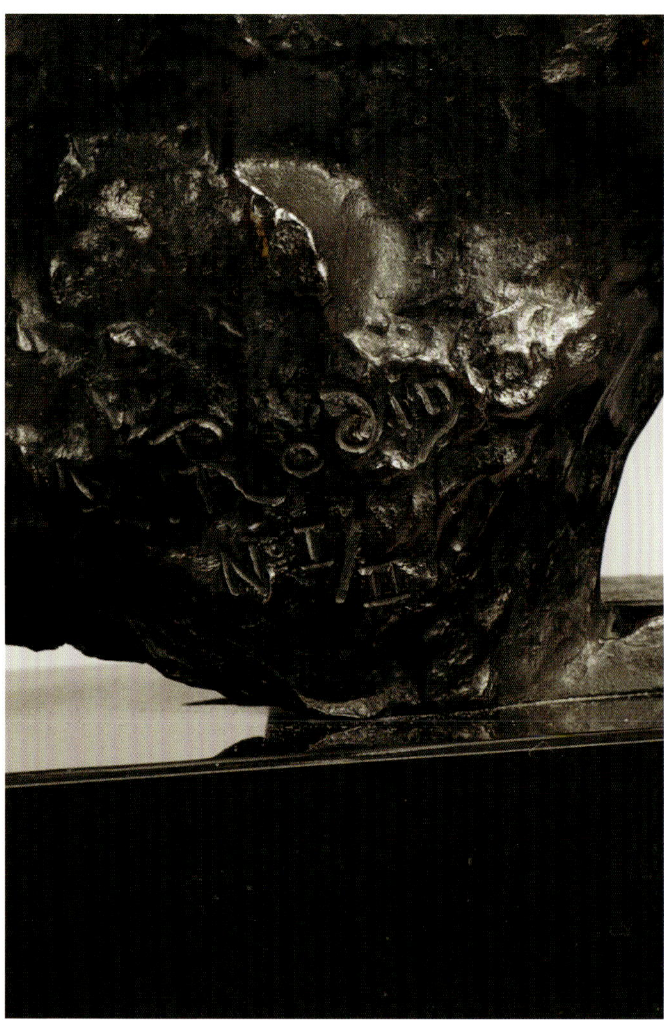

A lifelong advocate of Rodin and his work, Shaw said of the artist 'The Hand of God is his own hand'. Rodin requested that Shaw's portrait bust be included in an exhibition at the New Galleries in London as homage to the British collectors who supported him. Shaw presented the marble bust to the Municipal Gallery of Modern Art in Dublin in October 1908 but retained this bronze version for his own collection.

In 1914 Shaw wrote a letter of authorisation for Rodin to recast his portrait 'Please do as many replica casts as you want; the work is yours, the honour is mine: I'm proud to be known as your model; you are the only man next to whom I feel truly humble.'

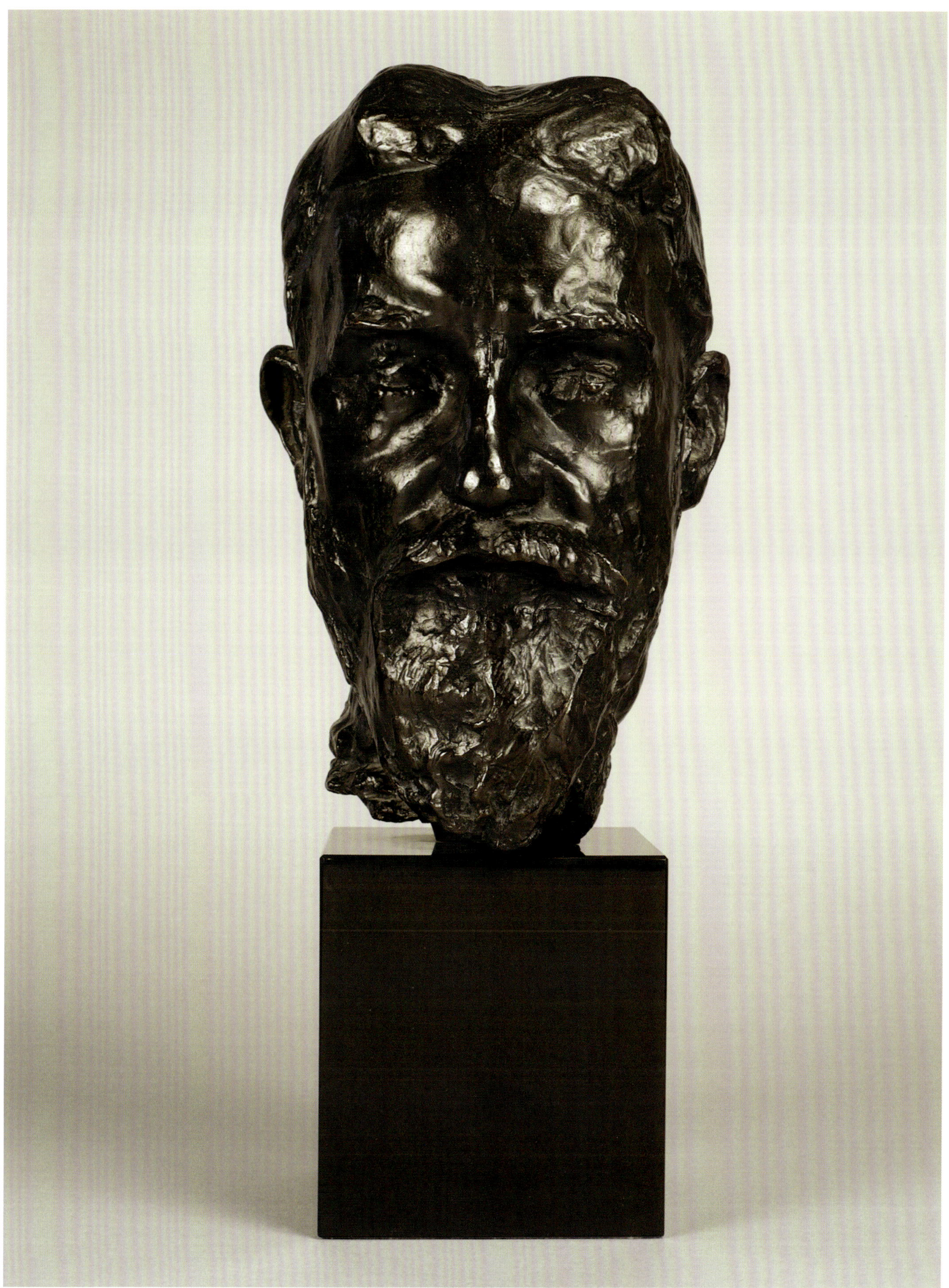

Head of Eustache de Saint Pierre, Study Type A Large Model

Tête d'Eustache de Saint-Pierre, Étude Type A Grande Modèle

Signed A. Rodin
Inscribed © by Musée Rodin 1974 and Georges Rudier Fondeur Paris
Bronze with a green and brown patination
Height: 13⅜ inches (35 cm)

Provenance:
Musée Rodin, Paris
Private Collection, USA
Robert Bowman Gallery, 2006
Private Collection, Turkey

Conceived 1886–1886, this example was cast in 1974. The Alexis Rudier foundry cast three or four un-numbered examples between 1910–1930 for Rodin and then the Musée Rodin. A further ten casts were made Musée Rodin by the Georges Rudier foundry between 1968 and 1976.

It is interesting to note that the town council of Calais who commissioned Rodin had originally envisaged a monument to just one burgher, Eustache de Saint Pierre. According to Froissart's Chronicles he was the leader and greatest hero of the story:

'…The richest burgher in the town, Sir Eustache de Saint-Pierre, got up and said: 'Gentlemen, it would be a great shame to allow so many people to starve to death, if there were any way of preventing it. And it would be highly pleasing to Our Lord if anyone could save them from such a fate. I have such faith and trust in gaining pardon and grace from Our Lord if I die in the attempt, that I will put myself forward as the first. I will willingly go out in my shirt, bareheaded and barefoot, with a halter (noose) around my neck and put myself at the mercy of the King of England.

'…Another very rich and much respected citizen, called Jean d'Aire…rose up and said he would keep him company. The third to volunteer was Sir Jacques de Wissant [sic], who was very rich both by inheritance and by his own transactions; he offered to accompany his two cousins, and so did Sir Pierre his brother. Two others completed the number, and set off dressed only in their shirts and breeches, and with halters round their necks, as they had been told.'

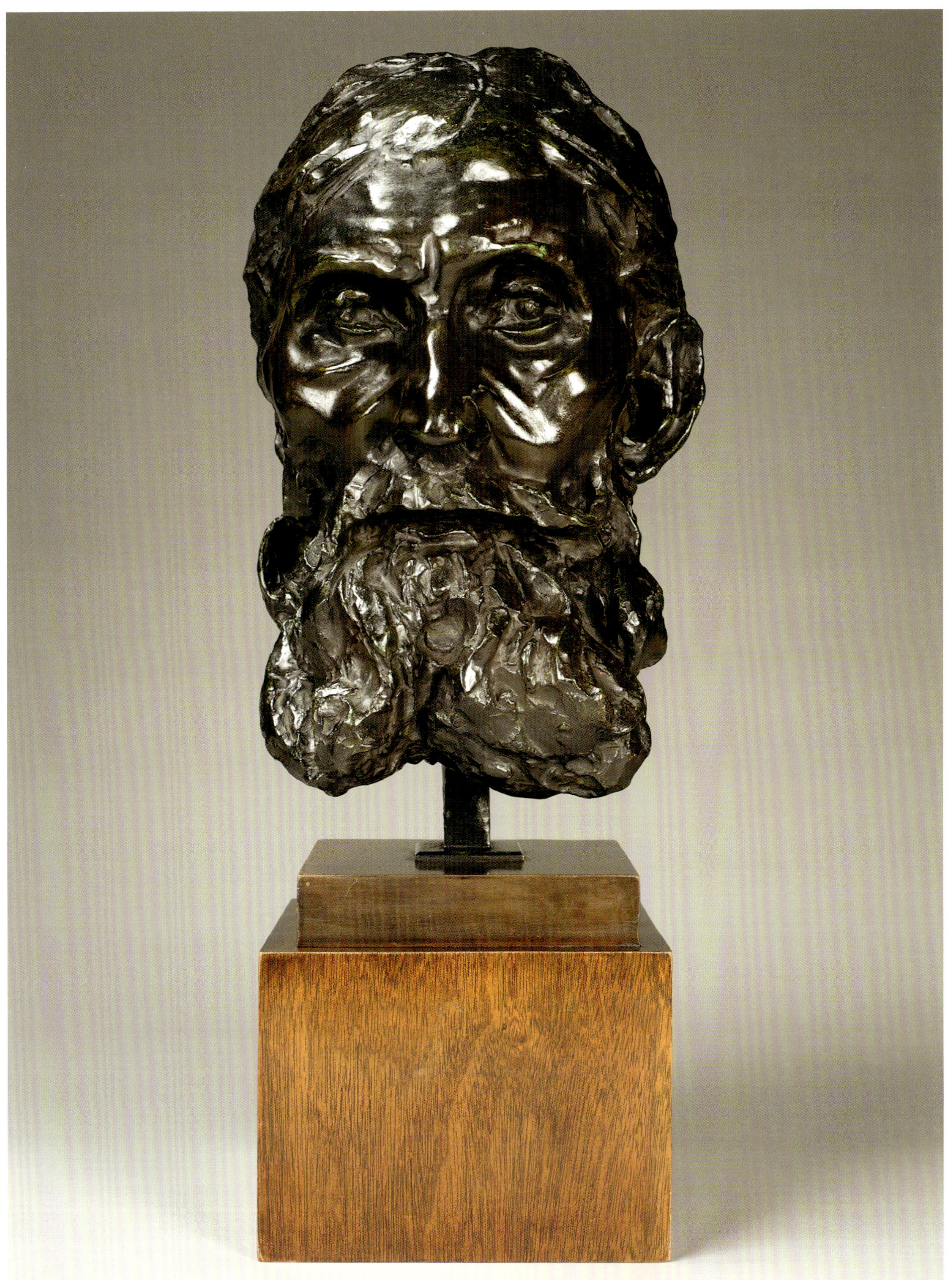

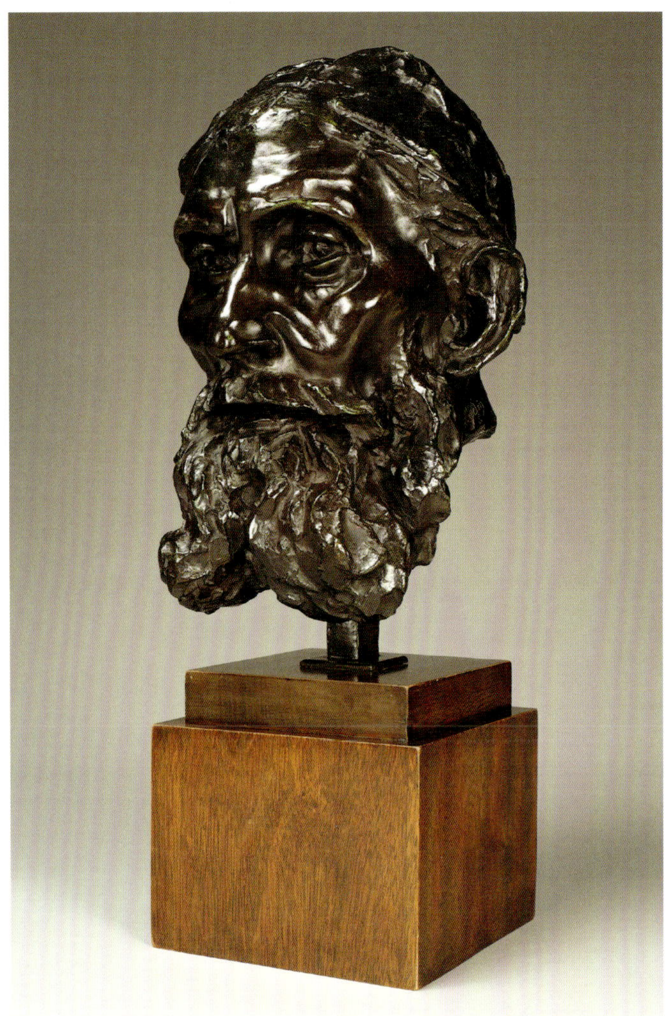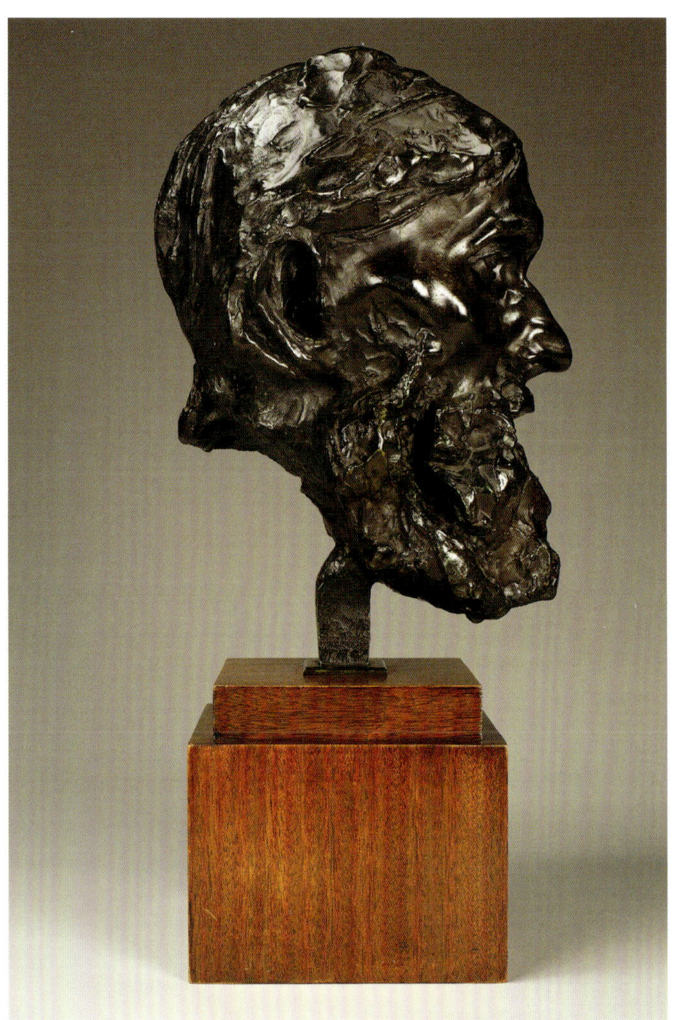

As with his studies of hands, Rodin considered his expressive heads as independent works in their own right. Rodin preferred using models of strong character rather than physical perfection. This humanised the subjects making for a more accessible and therefore more moving image, rather than something idealised and remote.

Rodin used different models for different parts of the figure, even repeating some elements on more than one burgher. But it was the heads; expressive and emotive that defined the figures as distinct individuals.

Rodin believed there were regional physical characteristics and therefore for *Saint-Pierre* he asked his friend the painter Jean-Charles Cazin who was born in the Pas-de-Calais region to pose for him for the head.

Type A Head is believed to be a truer portrait of Cazin than the *Final Head* with its sharper features enhanced by Rodin's impressionistic modelling.

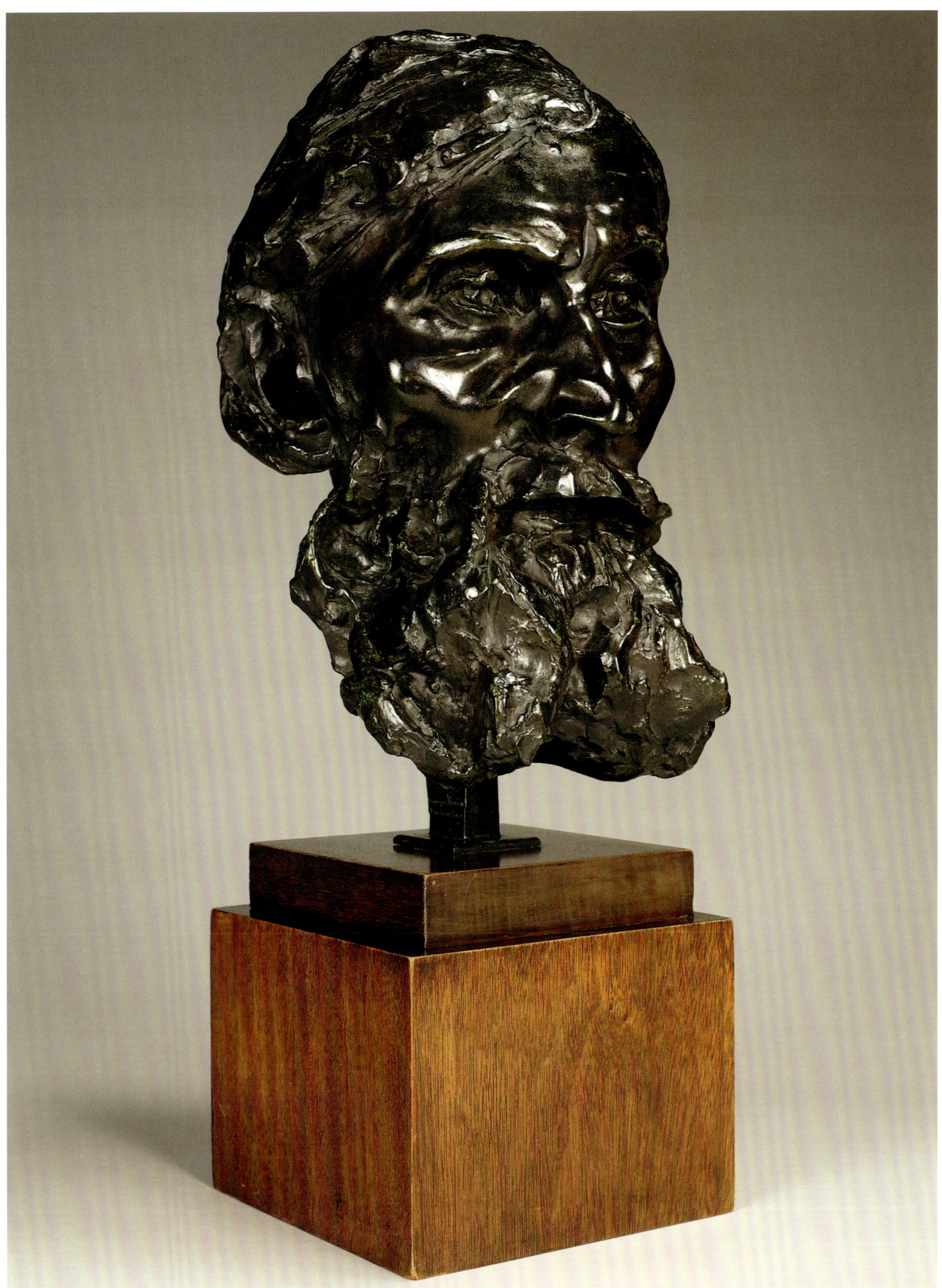

Gustav Mahler Head Type A

Gustav Mahler Tête, Type A

Signed A. Rodin and with repeat raised interior signature
Inscribed © Musée Rodin 1965 and Georges Rudier fondeur, Paris
Bronze with brown patination
Height: 19 inches (48.2 cm)

Provenance:
Musée Rodin Paris, executed October 1965
J. Floch New York, November 1965
Bella & Sol. Fishko, New York, 1966
Galerie Claude Bernard, Paris
Baron Von Banfield, Paris, artistic director of Teatro Verdi in Trieste
Robert Bowman Gallery, 2011
Private Collection, UK

Conceived in 1909, this example cast in 1965. Ten bronze casts of Gustave Mahler Head Type A were made between 1911 and 1954. A further ten casts were made by the Georges Rudier foundry between 1958 and 1966.

Gustav Mahler (1860–1911) was one of the leading composers and conductors of his age. He was married to Alma Mahler, whose stepfather was the Secessionist painter Carl Moll. Moll wanted Rodin to create the portrait of the composer after his departure from the Vienna State Opera in 1907.

Moll wrote: I want to tell you…how happy I am that you have been so kind as to fulfill my wish of making a bust of Mahler for me. You cannot imagine how much we love this man and how satisfied we are that the only artist who can understand his mind – through congeniality – is now doing his portrait. I was sure that the work would not involve a sacrifice on the maestro Rodin's behalf, because I can see how interesting this head of Mahler must be for an artist – even more so for Rodin.

Mahler sat for the portrait in Rodin's studio. Rodin was greatly impressed by his appearance, and concurred with Moll's enthusiasm for the project saying: I find his features remarkable. There is a suggestion not only of the Eastern origin, but of something even more remote, of a race now lost to us—the Egyptians in the days of Rameses.

The commission came at a time when both Mahler and Rodin were internationally successful and at the height of their distinguished careers. Mahler sat a dozen times for the sculptor, leading to a great mutual respect between the two.

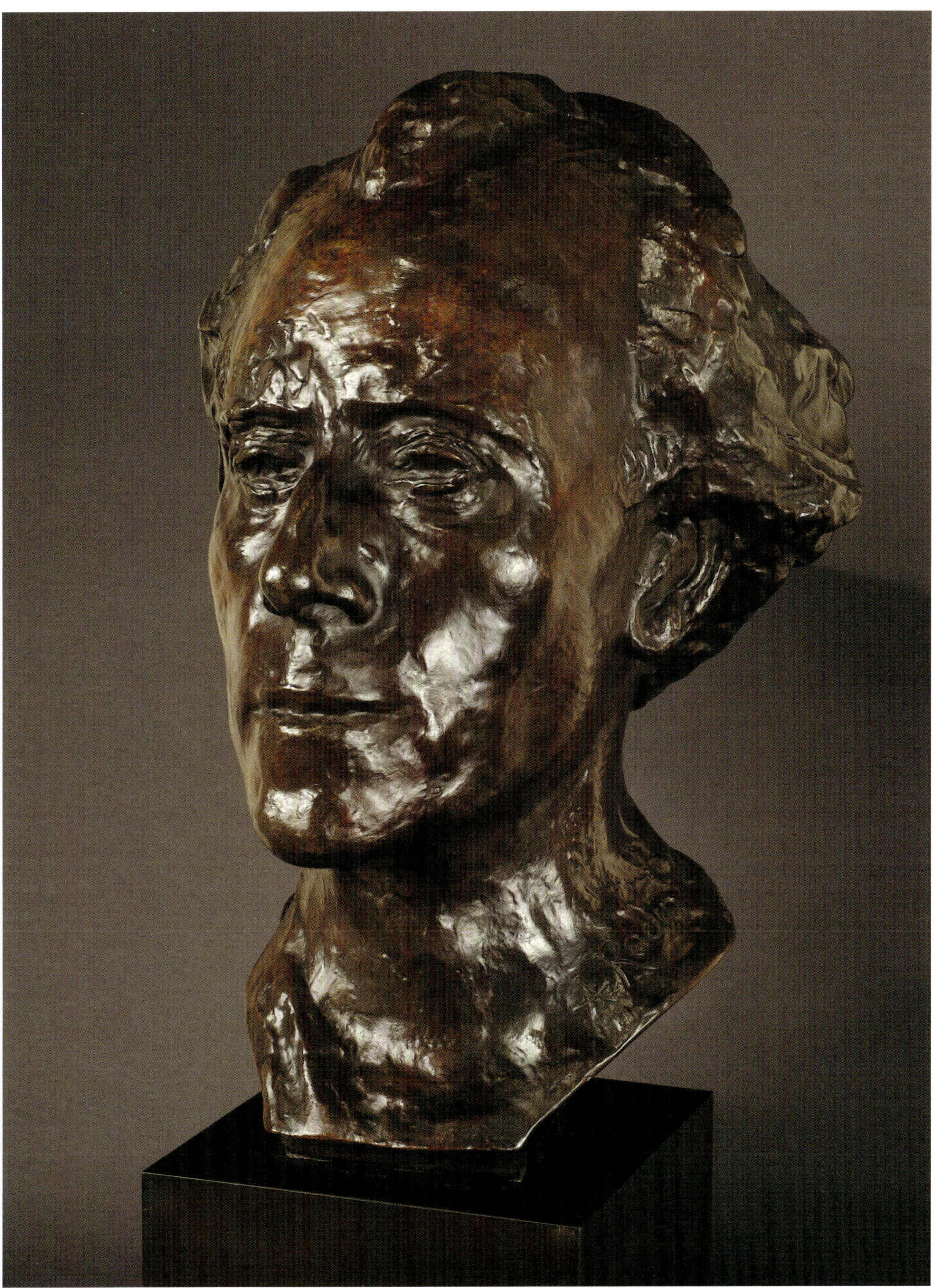

Gustave Geffroy

Gustave Geffroy

Signed A. Rodin and with repeat raised interior signature
Bronze with a rich dark-brown patination
Height: 13.4 inches (34 cm)

Provenance:
Sir John Lavery (1856–1941), acquired directly from the artist
Eileen Lavery (daughter of Sir John Lavery)
Thence by Descent
Robert Bowman Gallery, 2008
Private Collection, Ireland

Conceived and cast in 1905. The only other recorded lifetime cast also dates from 1905 and was acquired by the Musée du Luxumbourg in 1906, then transferred to the Louvre in 1929, the sculpture currently resides in the collection of the Musée D'Orsay. A posthumous edition of 12 castings was made for the Musée Rodin by the Georges Rudier foundry from 1955.

The eminent art critic Gustave Geffroy (1855–1926) was a close friend and ally of the Impressionists. He wrote a biography on Monet and promoted the works of Cezanne. Since his first article on Rodin in La Justice in 1883, Geffroy became a loyal supporter of the artist and followed his career with great interest.

A public appeal fund was launched in 1904 to offer an enlargement of *The Thinker* to the City of Paris, which at that time had no public monument by Rodin. Gustave Geffroy was appointed treasurer of the fund. Monet made a donation of two hundred francs to the fund, a considerable amount of money, as the artist had a relatively modest income at the time.

Their professional paths crossed again when Geffroy was appointed Director of the tapestry works Manufacture des Gobelins in 1908. Geffroy asked Rodin and other artists, including Monet and Redon, to give designs to help revitalise the workshop. Rodin had worked at the theatre de Gobelins in the 1860s, as a struggling artist, and it was here that he met his life partner Rose Beuret who was working there as a seamstress.

Geffroy wrote extensively about the importance of Rodin and his work, with his articles appearing in numerous periodicals including Les Lettres et les Arts, La Revue des Beaux-Arts et des Lettres, La Revue Politique et Litteraire, La Vie Artistique and Le Figaro.

'New positions! It is through these, in limiting oneself to the technique of a craft and the materiality of art, that Rodin's unheard of boldness and pro- found originality can be demonstrated... for him, the positions of the human body could not be reduced to a few types.'

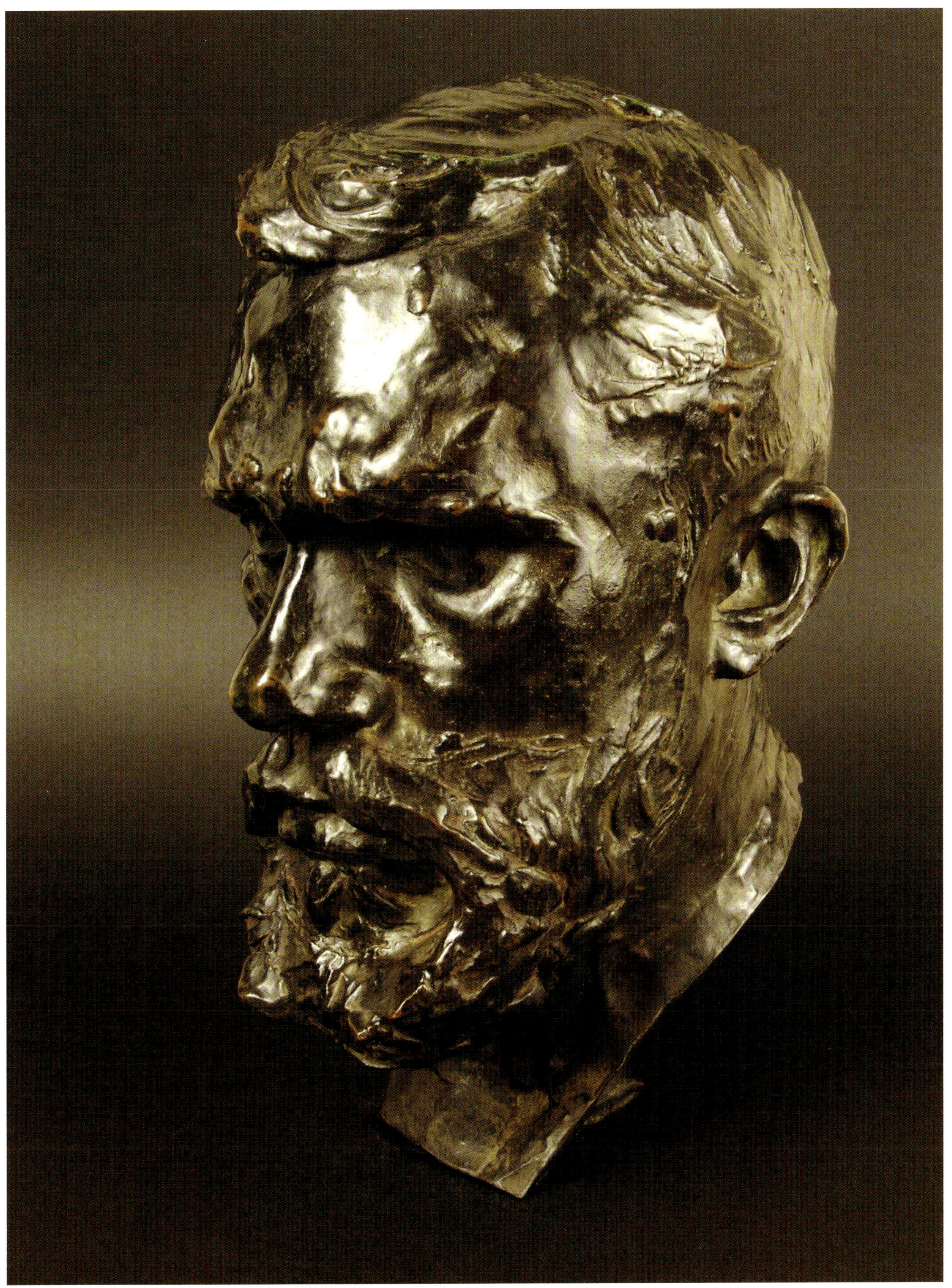

The two men also shared a deep fascination with the works of Honoré de Balzac and Victor Hugo; Geffroy would invite Rodin to literary evenings whilst in August 1891 they travelled (along with Carrier) to the Channel Islands, visiting the sites that had inspired Victor Hugo.

In 1903 Rodin had been elected President of the International Society of Sculptors, Painters and Gravers taking over from the late James Abbot McNeill Whistler. Sir John Lavery RA, the first owner of this cast of Geffroy, was the Vice President.

Irish born Sir John Lavery came from humble beginnings but rose to become one of the most prominent portrait painters of the Edwardian British aristocracy and the most glamorous and international of the Glasgow School. After being elected ARA in 1911, he spent time as an Official War Artist during the First World War. He was knighted in 1918 and became RA in 1921.

After receiving a commission from the Queen, Lavery moved to London where he became great friends with Whistler, an artist who had himself been championed by Geffroy in an article in La Gauloise where he urged the French Government to purchase the portrait of the Artist's mother, Arrangement in Grey & Black. It was Whistler and Lavery who co-founded the International Society of Sculptors, Painters and Gravers.

This cast of Geffroy was made in 1905, and correspondence between Lavery and Rodin includes a letter of the 16th November 1905, now archived in the Musée Rodin:

'Dear President...I am making myself a little socle for Geffroy like the one at the Salon d'Automne. Thus I will always have the pleasure of seeing it properly displayed at my home. I extend to you, my dear master, my sincerest best wishes, John Lavery.'

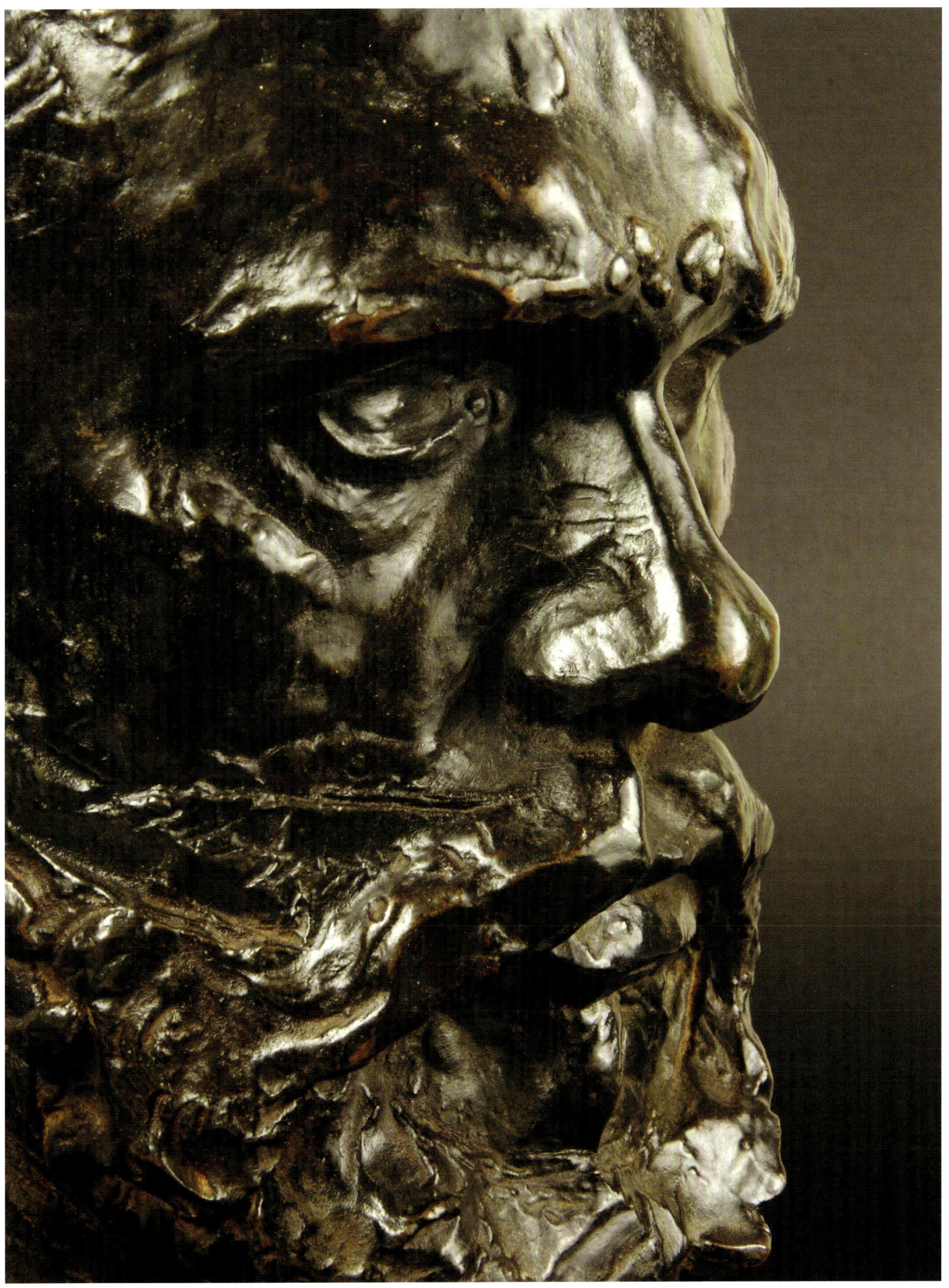

Mask of Hanako, Study Type E

Masque d'Hanako, Étude Type E

Signed A. Rodin
Inscribed © Musée Rodin 1956 and Georges Rudier Fondeur Paris
Bronze with a brown and red patination
Height: 7 inches (17.8 cm)

Provenance:
Musée Rodin, Paris
Gallery Browse and Delbanco, London
Browse and Derby, London
Private Collection
Robert Bowman Gallery, 2006
Private Collection, Turkey

Conceived between 1907 and 1908, this example cast in 1956. A few examples of this work were produced by the Alexis Rudier foundry prior to 1910. Seven casts were made for the Musée Rodin by the Alexis Rudier foundry between 1917 and 1950 and a further ten casts by the Georges Rudier foundry between 1954 and 1956.

Unlike Degas who was interested by dancers purely as subject matter, Rodin was drawn to dancers for what they taught him about movement. During his last decade of life, Rodin rarely tackled large works; possibly they were too difficult for him physically. This was however the period when he modelled many dancers.

Rodin portrayed the Japanese actress Ohta Hisa (1868–1945), known as Hanako, more often than any other sitter. No less than fifty-eight different heads and masks of her were modelled between 1907 and 1911, now preserved along with drawings in the Musée Rodin, Paris. This extensive collection conveys the impression that Rodin was studying someone who became a treasured friend and that the studies were intended for intimate viewing.

In 1906, while in Marseilles to study the Royal Cambodian dancers, Rodin met the thirty-seven year old Geisha. She belonged then to a troupe directed by the modern dance pioneer, Loie Fuller, who gave her the name 'Hanako', meaning 'little flower'.

Rodin was astounded by Hanako's skill in holding difficult poses but it was the mobility of her facial features that fascinated him the most. He found her Kabuki-style expressions of torment and fury particularly compelling. Judith Cladel, Rodin's friend and biographer described one of Hanako's sittings:

'Hanako did not pose like other people. Her features were contracted in an expression of cold, terrible rage. She had the look of a tiger, an expression thoroughly foreign to our occidental countenances. With the force of will the Japanese display in the face of death, Hanako was able to hold this look for hours.'

This mask Type E however shows a softer more thoughtful expression, which Hanako said was modelled when she and the artist were out walking together.

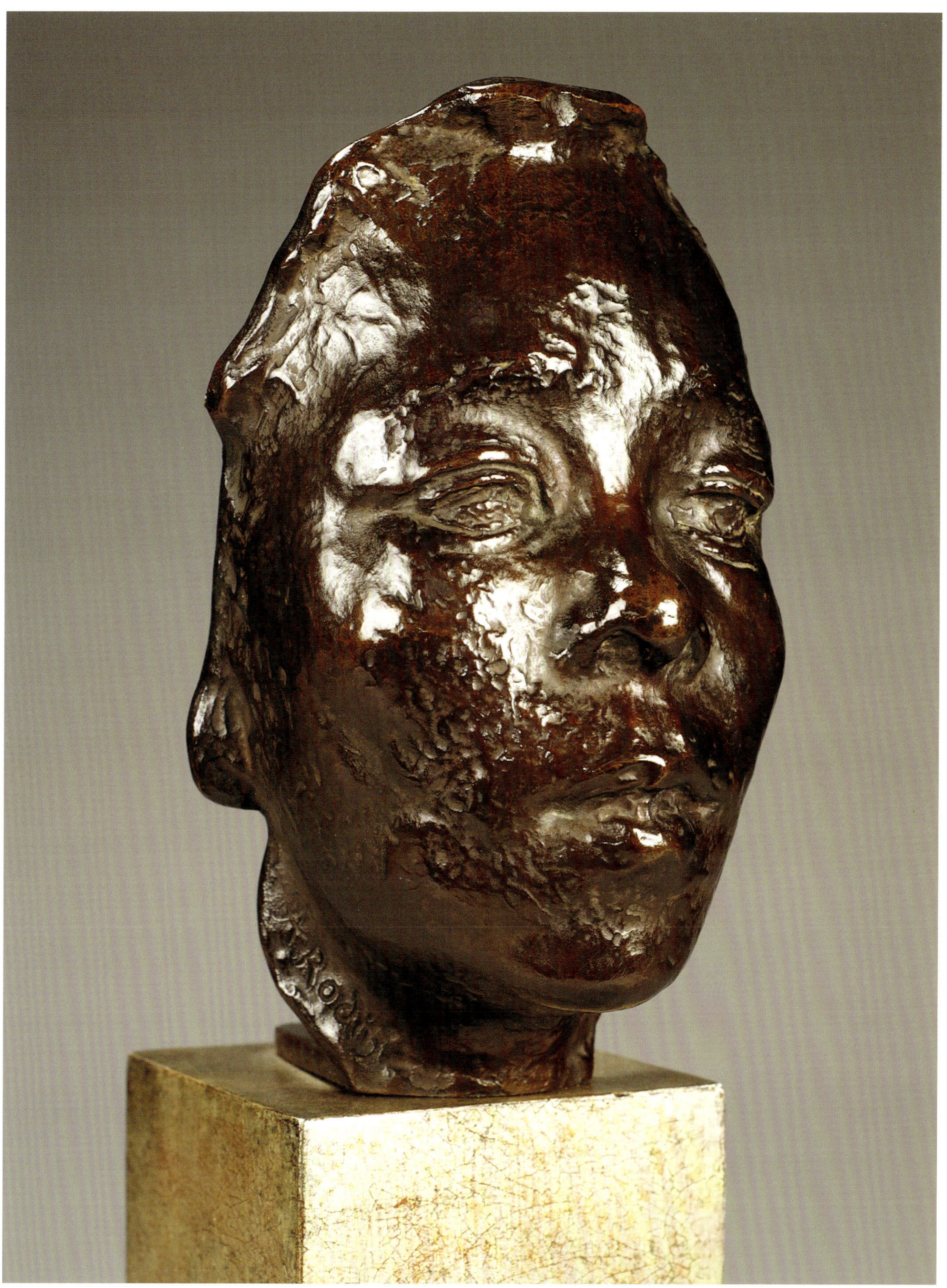

Rose Beuret (Mask of Madame Rodin)

Rose Beuret (Masque de Madame Rodin)

Signed A. Rodin with repeat raised interior signature
Inscribed Alexis Rudier Fondeur Paris
Bronze with a rich brown patination
Height: 10½ inches (27 cm)

Provenance:
M.Hans Hermann Vogel Chemnitz acquired from Rodin on the 5th October 1913
Auction Sale Karl & Faber, Munich 1962
Hella Tischer, Germany.
Auction Sale Christies London, 28 June, 1988 lot 118
Private Collection, Miami Florida.

Conceived in 1882, the present example was cast in 1913. Twenty-three lifetime casts of this model were made. The first of these was cast by Griffoul, a futher three by Philippet and seventeen by the Alexis Rudier foundry. A further twelve casts were made for the Musée Rodin, six by Alexis Rudier between 1917 and 1945, three by Susse between 1969 and 1974 and four casts by Georges Rudier Foundry between 1969 and 1981.

Rose Beuret met Auguste Rodin in 1864 when she was employed as a seamstress at the Théâtre des Gobelines in Paris. She soon became Rodin's mistress and by 1866 had given birth to a son named Auguste. Rodin's dedicated life partner was trusted with the care and keeping of his clay models and domestic affairs, yet Rodin did not marry Beuret until 1917 a few days before he died.

Early on in his career Rodin could not afford to pay professional models and Rose Beuret became his muse for such works as *Mignon* and *Bellona*. *The Mask of Madame Rodin*, conceived around 1882, shows Rose aged about forty years old. Her closed eyes and serious expression contrast to the lively, fiery Rose shown in *Mignon* and *Bellona*. Rodin exhibited this work for the first time at the Pavillon de l'Alma in 1900. As of 1904, the *Mask of Madame Rodin* was exhibited at multiple events, most famously at the International Exhibition of Fine Arts in Düsseldorf.

After the scandal caused by the *Age of Bronze*, where Rodin was accused of making body casts, he was keen to avoid controversy. His portrait of Rose Beuret is therefore slightly smaller than life-size and there is little in the way of sharpness to the features or hair.

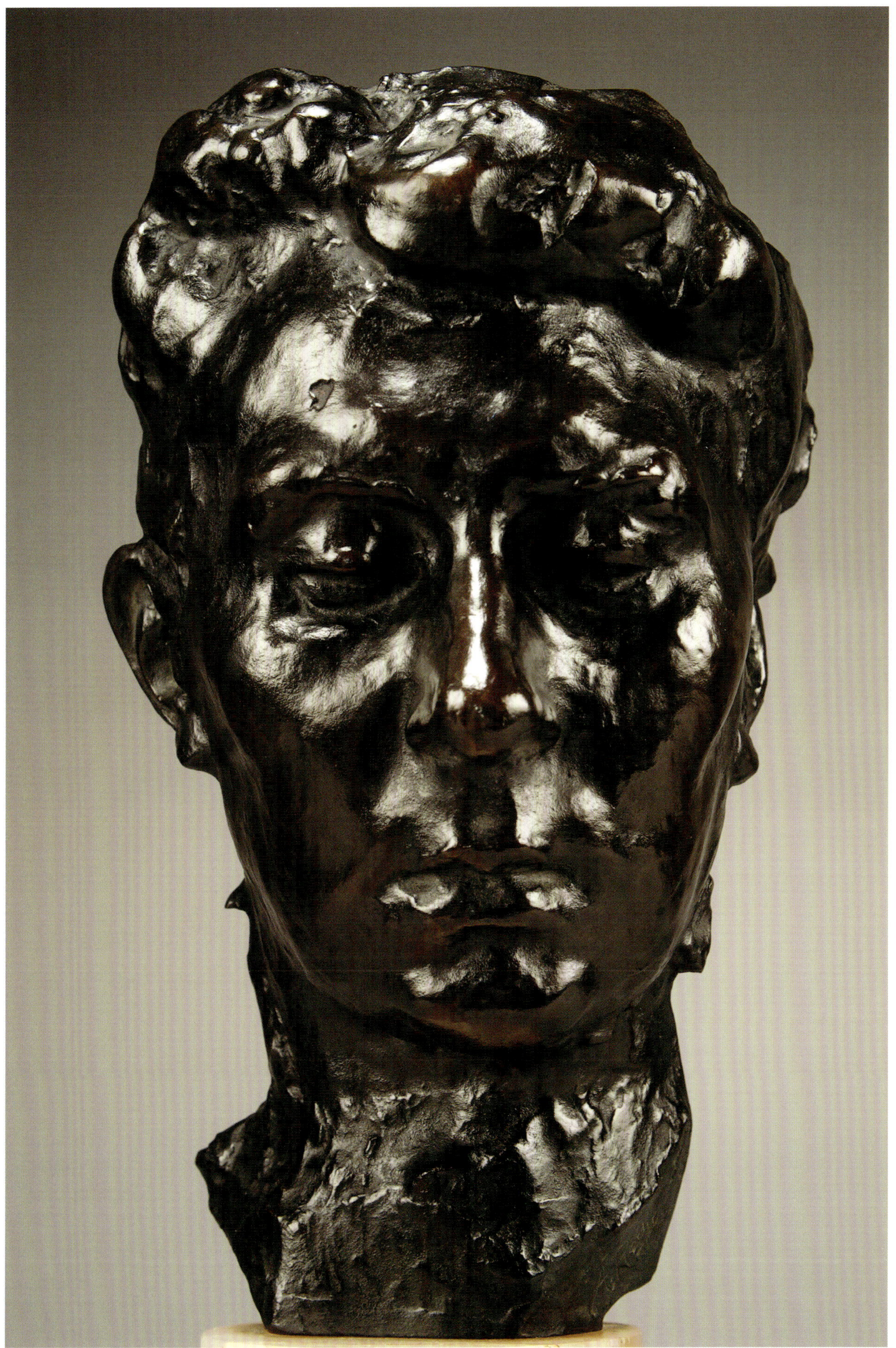

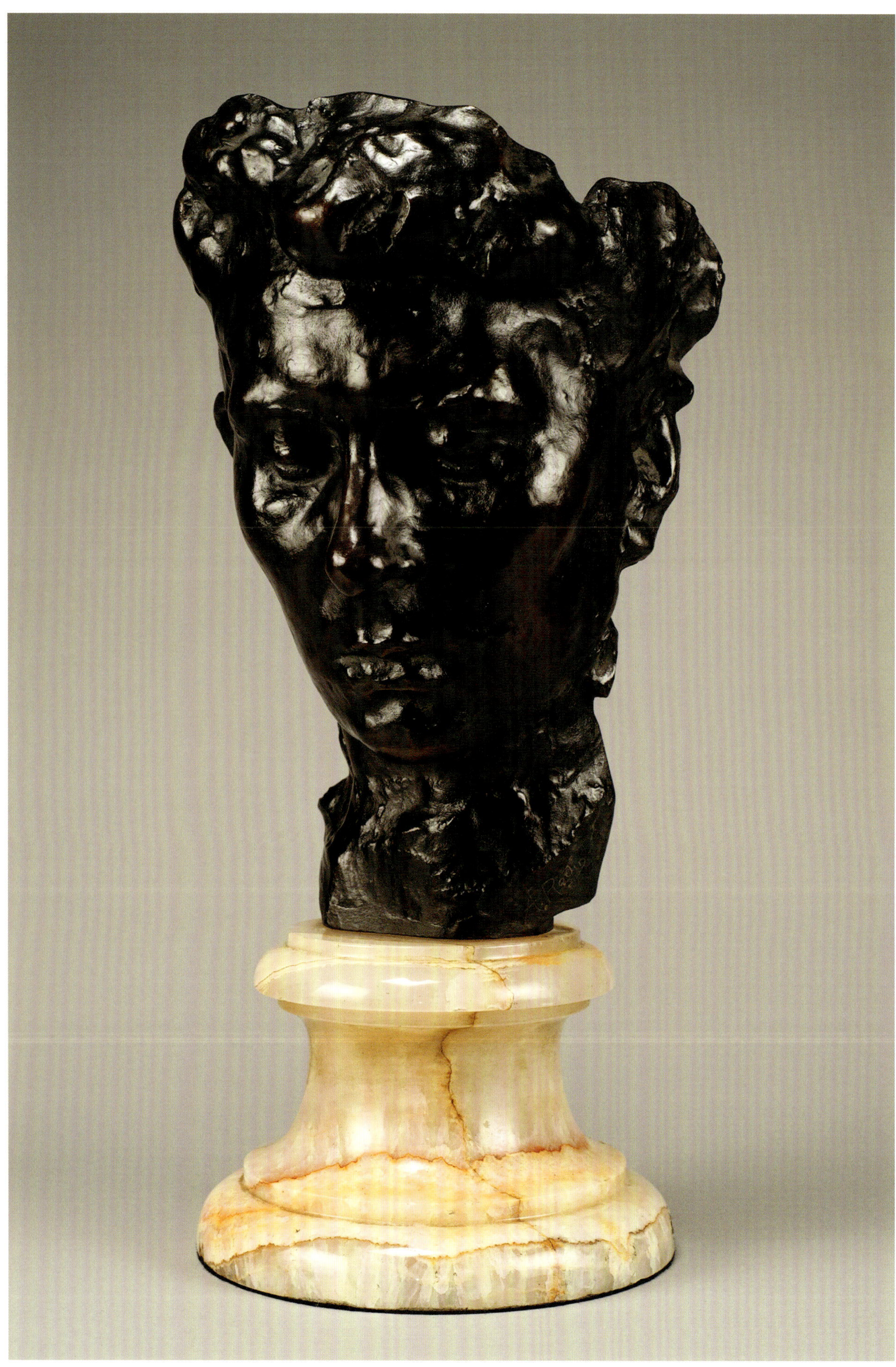

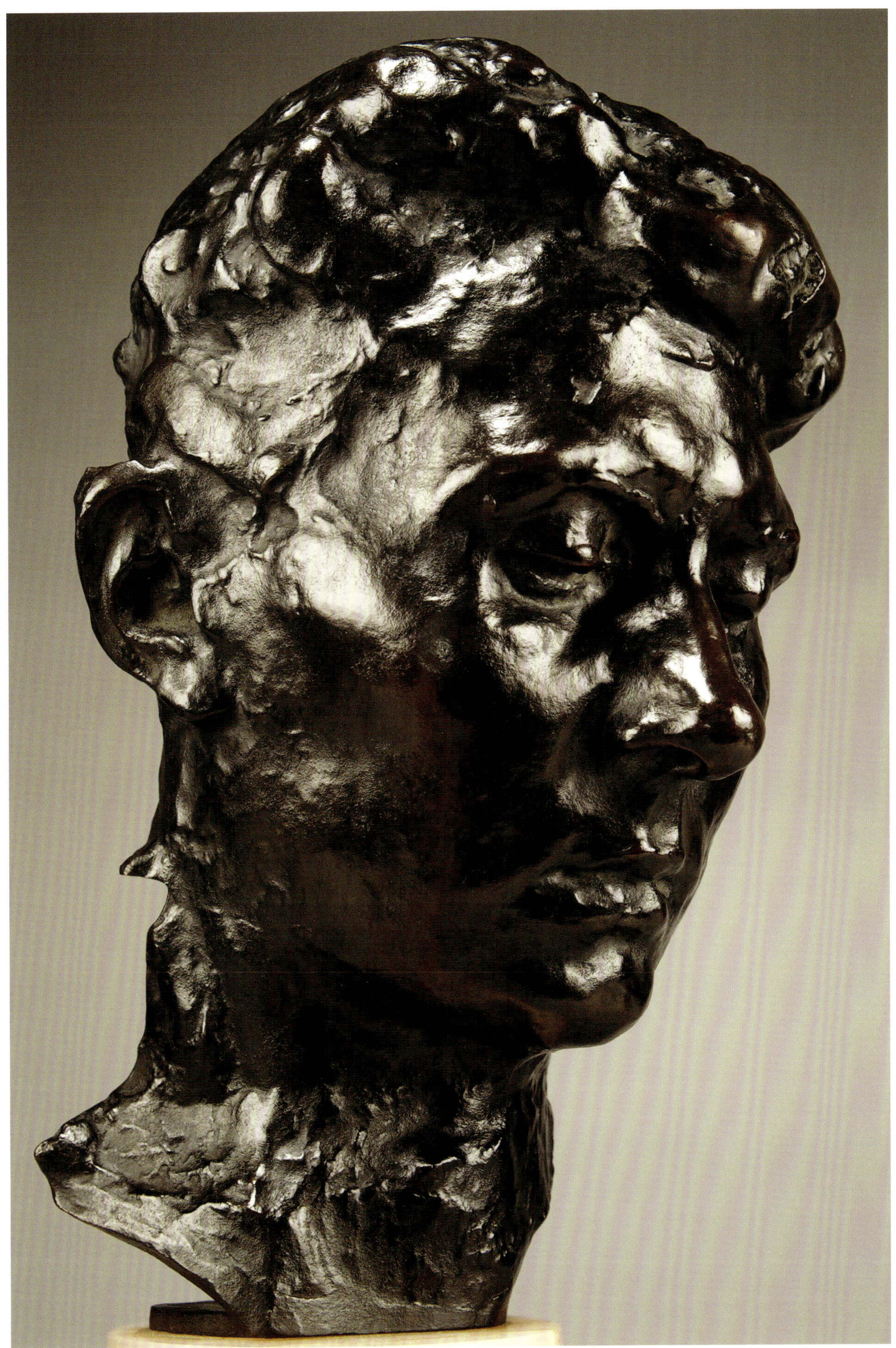

Bust of Camille Claudel

Tête de Camille Claudel

Signed A. Rodin
Inscribed © by Musée Rodin 1963 and Georges Rudier Fondeur Paris
Bronze with a rich dark brown and green patination
Height: 10⅝ inches (27 cm)

Provenance:
Musée Rodin, Paris.
Dominion Gallery, Montreal (acquired above, June 1963)
Bruton Gallery, London (1993)
Anon. Sale, Sotheby's, New York, 17 Nov. 1998, lot 479.
Private Collection
Robert Bowman Gallery, 2012
Private Collection, UK

Conceived circa 1882, this example was cast in 1963. There is one known lifetime cast of this work, possibly executed by the Françoise Rudier foundry in 1895. The Musée Rodin then continued the edition with eleven casts executed by the Georges Rudier foundry between 1955 and 1964.

Rodin met Claudel in 1882, after he took over from Alfred Boucher as supervisor of a small group of female sculptors based at a studio in Rue Notre-Dame des Champs, Paris. By all accounts Claudel was the most prominent member of the collective and according to Jessie Lipscomb (a fellow sculptor), she chose the models, explained the poses, and handed out the work to the others.

Rodin and Claudel soon became lovers and greatly inspired one another. 'I have said that Mademoiselle Camille Claudel was Rodin's pupil', explained Mathias Morhardt in 1898. 'It would be nearer the truth to say that she became his perceptive and sagacious co-worker'. Indeed, Rodin so trusted Claudel, that he asked her to assist him with the modeling of the hands and feet on his monument to *The Burghers of Calais*. Claudel also became a significant artist in her own right and her works *La Valse*, *L'implorante* and *L'abandon* are widely regarded as a masterpieces of late 19th century sculpture.

The present work was modelled shortly after Rodin met Claudel in 1882, with Rodin later using the same face in a number of allegorical portraits including *Thought*, *Farewell* and *The Convalescent*. He did not exhibit the piece during his lifetime.

Rodin's romantic relationship with Claudel lasted from shortly after the couple met, until around 1892, although they saw each other regularly until 1898. By 1905 Claudel had begun to display signs of mental illness and began a secluded life in her studio. In 1913, after the death of her father and at the instruction of her brother, she was committed to a psychiatric hospital. Although she showed continual signs of recovery and the doctors recommended that she was allowed to leave the hospital, Claudel's family insisted that she remained interned. She died in 1943 after thirty years in institutional care.

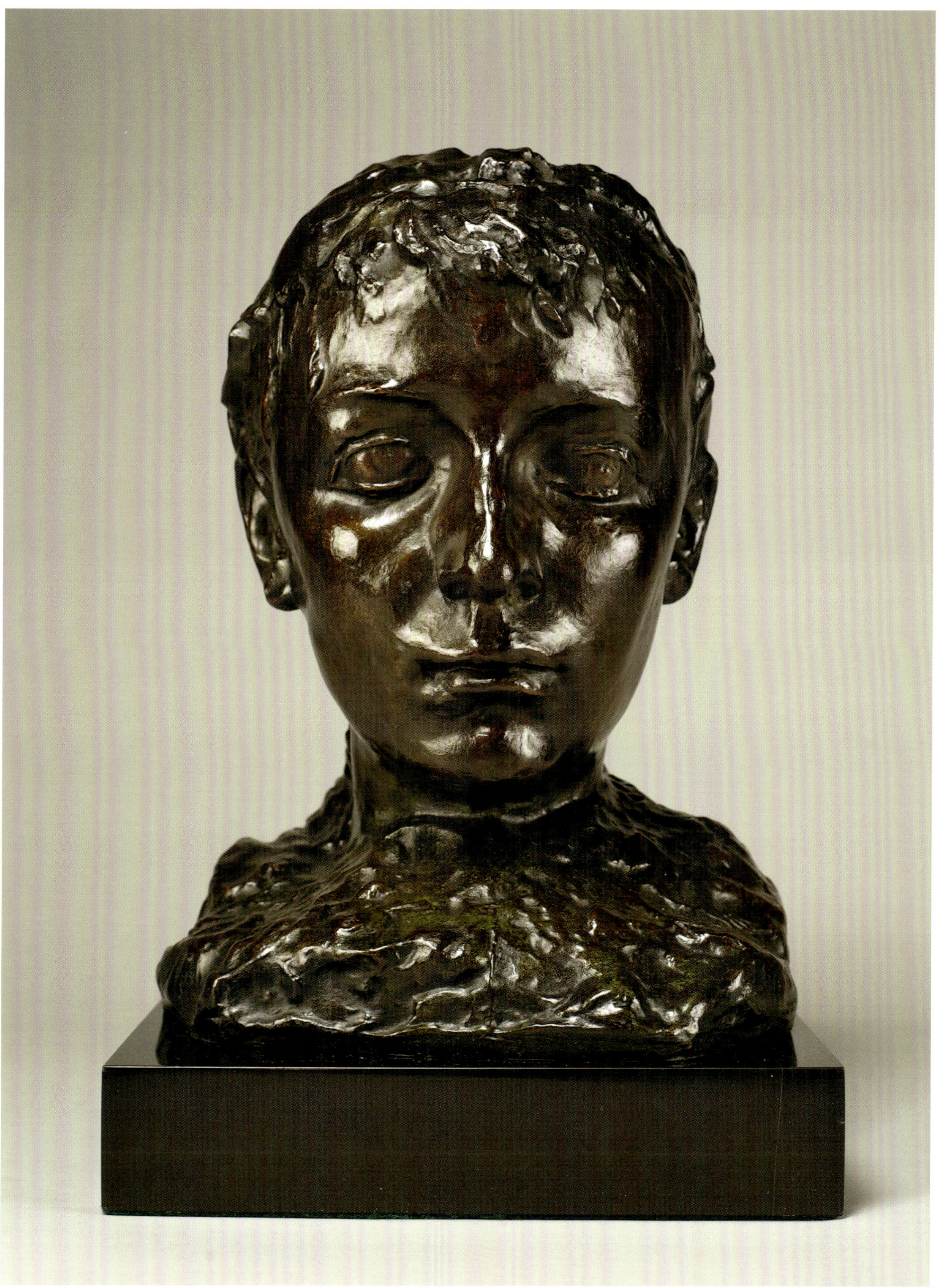

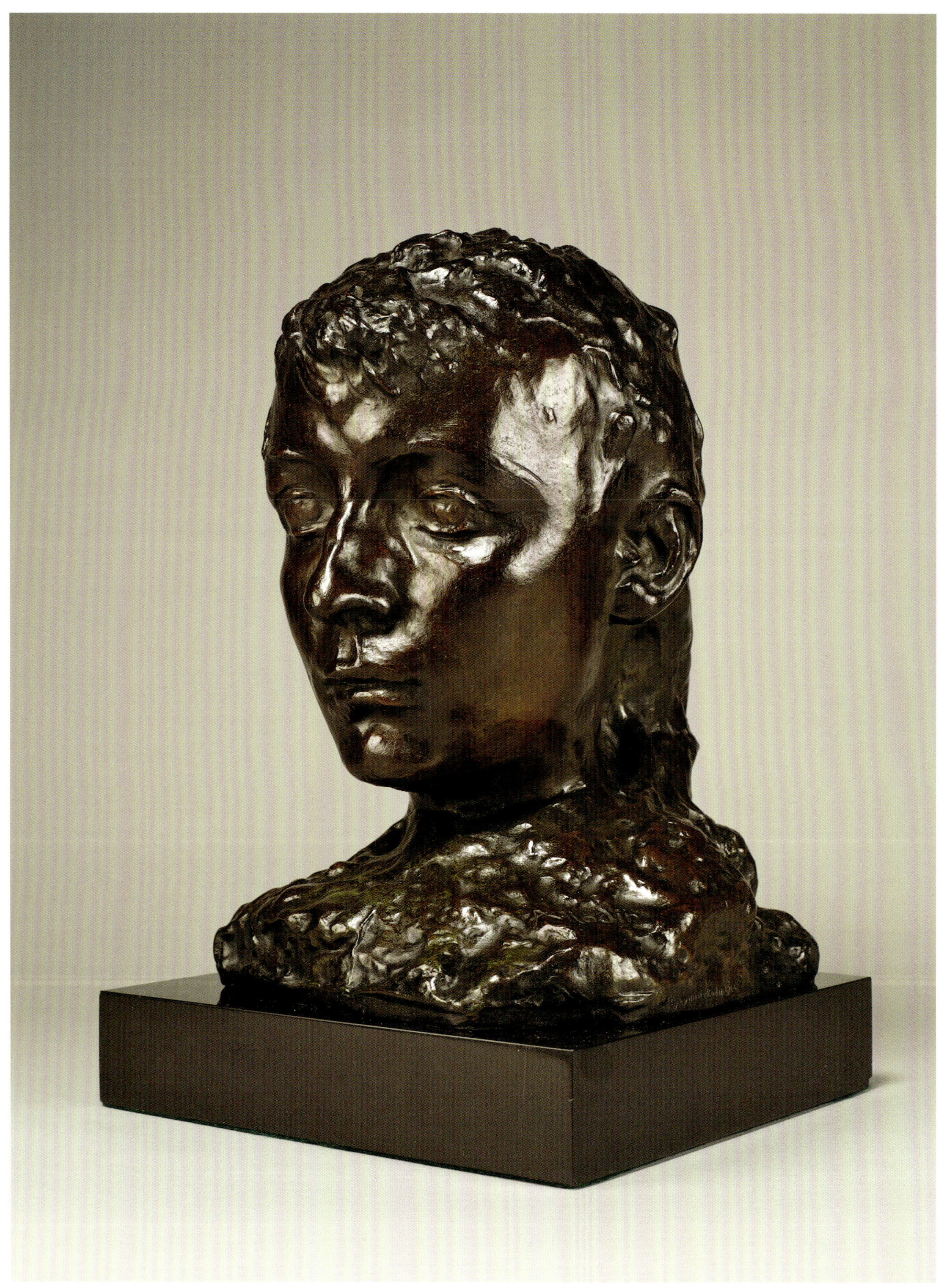

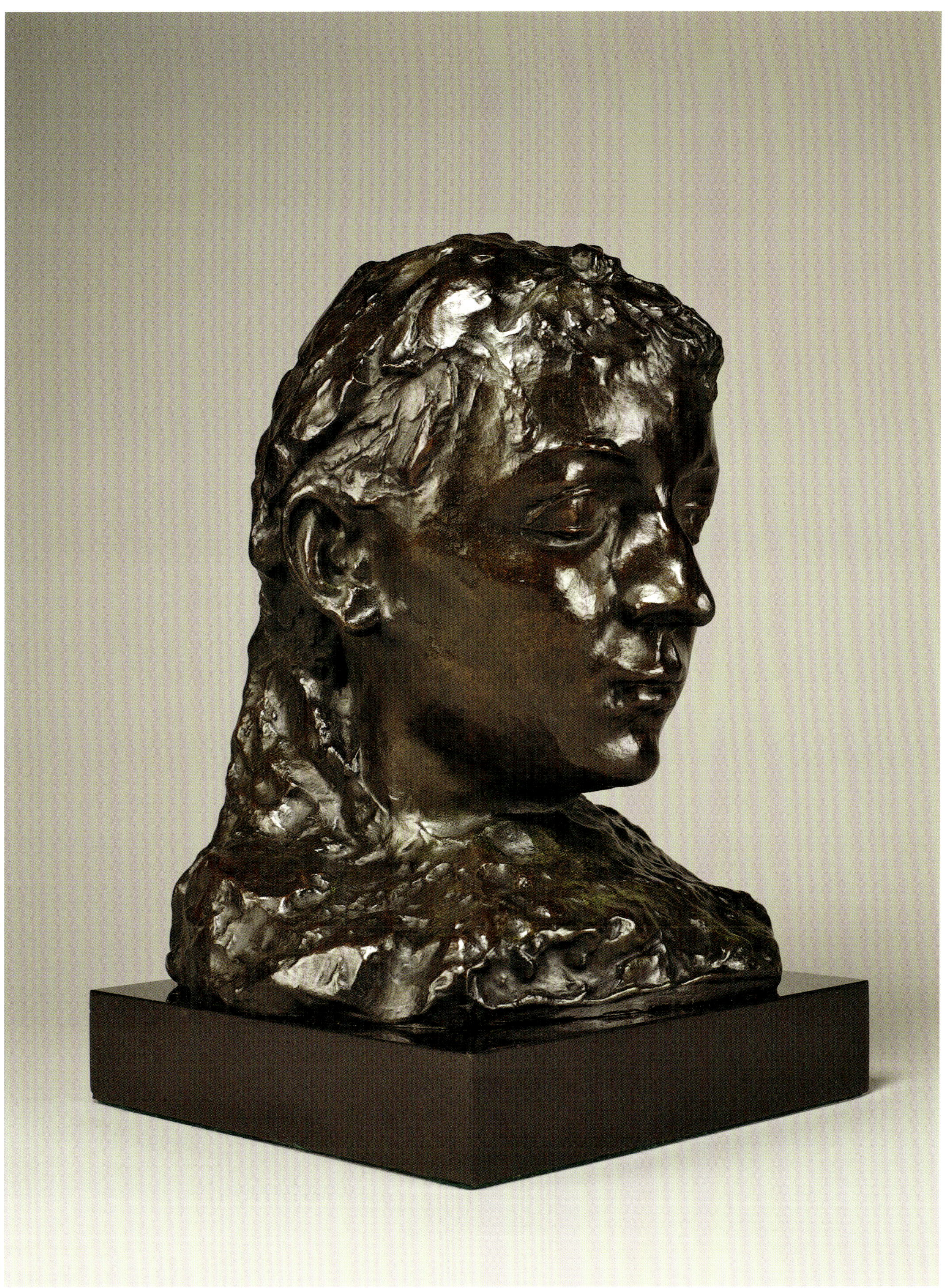

Head of Lust

Tête de la Luxure

Signed A. Rodin with repeat raised interior signature
Inscribed Alexis Rudier Fondeur Paris
Bronze with a rich dark green, black and brown patination
Height: 14¾ inches (37.3 cm)

Provenance:
Galerie Haussman, Paris, acquired from the Musée Rodin in 1918 for 3000 francs
Boghos Nubar Pasha, Paris
Private Collection, Switzerland (by descent from the above)
Acquired from the above
Robert Bowman Gallery, 2005
Private Collection, Turkey

Conceived in 1882, this example was cast between 1917 and 1918. Although this is a rare sculpture, it is unknown exactly how many bronzes were made.

The present bust is taken from *Crouching Woman*, which was one of the earliest figures Rodin modelled for *The Gates of Hell*. The full figure is often compared with Michelangelo's *Crouching Youth*, which Rodin likely knew from reproductions.

The model for *Crouching Woman* was Adèle, who was immortalised in the *Torso of Adèle* and later in one of Rodin's most well-known and sensuous works, *Eternal Spring*.

In the present bust, the face appears almost in profile with the neck almost at right angles as the model's head hangs languorously to her right. A similar effect can be seen in *Meditation*, *Caryatid a L'Urn* and *The Shade*, all of which were modelled during the same period.

As was often the case when the sculptor amended or reused parts of an existing sculpture, here Rodin makes no attempt to disguise the slab like panel on the right cheek where the woman's head had formerly lain against her leg. In doing so the work not only takes on a new identity away from the body, but also becomes a manifestation of the very sculptural process that created it.

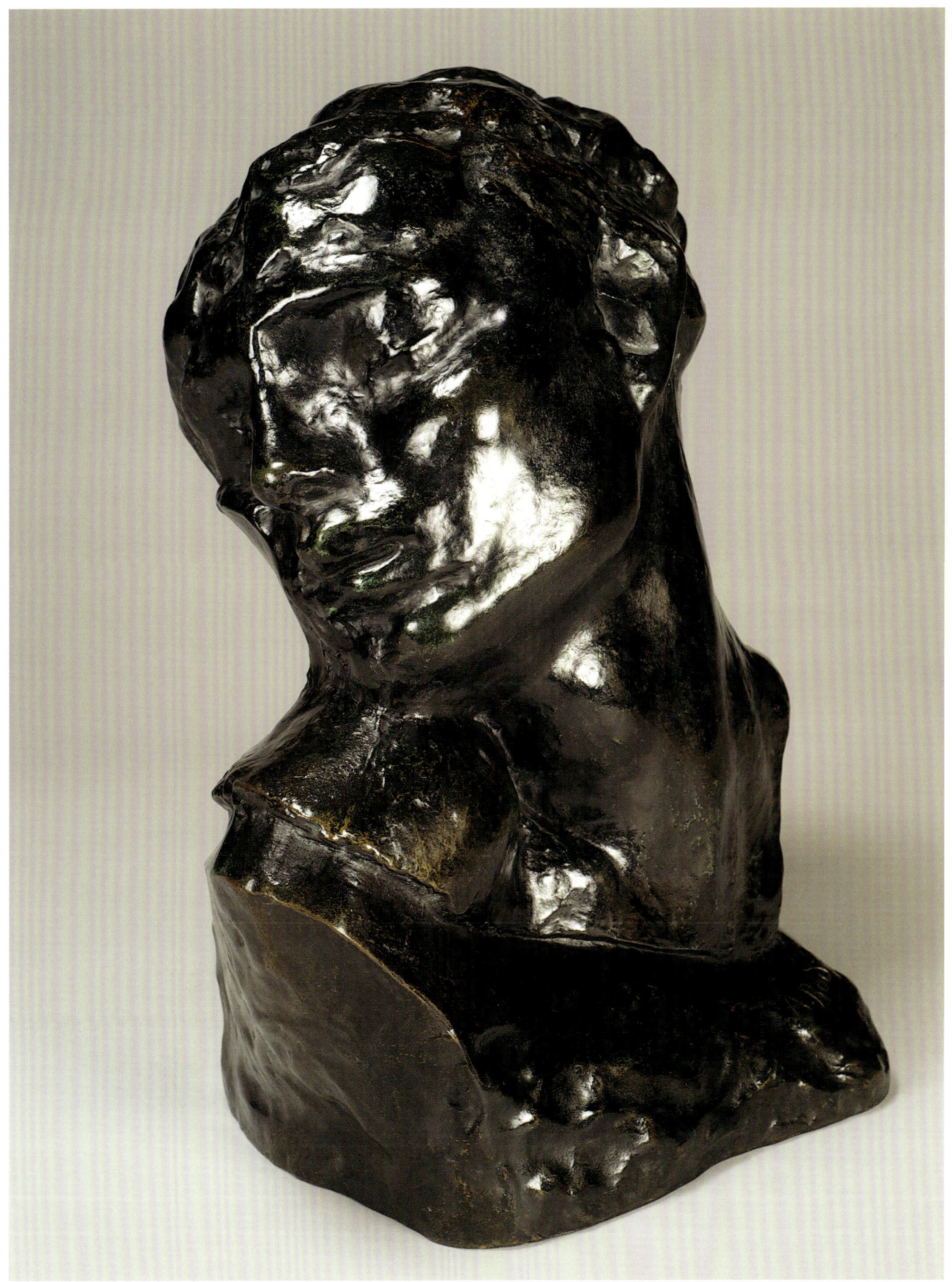

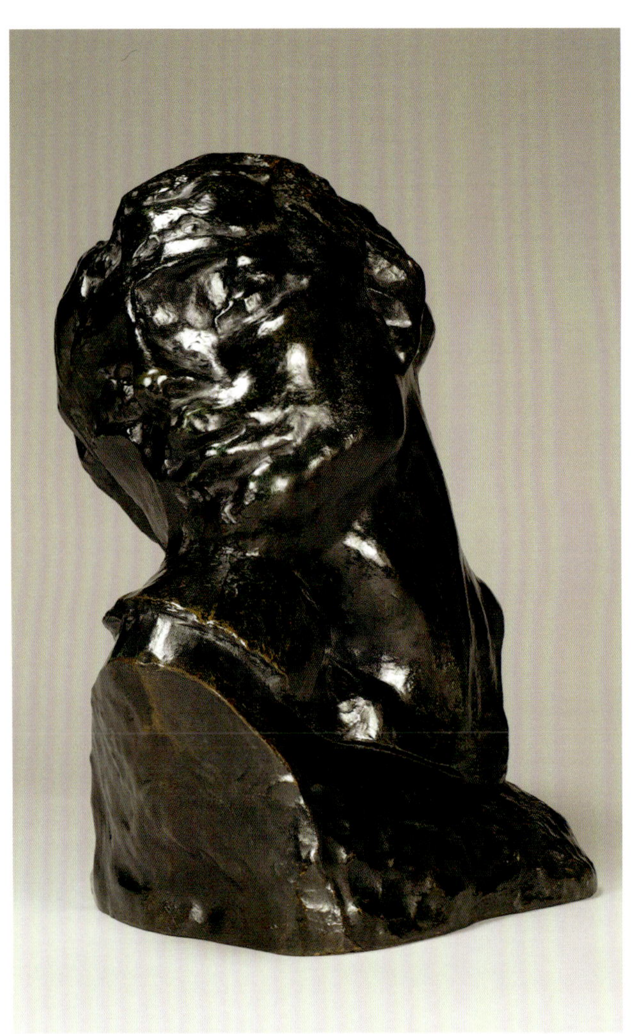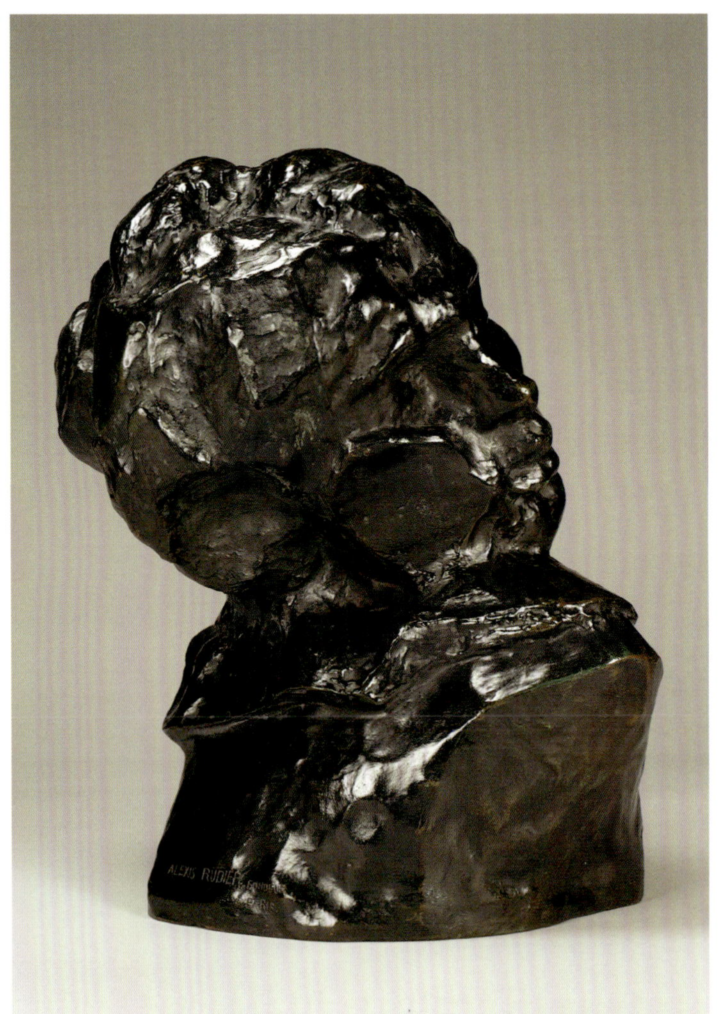

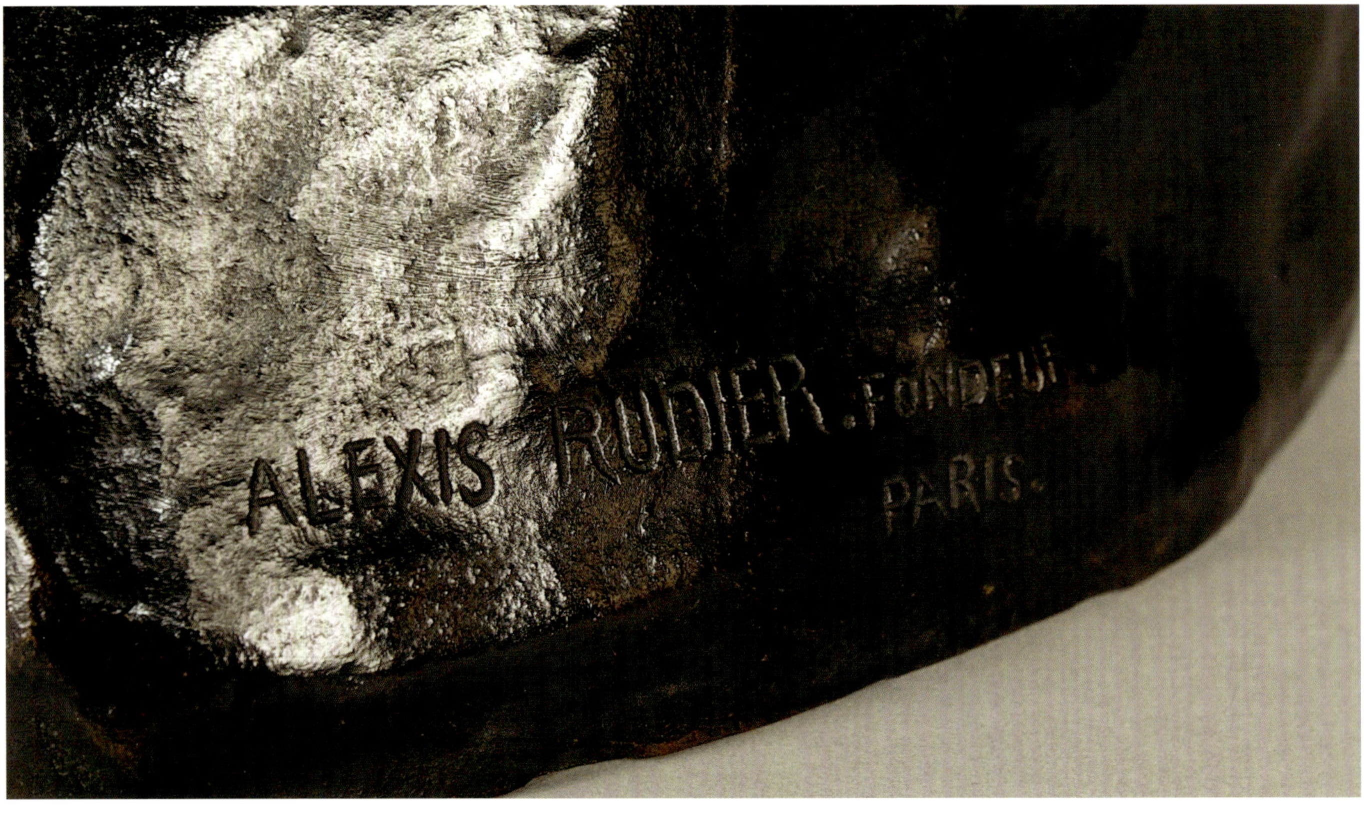

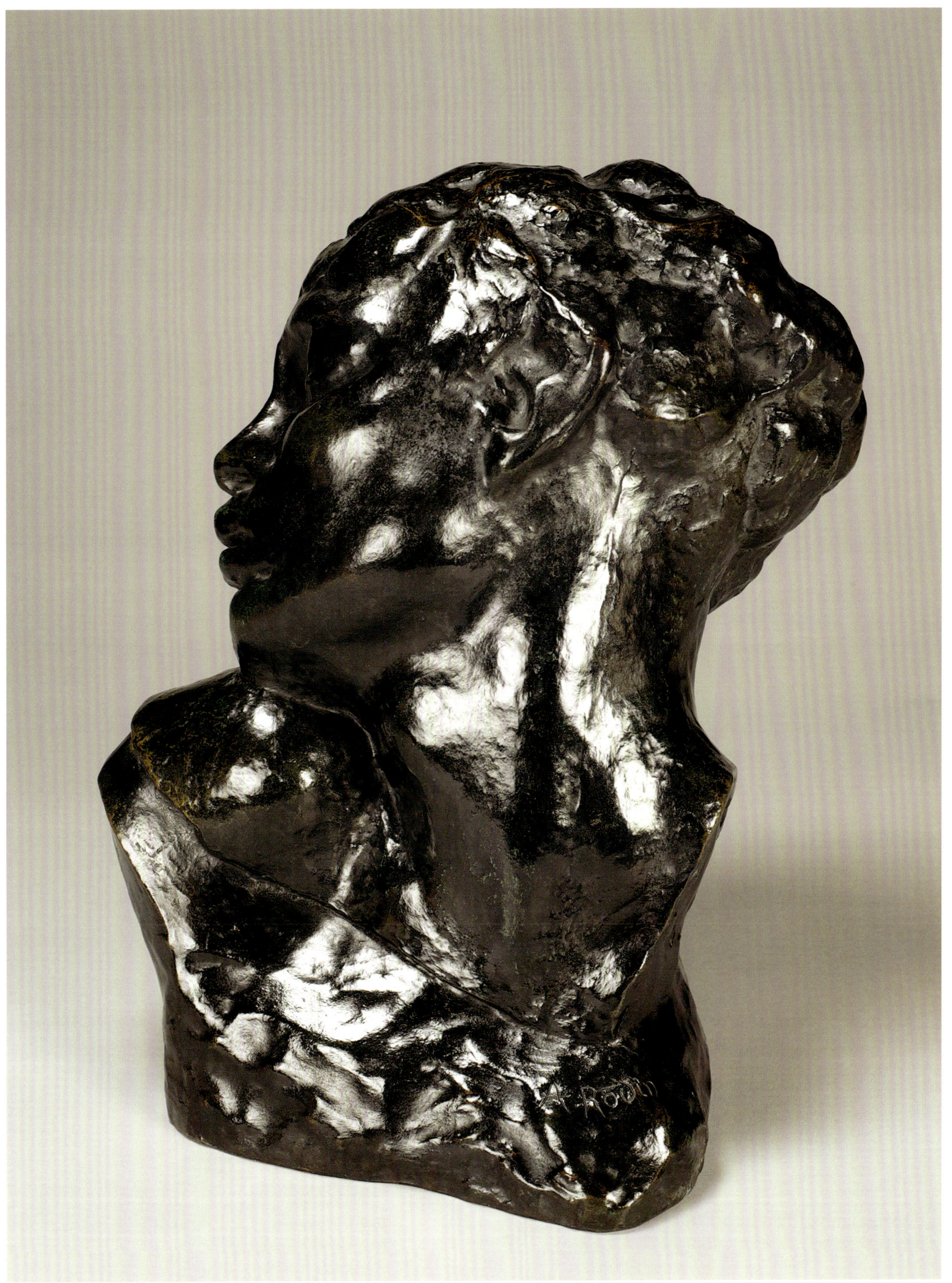

Bust of the Age of Bronze, Medium Model

Buste de l'Age d'Airain, Moyen Modèle

Signed Rodin
Patinated terracotta
Height: 8½ inches (21.2 cm)

Provenance:
Promised gift of Rodin to Auguste Neyt, the sitter for the model
Leonce Benedicte, executor of the Rodin's estate
Mr and Mrs Auguste Neyt, 1924
Thence by Descent
Private Collection, USA

This rare and fine bust is the head of of the controversial figure known as the age of bronze. When Rodin first exhibited the work in 1877, having modelled it the year before, he was accused of having cast the work directly from life, in other words taking a cast of a living human body and casting in bronze. Rodin gained two significant benefits from this initial rejection however, firstly the work became notorious and definitely increased his reputation and secondly he learnt never to produce works exactly to life scale to avoid the accusation ever being placed again.

Rodin re-united with his model for the sculpture, Auguste Neyt, 30 years after he sat for Rodin. To commemorate the meeting Rodin promised Neyt a terracotta bust of the sculpture. The gift was finally recieved by the model in 1924 from the executor of Rodin's estate.

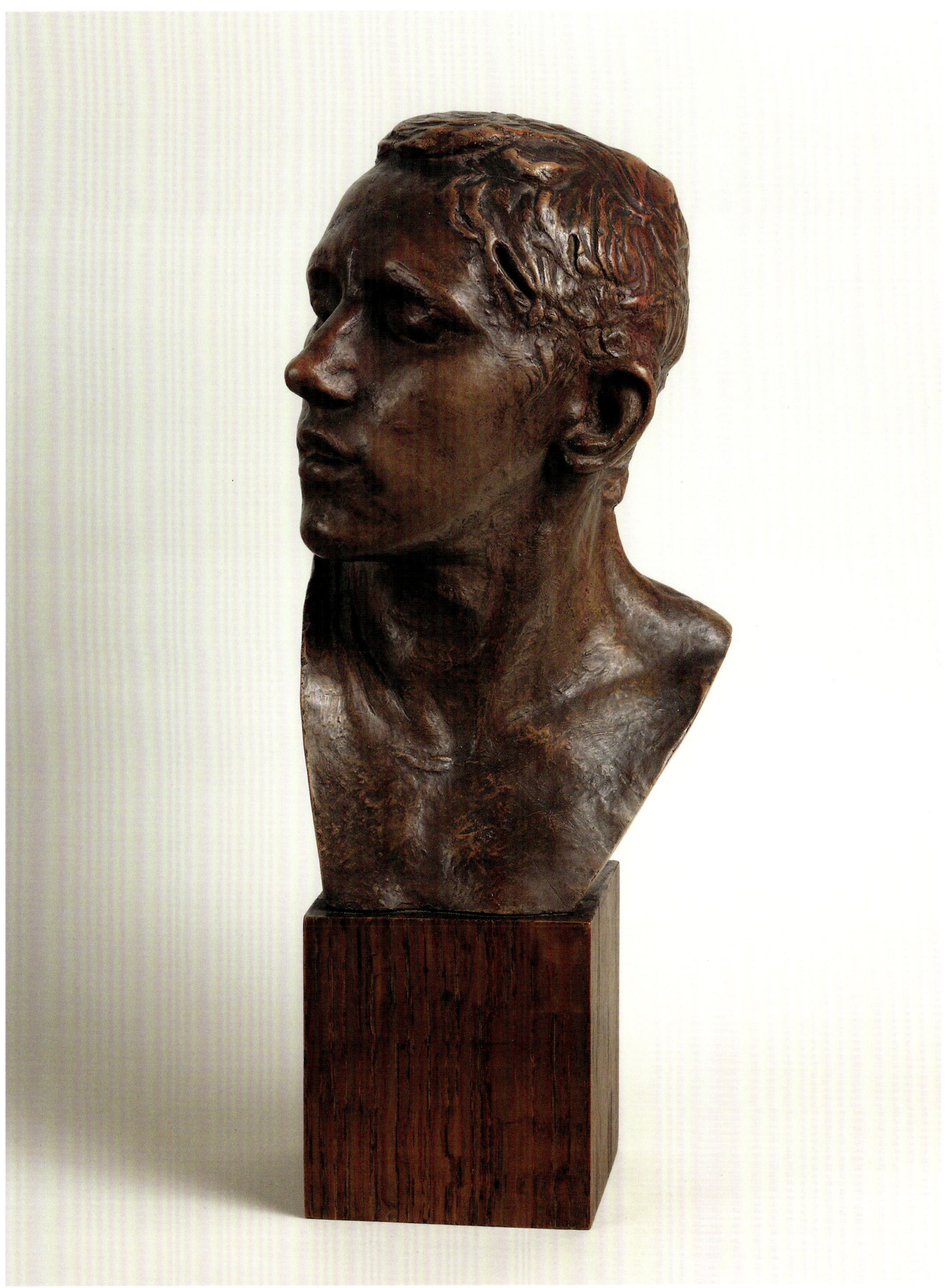

Victoria and Albert Museum Torso

Torse Victoria and Albert Museum

Signed A. Rodin
Inscribed © Musée Rodin 1979 and Fondeur Coubertin
Numbered 4
Bronze with a black and dark green patination
Height: 24¾ inches (63 cm)

Provenance:
Purchased from the Musée Rodin by Dr John Igini, Chicago
Carol Igini, Chicago
John May, England
Robert Bowman Gallery, 2010
Private Collection, Hong Kong

Conceived between 1900 and 1905, this example was executed in 1979. The only known lifetime cast was made by the Alexis Rudier foundry and given to the Victoria and Albert Museum in 1914 by Rodin. The Coubertin foundry made an edition of twelve casts for the Musée Rodin between 1978 and 1982.

This torso is a fragment of the figure entitled *Eve Eating the Apple* (1887). It started as a seated torso with legs but when Rodin had the torso enlarged he sliced it diagonally through the abdomen. The work was then mounted on a slightly flared base.

Rodin commented 'I often asked a model to sit on the ground with her back to me, gathering her arms and legs in front of her. In that position only the silhouette of the back, which gets thinner at the waist and widens at the hips, can be seen and that represents an exquisitely shaped vase, the amphora which contains future life within its sides.'

This almost abstract work shows Rodin at his most modern. The free approach to form clearly illustrates the sculptor as a pioneer, anticipating the developments to of later twentieth century sculpture.

The only known life time cast was given by Rodin to the Victoria and Albert Museum in 1914 and stands on its original plinth cast from a pillar that belonged to the sculptor. The work was one of eighteen sculptures gifted by Rodin to the V&A in honour of the French and British soldiers killed in the war. It is unique amongst public collections as the sculptures were selected by Rodin himself, who described them as the collection he had been making all his life.

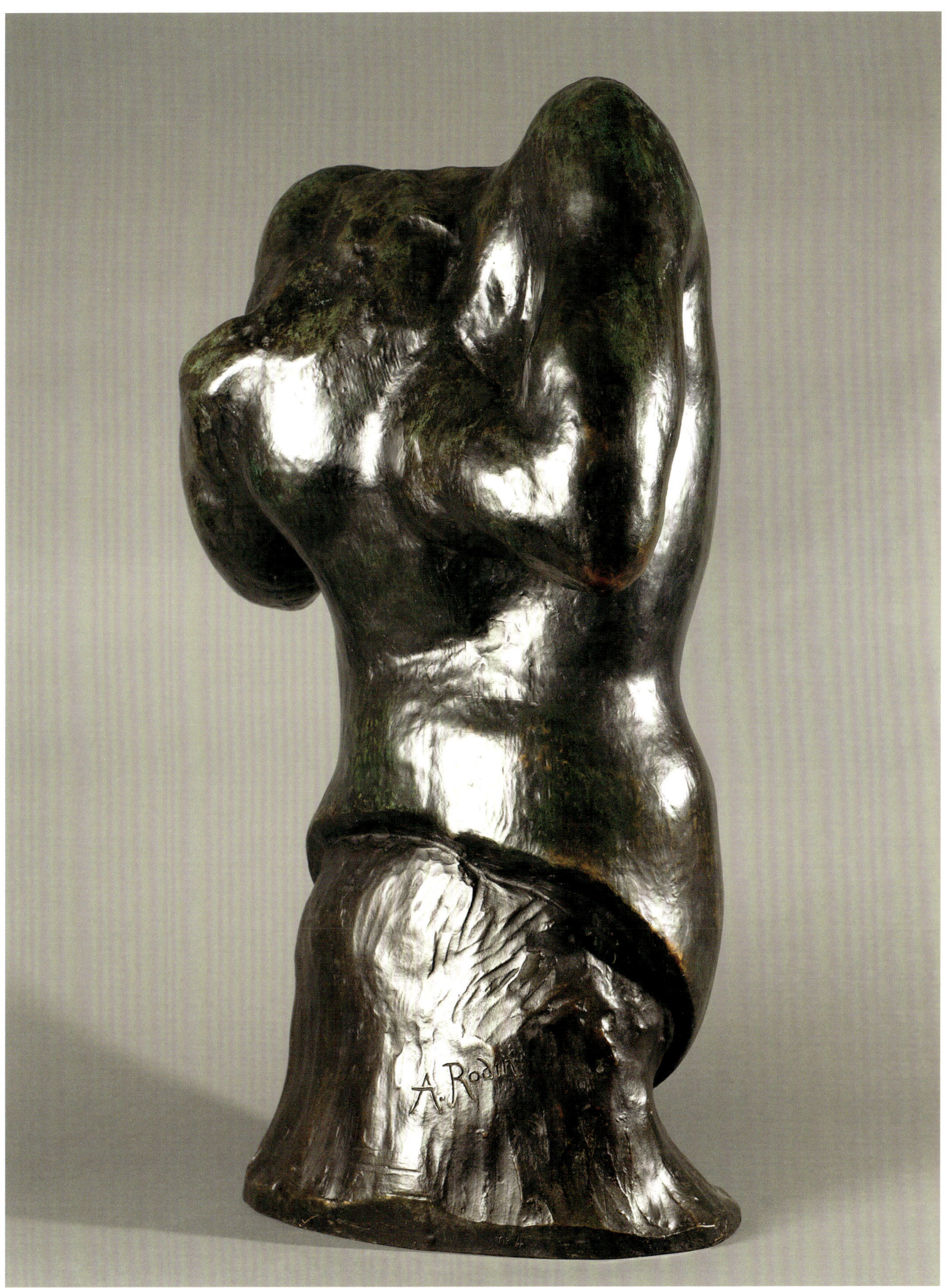

Torso of a Man, Study Type A, Small Model

Torse d'homme, Etude Type A, Petit Modele

Signed A. Rodin
Inscribed © by Musée Rodin 1970 and Georges Rudier Fondeur Paris
Numbered 5
Bronze with a rich green and dark brown patination
Height: 7¼ inches (18.5 cm)

Provenance:
Musée Rodin, Paris
Galerie Gerald Cramer, Lausanne. Acquired January 1971
Private Collection, Switzerland
Robert Bowman Gallery, 2011
Private Collection, UK

Conceived in 1900, this example was cast in 1970. This model was never cast during Rodin's lifetime. The Georges Rudier foundry made thirteen casts for the Musée Rodin between 1967 and 1975.

This small-truncated *Torso* is taken from the male figure in Rodin's earlier model *Man and his Thought*. The two figures, one male and one female, which comprised *Man and his Thought*, were originally incorporated into *The Gates of Hell* where they were used to support the upper cornice. The work was never cast in bronze and only a single marble, now in the National Gallery, Berlin, was carved. The present torso is typical of Rodin's move towards simplified and fragmented works, which he continued to produce throughout the later part of his career.

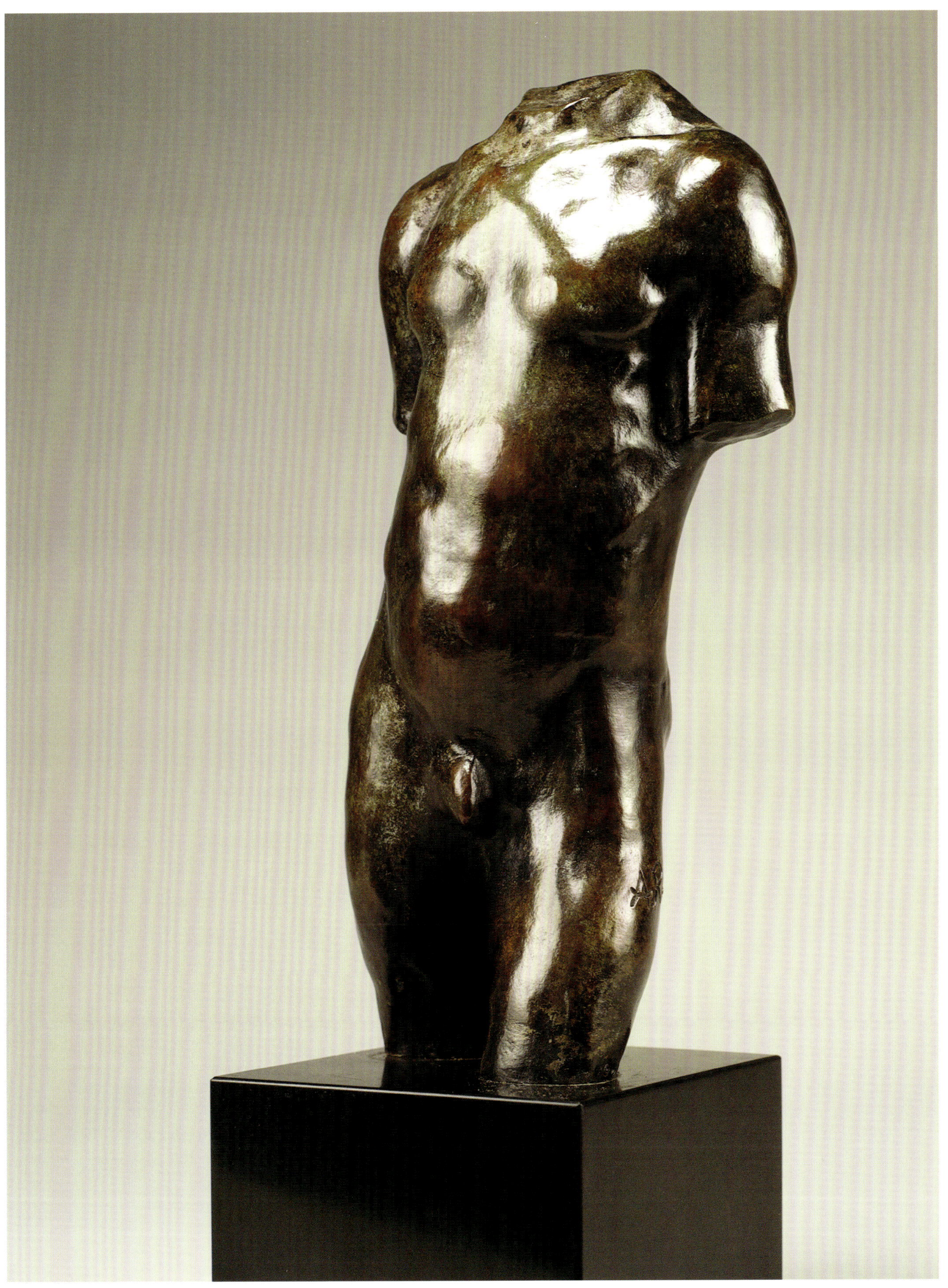

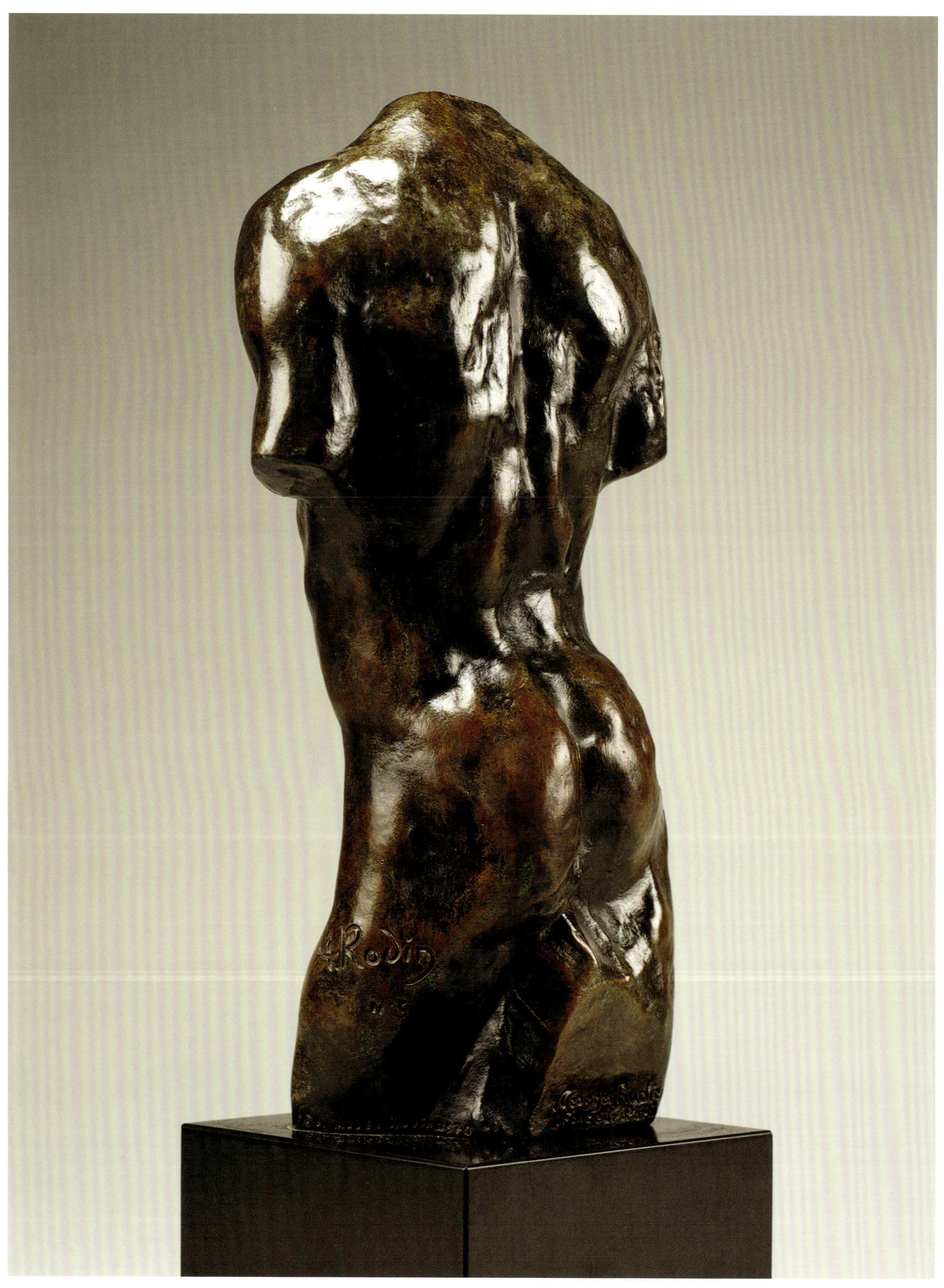

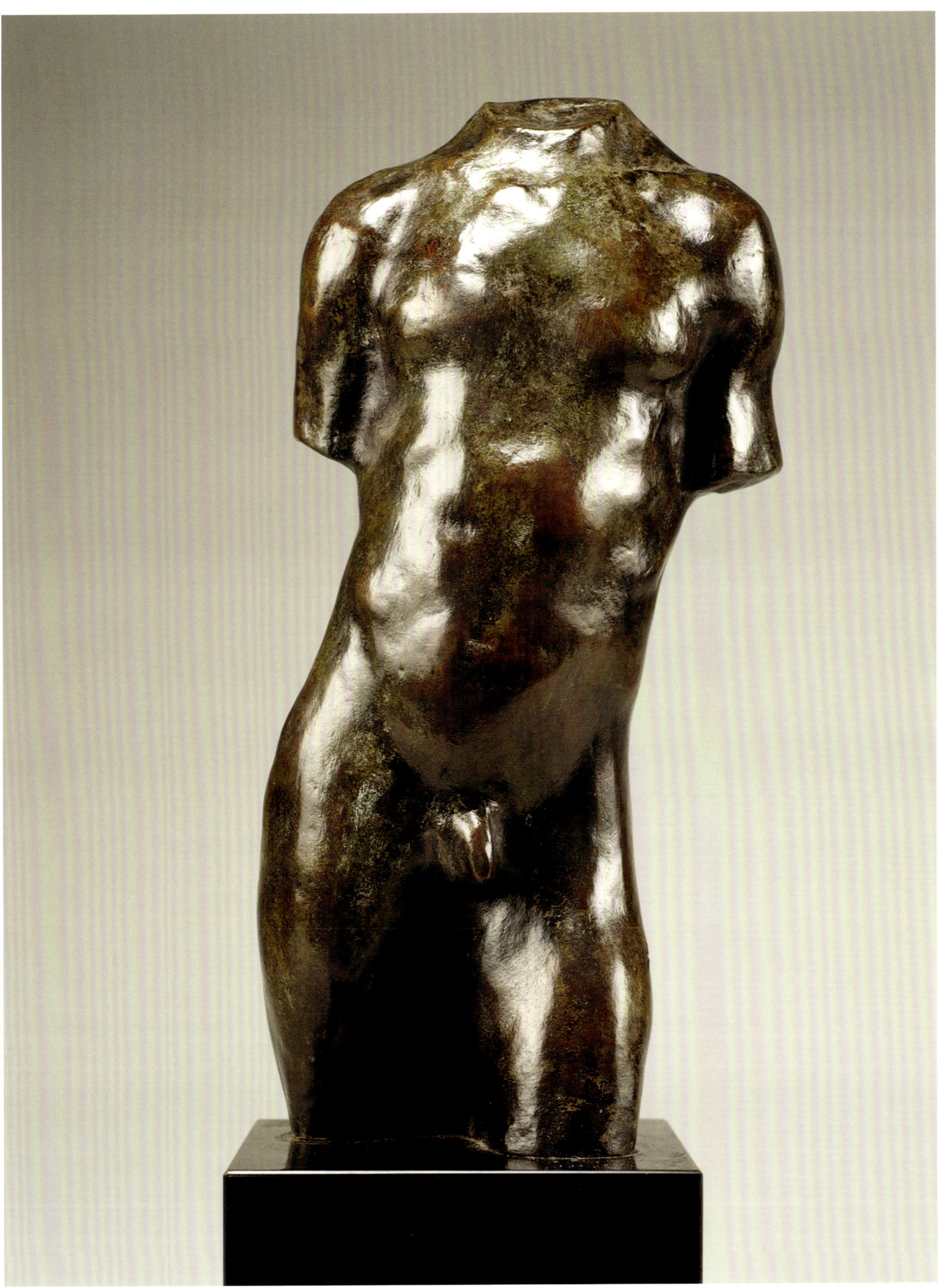

Male Torso Of Giganti

Torse D'Homme Giganti

Signed A. Rodin
Inscribed © by Musée Rodin 1966 and Georges Rudier Fondeur, Paris,
Bronze with a rich mid brown patination with green highlights
Height: 11 inches (28 cm)

Provenance:
Musée Rodin, Paris
Galerie Claude Bernard, Paris acquired 1966
Consons Inc. N.Y.
Dominion Gallery, Montreal 1967, Exhibited in the Cinquantenaire de la Mort D'Auguste Rodin, illustrated Exhibition catalogue p.58
Private Collection, Connecticut, USA
Robert Bowman Gallery, 2010
Private Collection, UK

Conceived in 1882 there were three examples of this work cast between 1902 and 1952 by the Alexis Rudier Foundry. A further ten casts were made by the Georges Rudier foundry between 1966 and 1974.

This small muscular torso demonstrates the close relationship between Rodin, Camille Claudel and the English sculptress Jessie Lipscomb, who each asked the same Italian model, a Neapolitan called Giganti, to pose for works during the mid 1880s.

As was typical, Rodin first modelled the entire figure before truncating the sculpture and working on an independent head and a torso. Lipscomb concentrated on the head, modeling a realistic likeness and Claudel made a plaster study, which she exhibited in 1885 at the Salon des Artistes Français.

Rodin's *Torso* was first exhibited in 1897 at the First International Exhibition of Fine Art Arts in Dresden where it was purchased by the German state.

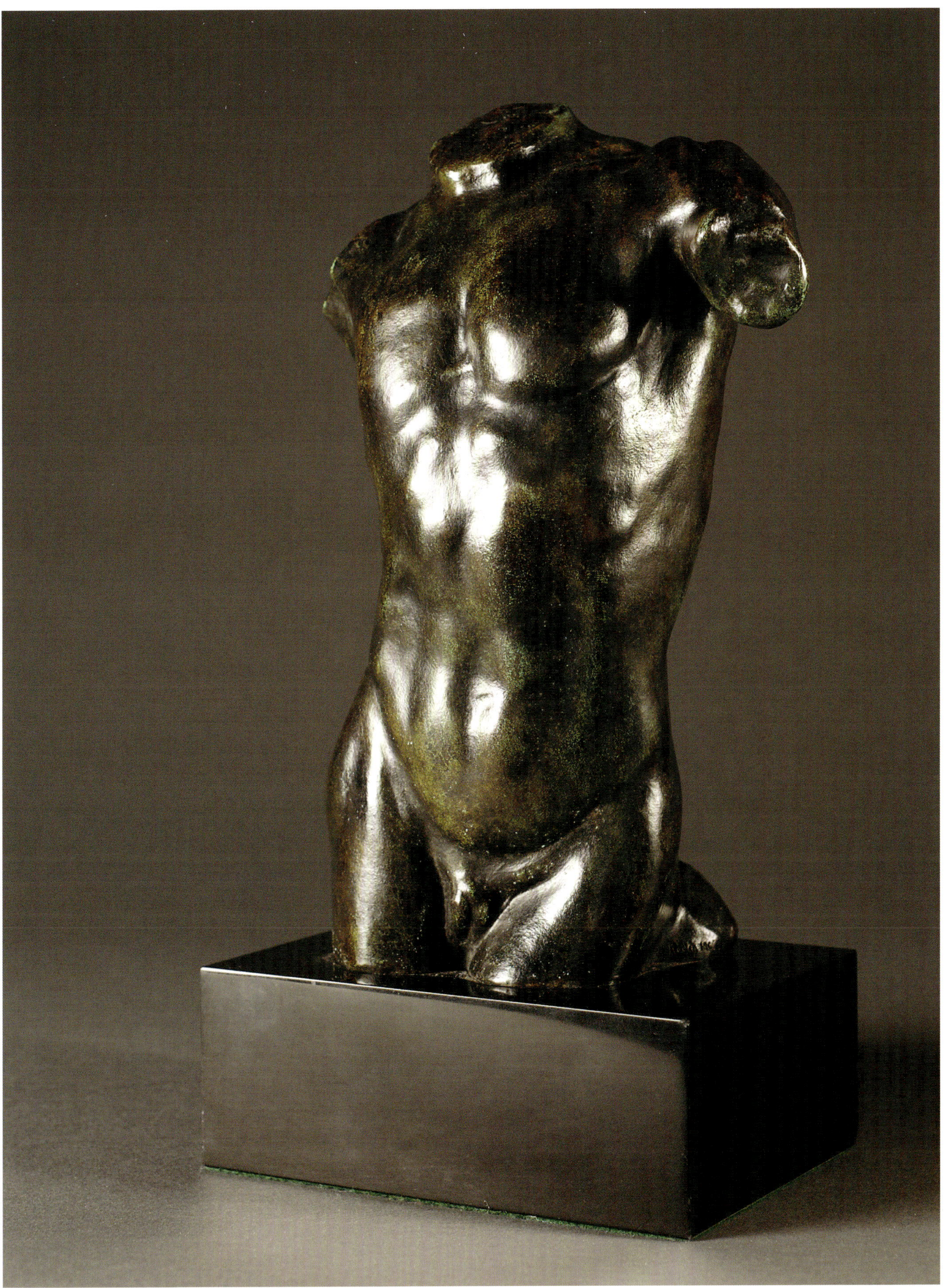

Torso of The Falling Man

L'Homme Qui Tombe, Torse

Signed A. Rodin
Inscribed © by Musée Rodin 1972 and Georges Rudier Fondeurs Paris
Numbered 7
Bronze with a rich dark green and black patination
Height: 40⅛ inches (102 cm)

Provenance:
Musée Rodin, Paris;
Feingarten Galleries, Los Angeles
Private Collection, United States
Robert Bowman Gallery, 2010
Private Collection, Norway

Conceived in 1904, this example cast 1972. This work was never cast in Rodin's lifetime. Thirteen casts were made by the Georges Rudier foundry for the Musée Rodin between 1967 and 1981.

This present work derives from the figure of the *L'homme Qui Tombe*, which hangs from the lintel on the left hand door of *The Gates of Hell*.

In this truncated form, the work has been produced in two sizes. The first version is in the original scale and the present monumental version, also known as *Torso of Louis XIV* or *Marsyas*, was conceived in plaster and first exhibited in Dusseldorf in 1904.

Rodin became increasingly interested in the idea of paring down his sculptures to their bare essentials, often by removing limbs or the head. This approach was an attempt to uncover what he considered the very essence of the human form and as such, differed from the work of Neo-classical artists who often replicated the fragmented monuments of antiquity.

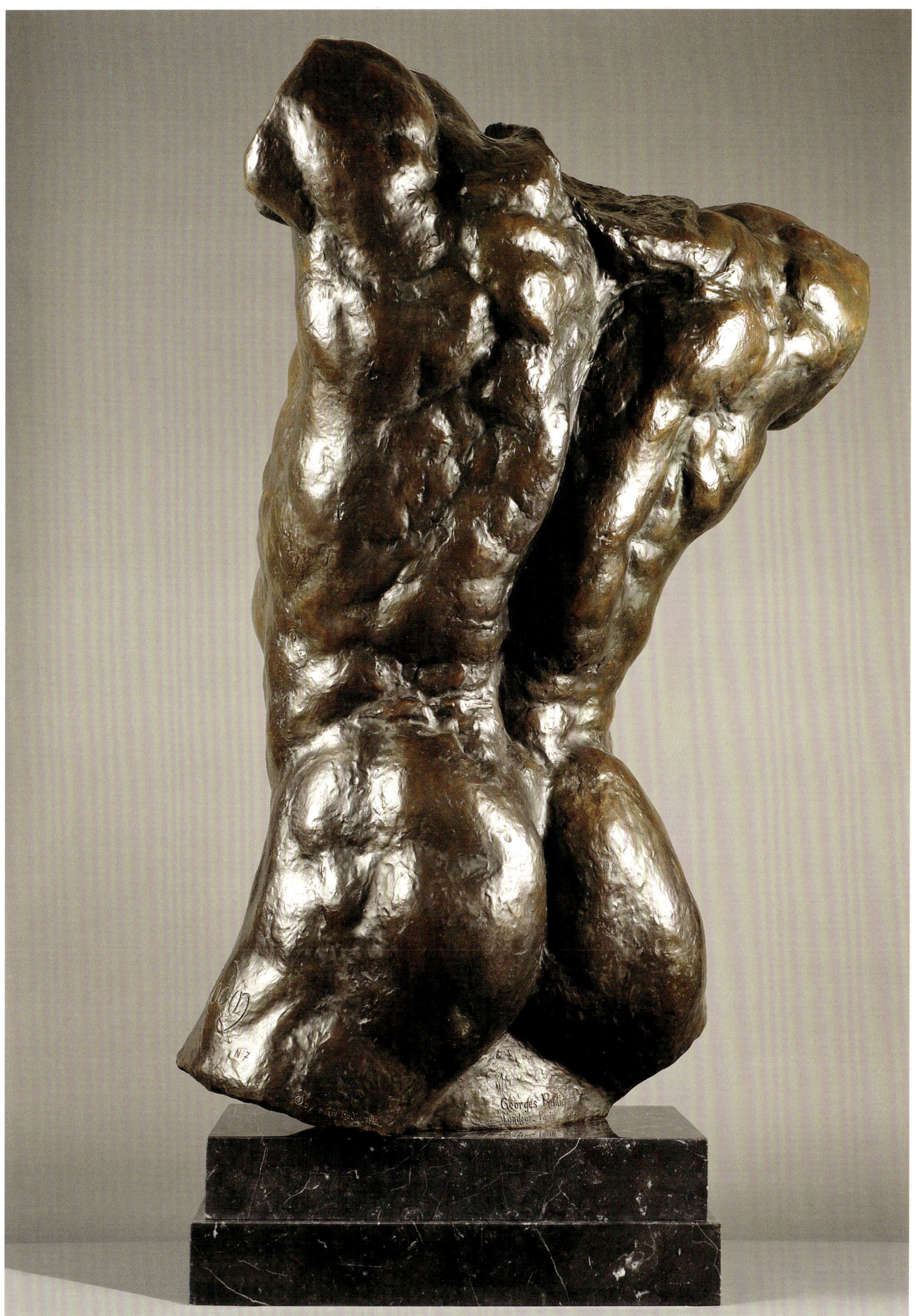

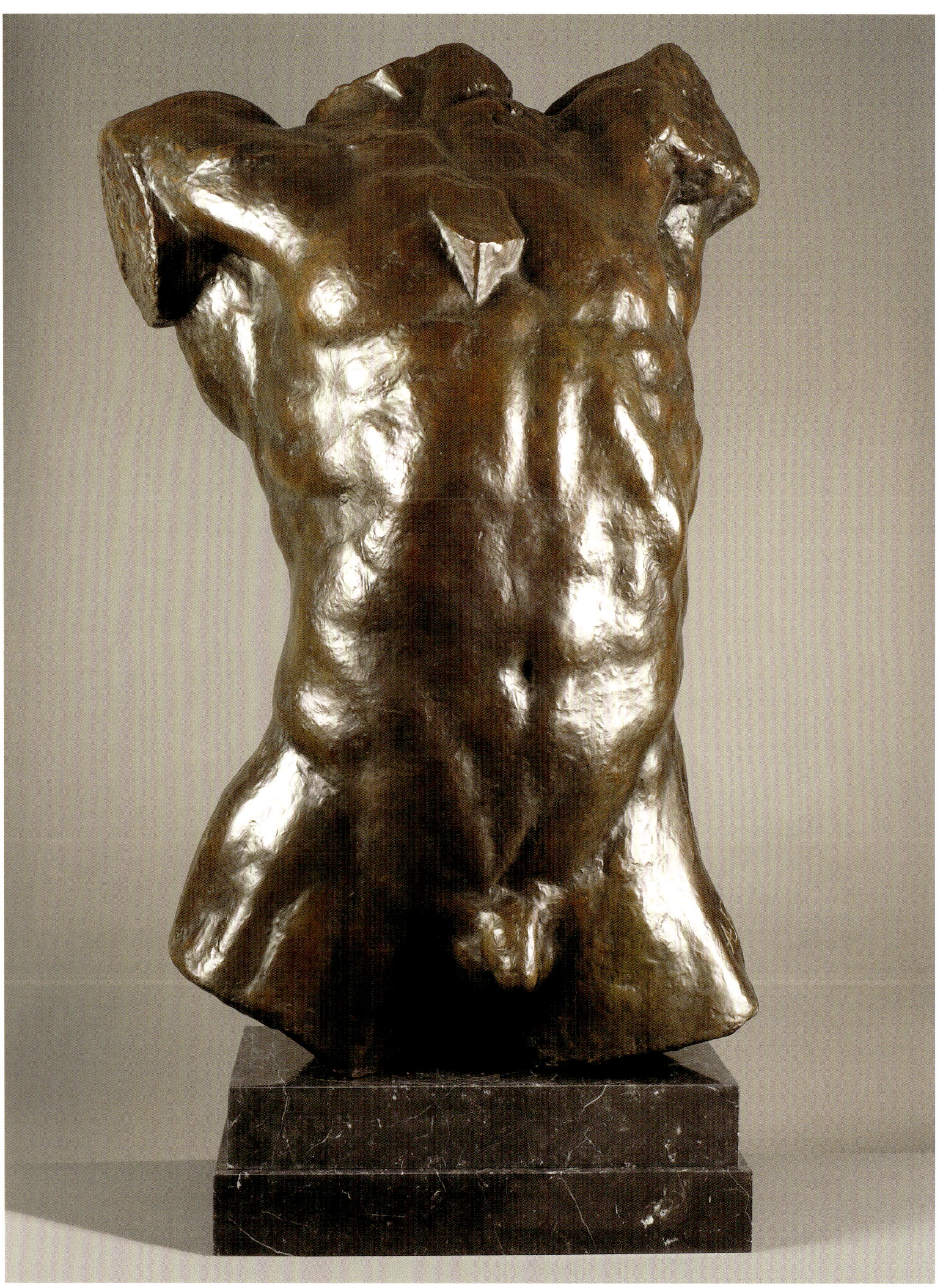

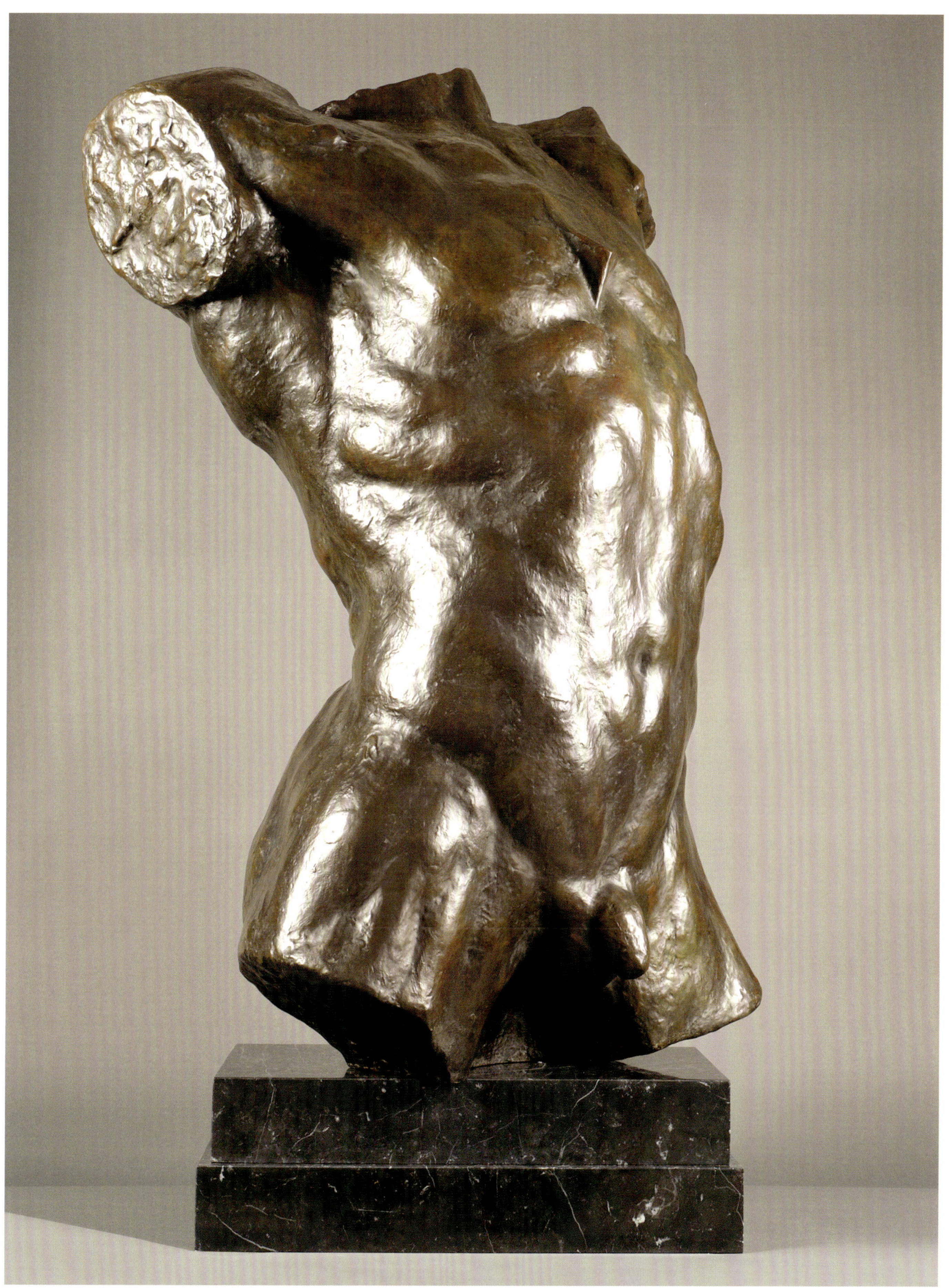

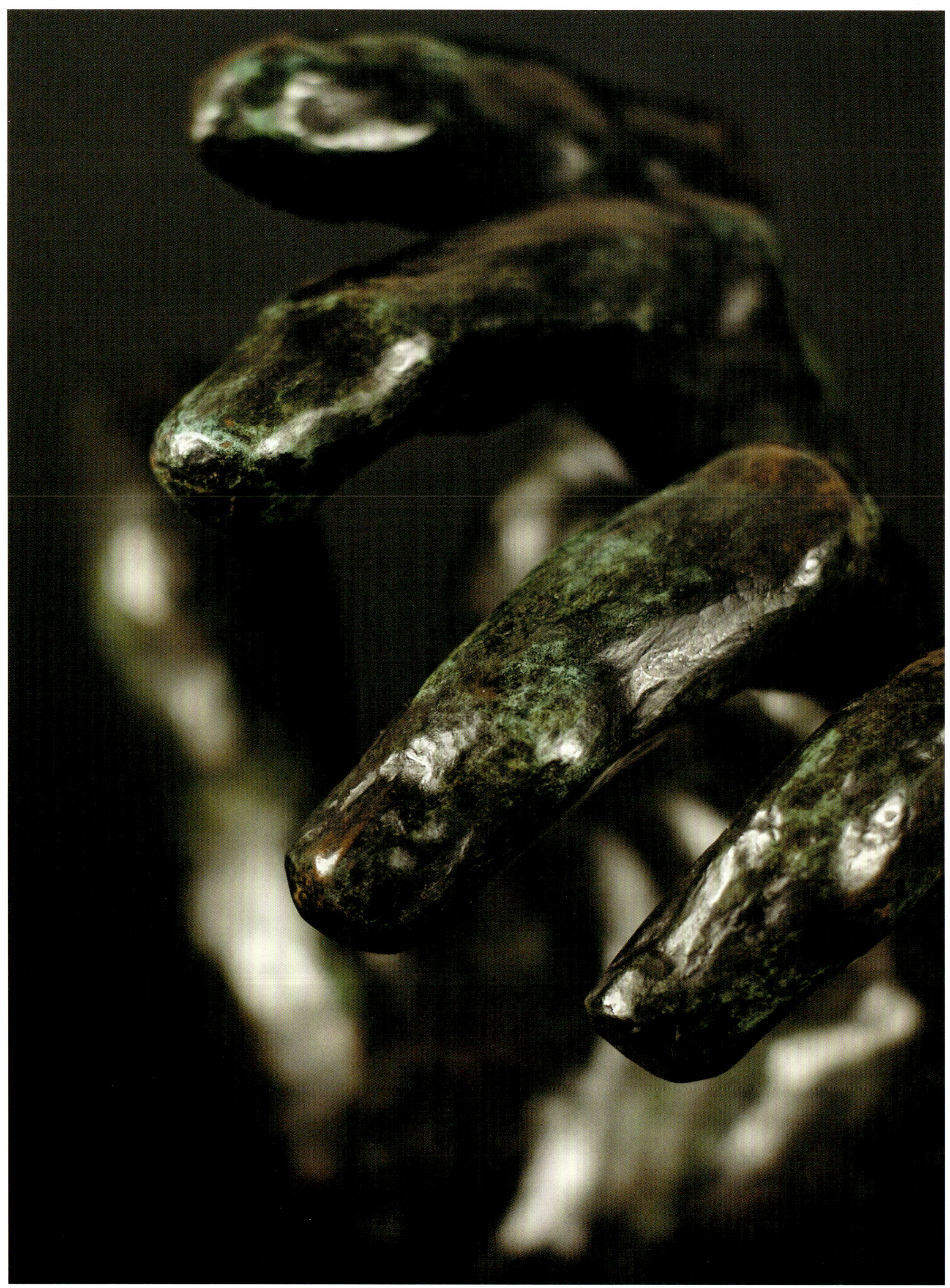

Rodin sculpted hands more than he did any other part of the body. He used them to convey powerful emotions, both on their own and when grouped with other sculptures. Gustave Kahn, a contemporary, described him as 'the sculptor of hands, of furious, clenched, angered, damned hands'.

In 1912 Rodin staged an exhibition comprised solely of hands. He defended himself against the barrage of criticism by saying:

'Have not the public and critics who serve the public reproached me enough for exhibiting simple parts of the human body?... Can they not imagine that an artist must apply himself to giving as much expression to a hand or a torso as to a face and that it was logical for an artist to exhibit an arm rather than a bust arbitrarily deprived by tradition of arms, legs, and abdomen? Expression and proportion, the ends are there. The means are modeling... it is by modeling that the flesh lives, vibrates, struggles and suffers'.

Whilst studying at the Petite École, in the 1850s, Rodin would have studied human anatomy and later, during the 1880s, he became interested in the pioneering Eadweard Muybridge's photographic studies of hands in motion.

Nevertheless, Rodin's interest in hands went far further than a mere interest in the human form. The sculptor believed that his own talent was God-given and flowed through his hands. As such his models of hands came to symbolize the very process of creation, of God as creator of man. In turn each of the hand models takes on its own identity and displays a strong sense of emotion.

Sketch of the Left Hand of Pierre and Jacques Weissant

Esquisse de Main Gauche pour Pierre et Jacques de Weissant

Signed A. Rodin with repeat raised interior signature
Inscribed © Musée Rodin 1970 and Georges Rudier Fondeur Paris.
Bronze with a green, dark green and black patination
Height: 10⅜ inches (26.5 cm)

Provenance:
Musée Rodin, Paris
Dominion Gallery, Montreal, acquired from the above 1970
Anonymous sale, Sotheby's, London, 21 April 1971, Lot 42 (incorrect measurements and numbering given)
Christies London, 6th December 1983, Lot 314
Gustav Zumsteg Collection
Robert Bowman Gallery, 2006
Private Collection, Turkey

Conceived between 1885–1887, this example was cast in 1970 by the Georges Rudier foundry for the Musée Rodin as part of an edition of eleven.

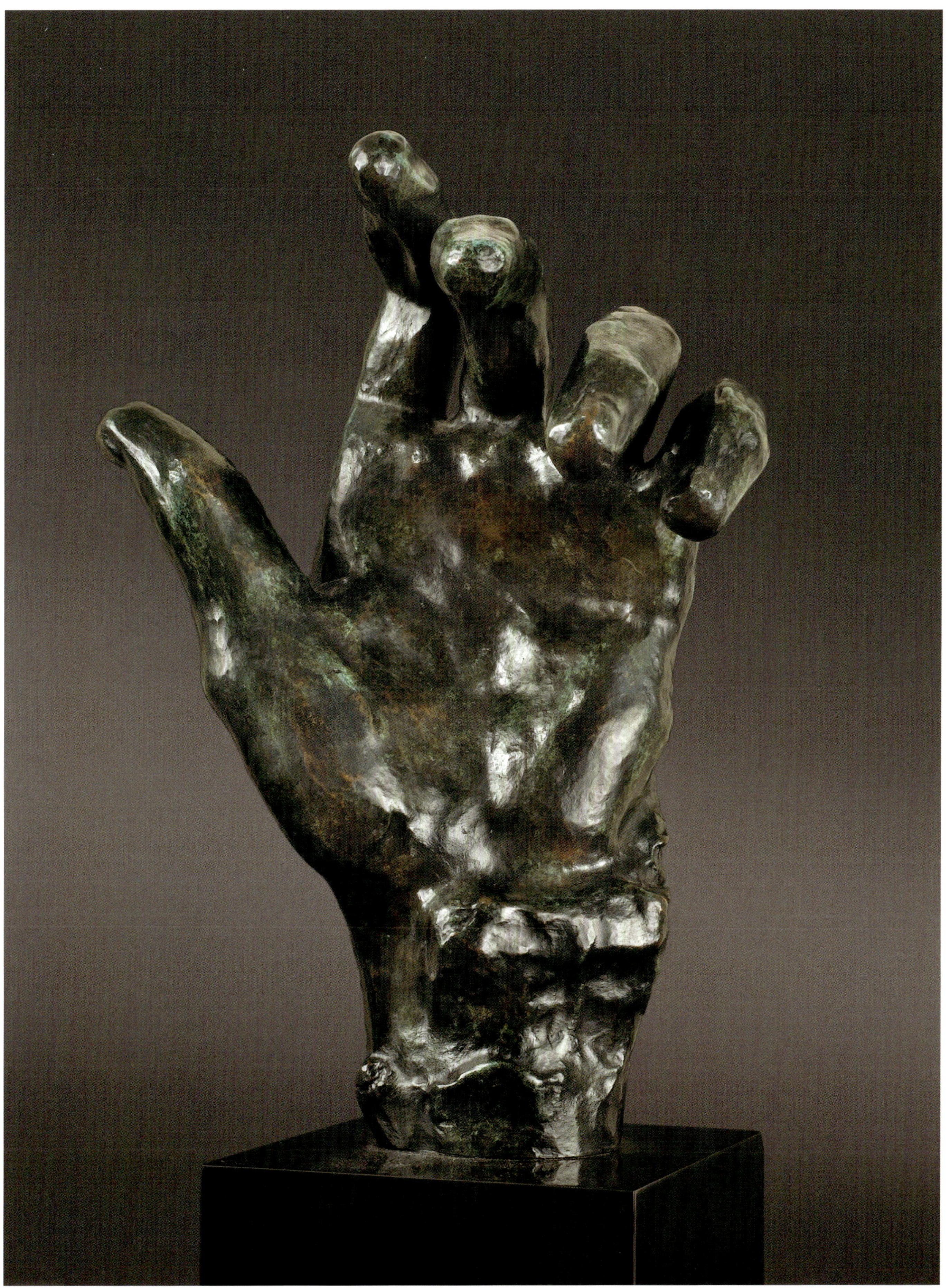

Left Hand 37

Main Gauche 37

Signed A. Rodin
Inscribed © by Musée Rodin 1966 and Georges Rudier Fondeur Paris
Bronze with a rich dark brown patination
Height: 5 inches (13 cm)

Provenance:
Musée Rodin, Paris
Flacs Collection, Paris
Private French collection, by Descent.

Conceived in 1901, this example was cast in 1966 by the Georges Rudier foundry for the Musée Rodin as part of an edition of twelve. No lifetime casts were made.

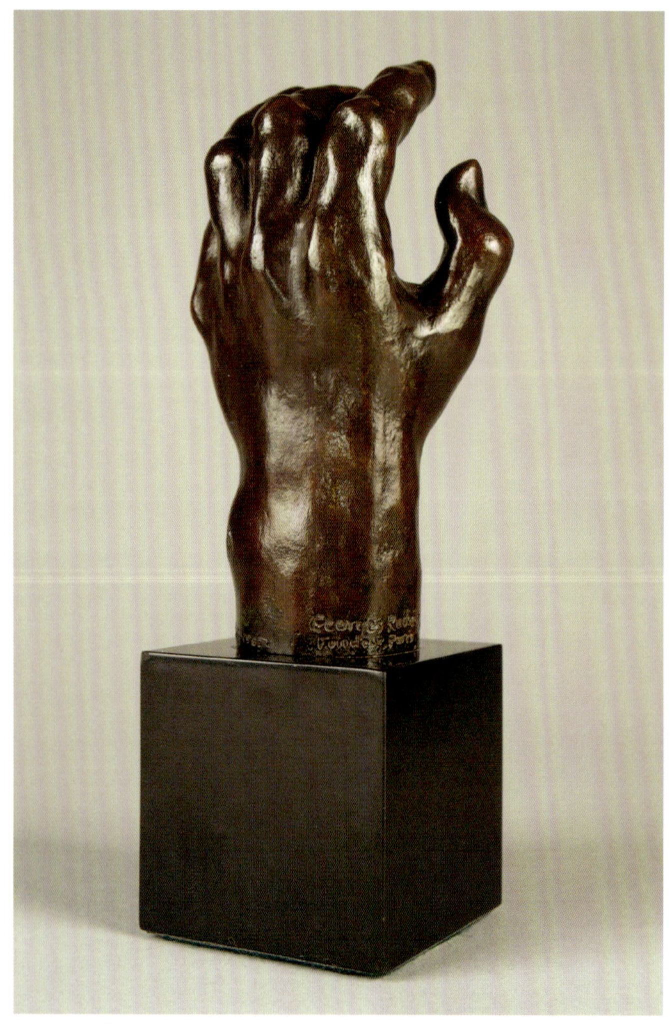

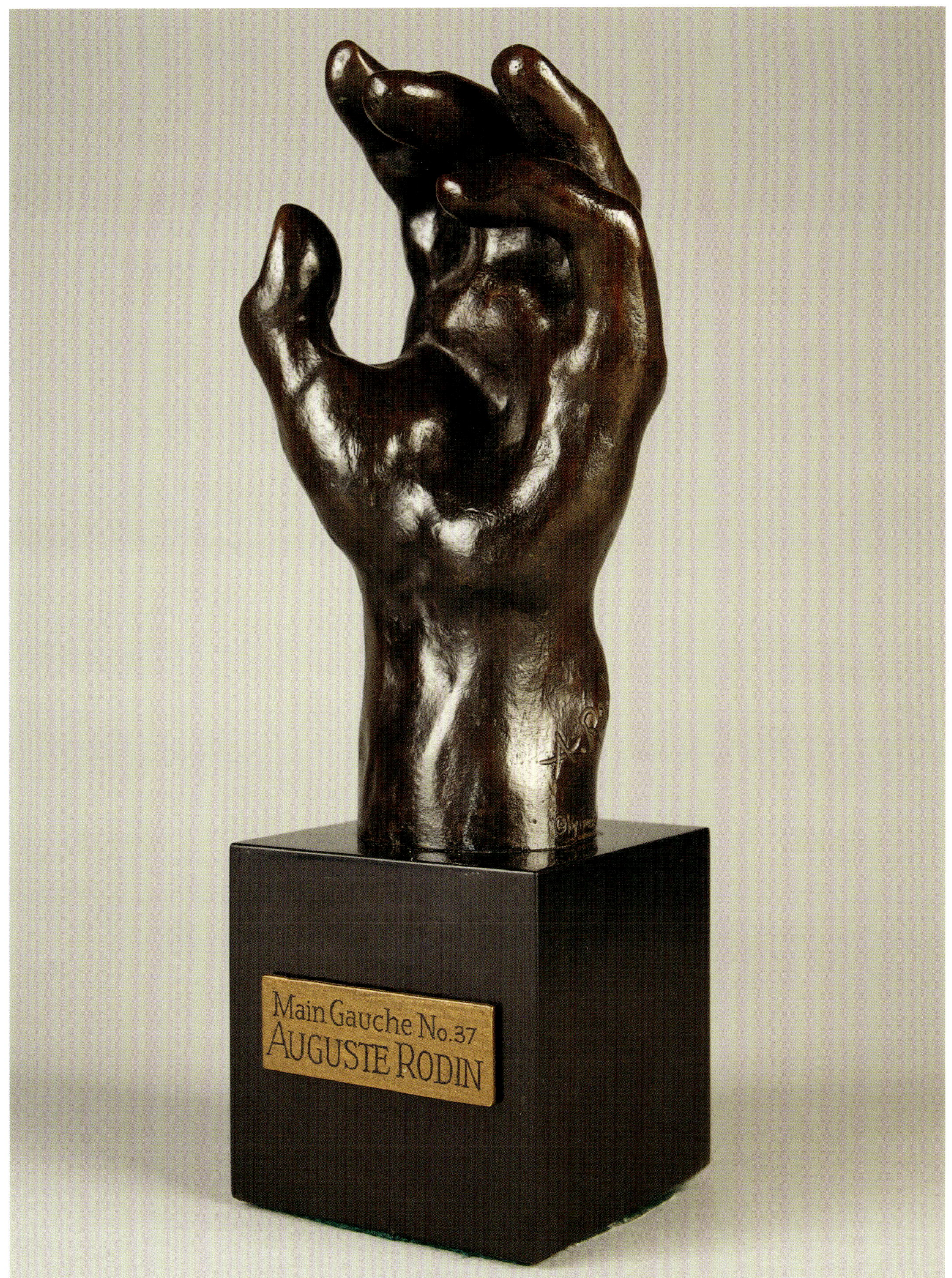

Main Gauche No.37
AUGUSTE RODIN

Right Hand 13

Main Droit 13

Signed A. Rodin and
Inscribed G. Rudier
Bronze with a rich brown patination
Height: 3⅜ inches (8.5 cm)

Provenance:
Purchased from Musée Rodin, Paris in 1963
By Descent

According to a letter from Cecile Goldscheider, Conserveteur of the Musée Rodin, dated 18 October 1963, sold with this work, this bronze is one of a limited edition of twelve and is listed under inventory no. 1.571. There are no previous editions.

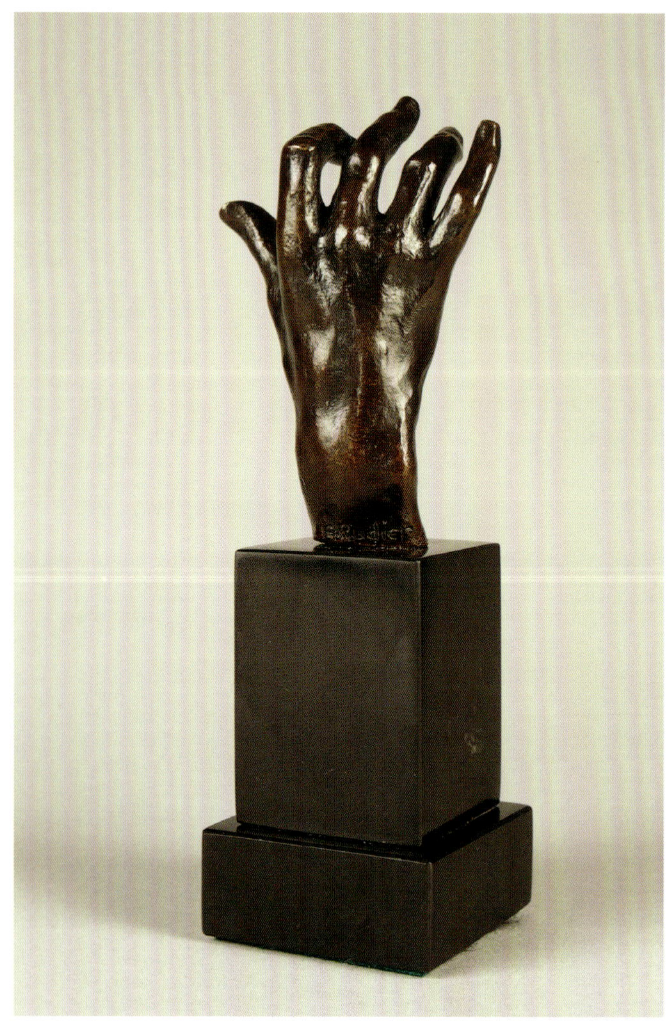

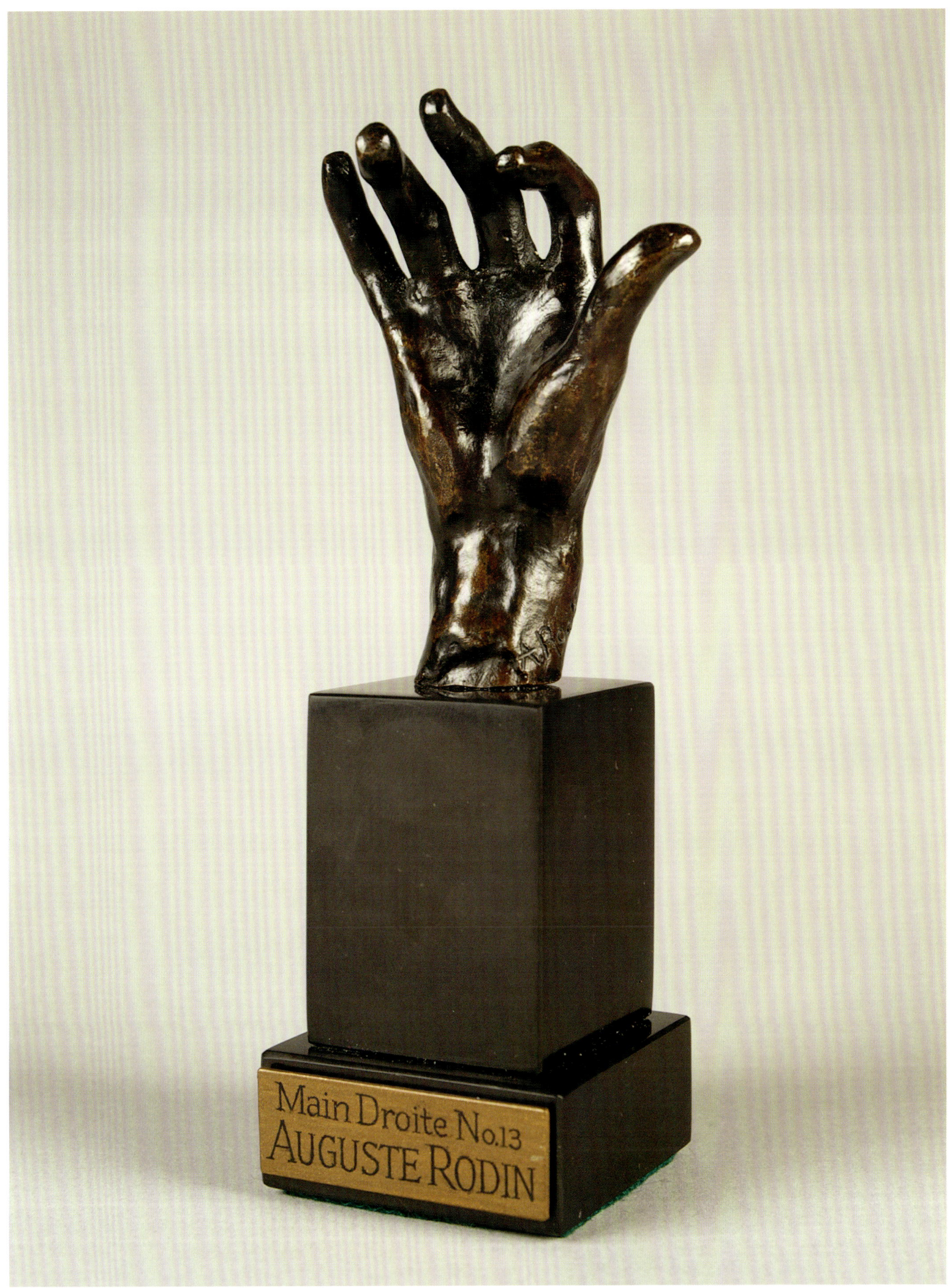

Main Droite No.13
AUGUSTE RODIN

Right Hand 27

Main Droite 27

Signed A. Rodin
Inscribed © by Musée Rodin and G Rudier Fondeur Paris
Bronze with a dark brown and green patination
Height: 6¼ inches (15.7 cm)

Provenance:
Musée Rodin, Paris
Roland Browse and Delbanco, London
Richard Mc Dougall, London
Private Collection, London

Conceived circa 1878, this example cast in 1960. Two casts were made for the Musée Rodin by the Alexis Rudier foundry in 1927 and 1949. A further eleven casts were made by the Georges Rudier foundry between 1960 and 1965.

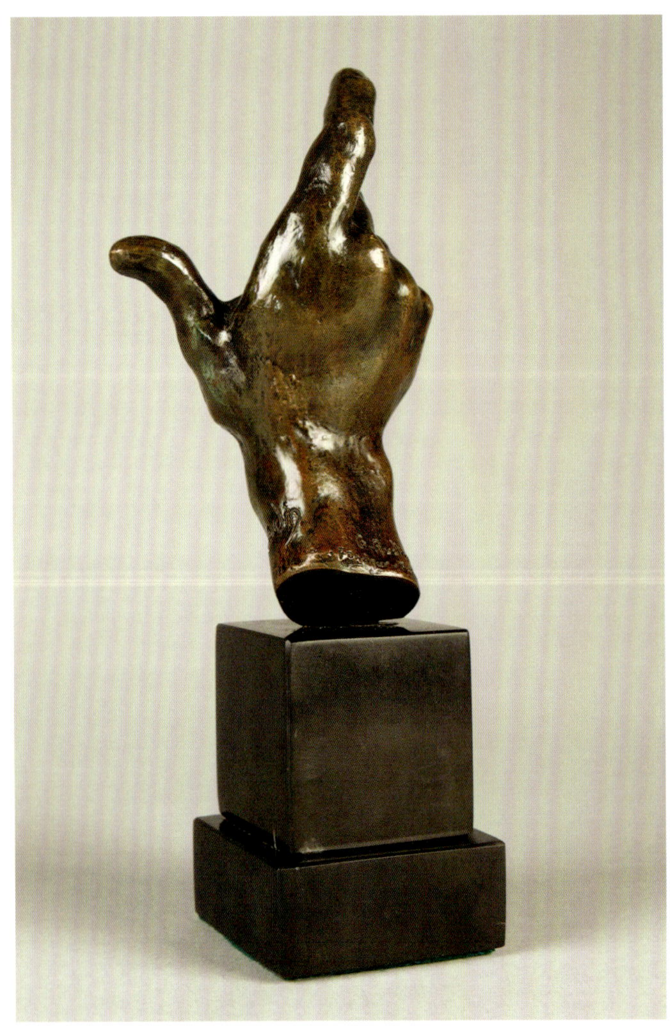

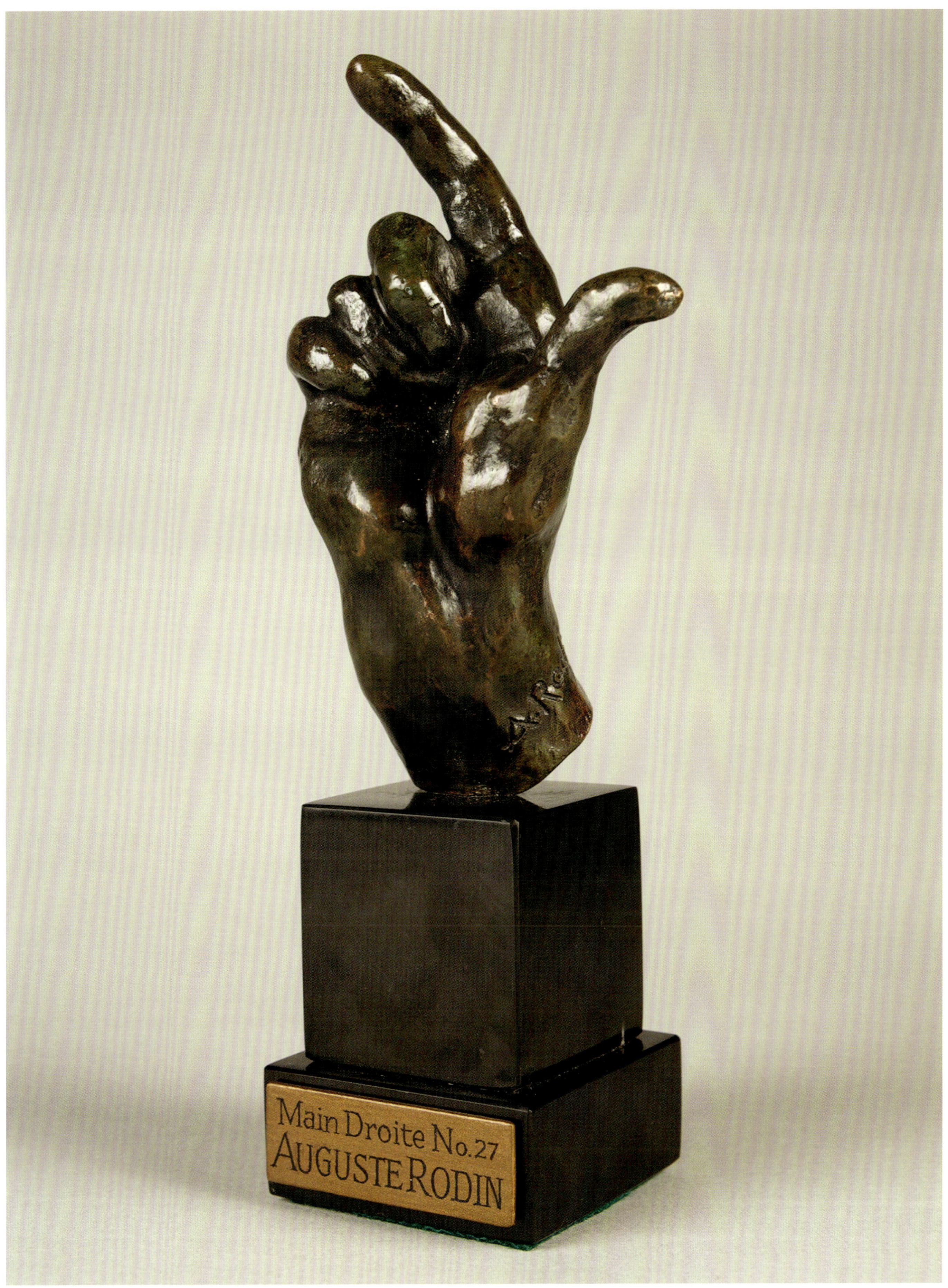

Main Droite No.27
AUGUSTE RODIN

Left Hand 26

Main Gauche 26

Signed A. Rodin
Inscribed © by Musée Rodin and Georges Rudier Fondeur Paris
Bronze with a dark brown and green patination
Height: 6¼ inches (15.7 cm)

Provenance:
Musée Rodin, Paris
Private Collection, France

Conceived before 1901. This model was never cast during Rodin's lifetime. Thirteen casts were made for the Musée Rodin. The Alexis Rudier foundry made a single cast in 1949, then the Georges Rudier foundry made twelve casts between 1953 and 1961.

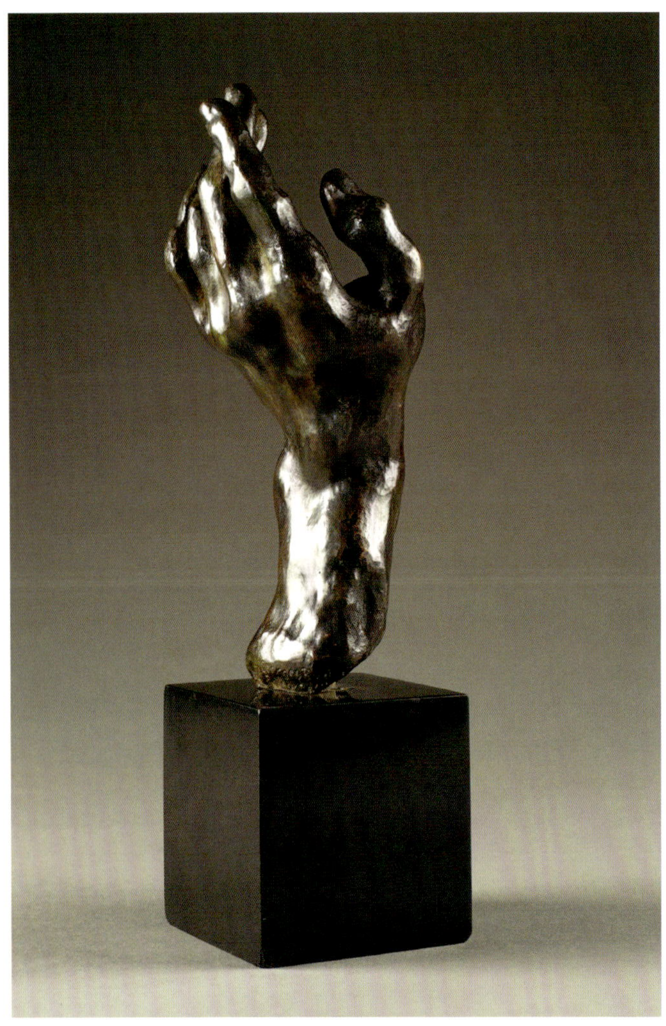

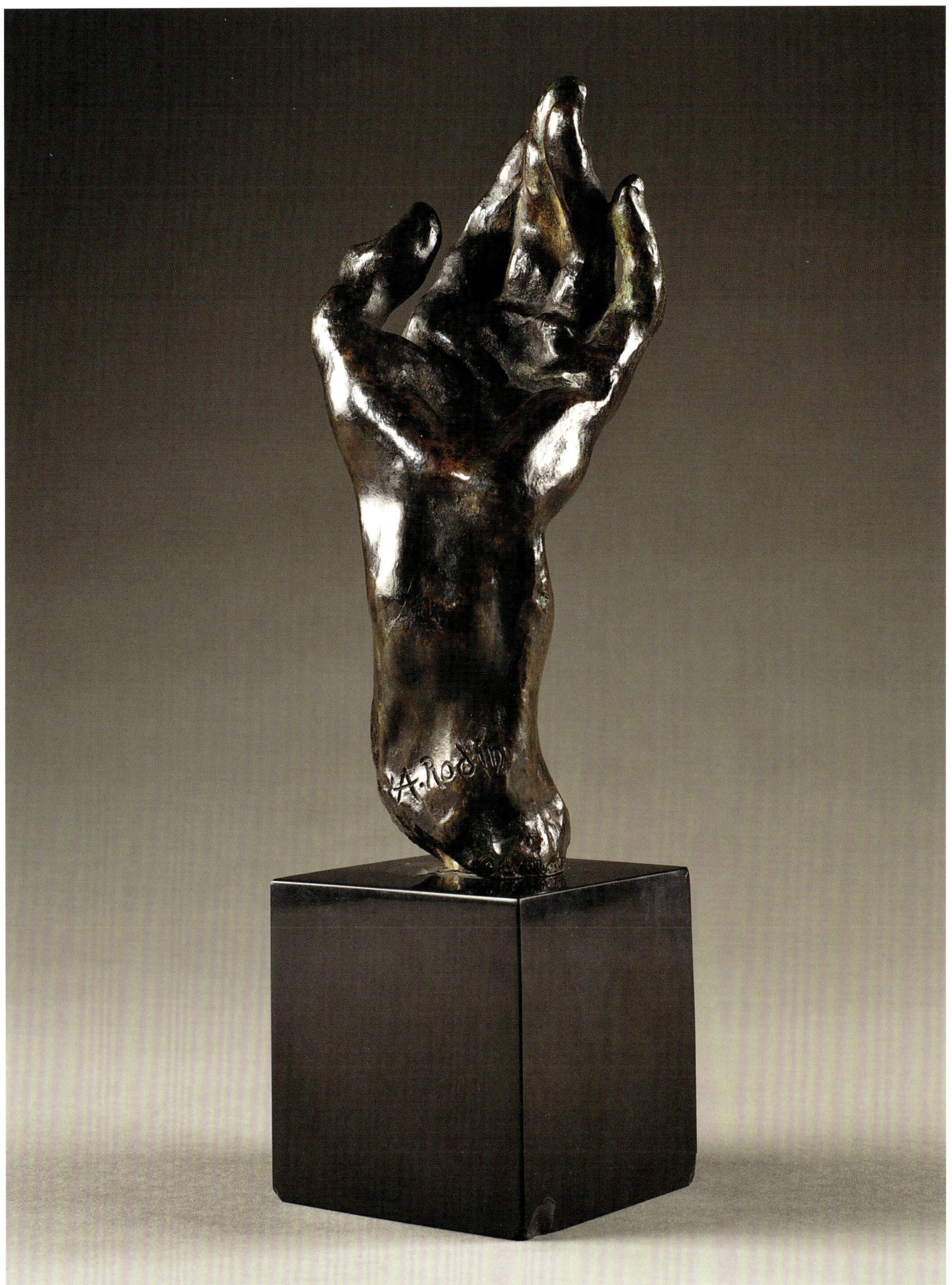

Left Hand 19

Main Gauche 19

Signed A. Rodin
Inscribed G. Rudier Fond Paris
Bronze with a rich brown patination
Height: 3½ inches (9 cm)

Provenance:
Purchased from Musée Rodin, Paris in 1968.
Private Collection, France

According to a letter from Cecile Goldscheider, conservateur of the Musée Rodin, dated 3rd March 1968, sold with this work, this bronze is one of a limited edition of 12. There are no previous editions.

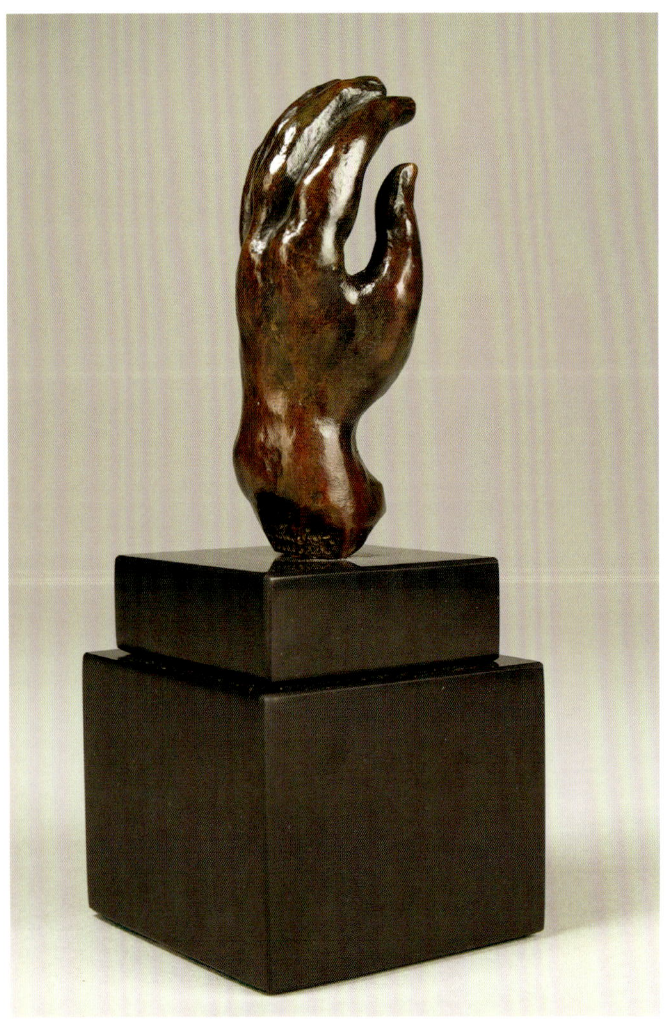

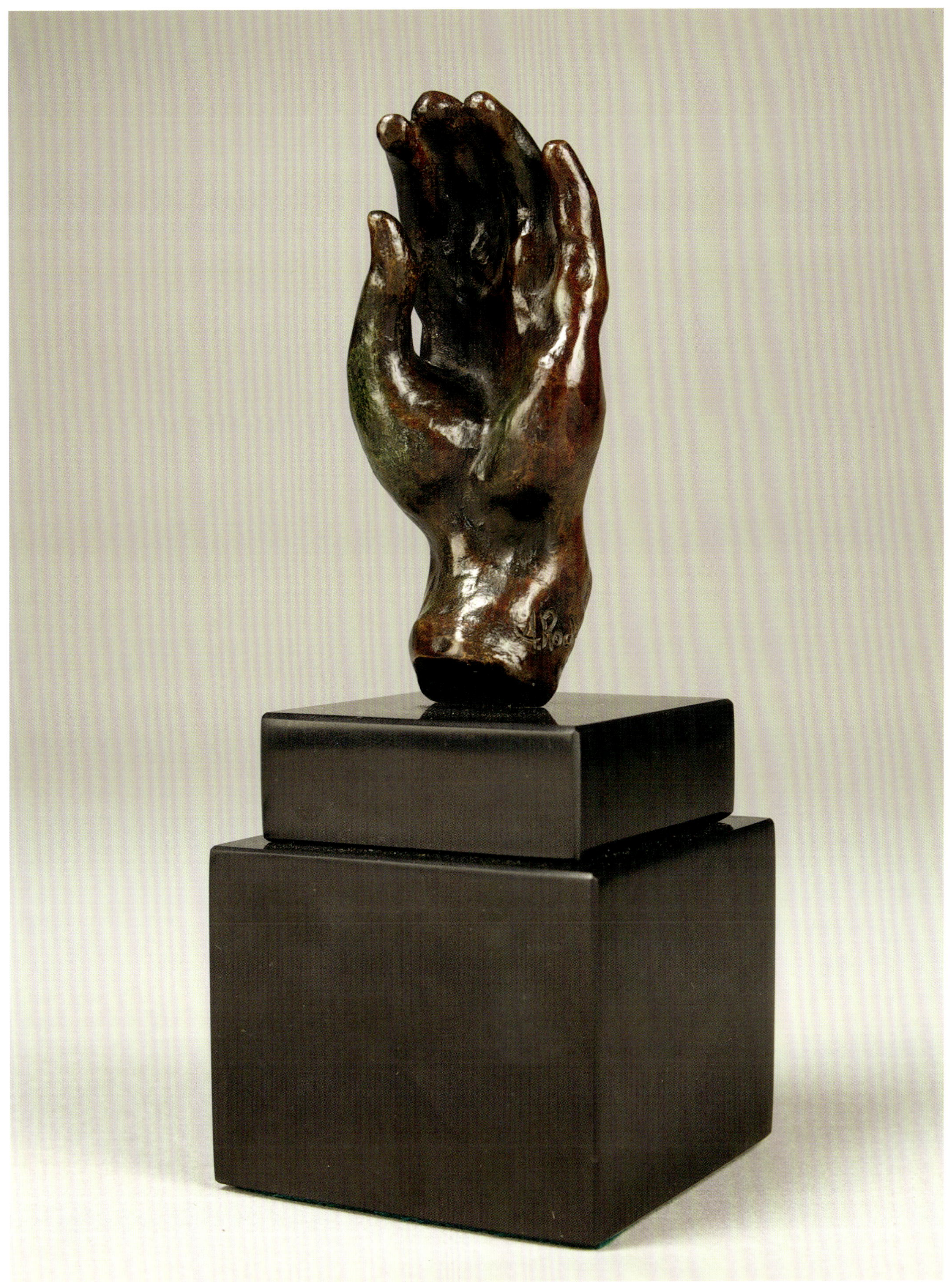

Cathedral, Large Model

Cathédrale, Grand Modele

Signed A. Rodin with repeat raised interior signature
Inscribed © by Musée Rodin 1955 and Georges Rudier Fondeur Paris
Bronze with a rich dark brown and green patination
Height: 25¼ inches (63.7 cm)

Provenance:
Musée Rodin Paris
Casino-Palais de la Méditerranée, Nice acquired from the above 1956
Private Collection, Normandy, France.
Private Collection, Nice, France. Acquired from the above in 1980
Robert Bowman Gallery, 2013
Sotheby's New York, 6th November 2013, Lot 37

Conceived in 1908, this example was cast in 1955. No lifetime casts of this work were made. In total sixteen casts were made for the Musée Rodin. The first three casts by the Alexis Rudier foundry between 1925 and 1945, then thirteen casts by the Georges Rudier foundry between 1955 and 1966.

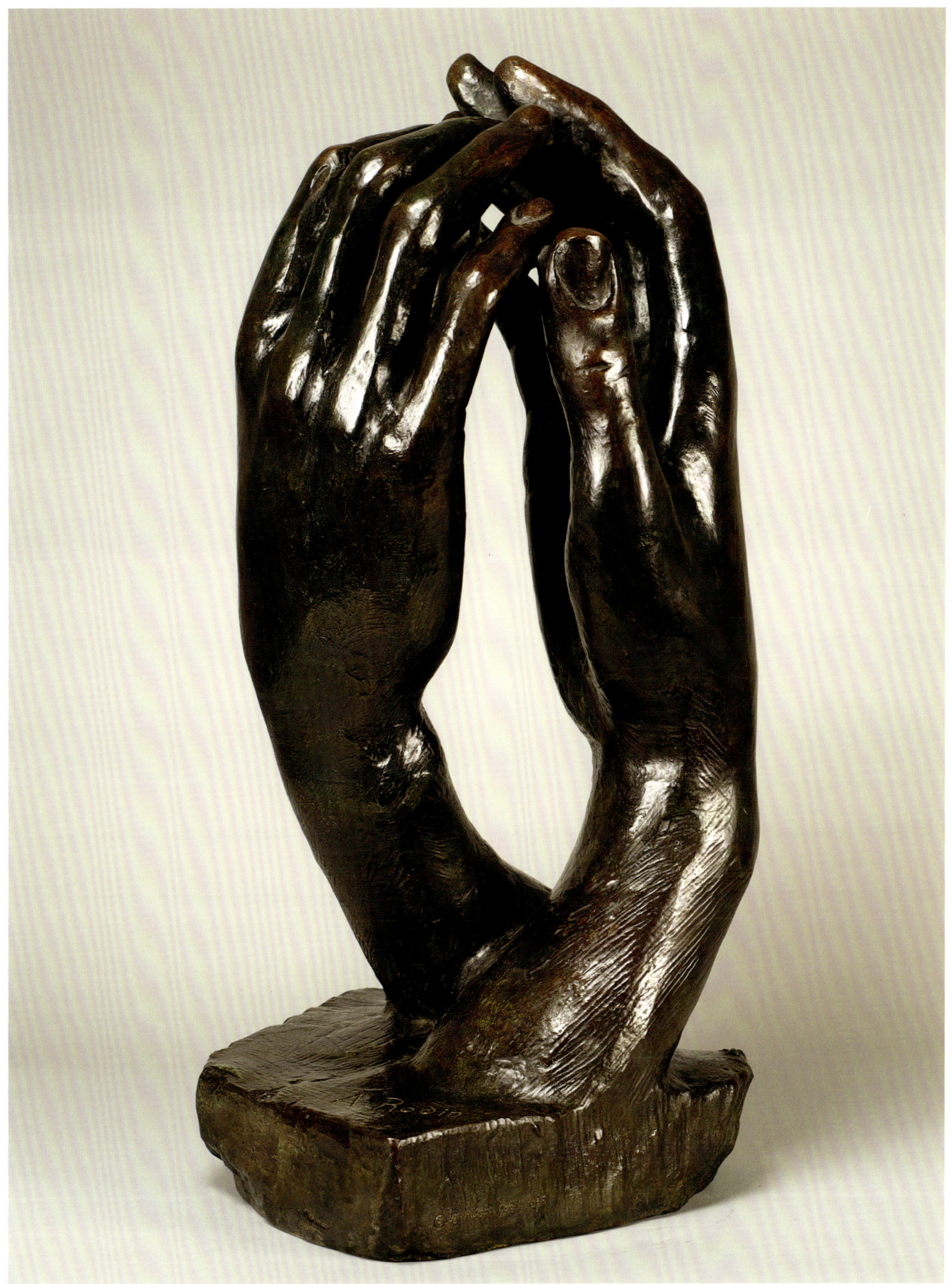

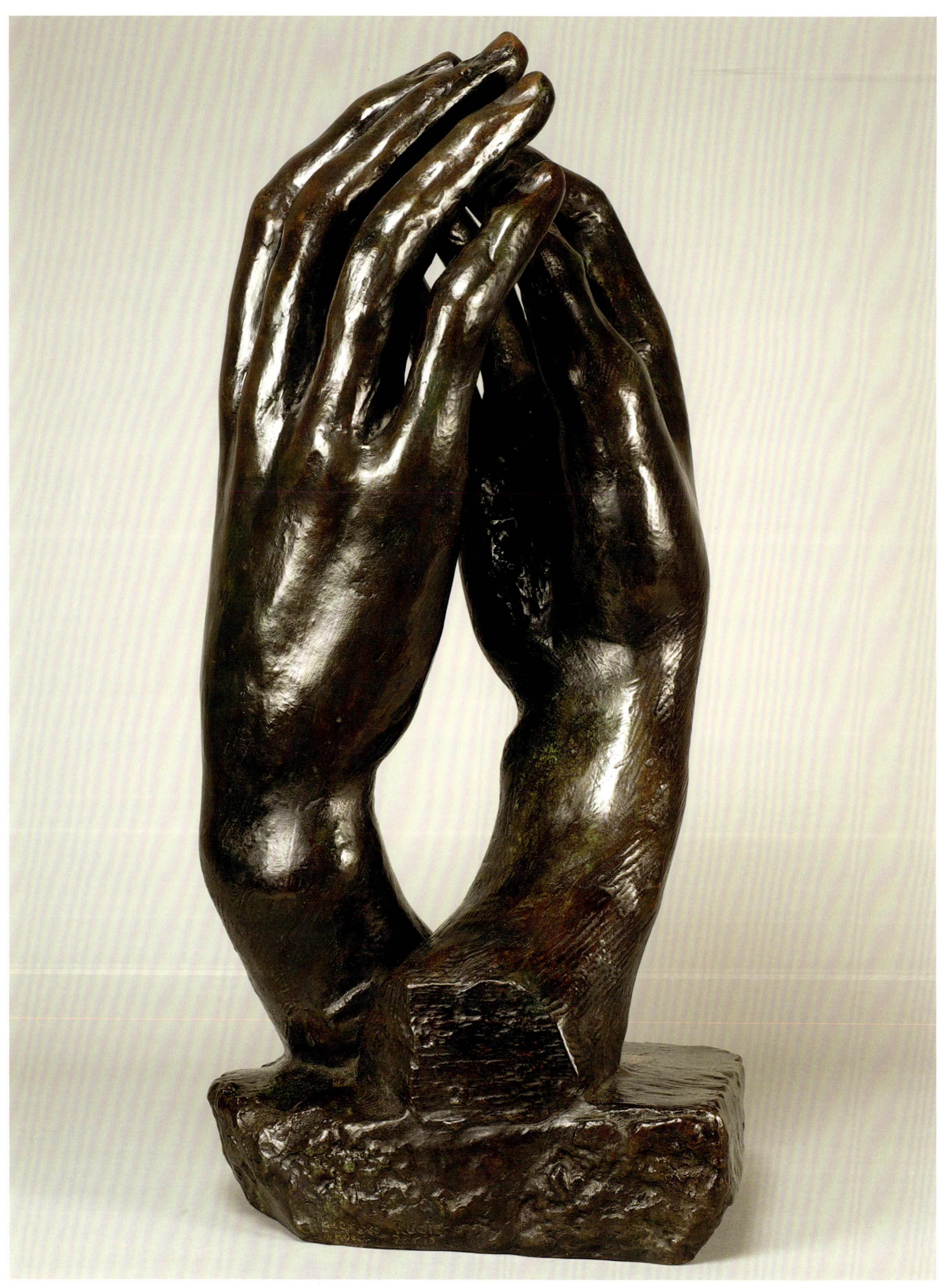

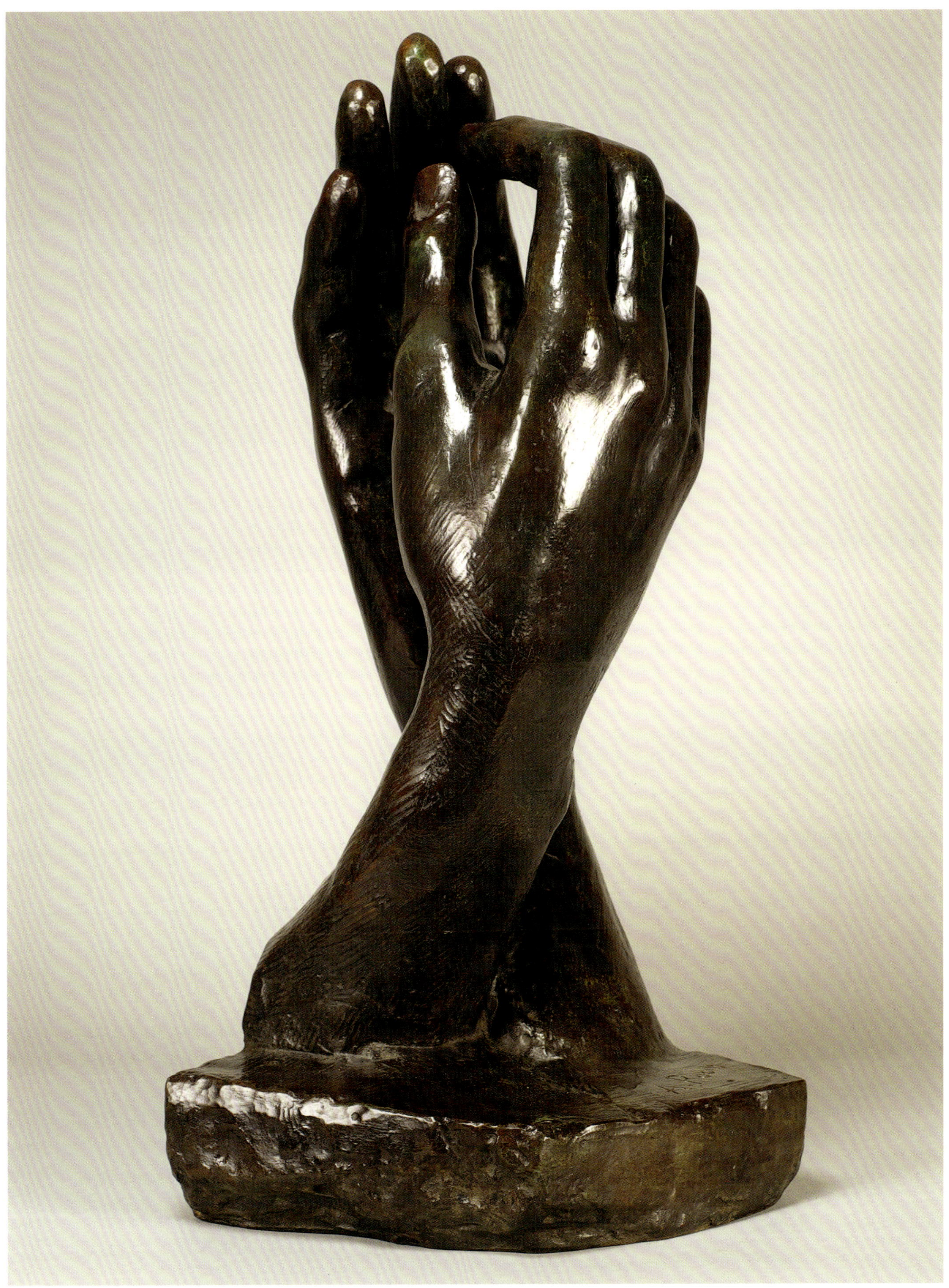

Index of Sculptures

BOWMAN SCULPTURE

6 Duke Street St James's, London SW1Y 6BN
Tel. +44 (0) 207 930 0277

gallery@bowmansculpture.com
www.bowmansculpture.com